Archaeologies of

BLACKWELL STUDIES IN GLOBAL ARCHAEOLOGY

Series Editors: Lynn Meskell and Rosemary A. Joyce

Blackwell Studies in Global Archaeology is a series of contemporary texts, each carefully designed to meet the needs of archaeology instructors and students seeking volumes that treat key regional and thematic areas of archaeological study. Each volume in the series, compiled by its own editor, includes 12–15 newly commissioned articles by top scholars within the volume's thematic, regional, or temporal area of focus.

What sets the *Blackwell Studies in Global Archaeology* apart from other available texts is that their approach is accessible, yet does not sacrifice theoretical sophistication. The series editors are committed to the idea that usable teaching texts need not lack ambition. To the contrary, the *Blackwell Studies in Global Archaeology* aim to immerse readers in fundamental archaeological ideas and concepts, but also to illuminate more advanced concepts, thereby exposing readers to some of the most exciting contemporary developments in the field. Inasmuch, these volumes are designed not only as classic texts, but as guides to the vital and exciting nature of archaeology as a discipline.

Archaeologies of the Middle East

Critical Perspectives

Edited by

Susan Pollock and
Reinhard Bernbeck

Blackwell Studies in Global Archaeology

Blackwell
Publishing

BLACKWELL PUBLISHING
350 Main Street, Malden, MA 02148-5020, USA
108 Cowley Road, Oxford OX4 1JF, UK
550 Swanston Street, Carlton, Victoria 3053, Australia

First published 2005 by Blackwell Publishing Ltd

Library of Congress Cataloging-in-Publication Data

Archaeologies of the Middle East : critical perspectives / edited by Susan
Pollock and Reinhard Bernbeck.
    p. cm. – (Blackwell studies in global archaeology)
  Includes bibliographical references and index.
  ISBN 0-631-23000-9 (hardback : alk. paper) – ISBN 0-631-23001-7
(pbk. : alk. paper) 1. Archaeology – Middle East – History. 2. Middle
East – Antiquities. I. Pollock, Susan, 1955– II. Bernbeck, Reinhard,
1958– III. Series.

DS56.A735 2005
939'.4'0072 – dc22

2004008966

A catalogue record for this title is available from the British Library.

Set in 10 on 12½ pt Plantin
by SNP Best-set Typesetter Ltd, Hong Kong
Printed and bound in the United Kingdom
by T.J. International Ltd, Padstow, Cornwall

The publisher's policy is to use permanent paper from mills that operate a
sustainable forestry policy, and which has been manufactured from pulp
processed using acid-free and elementary chlorine-free practices. Furthermore,
the publisher ensures that the text paper and cover board used have met
acceptable environmental accreditation standards.

For further information on
Blackwell Publishing, visit our website:
www.blackwellpublishing.com

Contents

Figures

Tables

List of Contributors

Reinhard Bernbeck is Associate Professor of Anthropology at Binghamton University. His specialty is the archaeology of the ancient Near East. He has directed and participated in field projects in Syria, Jordan, Turkey, and Iran. He is interested in historiography and theories of praxis and also remains committed to a historical materialist view of the past.

Petr Charvát is Director of Research at the Oriental Institute (Academy of Sciences of the Czech Republic) in Prague. He also holds part-time appointments at Charles University (Prague) and Western Bohemian University (Plžen). He has done fieldwork in Egypt, Lebanon, Turkey, Iraq, and Sri Lanka. His main research focus is the emergence of statehood and literacy from a general anthropological perspective and with respect to the cuneiform-using regions of ancient southwestern Asia.

Meredith S. Chesson is Assistant Professor of Anthropology at the University of Notre Dame. Her specialty is the archaeology of the Middle East, particularly the southern Levant. She has done fieldwork in Jordan, Cyprus, Italy, Canada, and the United States. Her research focuses on the emergence of social differentiation in early complex societies, urbanism, and mortuary practices.

Israel Finkelstein is Professor of Archaeology at Tel Aviv University and the co-director of the Megiddo Expedition. His field of research is the Levant in the Bronze and Iron Ages.

Jean-Daniel Forest is Chargé de Recherche at the Centre National de la Recherche Scientifique, Paris. He has conducted extensive fieldwork in Iraq, spanning the earliest village communities to state and urban societies. His research focuses on social, political, and religious dimensions of early Mesopotamian state societies and their antecedents.

Ian Kuijt is Associate Professor of Anthropology at the University of Notre Dame, with a specialty in the archaeology of the Middle East and western North America.

He has extensive fieldwork experience in Canada, the United States, Israel, Jordan, and parts of Europe. His research contributes to studies of the emergence of social inequality and food production, political economy, and identity within hunter-gatherer, foraging, and farming communities.

Mario Liverani is Professor of History of the Ancient Near East at the University of Rome "La Sapienza." He is the author of many books and articles on economic, social, and political history and on ancient and modern historiography. He has conducted fieldwork in Syria, Turkey, and presently in the Libyan Sahara.

Susan Pollock is Professor of Anthropology at Binghamton University, with a specialty in archaeology of the Middle East. She has conducted fieldwork in Iran, Turkey, and Iraq. Her research contributes to studies of political economy, ideology and representation, and archaeology in the media.

Jennifer Ross is Assistant Professor of Art and Archaeology at Hood College in Frederick, Maryland. Her research focuses on the social construction and functions of technological and artistic production. She excavates in Turkey, most recently at Çadır Höyük.

John Shea is Associate Professor of Anthropology at Stony Brook University. His areas of expertise include Paleolithic archaeology and paleoanthropology of the Middle East and Africa. He has directed fieldwork in Israel, Jordan, Tanzania, and Ethiopia. His research interests focus on lithic analysis and hominid/human adaptive radiations.

Sharon Steadman is Associate Professor in the Department of Anthropology and Sociology at the State University of New York at Cortland. Her research is centered on the study of architecture and the use of space. She is presently co-director of excavations at the site of Çadır Höyük in central Turkey.

Caroline Steele is an independent scholar. She has worked on excavations in Turkey, Iraq, and Syria. Her primary research interests lie in early urban societies of Mesopotamia and in the intersection of politics, human rights, and archaeology.

Marc Verhoeven is Visiting Associate Professor at the University of Tokyo. His specialty is the prehistory of the Near East. He has conducted fieldwork at Neolithic Tell Sabi Abyad in Syria. His main research interests are prehistoric symbolism, ritual, ideology, and the uses of ethnography for understanding the past.

Adel Yahya is Director of the Palestinian Association for Cultural Exchange (PACE), an organization established in 1996 to protect Palestinian cultural heritage. In addition to his active involvement in educating and involving local people in archaeology, he has conducted research on the Iron Age in the Levant.

Paul Zimansky is Professor of Archaeology at Boston University, specializing in the archaeology and history of the Bronze and Iron Age Near East. He has excavated in Iran, Iraq, Syria, and Turkey and published extensively on the civilization of Urartu (Ararat) in eastern Anatolia.

 # Series Editors' Preface

This series was conceived as a collection of books designed to cover central areas of undergraduate archaeological teaching. Each volume in the series, edited by experts in the area, includes newly commissioned articles written by archaeologists actively engaged in research. By commissioning new articles, the series combines one of the best features for readers, the presentation of multiple approaches to archaeology, with the virtues of a text conceived from the beginning as intended for a specific audience. While the model reader for the series is conceived of as an upper-division undergraduate, the inclusion in the volumes of researchers actively engaged in work today will also make these volumes valuable for more advanced researchers who want a rapid introduction to contemporary issues in specific sub-fields of global archaeology.

Each volume in the series will include an extensive introduction by the volume editor that will set the scene in terms of thematic or geographic focus. Individual volumes, and the series as a whole, exemplify a wide range of approaches in contemporary archaeology. The volumes uniformly engage with issues of contemporary interest, interweaving social, political, and ethical themes. We contend that it is no longer tenable to teach the archaeology of vast swaths of the globe without acknowledging the political implications of working in foreign countries and the responsibilities archaeologists incur by writing and presenting other people's pasts. The volumes in this series will not sacrifice theoretical sophistication for accessibility. We are committed to the idea that usable teaching texts need not lack ambition.

Blackwell Studies in Global Archaeology aims to immerse readers in fundamental archaeological ideas and concepts, but also to illuminate more advanced concepts, exposing readers to some of the most exciting contemporary developments in the field.

Lynn Meskell and Rosemary A. Joyce

Acknowledgments

The editors would like to thank a number of individuals who contributed directly to this book. Norman Yoffee read and commented on the manuscript at short notice. Stanley Kauffman of Binghamton University's Educational Communications Center produced the maps in chapters 1 and 2. Lynn Meskell and Rosemary Joyce invited us to contribute a book to their series and offered encouragement throughout the project. Jane Huber and her assistants at Blackwell were unwaveringly enthusiastic and supportive. We wish especially to thank all of the authors for their contributions, from which we have learned much, and for their patience throughout the process of producing this book. Finally, we wish to acknowledge the continuing intellectual inspiration of our colleagues, especially Charles Cobb, Carmen Ferradas, Randall McGuire, and Ann Stahl, and students in the Anthropology Department at Binghamton. We recognize our intellectual indebtedness to many more people, both professional colleagues and friends from all walks of life, without whose input, whether intended or not, this book could not have been conceived in the way it was.

1

Introduction

Susan Pollock
and Reinhard Bernbeck

It is ever more common these days for archaeologists to acknowledge that their profession is a Western product that emerged, like so many other academic disciplines, in the context of the European Enlightenment. The fact that archaeology is now practiced throughout much of the world, not just by Westerners but by a growing cadre of indigenous professionals, is a result of colonialism and imperialism. Westerners made the study of the material remains of the past a tool in their own political ambitions and at the same time demonstrated its utility to their subjects in their own quests for independence and national identities (Trigger 1984; Kohl and Fawcett 1995).

Although its object of study is the past and the lives of dead people, archaeology is a social practice that is thoroughly embedded in the contemporary world. Archaeologists invariably work among and often directly with people who reside in the areas where their fieldwork is conducted. The structure of the discipline and of academia in general gives some people the rights to excavate, curate, and study archaeological remains, while others are consigned to roles as consumers of the interpretations thereby produced. The ways in which archaeologists interpret their findings owe much to current ideas about knowledge production within the profession, and these tend to privilege certain topics and approaches over others.

The theme of archaeology's embeddedness in the contemporary world runs throughout the contributions to this book. A number of authors treat directly the connections between modern-day politics and the social context of archaeological practice. The choice of topics to include was itself very much a product of the current issues of concern in archaeology of the Middle East and the editors' and authors' readings and evaluations of them. In this way, like all books, the contents of this one are highly selective.

It perhaps needs little mention that any book on the archaeology of the Middle East, especially a single-volume work, cannot possibly pretend to be comprehensive. Our aims as editors have been threefold: to foreground the sociopolitical contexts and ideological implications of archaeological work, to explore various themes and approaches to archaeological interpretation that have not received much atten- tion in the archaeology of the region, and to address controversial issues as well as conventional ones in novel ways. We have not sought to produce an absolute coher- ence in presentation or viewpoints; any such harmony would be an artificial paper- ing over of real differences in the field. We as editors do not agree with all of the authors' arguments, and some authors disagree with the interpretations of others in the book. This is, we believe, a positive state of affairs in an intellectually vibrant field.

What we have *not* attempted to do in this book is to strive for coverage of all periods nor of all parts of the Middle East, nor have we selected a specific range of periods or single region for in-depth treatment. Rather, we have emphasized over- arching themes that are also of broad relevance to archaeology as a whole and, in doing so, endeavored to touch on a diversity of times and places in the Middle East. Nonetheless, this book, like so many others, tends to privilege those periods and places where "momentous" changes – according to archaeologists' current inter- pretations – are thought to have occurred, to the detriment of "in-between" periods in which, by contemporary definitions, not much of consequence happened.[1] The authors do not for the most part present systematic overviews of major sites or sets of data, but rather they treat issues and topics that are predicated upon the exis- tence and analysis of such data. For non-specialists in the field, we recommend using this book in conjunction with an overview text (for example, Roaf 1990; Kuhrt 1995; Sasson et al. 1995) in order to delve further into the evidence on which the interpretations and positions presented here are based.

The Middle East has been, and continues to be, in the forefront of much of the world's political calculations and promises to remain so for the foreseeable future. It is a region that is home to continuing violent conflicts between governments and variously defined social, religious, and ethnic groups, contexts in which archaeol- ogy frequently plays (willingly or not) a salient role (Meskell 1998; Silberman 1989; Scham 2001; Bernbeck and Pollock 2004). These ongoing conflicts play a sub- stantial part in shaping the conditions in which knowledge about archaeology of the region is produced and used. More than one chapter grapples with the effects of public perceptions about the Middle East on the study of the ancient history and archaeology of the region (see also Said 1981). It is a cruel irony that this book was in the process of completion during Gulf War II, not long after the U.S.-led inva- sion of Afghanistan, and amidst the continuing violence in Israel and the Occupied Territories. The implications and responsibilities for those of us who work in and study the remains of the past in this region are immense.

On a more strictly academic level, at various times in its history Near Eastern archaeology has stood in the theoretical and methodological forefront of the disci- pline of archaeology. It would, however, be difficult to argue for such a prominent position for the field these days (cf. Yoffee 1995). Many of the general themes that are sources of vibrant debate in other parts of the world – for example, whether emphasis is placed on study of individuals and small groups or on larger collectivi- ties, or on questions of meaning as opposed to external causalities of change – have resulted as yet in little sustained debate in archaeology in the Middle East. By broaching some of these issues here and seeking to examine older topics in novel ways, we hope to push the boundaries of the field and encourage work that engages with problems central to the discipline of archaeology as a whole.

As editors, we have found ourselves confronted with several challenges to our initial, idealistic conceptions of what a book with such goals should look like. The political economy of book production in the U.S. today dictates that total length be held within relatively narrow limits, due to cost as well as marketing assumptions about how much particular audiences are prepared to read. These limits placed constraints on the number of contributions and the lengths of each chapter. We would have liked the book to be more diverse in its geographic and temporal coverage and in the topics covered: there is, for example, little or no discussion of Iran or the Gulf states or of "Islamic archaeology." A second problem that we confronted was the difficulty in finding authors willing to write about certain topics. This was particularly challenging for some of the controversial issues, especially those that touch directly on the intertwining of archaeology and modern political issues, presumably due to individuals' concerns about limiting future research or even jeopardizing a career.

One of the distinctive aspects of the study of the ancient Near East is imparted by the variety of practitioners who participate in it. These include archaeologists – whether trained anthropologically or in culture historically oriented traditions – but also art historians, ancient historians, and scholars with specialties in the study of ancient languages. The contributors to this volume include scholars from all of these fields. These different specialties and associated educational backgrounds hold the potential to produce a truly vibrant field of study, in which similar issues may be viewed from quite different perspectives and the topics emphasized and questions posed may vary considerably. Both women and men are actively engaged in the field, but despite our efforts, we were unable to achieve a true gender balance among our contributors. However, the place where this volume is least successful in representing the actual balance of the field's practitioners is geographic: although both European and North American scholars are well represented, only two contributors are Middle Easterners.

Geographic Overview

The Middle East has no hard and fast geographic boundaries. It is a modern political designation that extends from Turkey to Iran or Afghanistan and southwards to Saudi Arabia and the Gulf states (see figure 1.1). Most scholars use the term Near East to designate this same region in pre-modern times.[2] In this book, we use "Middle East" whenever we speak of modern-day entities and practices ("Western Asia" might be another alternative) but retain "Near East" for references to ancient times (e.g., the ancient Near East).

The Middle East encompasses much geographic and environmental diversity. However, the region as a whole shares some general climatic characteristics,

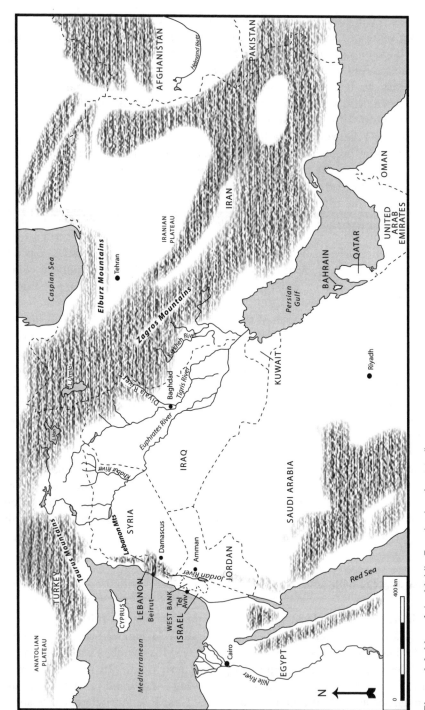

Figure 1.1 Map of the Middle East (authors' original)

especially hot, dry summers and cool to cold, moist winters. Paleoclimatic data indicate that during the early Holocene the rainy season lasted longer than today, along with higher summer and cooler winter temperatures. The transition to somewhat less favorable modern climatic conditions began approximately 6,000 years ago (COHMAP 1988; Hole 1994; Wilkinson 2003:ch. 2).

Geographers and botanists have divided the Middle East into a number of zones, based on features of the natural vegetation and topography.[3] These include the flat, alluvial plains of lowland Iraq, which are classified as sub-desert, with limited, scrub vegetation except in the immediate proximity of rivers; the rolling hills of northern Iraq and Syria and the foothills of the Taurus and Zagros mountains, with steppe vegetation; the high mountains and mountain valleys of the Taurus, Zagros, and Elburz ranges, which support forest vegetation and grassland; the high plateaus of Iran and Anatolia, the former a near desert, the latter characterized by steppe and grassland vegetation; and the coastal plains of the Mediterranean, Caspian Sea, and the Persian Gulf, each with a distinctive vegetational profile (scrub forest along the Mediterranean, sub-tropical vegetation at the Caspian shores, and salt-tolerant plants along the Gulf).

The distributions of wild plants and animals, the land and water resources necessary to support agriculture and animal husbandry, and raw materials including various types of stones, metals, and woods are often argued to be key to understanding historical developments in the region. The Fertile Crescent – an arc extending from modern-day Israel in the southwest up through Jordan, Lebanon, and Syria, over to Iraq, and down the line of the Zagros mountains in Iran – is generally acknowledged to be the area where the early domesticates, including cereals (especially wheat and barley), legumes, sheep, goats, cattle, and pigs, were developed from wild populations. Other wild plants, including fruits, nuts, and legumes, as well as animals, such as gazelle, onager, and a variety of deer, were available in and around the Fertile Crescent and were important sources of food and other materials.

The considerable topographic diversity of many parts of the Middle East as well as the early domestication of animals amenable to being herded over considerable distances (principally sheep and goat) have played a key role in settlement strategies from the distant past to the present. Sheep and goat can graze and browse in areas where agriculture is impractical, allowing the use of large stretches of land that would otherwise yield only limited food resources usable by people. Seasonal transhumance, especially movements between lowlands and highlands, has long been practiced in parts of the Middle East, allowing more effective use of available resources, separation of flocks from fields at critical times in the growing season, and as a political strategy to avoid the predations of rapacious governments. Pursuing a range of modes of subsistence and degrees of mobility has enabled Middle Eastern peoples to remain flexible in the face of the vagaries of harsh environments and political systems (Rowton 1973; Adams 1974, 1981; Henry 1989; Wilkinson 2003).

The distributions of other natural resources, especially stones, metal ores, high quality woods, and water, have also influenced the history of the Middle East. The absence of metals and dearth of stone and wood in the alluvial lowlands of Mesopotamia (present-day Iraq) are widely cited, especially in contrast to the presence of these materials in the surrounding mountain and plateau regions (Algaze 1989). Although a number of scholars have argued compellingly that the poverty of natural resources in the Mesopotamian lowlands has been exaggerated (Van de Mieroop 2002), there is little question that exchange, alliances, and military adventures have all been spurred by, among other things, the desire for resources that were not locally available. Already in Paleolithic times, items such as marine shell were exchanged over long distances (Hole and Flannery 1968:160), a testimony to the scale of interactions well before the appearance of state and urban societies or even village communities.

Modes of transportation, of people and goods, are key to permitting and constraining interactions among people. The first attestations of domesticated pack animals – donkeys – date to the fourth millennium B.C.E.; the camel was not domesticated until much later. Prior to the fourth millennium, overland transport was dependent on the human back. Riverine transport by boat has been used since at least the late fifth millennium B.C.E. (Safar et al. 1981), a far easier and more effective way to move people and goods than overland, at least in the downstream direction. Maritime movements became important in the third millennium, if not earlier.

Brief History of Archaeological Work in the Middle East

Some of the earliest explorations of archaeological remains in the Middle East at the beginning of the 19th century occurred well before archaeology existed as a clearly defined field of study.[4] Two principal and interrelated driving forces underlay the early explorations. One was colonialism, with its attendant efforts to maintain control over knowledge production in colonial holdings and to appropriate resources of all kinds for the benefit of the colonizers. In the case of archaeology, colonialism's impact is evident in the race to fill European museums with unusual and exotic treasures and in expeditions and even "educational travel" that sought to catalog and systematize knowledge of everything from flora to fauna to ancient monuments, the most famous being Napoleon's in Egypt. The second inspiration for archaeological work in the Middle East was the Bible. Numerous individuals traveled to the region – especially the areas that are today Israel, Jordan, and the Palestinian territories – in a quest to identify places known from the Bible and thereby authenticate, if indirectly, biblical stories.

Together, these two sources of motivation – colonial sovereignty and religiously inspired travels – contributed to the construction of the ancient (pre-Islamic) Near Eastern past as being part of Western heritage, the famous "cradle of [our] civilization" (Bahrani 1998; Pollock, Steele, this volume). This endeavor was made all the easier by the fact that there were very few native Middle Eastern archaeologists or other scholars interested in the pre-Islamic past prior to the nationalist movements of the 20th century, thus eliminating any likely counter-claims to the appropriation of the Middle Eastern past by the West.

The early practitioners of archaeology included diplomats, military officers, missionaries, mining engineers, and businessmen. Monumental stone architecture, most notably from northern Mesopotamia (Iraq), and inscribed artifacts were the subject of much of the earliest scholarly attention. Already in the 1770s, Carsten Niebuhr, the one surviving member of an ill-fated expedition to Persia (Iran), had copied cuneiform inscriptions still standing at the Achaemenid capital of Persepolis. These and subsequently discovered examples from Mesopotamia formed the basis upon which a variety of individuals in western Europe began the attempt to decipher the script – cuneiform – and the ancient languages it was used to write (Zimansky, this volume).

The earliest work relied principally on studies of standing monuments, but by the middle of the 1800s, excavations – albeit more like treasure hunts by today's standards – were becoming increasingly common. They were predicated on the growing realization that the mounds dotting the landscape in many areas held archaeological remains. It was not, however, until nearly the end of the 19th century, in Petrie's work at Tell el-Hesi, that what we today consider a basic principle – attention to stratigraphy – began to be incorporated into excavations. A further methodological breakthrough around the turn of the 20th century allowed excavators for the first time to distinguish mudbrick, one of the most common building materials used in the region in the past.

Already by the turn of the 20th century, one of the enduring characteristics of archaeology of the Middle East was well established: the involvement of a mixture of archaeologists, architects, art historians, and philologists. This diversity of different scholarly interests and backgrounds has, on the one hand, resulted in a variety of different approaches to the subject matter, including emphases on different kinds of research questions and use of a variety of kinds of data to answer them. On the other hand, different specialists have all too often remained isolated in their work, either ignorant of what others are doing in related fields or dismissive of those approaches as less useful or reliable than their own (see Zimansky, this volume). These divisions tend to be perpetuated in many educational programs that track students in one direction, with little or no exposure to related fields.

Anthropological approaches to the study of the ancient Near East were relatively late in coming, and they remain to this day in the minority. Although it is rarely possible – or even helpful – to identify the "first" example of a particular approach, Robert Braidwood is often credited with introducing anthropological archaeology in the Middle East in the context of his investigations of early village life and the beginnings of agriculture. Although some elements of anthropological archaeology have become more or less routine in the region – especially systematic regional settlement surveys, pioneered in the 1930s (Jacobsen and Adams 1958; Adams 1962, 1965; see now Wilkinson 2003; Steadman, this volume) – much of the work conducted is rooted in European (as distinct from American) scholarly traditions that emphasize archaeology's connections to history and art history rather than to anthropology (Bernbeck and Pollock 2004). The contributors to this volume represent both of these "schools" – the Americanist anthropological tradition and the European historical one – helping, we believe, to promote a dialogue between different perspectives and multiple archaeologies in our studies of the ancient Near East.

Looking to the Future

We hope that the papers in this book will encourage a rethinking and ultimately some changes in the practice of scholars concerned with the ancient Near East and in this way will also impact the field's contributions to broader scholarship and to non-academic discourse. Although there are many directions to which these papers point in their critiques and suggestions for constructive reassessment, we identify two principal areas that seem to us key.

The first of these is the realm of fieldwork, generally thought to be the bread and butter of archaeology as well as the practice that ultimately produces the material on which assyriologists, ancient historians, and art historians work. Several of the authors call for a more self-critical fieldwork practice, not so much in terms of the ways in which field methods impact the results of our research but rather in the ways in which archaeologists and their work are interwoven with people who live in the areas where we work. Second, the range of different approaches to interpreting the material record of the ancient Near East taken by the authors in this volume presents a challenge to readers and one with which we hope readers will engage. As one peruses these diverse approaches to the study of the past, it is perhaps not of primary importance whether or not one agrees with each author's arguments. Instead of striving to promote the "best" – often equated with the newest – approach, the central point is to appreciate the multiplicity of ways in which understandings of the past can be achieved through a range of different perspectives that are all too often marginalized in our teaching and scholarship.

NOTES

1   Zeder (1994) has made a compelling case concerning the common neglect of village-based societies in Mesopotamia "after the [Neolithic] revolution." One could also point to the dearth of research on the Kassite period (ca. 1600–1150 B.C.E.) , a time during which there is relatively little evidence of war or expansionary politics in southern Mesopotamia, to suggest that "peacetime" is not seen as a stimulating research topic.
2   The terms Near East, Middle East, and Far East are legacies of European involvement with these parts of the world and especially of British colonialism. Each referred originally to a different geographic area. The Near and Middle East designations quickly became conflated in popular parlance, and "Near East" has fallen out of common usage, except among scholars of the ancient world.

3 It should be pointed out that in many, if not most, areas of the Middle East "natural" vegetation is something that can only be reconstructed hypothetically – thousands of years of human occupation and alteration of the vegetation have created a thoroughly anthropogenic environment.

4 Specification of an exact beginning of archaeological exploration is arbitrary, as it depends entirely on one's definition of such enterprises. However, prior to the early 19th century there are only isolated examples that might be considered archaeological, and hence we use the generally accepted reference to the early 1800s. It is worth mentioning, however, that there were occasional explorations of antiquities in ancient times, the best-known example being the Neo-Babylonian king Nabonidus, who commissioned excavations at Ur from which he retrieved ancient clay tablets.

REFERENCES

Adams, Robert McCormick, 1962 Agriculture and Urban Life in Early Southwestern Iran. Science 136:109–122.

Adams, Robert McCormick, 1965 Land Behind Baghdad. Chicago: University of Chicago Press.

Adams, Robert McCormick, 1974 The Mesopotamian Social Landscape: A View from the Frontier. *In* Reconstructing Complex Societies: An Archaeological Colloquium. C. B. Moore, ed. pp. 1–12. Bulletin of the American Schools of Oriental Research, Supplement 20.

Adams, Robert McCormick, 1981 Heartland of Cities. Chicago: University of Chicago Press.

Algaze, Guillermo, 1989 The Uruk Expansion: Cross-cultural Exchange in Early Mesopotamian Civilization. Current Anthropology 30:571–608.

Bahrani, Zainab, 1998 Conjuring Mesopotamia: Imaginative Geography and a World Past. *In* Archaeology under Fire: Nationalism, Politics and Heritage in the Eastern Mediterranean and the Middle East. Lynn Meskell, ed. pp. 159–174. London: Routledge.

Bernbeck, Reinhard, and Susan Pollock, 2004 The Political Economy of Archaeological Practice and the Production of Heritage in the Middle East. *In* The Blackwell Companion to Social Archaeology. Lynn Meskell and Robert Preucel, eds pp. 335–352. Oxford: Blackwell.

COHMAP Members, 1988 Climatic Changes of the Last 18,000 Years: Observations and Model Simulations. Science 241:1043–1052.

Henry, Donald, 1989 From Foraging to Agriculture: The Levant at the End of the Ice Age. Philadelphia: University of Pennsylvania Press.

Hole, Frank, 1994 Environmental Instabilities and Urban Origins. *In* Chiefdoms and Early States in the Near East: The Organizational Dynamics of Complexity. Gil Stein and Mitchell Rothman, eds. pp. 121–151. Madison: Prehistory Press.

Hole, Frank, and Kent Flannery, 1968 The Prehistory of Southwestern Iran: A Preliminary Report. Proceedings of the Prehistoric Society 33:147–206.

Jacobsen, Thorkild, and Robert McCormick Adams, 1958 Salt and Silt in Ancient Mesopotamian Agriculture. Science 128:1251–1258.

Kohl, Philip, and Clare Fawcett, eds., 1995 Nationalism, Politics, and the Practice of Archaeology. Cambridge: Cambridge University Press.

Kuhrt, Amélie, 1995 The Ancient Near East c. 3000–330 B.C. 2 vols. London: Routledge.

Meskell, Lynn, ed., 1998 Archaeology under Fire: Nationalism, Politics and Heritage in the Eastern Mediterranean and the Middle East. London: Routledge.

Roaf, Michael, 1990 Cultural Atlas of Mesopotamia and the Ancient Near East. New York: Facts on File.

Rowton, Michael, 1973 Autonomy and Nomadism in Western Asia. Orientalia 42:247–258.

Safar, Fuad, Mohammad Ali Mustafa, and Seton Lloyd, 1981 Eridu. Baghdad: State Organization of Antiquities and Heritage.

Said, Edward, 1981 Covering Islam: How the Media and the Experts Determine How We See the Rest of the World. New York: Pantheon.

Sasson, Jack, John Baines, Gary Beckman, and Karen Rubinson, eds., 1995 Civilizations of the Ancient Near East. New York: Charles Scribner's and Son.

Scham, Sandra, 2001 The Archaeology of the Disenfranchised. Journal of Archaeological Method and Theory 8:183–213.

Silberman, Neal Asher, 1989 Between Past and Present: Archaeology, Ideology, and Nationalism in the Modern Middle East. New York: Henry Holt.

Trigger, Bruce, 1984 Alternative Archaeologies: Nationalist, Colonialist, Imperialist. Man n.s. 19:355–370.

Van de Mieroop, Marc, 2002 In Search of Prestige: Foreign Contacts and the Rise of an Elite in Early Dynastic Babylonia. *In* Leaving No Stones Unturned: Essays on the Ancient Near East and Egypt in Honor of Donald P. Hansen. Erica Ehrenberg, ed. pp. 125–137. Winona Lake, IN: Eisenbrauns.

Wilkinson, Tony J., 2003 Archaeological Landscapes of the Near East. Tucson: University of Arizona Press.

Yoffee, Norman, 1995 Political Economy in Early Mesopotamian States. Annual Review of Anthropology 24:281–311.

Zeder, Melinda, 1994 After the Revolution: Post-Neolithic Subsistence in Northern Mesopotamia. American Anthropologist 96:97–126.

2
A Cultural-Historical Framework

Reinhard Bernbeck
and Susan Pollock

Although the goal of this book is not to present a single historical narrative of the ancient Near East, non-specialist readers may find the need for a framework within which to place the individual contributions. In this chapter, we offer a culture-historical overview of the ancient Near East. It cannot be overemphasized that, due to its brevity, this summary touches only on certain "highlights" and even these only in a most cursory fashion. Because the objective of this overview is to offer a basic background culture history, we do not endeavor to challenge standard inter-pretations and conventional wisdom; that task is left to authors of individual chap-ters. For locations of sites mentioned here and elsewhere in the book, see figures 2.1–2.2. In what follows, we have kept to the usual names given to periods. Espe-cially for historical times, this has the drawback of focusing on dynasties, implying that changes of rulers and elite concerns are the most fundamental traits of history. We do not subscribe to such a top-down view, but we have adhered to these con-ventions for convenience of reference.

Paleolithic

The archaeological record in the Middle East extends back to the Lower Paleolithic. There have been numerous isolated finds of Acheulean handaxes but few sites and no hominid remains, a situation that is probably attributable to the vagaries of site discovery as well as preservation.

During the Middle Paleolithic period the Middle East comes to occupy a place at the forefront of debates concerning relationships between Neandertals and fully modern humans (*Homo sapiens sapiens*). The region plays an important role because of its location at a key geographic crossroads between Africa, Asia, and Europe as well as the unexpectedly early dates for modern human skeletal remains (Shea, this volume). The Middle Eastern evidence raises important issues about hominid

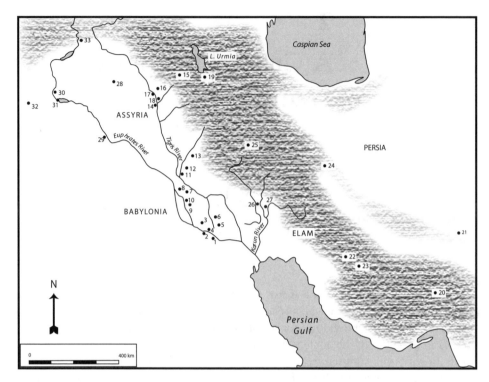

Figure 2.1 Map of Mesopotamia and Iran with archaeological sites marked. Key to sites: 1 Ur; 2 Ubaid; 3 Uruk; 4 Oueili; 5 Lagash; 6 Telloh; 7 Kish; 8 Babylon; 9 Nippur; 10 Abu Salabikh; 11 Asmar; 12 Khafajah; 13 Abada; 14 Assur; 15 Shanidar; 16 Gawra; 17 Nineveh; 18 Nimrud; 19 Hajji Firuz; 20 Yahya; 21 Shahdad; 22 Malyan; 23 Persepolis; 24 Sialk; 25 Godin; 26 Susa; 27 Chogha Zanbil; 28 Brak; 29 Mari; 30 Mureybit; 31 Abu Hureyra; 32 Ebla; 33 Çayönü (authors' original)

evolutionary pathways, social interactions between different types of hominids, and relationships between behavioral and physical characteristics.

Neolithic

The Middle East was one of the first regions in the world where people began to select and care for plants and animals, ultimately leading to their domestication, and where decreased mobility translated into the beginnings of more sedentary, village-based life. Associated with these transformations was a wide range of symbolic and ideological changes that have only recently become a serious focus of research (Kuijt and Chesson, this volume). Some scholars regard these latter as the driving force of Neolithic change (Hodder 1990; Cauvin 1994), whereas others have argued that economic (Childe 1928), demographic or ecological (Flannery 1969) variables were key. These enormously significant economic, social, and symbolic changes *in toto* characterize what V. Gordon Childe (1941) long ago labeled the

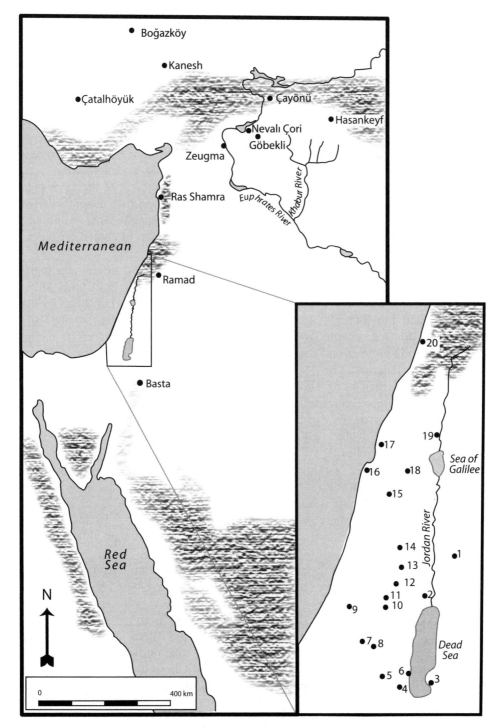

Figure 2.2 Map of the Levant and southeastern Turkey with archaeological sites marked. Key to sites: 1 'Ain Ghazal; 2 Jericho; 3 Dhra'; 4 Nahal Hemar; 5 Arad; 6 Masada; 7 Lachish; 8 Hebron; 9 Miqne-Ekron; 10 Jerusalem; 11 Gibeon; 12 Bethel; 13 Shiloh; 14 Shechem; 15 Megiddo; 16 El Wad, Skhul, Tabun, Kebara; 17 Akko; 18 Qafzeh; 19 Hazor; 20 Byblos (authors' original)

"Neolithic Revolution" but which might better be referred to as the process of neolithization.

The arc of the Fertile Crescent was the principal locus for this suite of changes, but neolithization did not occur simultaneously or uniformly throughout the area. The Levant and middle Euphrates Valley saw the first efforts at managing wild cereals and legumes, that ultimately resulted in their domestication. In the Zagros and Taurus mountain valleys and foothills, human intervention that led to domestication focused first on animals, especially goats, sheep, pig, and, somewhat later, cattle. Villages, the existence of which implies a less mobile way of life, appear in the Levant in the Natufian period, as does impressive architecture in southeastern Turkey prior to the occurrence of morphologically domesticated plants or animals. In the Zagros mountains the management and domestication of animals seems to have begun before the first sedentary villages appear.

Numerous models have been proposed to explain why food production (agriculture and animal husbandry) began when and where it did (e.g., Childe 1928; Braidwood 1960; Flannery 1969; Moore 1982; Hole 1989a). Rather than viewing sedentism and mobility as two clear-cut, dichotomous categories, scholars are increasingly drawing on ethnographic as well as archaeological literature to recognize a multitude of types and degrees of mobility. A traditional indicator of sedentariness is architecture. The earliest communities in which people constructed dwellings, rather than using naturally occurring shelters such as caves and overhangs, contain semi-subterranean, single-room, round abodes with walls of poles and reeds or reed mats. By Pre-Pottery Neolithic B (PPNB), villages consisted of multi-roomed, rectangular structures constructed of mudbrick that may have housed extended families (Byrd 2000; Moore et al. 2000). Although architecture can reveal a wide range of information on social organization and relations, it is increasingly evident that it does not, by itself, allow the specification of degrees or types of sedentism. Recent studies are focusing primarily on biological indicators that can show whether there was year-round occupation – and, by inference, if there was not – and the occurrence of debris-strewn floors as signs of short-term occupation.

During the period when the principal transformations from hunting-gathering, highly mobile lifeways to more sedentary, agricultural, village-based life were taking place in many locations across the Fertile Crescent, there were also spectacular changes in communal and regional ritual practices. In addition to the oft-cited skull separation, plastering, and display that characterize the PPNB in the Levant (see Verhoeven, Steadman, this volume), there appeared an abundance of figurines and statuary throughout the Fertile Crescent (Kuijt and Chesson, this volume). In the foothills of the Taurus mountains, aceramic Neolithic sites such as Nevalı Çori, Çayönü, and Göbekli Tepe have revealed an awesome array of non-domestic buildings, carved stone stelae with representations of animals, mythical beasts, and anthropomorphic elements, and sculptures (Hauptmann 1999; Özdoğan 1999; Schmidt 2000). These and other indications of ritual practices suggest that the numerous changes in daily living – new ways of acquiring and undoubtedly also preparing food, different kinds of communities and attachments to places – involved the establishment of a new habitus and its transmission to successive generations by means of elaborate and regionally variable forms of ritual.

In the Levant, the aceramic Neolithic was followed by the abandonment of many communities, including some of the largest, presumably in favor of a more mobile way of life. Some scholars have suggested that these abandonments were due to localized resource depletion as a result of farming, fuel cutting, and grazing (Köhler-Rollefson 1992). In the rolling hills of northern Syria, Iraq, and southeastern Turkey, Neolithic villages continued to flourish, in a series of cultural traditions known as Hassuna, Samarra, and Halaf. Some researchers have sought the beginnings of sociopolitical hierarchies in these later Neolithic traditions, with an emphasis on the exchange of elaborately painted pottery thought to have been produced by specialists (Davidson and McKerrell 1976; LeBlanc and Watson 1973; Watson 1983). Others have investigated the historical trajectory of modes of production and their social implications, examining the organization of labor required to construct buildings and make pots, the implications of village layout, and the locations of productive activities and storage facilities (Bernbeck 1994, 1995). In the last decade there has been increased attention to patterns of subsistence and settlement during the later Neolithic, with the recognition that they were much more variable than once thought, including localized emphases on wild resources and different patterns of mobility (Akkermans 1993; Zeder 1994; Bernbeck et al. n.d.).

By Samarran times (ca. 6400–5800 B.C.E.) people were practicing irrigation agriculture, as indicated by plant remains recovered, the locations of agricultural settlements in areas where rainfall farming is unlikely to have been feasible, and the remains of irrigation channels (Oates and Oates 1976). By 5500 B.C.E., if not before, settlements extended into the alluvial Mesopotamian plains, generally believed to indicate that irrigation agriculture was well enough developed to permit people to settle in this presumably inhospitable environment. However, recent paleoclimatic data suggest that southern Mesopotamia may have supported a moister environment at the time, with marshes, flood basins, and a high water table that could sustain a variety of subsistence practices including flood-recession agriculture (Sanlaville 1989; Wilkinson 2003:87–89). Coincident with settlement of the alluvial lowlands came large, free-standing, tripartite structures that may have housed extended families. This residential pattern contrasts markedly to the one in dry-farming areas where agglutinative architecture, probably housing smaller stem families, prevailed (Bernbeck 1995).

Chalcolithic

The early occupation of the southern Mesopotamian plains has been dubbed the Ubaid tradition (ca. 6000–4000 B.C.E.), distinguished by particular styles of architecture (especially the tripartite house with long central hall and smaller rooms on the two long sides), pottery, and other artifacts such as seals. Similar pottery – characterized by black to brown painting on a well-fired, buff-colored body – extends well into the Zagros mountain valleys of Iran, the northern Mesopotamian plains of Syria and Iraq, and the Taurus foothills of Turkey. These material culture similarities suggest widespread communication and interactions, although their character remains unclear, especially in light of the limited evidence for substantial long-distance exchange (Pollock 1999:81–86; Frangipane 2001; Nissen 2001).

In some areas, especially in southern Mesopotamia and the lowland plains of southwestern Iran, the Ubaid period saw the emergence of a small number of settlements markedly larger than most others and distinguished by the presence of temples, central storehouses, and cemeteries. At some sites, including small ones such as Tell Abada in central Iraq, there are indications that one household stood out from others, based on its size and unusual concentrations of artifacts and associated burials. This distinction continued over generations. Despite the dearth of exotic or other obvious "luxury" goods and low degrees of mortuary differentiation – except in lowland southwestern Iran – the presence of these "temple towns" and limited residential differentiation have convinced many researchers that Ubaid societies in southern Mesopotamia and southwestern Iran saw the emergence of hierarchical social structures, whether based on ritual or political differentiation (Jasim 1989; Pollock 1989; Hole 1989b; Stein 1994; Wright 1994 [1983]).

Substantial copper-based metallurgy is indicated by finds of metalwork of various kinds in fifth millennium sites in Turkey, northern Iraq, the Levant, and Iran. Most metalworking seems to have occurred in those areas where sources of ore were present (Moorey 1994:255–256; Chegini et al. 2000).

The fourth millennium B.C.E. saw the emergence of urbanized societies, which scholars traditionally characterize as states (but see Forest, this volume), in southern Mesopotamia and surrounding areas. In the alluvial lowlands there was an explosion of settlements, in sheer numbers and in size, during this time, which is known as the Uruk period. By the end of this period, the largest city, Uruk, extended over more than 200 ha. and was probably home to at least 20,000 residents. Recording technologies underwent rapid development, with the elaboration of clay tokens and the first appearances of cylinder seals (cylinders with the designs carved around their circumference and rolled to leave an impression [Charvát, this volume]), clay bullae containing tokens, and clay tablets with numerical signs and ultimately writing (Zimansky, this volume). Seals as well as other artifacts bearing iconography depict images of physical violence by some people against others as well as scenes of hierarchy and dominance. There is widespread evidence for tribute in labor and products, with dependent labor compensated in the form of food rations.

Southern Mesopotamia remained a heavily agrarian society in this as well as subsequent periods. Wool production seems to have achieved major importance during Uruk times, with the weaving of woolen textiles becoming a major Mesopotamian industry for both local consumption and export (Green 1980; McCorriston 1997; Pollock 1999:103–110). Domesticated donkeys appeared in Mesopotamia at this time, marking a significant breakthrough in overland transportation possibilities: a pack of loaded donkeys could transport substantial quantities of goods or people over long distances (Wright 2001:127), although boats – attested at least since Ubaid times – were probably often the preferred means.

By the middle of the Uruk period, southern Mesopotamian-style pottery, seals, and architectural styles begin to turn up in distant areas, including the middle Euphrates Valley, Taurus foothill zone of southeastern Turkey, northern Mesopotamian plains, and valleys of the Zagros mountains. By Late Uruk numerical tablets are also found in areas far distant from the alluvial lowlands. Interpretations of this "Uruk expansion" remain debated. Many scholars have argued for some kind of colonization of "the peripheries" by southern Mesopotamian state(s) for purposes of controlling resources, especially raw materials unavailable in the alluvial lowlands (Algaze 1993, 2001). Others have contested this notion, contending that southern states were not able to exert substantial political or economic control over such long distances or that there are other equally plausible ways to account for the observed similarities in material culture (Stein 1999; Rothman 2001). Regardless of the ultimate explanation for the widespread appearance of similar artifact and architectural styles, it is clear that interregional interactions were extensive during the fourth millennium, reaching not only the areas already mentioned but even as far as Egypt, where several of the distinctive Uruk clay cones – a form of architectural decoration – as well as occasional other Mesopotamian items have been found (von der Way 1987).

Increased research in the "peripheral" areas of Turkey, northern Syria and Iraq, and western and central Iran has shown that there were indigenous Late Chalcolithic traditions in most of these regions. These local traditions exhibit distinctive administrative, political, and economic systems and their own forms of internal hierarchy and inequalities, based on the exploitation of locally available resources. In areas near sources of ores, copper-based metallurgy developed into substantial industries (Chegini et al. 2000; Frangipane 2001; Malek Shahmirzadi 2002). In many regions agriculture, based primarily on rainfall farming rather than the irrigation-based cultivation that characterized the alluvial lowlands, was highly productive.

In the Levant, copper-based metallurgy was a major industry, probably involving a high degree of specialized production. Nonetheless, settlements exhibit little internal residential differentiation and few public buildings. The metal artifacts produced were not primarily tools but rather items used for display and ornamentation (Levy 1986; Kerner 2001).

Third Millennium B.C.E.

During the first two-thirds of the third millennium, there was pronounced urbanization in many parts of the Near East, although the extent to which it occurred at the expense of rural settlement varied from region to region. The alluvial lowlands of southern Mesopotamia saw a hyperurbanization in which towns and walled cities grew to massive proportions, apparently through the incorporation of former village dwellers. The Early Dynastic period (ca. 2900–2350 B.C.E.)

was distinguished by city-states – politically distinct entities with relatively small territories that included one or a few cities and a rural hinterland. The political landscape was the scene of shifting alliances as well as chronic conflict, occasionally breaking out into war, despite the overarching cultural and economic ties among city-states (Postgate 1992). Southern Mesopotamia was characterized by an "oikos" economy in which large, hierarchically organized households – whether in the hands of wealthy elites or institutions such as temples – controlled land, other means of production, and a dependent labor force that produced much of what the household consumed (Pollock 1999:ch.5). There is evidence for flourishing trade in a wide range of materials and finished products, with metals, stones, exotic woods, and other items reaching the lowlands, in exchange for textiles, grain, and fish.

In northern Mesopotamia substantial urbanization also occurred during this time, although cities tended to be smaller than in the South. Many consisted of a high citadel, where administrative and cultic activities were located, and a more extensive, residential "lower town." Most cities were walled, and many were circular in shape (*Kranzhügel*; Weiss 1986). Many, but by no means all, of the urban centers of northern Mesopotamia were located in areas where rainfall-based farming was possible. In many areas, good pasturage for animals was also available. In addition to agrarian production, long-distance exchange and the specialized craft production that supported it helped fuel the establishment and growth of urban settlement in the region (Heinz 2002). Rural settlements, which remained a much more visible part of the landscape than in the South, also included specialized communities where agricultural surpluses were accumulated and stored (Schwartz 1994).

The first half of the third millennium was also a time of urbanization in the Levant, but urban centers were modest in size and their growth was accompanied by substantial ruralization, involving considerable population increase in rural areas (Falconer 1994). Important exchange connections linked coastal Levantine cities with Egypt, the products of which entered into overland trade within northern Mesopotamia and thence to the alluvial lowlands, Iran, and beyond.

In southern and western Iran, a set of material culture distinct from that characteristic of Mesopotamia, and including a writing system known as Proto-Elamite, was in use. Elam and Awan coalesced as political entities, partly in response to periodic threats from the Mesopotamian city-states of Lagash and Kish. Trade between Iran and Mesopotamia and booty resulting from raids are attested by the presence of durable items, including "intercultural style" stone vessels, produced at places such as Tepe Yahya in southern Iran, as well as lapis lazuli from Badakhshan (Afghanistan) and carnelian, which were worked into beads and seals at Shahr-i Sokhta and other places. Goods were moved by overland transport as well as by river and sea-borne routes (Kohl 1978; Potts 1994:37; Potts 1999).

The landscape of relatively small, politically autonomous states throughout much of the Near East was substantially altered with the rise to power of the Akkadian dynasty (also known as Sargonic after the first king, Sargon) in Mesopotamia. Named for the capital, Akkad, its five principal kings were able to bring much of

Mesopotamia under the rule of a single state, often considered to be the first empire (Liverani 1993, and this volume; Forest, this volume). The conquests of the Sargonic kings, especially Naram-Sin, resulted in the imposition of royally appointed Mesopotamian governors and military garrisons in places as distant as northern Syria and western Iran. However, like later empires in the ancient Near East, the Sargonic one is best characterized as a network of nodes and links, with large areas in between that were not dominated by the imperial center.

Substantial tribute as well as booty from foreign conquests flowed into Mesopotamia under the Sargonic reign. Commercial ties were also promoted, and in Sargonic-period texts we read of maritime trade with the lands of Magan (the Oman peninsula) and Meluhha (Indus Valley). A wide variety of goods were traded, including copper, silver, gold, tin, carnelian, lapis, ivory, pearls, woods, linen, and exotic animals such as apes and birds.

The Akkadian conquests in northern Mesopotamia brought about substantial destruction in some major cities in the region, resulting in temporary abandonments. In other cases, as at Mari and Brak, new buildings were constructed by Akkadian overlords. Texts tell of the appointment of daughters of the Mesopotamian kings as high priestesses in key cities, a practice also followed within the Mesopotamian heartland. Southern rule led to a reorientation of trading relationships toward the imperial center. In places where the Akkadian rulers were unable to control trade routes, these were disrupted, in an apparent attempt to monopolize trade. These efforts coincided with a temporary decline in Levantine trade with Egypt (Heinz 2002).

Southwestern Iran – lowland Elam – fell under the direct control of the Akkadian kings and was governed by Mesopotamian officials. A military garrison was established at Susa, and much of the daily as well as administrative material culture found there is stylistically similar to that from Mesopotamia. Some texts were written in Akkadian.

Frequent rebellions, both within Mesopotamia and outside it, challenged Sargonic rule, and when the empire finally fell apart, approximately 100 years after Sargon's ascent to power, Mesopotamia returned to a political landscape of independent city-states similar to that of the Early Dynastic period. Not long after, ca. 2100 B.C.E., a dynasty based in the southern city of Ur once again created a substantial empire, which scholars today refer to as Ur III (or Third Dynasty of Ur). Under the Ur III kings, the core of the empire in southern Mesopotamia was divided into a series of administrative provinces, each headed by a governor appointed by the king but derived from a local family. Northern Mesopotamia, including the area around Assur, and western Iran (Elam and Awan) were conquered and placed under the control of military governors. A complex structure of taxation was imposed, with an elaborate bureaucracy to administer it. Systems of weights and measures, the writing system, and the calendar were highly standardized, in part to train a scribal class. The Ur III state maintained trade ties to foreign lands, and there are indications of independent merchants who were employed to organize trade on behalf of the state. Highland Elam, including the city of Anshan, was at times bound to Ur through marriages of local rulers to daughters of the Ur kings; on other occasions, military attacks – perhaps aimed at acquiring booty – were launched against Elam.

As the Ur III state expanded its control into neighboring highland regions inhabited in part by nomadic groups, conquests were followed by demands for tribute. As a result of growing demands placed upon them, people living in these regions moved increasingly into the lowlands in hopes of finding a more secure life there. These movements of Amorites into Mesopotamia are documented in Ur III texts, and ancient scribes blamed Amorite "invasions" for the gradual collapse of the central government around 2000 B.C.E., although internal problems, probably related to the overblown bureaucracy, also played a role. Under its last king, Ibbi-Sin, the Ur III state weakened substantially, and the king was ultimately captured and taken as prisoner to Elam (Charpin 1995; Kirsch and Larsen 1995; Potts 1999).

The late third millennium saw an abandonment of urban communities in the Levant. Although agriculture and small villages were not totally forsaken, there was a heavy emphasis on mobile pastoralism (Dever 1992; Haiman 1996). Urban centers reappeared in the early second millennium. Although these Middle Bronze Age urban communities were home to a larger proportion of the population than had been the case in the Early Bronze Age of the third millennium, they, too, do not seem to have been able to dominate the rural settlements around them, which maintained a considerable degree of self-determinacy (Falconer 1994).

Second Millennium B.C.E.

A series of regional states arose during the first half of the second millennium, several of which intermittently gained substantial control over both neighboring and more distant regions through a combination of conquest and alliances. The first of these were the southern city-states of Isin and Larsa and the northern one of Assur; they were followed by Mari, on the western Euphrates, and Babylon. Cross-cutting the individual political units and their changing alliances and rivalries was an "internationalization" supported by trade, intermarriage, and regular travels on the part of professionals, including scribes, doctors, musicians, and diviners. Many of these city-states were controlled by dynasties bearing Amorite names, widely assumed to represent the settling down of former nomads who had gradually moved into the alluvial lowlands over centuries (Charpin 1995; Kuhrt 1995; Whiting 1995).

The Amorite conqueror, Shamshi-Adad I, took power in Assyria in the mid-19th century and from a base on the Tigris not far from Assur conquered other city-states including Mari, Nineveh, and Shubat-Enlil. Assur's wealth and power derived to a substantial degree from trade with Anatolia in tin, textiles, silver, and gold, a commercial connection that is particularly well documented through texts found at the site of Kültepe/Kanesh in Anatolia. The merchant-capital-based trade was run by merchants from Assur, some of whom settled in Kültepe/Kanesh to further their family businesses, and in doing so adopted the local culture so thoroughly that their material remains are almost completely indistinguishable archaeologically from those of the native inhabitants (Özgüç 1963). Merchandise was transported by donkey caravans, with tin and textiles brought into Anatolia from Assur and silver and gold moved in the opposite direction. Merchants in Assur bought tin – perhaps coming from Iran – and textiles for silver and sold them in Kanesh for larger quantities of silver and gold. Control over the tin trade was lucrative, since sources of tin were few and demand for it, as a constituent of bronze, high (Yoffee 1981; Larsen 1987; Veenhof 1995).

Of the various competing states, it was Babylon that achieved the most extensive political control. Under king Hammurabi, Babylon began to expand its territory around 1760 B.C.E., until it controlled an area approximately the size of the Ur III empire. Like most of the smaller political entities that it incorporated, the Old Babylonian state was concerned to ensure that ample supplies of silver, gold, copper, tin, lapis, carnelian, exotic woods, horses, etc. would find their way to Babylon. Both private merchants and others associated with the state were involved in trading ventures. The extensive polity assembled under Hammurabi did not much outlast his death, as was also the case with the Old Assyrian state under Shamshi-Adad.

The time between ca. 1600 and 1200 B.C.E. is exceptional because of the relative stability, despite conflicts, and the establishment of diplomatic relationships between a number of major polities, among them Egypt, the Hittites in Anatolia, the Kassite dynasty in Babylonia, and Hurri-Mittani in northern Syria. The best information on these connections comes from Egyptian texts at Tell el-Amarna, Pharaoh Akhenaten's capital. Rulers and their elite apparently sent highly prized goods such as gold, lapis lazuli, and horses to one other and often received similar items in return. The function of these gifts was less their use-value than the prestige that came with giving them away, thus enhancing relationships with other friendly regimes (Liverani 1979).

There were, of course, episodes of war. The Hittites established a powerful state in central Anatolia, the capital of which was Hattusha. This dynasty, which lasted from ca. 1650–1200 B.C.E., fought with the Hurri-Mittani, Egyptians and especially their internal enemy, the Kashkaeans, a sort of guerrilla group living in the mountains north of Hattuša.

Hittite culture and religion display a tradition fundamentally different from Mesopotamia. The language was Indo-European, written in cuneiform (Zimansky, this volume). Deities were worshiped near springs and in rock chambers as well as at other prominent natural spots, and magic played an important role (Haas 1994; Klinger 2002). Hittite ideology forced the king to worship all deities of his empire in their location. This necessitated unmanageably long travels and was finally solved by building numerous temples in the capital, requiring a considerable extension of the city (Neve 1996; Seeher 2002).

The southeastern border of the Hittite realm became the home of the Mittani kingdom. At the time of its greatest extension, Hurro-Mittani domination reached from the Mediterranean coast in the west across the northern Syrian steppes to the edge of the Zagros mountains in the east (Wilhelm 1982). The region was settled by a Hurrian-speaking population, although members of the elite had Indo-Iranian names, and in one written contract, Indo-Iranian gods are mentioned. The capital of the kingdom, Waššukanni, has not yet been identified, and other evidence about this polity is scanty. Our limited state of knowledge about them has led to a highly simplified historiography, according to which Hurrian lower classes were ruled by an Indo-Iranian elite. The desire to confirm Mittani domination over Hurrians through archaeology has resulted in misguided, often racist attempts to identify an ethnically distinct "Hurrian" culture (Diakonoff 1972; Kammenhuber 1977; Barrelet 1978; Börker-Klähn 1988).

Before Mittani power was established, a Hittite king had attacked Babylon, putting an end to the Old Babylonian dynasty and taking away the statue of the main god, Marduk. The ensuing political vacuum was soon filled by the Kassites who established a new dynasty in Babylon and emerged as a power to be reckoned with for the next 400 years. Judging by their names Kassites were neither of Sumerian nor Semitic origin. In contrast to their predecessors, the Kassite dynasty was able to achieve long-lasting political control over southern Mesopotamia, only being overthrown by Elamite invaders in the twelfth century B.C.E. Kassite kings undertook substantial building programs and restorations in several old southern Mesopotamian cities, often following earlier architectural traditions. They also promoted traditional Babylonian religious rituals. Connections with Egypt were advanced by regular contacts and royal marriages that were accompanied by lavish gift-giving as well as more formal trading ties. The distances over which trade and gift-giving connections reached are made clear by finds of Kassite seals at Thebes in Greece and a Mycenaean oxhide ingot in Mesopotamia (Brinkman 1972; Charpin 1995; Sommerfeld 1995).

In this period, the Levant was spotted with small, rarely independent city-states such as Ugarit, Kumidi, Hazor, or Gezer. Much of their richness was derived from their favorable locations along maritime or overland trade routes. These states typically consisted of a fortified city on the coast plus surrounding countryside with a population living in small villages. They had close ties with Egypt, which, for much of the second half of the second millennium, dominated the region (Weinstein 1981). Among the chief products of the Canaanite states were grain and wine.

Ugarit is of particular interest because of the large number of unique religious and mythological texts found there (Klengel et al. 1989:278–279; Tsumura 1999). Historically of major importance are letters from the last days of the city that report threatening ships of an unknown enemy. A connection has been drawn to those groups called by the Egyptians "Sea Peoples" (Drews 1993). Among these were the "Peleshet," known in the Bible as Philistines, who destroyed a number of cities along the southern Levantine coast and settled there, for instance at Ashkelon, Gaza, and Ekron. In the post-destruction layers, close stylistic similarity in ceramics with Mycenean products from the Aegean point to the origins of the "Sea Peoples" (Dothan 1992; Knapp 1992). However, this does not necessarily mean that the "Sea Peoples" were the cause of the breakdown of the Hittite and Mittani empires. Rather, they may have been the final stroke needed to bring down overspecialized societies heavily dependent on external relations.

Further east, on the upper Tigris, Assyria had risen to power with the Middle Assyrian empire (ca. 1365–1077 B.C.E.), after the demise of the Mittani. Assyrian expansion was oriented towards Babylonia as well as the west, where recent excavations have exposed palaces and fortress-like buildings of possibly defensive function (Kühne 1983; Akkermans and Rossmeisl 1990). Middle Assyrian kings began to put in place imperial policies of expansion that became the mainstay of later Neo-Assyrian imperialism: large-scale deportations (Freydank 1975) and the legitimation of war by invocation of the main god, Assur, who was turned into a war god (Nissen 1998:88).

Assyrian desires to take control of southern Mesopotamia did not lead to major successes but proved useful to a third party, the Elamites in southwestern Iran (ca. 1450–1100 B.C.E.). When the Middle Assyrian king Assur-Dan attempted to conquer Babylon unsuccessfully in 1161 B.C.E., the Elamite ruler Shutruk-Nahhunte followed immediately, conquering Babylonia and taking major monuments to his capital at Susa (Carter and Stolper 1984:32–43; Potts 1999:188–258). Many of these were excavated by French expeditions to Susa in the late 19th century C.E. and are of premier art historical and historical importance, such as the Codex Hammurabi and the "Naram-Sin Stele."

First Millennium B.C.E.

In the second millennium B.C.E., Assyria had never been able to subdue more than a relatively small territory. With the rise of the Neo-Assyrian empire (ca. 900–610 B.C.E.), much of the Near East was unified under one political power (Spek 1993; Parker 2001). The Assyrians conquered successively Babylonia, Syria, and Palestine. The Assyrian empire is known largely through excavations at several of the imperial capitals including Nineveh, Nimrud, and Dur Sharrukin (Mallowan 1966; Albenda 1986; Levine 1986). As opposed to earlier times, Assyrian kings often shifted their capital to a new site when coming to power, building major palaces and decorating them with orthostats, a Hittite tradition that the Assyrians refined. Traditionally orthostats had reliefs of court scenes; now, violent images of war, siege, destruction, killing, and deportation prevailed, accompanied by more solemn depictions of the king in rituals or during hunts. The reliefs often carry annalistic inscriptions, from which historical events – mostly campaigns against various enemies – can be gleaned (Reade 1980; Winter 1981; Villard 1988).

The expansion of the Neo-Assyrian empire occurred in several phases. In the ninth century, most military campaigns were aimed at regions west of the Assyrian heartland on the Tigris River. Partly, this may have been due to a desire to secure provisions of iron, a metal that quickly became of prime military importance in the early first millennium B.C.E. The end of the ninth and the first half of the eighth centuries B.C.E. can best be interpreted as a period of consolidation, with little further expansion (Bernbeck 1993). In the middle of the eighth century, Tiglat-Pileser III restructured the empire and established provincial districts (Garelli 1991). From his reign on, the empire continually expanded, leading to the conquest of Egypt under Assurbanipal (668–631). In the end, this proved fatal. The overstretching of resources resulted in a collapse of the empire in 614 B.C.E. (Lamprichs 1995).

Like all other kingdoms and empires of the ancient Near East, the Neo-Assyrian one consisted of not much more outside the imperial core than a network of "royal highways" (*harran šarri*; Kessler 1980) and nodes in the form of Assyrianized castles (Liverani 1988). Much of the interstices in this network was probably never dominated by the Assyrians, and this was one of the sources of their constant need to fight against internal enemies in addition to outward expansion. The core region, a territory completely under the power of the Assyrian rulers, was expanded over time. The massive interference of Assyrian power on all levels of life in this zone has only recently become clear with the synopsis of survey work in Upper Mesopotamia by Wilkinson and Barbanes (2000), which reveals a steep increase in the later Neo-Assyrian period of small, hamlet-sized and regularly spaced villages, often in ecologically marginal regions. This is most likely due to resettlement of deportees (Oded 1979).

Assyria was at war with four neighboring regional entities. Two of these, Babylonia and Urartu, were major states. Urartu, with its capital Tushpa on the shores of Lake Van, had been established in the ninth century B.C.E. by rulers with strong relations to Assyria, but afterwards developed independently into a rival of Assyria, vying to conquer small city-states on the upper Euphrates. At the end of the eighth century B.C.E., the Assyrian king Sargon II ravaged the kingdom but was unable to integrate it into his realm. Our sense of the historical events of these times is relatively sophisticated due to the fact that we have sources from political opponents at our disposal (Lanfranchi and Parpola 1990). Still, the Urartian language is not yet fully understood (Zimansky, this volume), and for most of its history, only monumental stone inscriptions have survived. However, recent stunning archaeological discoveries have significantly added to our knowledge about the later periods of this polity (Belli 1999; Çilingiroğlu and Salvini 2001). Urartu differs not just linguistically, but also in religious terms from lowland Mesopotamia. Stone stelae were placed on passes, road crossings, and salient natural points, but they lack reliefs, and the main god Haldi was not represented anthropomorphically (Salvini 1995; Zimansky 1995; Smith 2000, 2003).

Urartu's western neighbor was the central Anatolian kingdom of Phrygia. This entity, whose capital Gordion is well known for the incomparable riches of its royal tombs (Young 1981), had good relations with Assyria to the east as well as the Greeks to the west (Mellink 1965; Muscarella 1989). The Phrygian language, for which we do not have many sources, was an Indo-European one related to Greek and languages of other peoples then occupying the Balkans. Apparently, Phrygian culture had been established not long after the breakdown of the Hittite empire around 1200 B.C.E., making an historical link between these two events possible.

The Hittite court had always had strong political connections to Cilicia and Carchemish in the south and southeast, and it is in these regions that we see a continuation of Hittite culture in what is today known as the "Neo-Hittite kingdoms"

(Hawkins 2002). These were mostly small city-states in southeastern Anatolia. They continued the use of Luwian (hieroglyphic) writing on stone and the decoration of their palaces with orthostats (Bonatz 2001; Zimansky 2002). These city-states were interspersed with Aramaic ones (Glassner 2002:38). The latter are identifiable through names of the form "*Bit* X", where "*bit*" means "house, kin unit" and refers to a common (mythical) ancestor. Aramaic became important as an administrative language, largely due to its use of an alphabetic script, the precursor of later West Semitic scripts, including Hebrew. In contrast to Akkadian, Aramaic was written cursively on parchment, ostraka, or stone. Neo-Assyrians used Aramaic as a second administrative language (Klengel et al. 1989:342).

South of the Aramaic-Neo-Hittite realm, the Neo-Assyrians encountered a number of kingdoms well known from the Bible. Among those were Damascus, Hamath, Moab, Ammon, Edom, as well as Israel and Judah (Sauer 1986). At the time of Neo-Assyrian expansion, the Israelite state had disintegrated into a northern (Israel) and southern (Judah) kingdom (Finkelstein, this volume). Israel, with its capital Samaria, was ruled by the relatively powerful dynasty of Omri that had strong connections to the Phoenicians on the Mediterranean coast. This dynasty was followed by other kings at Samaria until the final destruction by the Assyrians in 722 B.C.E.. Judah, a smaller and economically less attractive state, was not touched by this attack (Finkelstein and Silberman 2001:169–228). Soon after, however, in 701 B.C.E., Sennacherib took revenge on the rebellious king Hesekiah and destroyed large parts of the Judaean countryside but left Jerusalem untouched. The reliefs of the destruction of Lachish, the second-ranked city of Judah, figured prominently in Sennacherib's palace in Nineveh (Ussishkin 1982, 2003). Judah survived the end of the Neo-Assyrian empire, but in 586, the Neo-Babylonian king Nebuchadnezzar II destroyed Jerusalem and its temple and took the urban elite into captivity in Babylonia.

Despite their might, brutality, and somewhat sadistic delight in decorating palaces with scenes of ultimate violence (Bersani and Dutoit 1985; Davis 1996:266–285), the Assyrian court was also a center where multiple cultures were melded into an impressive imperial art. Artisans from different regions created intricate ivory panels for furniture (Winter 1982). Elaborate jewelry of gold and precious stones was recently found in the burials of queens at Nimrud. Under Sennacherib, a major irrigation system was installed that diverted water from the Tigris River in the mountains of the Zagros (Jacobsen and Lloyd 1935). Many tablets, most famously Assurbanipal's library containing some 30,000 texts (Glassner 2002), provide important insights into literature, religion, astronomy, jurisprudence, and other spheres of intellectual life.

In the late seventh century B.C.E., the Medes, a tribe from the Iranian highlands, gained power and established a capital in Ekbatana (Frye 1984; Brown 1986). Together with southern Babylonian groups, they were able to put an end to the Assyrian empire. The mountainous regions became part of a short-lived Median kingdom, while the Neo-Babylonian kings (ca. 626–539 B.C.E.) were able to rule over much of the former Assyrian realm. Babylon again became a political and cultural center (Beaulieu 1995), and its most famous king, Nebuchadnezzar II, was responsible for such prominent buildings as the tower of Babel, a ziggurat (Schmid 1995). The end of the empire is shrouded in mystery. The last king Nabonidus, known also for his interest in the Mesopotamian past and his excavations of earlier temples, withdrew to the desert oasis of Teima, presumably for religious reasons. This gave the increasingly powerful Achaemenid king Cyrus II from the Iranian highlands the occasion to defeat the powerholder in Babylon, Nabonidus's son Belsazar (Beaulieu 1989).

Cyrus II was the founder of the vast Achaemenid ("Persian") empire (559–331 B.C.E.) that reached from western Anatolia to the Indus Valley in today's Pakistan. Larger than any earlier empire, it was plagued by frequent revolts, often several at a time in widely separate parts of the empire (Briant 1999). This necessitated military and administrative decentralization. The territory was divided into satrapies (extensive provinces), each of which was subdivided into smaller units (Wiesehöfer 1996:60–61). The rulers of a satrapy were normally from the royal family. Other unifying measures were the institutionalization of an administrative language, Aramaic, a single system of measurements, an empire-wide currency (Frye 1984:129–130), and the enlargement of the Assyrian network of royal highways (Nissen 1998:118).

Susa, Persepolis, Babylon, and Ekbatana were Achaemenid capitals (Briant 1988). Susa and Persepolis were the preferred cities, as evidenced in the layout and architecture of their vast palace complexes. Stone reliefs at Persepolis exhibit parallels to Assyrian precursors, such as mythical *lamassu*, genii guarding the entrances (cf. Panaino 2000). And while power over the periphery was still depicted in orthostats, it was represented through formalized scenes of tribute-giving by all 20 satrapies, rather than torture and violence, all the while keeping to the highly normative renderings of foreigners' clothing and hair styles typical of Assyrian imagery (Walser 1966; Root 1979; Roaf 1983). The focus on scenes of political economy rather than military character underscores Achaemenid preference for discipline and order as a means to rule, rather than sheer force.

Much of our knowledge about Achaemenid warfare and its failures at Marathon and Salamis is derived from well-known Greek sources, particularly Herodotus (cf. Högemann 1993). While Eurocentric historians have for the longest time blindly believed in the exactitude of accounts of heroic, victorious Greeks against the huge Persian army, recent assessments have cast serious doubt on both the rendering of the events as well as their importance to the Achaemenid empire (Young 1980; Wiesehöfer 1996:51–52). Long after these battles, the Achaemenid empire fell prey to Alexander III ("the Great"). Alexander's conglomeration of politically highly variable conquests (the Achaemenid realm, Macedonia, the Greek peninsula) disintegrated immediately after his death in 323 B.C.E. Much of the ancient Near East became part of the Seleucid empire (ca. 310–63 B.C.E.). The Levant was temporarily part of the Ptolemaic empire, centered on Egypt. Anatolia was the scene of various small polities (Armenia, Bithynia, Pontos).

The period following Alexander's conquests is still interpreted in standard literature as a "Hellenization" of the Orient. However, Alexander himself underwent an Orientalization during his short reign, in mundane elements such as clothing as well as in administrative policies (satrapies as provincial units, Greek and Aramaic as official languages of the bureaucracy; Frye 1984:142–143; Hauser 1995). The dominant idea of a deep-reaching Hellenization of the Near East is due to ethnocentric representations by ancient authors, the colonization policy of the Seleucid emperors, and present archaeologists' and historians' preconceptions (cf. Sherwin-White and Kuhrt 1993). And while the Seleucids founded major cities and gave them the prerogatives of *poleis*, settled them with immigrants from Macedonia and Greece, and furnished them with their traditional institutions (theater, agora, gymnasium), these did not bring a Greek culture of "democracy." As noted by one prominent historian, "to invent the free citizen was at the same time to invent the slave" (Vernant 2000:174). The focus on the archaeological identification of Greek foundations, from Anatolia to Afghanistan, has led to the neglect of contemporary non-Greek cities and the countryside that pervaded the interstices of this Greek network.[1] The few indications available about provincial conditions suggest that, contrary to traditional views, Seleucid power may have been relatively successful because of the loose ("federal") administrative structure, rather than the presence of Macedonian military garrisons (Wiesehöfer 1996:109).

The end of Seleucid power is attributed to the rise of Parthia in the east (ca. 270 B.C.E.–C.E. 227) and Rome in the west. In the second half of the second century B.C.E., the Parthian dynasty established itself as a political counterweight against Rome. The territory reached from Afghanistan to the upper Euphrates which was the border with Rome. Despite a dynasty that is one of the longest-lasting of the Near East, Parthian history is marginalized in Near Eastern historiography because written sources are scarce, and much of what we know is derived from the adversarial information of Roman authors (Ball 2000:12–13). During the Parthian reign, a shift is perceptible in Mesopotamia from Philhellenism to ideological recourse to the Achaemenids as political ancestors (Schippmann 1980:75–76). This may be reflected in the establishment of Ctesiphon, which was first a suburb of Seleucia on the Tigris, as capital. This move was apparently meant to draw inhabitants from the Greek *polis* to a newly founded, more "Iranian" city (Frye 1984:227).

Both the Parthian empire and the Roman client states at its western border profited from Rome's desires for spices, perfumes, silk, and other products from the Far East. The Silk Road's western starting points were such famously rich cities as Hatra, Palmyra, and (the recently irrevocably perished) Zeugma on the Euphrates (Wiesehöfer 1996:147; Kennedy 1998). While trade and urban life may have prospered, surveys indicate that agriculture was neglected and nomadism was on the rise (Adams and Nissen 1972:57; Bernbeck 1996:406–407).

Contemporary with the rise of the Parthian empire, the Levant was turned into a series of small client states of Rome. Judaea is the most famous among them, as a result of the detailed description of it from Flavius Josephus's account of the "Jewish War" (Smallwood 1976; Bernbeck, this volume), the stunning finds of religious texts at Qumran (Davies et al. 2002; Zangenberg 2003), and the intense long-lasting interest in Christian New Testament history that led to the early establishment of an archaeology of Palestine (Yahya, this volume). Most of the Roman client kingdoms had a double structure of Romanized cities, castles, and religious institutions that existed side-by-side with traditional villages, towns with local culture and temples for native deities (Safrai 1994). In Judaea, Herod "the Great" built major fortresses, among them the Masada, that are a mixture of Roman elements (baths with *caldarium* and *tepidarium*) and non-figural wall decoration and mosaics, in accordance with Jewish proscriptions (Lehmann 2003). In other kingdoms, deities such as the main Nabataean god Dushara were depicted either in their traditional form as a stone cube or as a personified image in the Graeco-Roman tradition (Ball 2000:46–47).

While we do not know much about the lower classes of other Roman client kingdoms, we are extremely well informed about Judaea. In the first century C.E., numerous messiahs emerged and incited revolts against the foreign occupation. Not only did these mostly peasant figures preach resistance against occupation forces, they also condemned urban Jewish collaborators. Crucifixion was the elite's answer to such threat, spurring more resistance (Hanson and Oakman 1998:86–95). Two major revolts in C.E. 70 and 135 led to the destruction of the Second Temple in Jerusalem and, finally, the complete Romanization of the city and a ban on access for all Jews (Isaac 1992).

Regions east of Judaea never became semi-independent client polities. They were too near to Rome's border with the powerful Parthian enemy and the unruly Arab tribes and were therefore directly controlled. Well known are the centers of the Dekapolis, a league of ten cities, including Gerasa and Gadara east of the Jordan River. Most of these cities already had a Hellenistic tradition and their western character became even more emphasized with Roman rule (Ball 2000:181–197). The importance of these frontier cities and of the *limes arabicus* on the eastern edge of the Roman empire were emphasized with the death of the last Parthian king in 224 C.E. and the expansion of the Sasanian empire (226–651 C.E.) towards the west.

First and Second Millennia C.E.

The Sasanian dynasty inherited much of the Parthian territory. In the East, it bordered the Kushana kingdom in today's eastern Afghanistan until its inclusion in the Sasanian empire in the mid-third century. The most important western neighbor was Rome and later the Byzantine realm. Armenia and other Anatolian regions were a bone of contention between Sasanians and Romans, with both sides attempting to keep the borderland under their influence. In the course of wars in the Sasanian west in the third century, the Romans repeatedly suffered devastating defeats (Schippmann 1990:19–24), and Shahpur I even captured the Roman emperor Valerian in C.E. 260 (Whitby 1994). On the same occasion, tens of thousands of Roman POWs were deported and settled in newly founded cities, among them Jundishahpur in the Susiana plain and Bishapur in the southern Zagros mountains. Jundishahpur soon became one of the foremost academic centers of late antiquity, attracting Greek philosophers who had become homeless after Justinian's closure of Plato's academy in Athens (cf. Potts 1989).

Sasanian kings, even more than the Parthians, saw themselves as heirs of the Achaemenid dynasty. They traced their origin back to the region of Persepolis, and reliefs were carved into the rock face below the façades of Achaemenid royal burials in the vicinity (Wiesehöfer 1996: 155). In other places as well, royal Sasanian reliefs and inscriptions were positioned in relation to Achaemenid landscape features (Bernbeck 2003). The Sasanians are known for palace architecture that influenced later Islamic building traditions, with monumental domes over square rooms as well as the *iwan*, a room with walls on three sides and a barrel-vault (Schippmann 1990:115–119).

Knowledge about living conditions of the lower classes in Sasanian times is limited. As for so many other periods, archaeological interest has so far concentrated on elites and large sites, palaces, and temples rather than the living quarters and villages (e.g. Simpson 2003). Surveys suggest rural-urban migrations (Wenke 1987:256), but also major administrative efforts to construct large-scale irrigation networks all over Mesopotamia and the Susiana Plain. It is unclear whether a failure in upkeep led to their ruin and concurrent decline of population, or whether the construction of the systems themselves are at the root of ecological problems (Adams 1981:205).

Religion played a major role both internally and in relation to the emerging Byzantine empire. Zoroastrianism became the Sasanian state religion under the high priest Kartir. Mani, the third century C.E. founder of Manichaeism, a syncretistic religion with elements of Zoroastrianism, Chaldaean beliefs, Judaism, early Christianity, and Gnosticism, was killed at the instigation of the magi (Zoroastrian priests; cf. Sundermann 1986:253–268). Manichaeism had spread quickly over a vast area reaching from Spain to China. Syncretistic religions attest to intense interchanges in spiritual matters; eastern ideas, for example, became highly influential for the development of Christian theology. The concept of a god as "pure" and "good," for example, has its origins in Zoroastrianism (Ball 2000:435).

From the early fourth century C.E. onwards, the Roman empire was divided administratively into an eastern and a western part, with Constantinople (Istanbul) as the eastern capital. This city became the core of the Byzantine empire (C.E. 610–1204) whose Near Eastern possessions included Anatolia and the Levant. The former *Provincia Palaestina* turned into a favored region in the fourth century, with financial resources flowing to the area because of its importance as the origin of Christianity, the official religion of the Byzantine state. In many places thought to have biblical significance, churches were built, most prominently the Church of the Holy Sepulchre in Jerusalem (Silberman 1995:11). Contemporary synagogues have also been discovered, especially in Galilee and the Golan (Hachlili 1988).

Based on a combination of historical data and survey evidence, the Levant and northern Mesopotamia seem to have witnessed an unprecedented economic boom and demographic growth during Byzantine times (e.g. Broshi 1979). This may, however, be due to mis-dating of ceramics, since much of the standard "Byzantine" ceramic material continues in use in the following early Islamic times (Whitcomb 1995:493–494). Thus, the stark contrast between dense settlements with terraced

fields and olive production in Byzantine times and a largely uninhabited early
Islamic landscape is overdrawn (but see Wilkinson 2003:171–172).

C.E. 622, the year of the prophet Mohammed's *hijrah* to Medina, marks the
beginning of the Islamic calendar and has been a convenient starting date for what
archaeologists often call the "Islamic period." However, this notion of a radical
historical-cultural divide, underscored by the swift conquest of Mesopotamia,
Sasanian Iran, Syria, and North Africa, has produced an ill-conceived historiography that puts the archaeology of the succeeding periods on the wrong track. The
concept of an "Islamic archaeology" is replete with orientalist preconceptions: a
period of more than 1,300 years is glossed over, although both written and archaeological data are much richer than for earlier periods. Moreover, much of what
counts as "Islamic archaeology" is merely an art history (e.g. Schick 1998) that
aims to create a space-time systematics at the level of specific rulers, rather than
contributing to anthropological-historical knowledge of social development (Insoll
1999:3–7).

Recently, however, change is apparent in excavation and survey projects with
interests in the archaeology of "Early Islam." Most archaeologists would include
under this term the Umayyad and Abbasid dynasties (C.E. 638–mid-13th century).
This period is of long-standing interest for its urban planning and architecture. The
earliest and most famous major public building from this period is the Dome of the
Rock in Jerusalem (Grabar 1990). The foundation of new cities in the vicinity of
older ones gave planners the opportunity of imposing an artificial urban layout. Such
new cities are characterized by some elements already known from late antiquity,
above all the two main thoroughfares crossing at a right angle in a settlement's center.
Elements of Sasanian origin also provide continuity, for example the decoration of
palaces and "castles" with stucco (Kröger 1982:22). On the other hand, the lack of
theaters, the mosques with their specific plans and installations, caravanserais, and
bazaars give these towns their own cultural characteristics. Archaeologists have variously focused on continuity with earlier periods (Meinecke 1996:141) and the inno-
vative potential of the Arab conquerors (Whitcomb 1995:491–492).

We do not know much about daily life in the Early Islamic period. The wide
range of analytical archaeological methods, such as faunal and paleobotanical analysis, absolute dating techniques, and spatial analysis of artifacts, are rarely considered worthwhile applying to Islamic remains (but see King and Cameron 1994;
Yahya, this volume). Regional research on early Islamic settlement often leads to
highly contradictory results. Areas with relatively well known ceramics display a
demographic increase in the Early Islamic period (Bartl 1994), whereas neighboring regions are often interpreted as almost deserted, most likely because orientalist assumptions impinge on the wrong chronological assignment of sherds.

In the Levant, the Crusader period marks a brief interlude (C.E. 1097–1291)
that has repercussions up to today. The Crusader polities in the Levant have traditionally been interpreted as well-integrated kingdoms in which gradually oriental-
izing Franks and the local population lived peacefully side by side. This older view
has been replaced by one that sees the European invaders as a population restricted
to their easily defensible castles and monumental monasteries, with practically no

communication with the surrounding villagers (Smail 1995; Gabrieli 1973). More recent research indicates that crusaders had access to undefended hamlets and manors, but that such contact was largely restricted to Christian localities (Ellenblum 1995:508–509).

Highly visible, forbiddingly militant-looking castles dot the landscape of the Levant and provide present inhabitants with a constant reminder of a past foreign occupation and clash of religions. Because of obvious analogies to the present, these archaeological remains need to be treated carefully, and any positive reference to the Crusader period in modern political or other contexts is insensitive and likely to engender further conflict (Scham 2002:26–27).

Disputed reasons for the first Crusade include the search for an outlet for over-population and rampant poverty in Europe, as well as the conquest of Jerusalem by the Seljuks, a Turkish tribe that had converted to Islam. This dynasty, which ruled over Mesopotamia and Anatolia, was followed by others with origins further east in Mongolia. The Mongolian conquests wrought havoc on the ancient irriga-tion systems in Mesopotamia and seriously reduced the region's population (Adams 1981:225–228). However, no similarly in-depth evidence is available from other regions. The political situation stabilized with the Ottoman dynasty (C.E. 1300–1923) that ruled over Mesopotamia, the Levant, and Anatolia. Iran was for much of this period governed by the Safavid dynasty. A theoretically informed archaeology with a socio-economic focus is not yet available for these periods, although a recent volume on Ottoman archaeology makes a fundamental step in that direction (Baram and Carroll 2000).

This chapter cannot end without a suggestion. Even the most recent past should not escape the critical eyes of archaeological scrutiny. From the early 20th century on, the Middle East has been subject to numerous wars, mass murder, and exter-nal political and economic pressures. These events are historically well known. However, archaeologists have generally avoided investigating their impacts on local populations, even though they may have more sophisticated means to do so than anyone else.

NOTE

1 There are probably many small settlements excavated which remain largely unpublished because such sites are mostly excavated with other goals in mind (for a recent exception see Parr 2003:251–276).

REFERENCES

Adams, Robert McCormick, 1981 Heartland of Cities. Chicago: University of Chicago Press.
Adams, Robert McC., and Hans J. Nissen, 1972 The Uruk Countryside. Chicago: Univer-sity of Chicago Press.

Akkermans, Peter M. M. G., 1993 Villages in the Steppe. Ann Arbor: International Mono-
    graphs in Prehistory.
Akkermans, Peter M. M. G., and Inge Rossmeisl, 1990 Excavations at Tell Sabi Abyad,
    Northern Syria: A Regional Center on the Assyrian Frontier. Akkadica 66:13–60.
Albenda, Pauline, 1986 The Palace of Sargon, King of Assyria. Paris: Éditions Recherche sur
    les Civilisations.
Algaze, Guillermo, 1993 The Uruk World System: The Dynamics of Expansion of Early
    Mesopotamian Civilization. Chicago: University of Chicago Press.
Algaze, Guillermo, 2001 Initial Social Complexity in Southwestern Asia: The Mesopotamian
    Advantage. Current Anthropology 42:199–233.
Ball, Warwick, 2000 Rome in the East. London: Routledge.
Baram, Uzi, and Lynda Carroll, eds., 2000 A Historical Archaeology of the Ottoman Empire.
    New York: Kluwer Academic/Plenum.
Barrelet, Marie-Thérèse, 1978 Le "cas hurrite" et l'archéologie. Revue Hittite et Asiatique
    36:23–34.
Bartl, Karin, 1994 Frühislamische Besiedlung im Balih-Tal / Nordsyrien. Berlin: Reimer.
Beaulieu, Paul-Alain, 1989 The Reign of Nabonidus, King of Babylon, 556–539 B.C. New
    Haven: Yale University Press.
Beaulieu, Paul-Alain, 1995 King Nabonidus and the Neo-Babylonian Empire. In Civiliza-
    tions of the Ancient Near East. Jack M. Sasson, John Baines, Gary M. Beckman, and
    Karen S. Rubinson, eds. pp. 969–980. New York: Charles Scribner's Sons.
Belli, Oktay, 1999 The Anzaf Fortresses and the Gods of Urartu. Geoffrey D. Summers and
    Ayça Üzel, trans. Istanbul: Arkeoloji ve Sanat Yayınları.
Bernbeck, Reinhard, 1993 Steppe als Kulturlandschaft. Berlin: Dietrich Reimer.
Bernbeck, Reinhard, 1994 Die Auflösung der Häuslichen Produktionsweise: Das Beispiel
    Mesopotamiens. Berliner Beiträge zum Vorderen Orient Band 14. Berlin: Dietrich
    Reimer.
Bernbeck, Reinhard, 1995 Lasting Alliances and Emerging Competition: Economic
    Developments in Early Mesopotamia. Journal of Anthropological Archaeology 14:1–
    25.
Bernbeck, Reinhard, 1996 Settled and Mobile Populations in the Southern Ğazira (3rd
    through 9th Centuries A.D.). In Continuity and Change in Northern Mesopotamia from
    the Hellenistic to the Early Islamic Period. Karin Bartl and Stefan Hauser, eds. pp.
    401–414. Berlin: Reimer.
Bernbeck, Reinhard, 2003 Der grüne Punkt im Alten Orient. In Müll. Facetten von der
    Steinzeit bis zum Gelben Sack. Mamoun Fansa and Sabine Wolfram, eds. pp. 35–46.
    Mainz: Philipp von Zabern.
Bernbeck, Reinhard, Susan Pollock, Susan Allen, Ana Gabriela Castro Gessner, Sarah Kielt
    Costello, Robert Costello, Melissa Foree, Margarita Gleba, Marie Goodwin, Sarah
    Lepinski, Carolyn Nakamura, and Sarah Niebuhr, n.d. The Biography of an Early Halaf
    Village: Fıstıklı Höyük 1999–2000. To appear in Istanbuler Mitteilungen.
Bersani, Leo, and Ulysse Dutoit, 1985 The Forms of Violence: Narrative in Assyrian Art and
    Modern Culture. New York: Schocken Books.
Börker-Klähn, Jutta, 1988 Die archäologische Problematik der Hurriter-Frage und eine
    mögliche Lösung. Xenia 21:211–247.
Bonatz, Dominik, 2001 Mnemohistory in Syro-Hittite Iconography. In Historiography in the
    Cuneiform World. Tzvi Abusch, Paul-Alain Beaulieu, John Huehnergard, Peter Machin-
    ist, and Piotr Steinkeller, eds. pp. 65–78. Bethesda, MD: CDL Press.
Braidwood, Robert, 1960 The Agricultural Revolution. Scientific American 203:130–148.

Briant, Pierre, 1988 Le nomadisme du Grand Roi. Iranica Antiqua 23:253–273.

Briant, Pierre, 1999 War, Persian Society and Achaemenid Empire. *In* Soldiers, Society and War in the Ancient and Medieval Worlds. Kurt Raaflaub and Nathan Rosenstein, eds. pp. 105–128. Cambridge, MA: Harvard University Press.

Brinkman, John A., 1972 Foreign Relations of Babylonia from 1600–625 B.C. American Journal of Archaeology 76:270–281.

Broshi, Magen, 1979 The Population of Western Palestine in the Roman-Byzantine Period. Bulletin of the American Schools of Oriental Research 236:1–10.

Brown, Stuart C., 1986 Media and Secondary State Formation in the Neo-Assyrian Zagros: An Anthropological Approach to an Assyriological Problem. Journal of Cuneiform Studies 38:187–217.

Byrd, Brian, 2000 Households in Transition: Neolithic Social Organization within Southwest Asia. *In* Life in Neolithic Farming Communities: Social Organization, Identity, and Differentiation. Ian Kuijt, ed. pp. 63–98. New York: Kluwer Academic/Plenum.

Carter, Elizabeth, and Matthew W. Stolper, 1984 Elam. Surveys of Political History and Archaeology. Berkeley: University of California Press.

Cauvin, Jacques, 1994 Naissance des divinités, naissance de l'agriculture. Paris: Centre National de la Recherche Scientifique.

Charpin, Dominique, 1995 The History of Ancient Mesopotamia: An Overview. *In* Civilizations of the Ancient Near East. Jack Sasson, John Baines, Gary Beckman, and Karen Rubinson, eds. pp. 807–829. New York: Charles Scribner's & Son.

Chegini, Naser, Morteza Momenzadeh, Hermann Parzinger, Ernst Pernicka, Thomas Stöllner, Rasool Vatandust, and Gerd Weisgerber, 2000 Preliminary Report on Archaeometallurgical Investigations around the Prehistoric Site of Arisman near Kashan, Western Central Iran. Archäologische Mitteilungen aus Iran und Turan 32:287–318.

Childe, V. Gordon, 1928 The Most Ancient East: The Oriental Prelude to European Prehistory. London: Kegan Paul.

Childe, V. Gordon, 1941 Man Makes Himself. Revised edition. London: Watts & Co.

Çilingiroğlu, Altan, and Mirjo Salvini, eds., 2001 Ayanis I. Ten Years' Excavations at Rusahinili Eiduru-kai. Rome: Istituto per gli Studi Micenei ed Egeo-Anatolici.

Davidson, Thomas, and Hugh McKerrell, 1976 Pottery Analysis and Halaf Period Trade in the Khabur Headwaters Region. Iraq 38:45–56.

Davies, Philip R., George J. Brooke, and Phillip R. Callaway, 2002 The Complete World of the Dead Sea Scrolls. London: Thames & Hudson.

Davis, Whitney, 1996 Replications. Archaeology, Art History, Psychoanalysis. Pennsylvania Park: Pennsylvania State University Press.

Dever, William G., 1992 Pastoralism and the End of the Urban Early Bronze Age in Palestine. *In* Pastoralism in the Levant. Ofer Bar-Yosef and Anatoly Khazanov, eds. pp. 83–92. Madison: Prehistory Press.

Diakonoff, Igor M., 1972 Die Arier im Vorderen Orient: Ende eines Mythos. Orientalia NS 41:91–120.

Dothan, Trude, 1992 People of the Sea: The Search for the Philistines. New York: Macmillan.

Drews, Robert, 1993 The End of the Bronze Age: Changes in Warfare and the Catastrophe ca. 1200 B.C. Princeton: Princeton University Press.

Ellenblum, Ronnie, 1995 Settlement and Society Formation in Crusader Palestine. *In* The Archaeology of Society in the Holy Land. Thomas E. Levy, ed. pp. 502–511. New York: Facts on File.

Falconer, Steven, 1994 Village Economy and Society in the Jordan Valley: A Study of Bronze

Age Rural Complexity. *In* Archaeological Views from the Countryside: Village Communities in Early Complex Societies. Glenn Schwartz and Steven Falconer, eds. pp. 121–142. Washington: Smithsonian Institution Press.

Finkelstein, Israel, and Neil A. Silberman, 2001 The Bible Unearthed. New York: The Free Press.

Flannery, Kent, 1969 Origins and Ecological Effects of Early Domestication in Iran and the Near East. *In* The Domestication and Exploitation of Plants and Animals. Peter Ucko and George Dimbleby, eds. pp. 73–100. London: Duckworth.

Frangipane, Marcella, 2001 Centralization Processes in Greater Mesopotamia: Uruk "Expansion" as the Climax of Systemic Interactions among Areas of the Greater Mesopotamian Region. *In* Uruk Mesopotamia & Its Neighbors: Cross-Cultural Interactions in the Era of State Formation. Mitchell Rothman, ed. pp. 307–347. Santa Fe: School of American Research.

Freydank, Helmut, 1975 Die Rolle der Deportierten im mittelassyrischen Staat. *In* Die Rolle der Volksmassen. Joachim Herrman and Irmgard Sellnow, eds. pp. 55–63. Berlin: Akademie-Verlag.

Frye, Richard, 1984 The History of Ancient Iran. Munich: C. H. Beck.

Gabrieli, Francesco, ed., 1973 Die Kreuzzüge aus arabischer Sicht. Barbara von Kaltenborn-Stachau and Lutz Richter-Bernburg, trans. Zürich: Artemis.

Garelli, Paul, 1991 The Achievement of Tiglath-Pileser III: Novelty or Continuity? *In* Ah, Assyria . . . : Studies in Assyrian History and Ancient Near Eastern Historiography Presented to Hayim Tadmor. Mordechai Cogan and Israel Eph'al, eds. pp. 46–51. Jerusalem: The Magnes Press.

Glassner, Jean-Jacques, 2002 La Mésopotamie. Paris: Société d'édition Les Belles Lettres.

Grabar, Oleg, 1990 The Meaning of the Dome of the Rock. *In* Studies in Arab History. Antonius Lectures, 1978–87. Derek Hopwood, ed. pp. 51–53. New York: St. Martin's Press.

Green, Margaret, 1980 Animal Husbandry at Uruk in the Archaic Period. Journal of Near Eastern Studies 39:1–35.

Haas, Volkert, 1994 Geschichte der hethitischen Religion. Leiden: E. J. Brill.

Hachlili, Rachel, 1988 Ancient Jewish Art and Archaeology in the Land of Israel. New York: E. J. Brill.

Haiman, Mordechai, 1996 Early Bronze Age IV Settlement Pattern of the Negev and Sinai Deserts: View from Small Marginal Temporary Sites. Bulletin of the American Schools of Oriental Research 303:1–32.

Hanson, K. C., and Douglas E. Oakman, 1998 Palestine in the Time of Jesus. Minneapolis: Fortress Press.

Hauptmann, Harald, 1999 The Urfa Region. *In* Neolithic in Turkey: The Cradle of Civilization. New Discoveries. Mehmet Özdoğan and Nezih Başgelen, eds. pp. 65–86. Istanbul: Arkeoloji ve Sanat Yayınları.

Hauser, Stefan R., 1995 Siehst Du die Zeichen an der Wand? Zum Ende altorientalischer Kultur. *In* Zwischen Euphrat und Indus. Aktuelle Forschungsprobleme in der vorderasiatischen Archäologie. Karin Bartl, Reinhard Bernbeck, and Marlies Heinz, eds. pp. 251–268. Hildesheim: Georg Olms.

Hawkins, J. David, 2002 Die Erben des Grossreichs I. Die Geschichte der späthethitischen Kleinkönigreiche Anatoliens und Nordsyriens im Überblick (ca. 1180–700 v.Chr.). *In* Die Hethiter und ihr Reich. Das Volk der 1000 Götter. Anonymus, ed. pp. 56–61. Stuttgart: Konrad Theiss.

Heinz, Marlies, 2002 Altsyrien und Libanon: Geschichte, Wirtschaft und Kultur vom Neolithikum bis Nebukadnezar. Darmstadt: Wissenschaftliche Buchgesellschaft.

Hodder, Ian, 1990 The Domestication of Europe: Structure and Contingency in Neolithic Societies. Oxford: Blackwell.

Högemann, Peter, 1993 Das alte Vorderasien und die Achämeniden. Ein Beitrag zur Herodot-Analyse. Wiesbaden: Dr. Ludwig Reichert.

Hole, Frank, 1989a A Two-Part, Two-Stage Model of Domestication. *In* The Walking Larder: Patterns of Domestication, Pastoralism, and Predation. Juliet Clutton-Brock, ed. pp. 97–104. London: Unwin Hyman.

Hole, Frank, 1989b Patterns of Burial in the Fifth Millennium. *In* Upon This Foundation – The Ubaid Reconsidered. Elizabeth Henrickson and Ingolf Thuesen, eds. pp. 149–180. Carsten Niebuhr Institute Publications 10. Copenhagen: Museum Tusculanum.

Insoll, Timothy, 1999 The Archaeology of Islam. Oxford: Blackwell.

Isaac, Benjamin H., 1992 The Limits of Empire. The Roman Army in the East. Oxford: Clarendon Press.

Jacobsen, Thorkild, and Seton Lloyd 1935 Sennacherib's Aqueduct at Jerwan. Oriental Institute Publications 24. Chicago: University of Chicago Press.

Jasim, Sabah Abboud, 1989 Structure and Function in an 'Ubaid Village. *In* Upon This Foundation – The Ubaid Reconsidered. Elizabeth Henrickson and Ingolf Thuesen, eds. pp. 79–90. Carsten Niebuhr Institute Publications 10. Copenhagen: Museum Tusculanum.

Kammenhuber, Annelies, 1977 Die Arier im Vorderen Orient und die historischen Wohnsitze der Hurriter. Orientalia NS 46:129–144.

Kennedy, David L., 1998 The Twin Towns of Zeugma on the Euphrates: Rescue Work and Historical Studies. Portsmouth: Journal of Roman Archaeology LLC.

Kerner, Susanne, 2001 Das Chalkolithikum in der südlichen Levante: Die Entwicklung handwerklicher Spezialisierung und ihre Beziehung zu gesellschaftlicher Komplexität. Rahden: Verlag Marie Leidorf.

Kessler, Karlheinz, 1980 Untersuchungen zur historischen Topographie Nordmesopotamiens. Wiesbaden: Dr. Ludwig Reichert.

King, G. R. D., and Averil Cameron, eds., 1994 The Byzantine and Islamic Near East, II: Land Use and Settlement Patterns. Princeton: Darwin Press.

Kirsch, Elisabeth, and Paul Larsen, 1995 Das Verhältnis zwischen Seßhaften und Nichtseßhaften in Mesopotamien am Ende des 3. und zu Beginn des 2. Jt. v. Chr. *In* Zwischen Euphrat und Indus: Aktuelle Forschungsprobleme in der Vorderasiatischen Archäologie. Karin Bartl, Reinhard Bernbeck, and Marlies Heinz, eds. pp. 148–164. Hildesheim: Georg Olms.

Klengel, Horst, and an authors' collective, 1989 Kulturgeschichte des alten Vorderasiens. Berlin: Akademie-Verlag.

Klinger, Jörg, 2002 Reinigungsriten und Abwehrzauber. Funktion und Rolle magischer Rituale bei den Hethitern. *In* Die Hethiter und ihr Reich. Das Volk der 1000 Götter. Anonymus, ed. pp. 146–151. Stuttgart: Konrad Theiss.

Knapp, A. Bernard, 1992 Bronze Age Mediterranean Island Cultures and the Ancient Near East, Part 1. Biblical Archaeologist 55:52–72.

Kohl, Philip, 1978 The Balance of Trade in Southwestern Asia in the Mid-Third Millennium B.C. Current Anthropology 19:463–492.

Köhler-Rollefson, Ilse, 1992 A Model for the Development of Nomadic Pastoralism on the Transjordan Plateau. *In* Pastoralism in the Levant. Ofer Bar-Yosef and Anatoly Khazanov, eds. pp. 11–18. Madison: Prehistory Press.

Kröger, Jens, 1982 Werkstattfragen iranisch-mesopotamischen Baudekors in sasanidisch-frühislamischer Zeit. *In* Künstler und Werkstatt in den orientalischen Gesellschaften. Adalbert Gail, ed. pp. 17–30. Graz: Akademische Druck- und Verlagsanstalt.

Kühne, Hartmut, 1983 Tall Šeh Hamad/Dur Katlimmu, die Wiederentdeckung einer mittelassyrischen Stadt. Damaszener Mitteilungen 1:149–164.

Kuhrt, Amélie, 1995 The Ancient Near East c. 3000–330 B.C. 2 volumes. London: Routledge.

Lamprichs, Roland, 1995 Die Westexpansion des assyrischen Reiches. Eine Strukturanalyse. Neukirchen-Vluyn: Neukirchner Verlag.

Lanfranchi, Giovanni B., and Simo Parpola, 1990 The Correspondence of Sargon II, Part II. Letters from the Northern and Northeastern Provinces. Helsinki: Helsinki University Press.

Larsen, Mogens T., 1987 Commercial Networks in the Ancient Near East. *In* Center and Periphery in the Ancient World. Michael Rowlands, Mogens T. Larsen, and Kristian Kristiansen, eds. pp. 47–56. Cambridge: Cambridge University Press.

LeBlanc, Steven, and Patty Jo Watson, 1973 A Comparative Statistical Analysis of Painted Pottery from Seven Halafian Sites. Paléorient 1:117–133.

Lehmann, Gunnar, 2003 Zwischen Umbruch und Tradition. Kultureller Wandel in Palästina während der römischen Kaiserzeit im Licht der archäologischen Quellen, ca. 40 v.u.Z. und 350 u.Z. *In* Zeichen aus Text und Stein. Stefan Alkier and Jürgen Zangenberg, eds. pp. 136–182. Tübingen: Francke Verlag.

Levine, Louis D., 1986 Cities as Ideology: The Neo-Assyrian Centers of Assur, Nimrud and Nineveh. Bulletin of the Canadian Society for Mesopotamian Studies 12:1–7.

Levy, Thomas E., 1986 Archaeological Sources for the Study of Palestine: The Chalcolithic Period. Biblical Archaeologist 49:82–108.

Liverani, Mario, 1979 Three Amarna Essays. Monographs of the Ancient Near East 1(5). Malibu: Undena Publications.

Liverani, Mario, 1988 The Growth of the Assyrian Empire in the Habur / Middle Euphrates Area: A New Paradigm. State Archives of Assyria Bulletin 2(2):81–98.

Liverani, Mario, ed., 1993 Akkad: The First World Empire. Padua: Sargon.

Malek Shahmirzadi, Sadegh, 2002 The Ziggurat of Sialk (in Farsi). Sialk Reconsideration Project, Report No. 1. Tehran: Iranian Cultural Heritage Organization.

Mallowan, Max E. L., 1966 Nimrud and its Remains. 2 Vols. New York: Dodd, Mead.

McCorriston, Joy, 1997 The Fiber Revolution: Textile Extensification, Alienation, and Social Stratification in Ancient Mesopotamia. Current Anthropology 38:517–549.

Meinecke, Michael, 1996 Die frühislamischen Kalifenresidenzen: Tradition oder Rezeption? *In* Continuity and Change in Northern Mesopotamia from the Hellenistic to the Early Islamic Period. Karin Bartl and Stefan Hauser, eds. pp. 139–164. Berlin: Reimer.

Mellink, Machteld, 1965 Mita, Mushki and Phrygians. Anadolu Araştırmaları 2(1–2):317–325.

Moore, Andrew M. T., 1982 Agricultural Origins in the Near East: A Model for the 1980s. World Archaeology 14(2):224–236.

Moore, Andrew M. T., Gordon Hillman, and Anthony Legge, 2000 Village on the Euphrates: From Foraging to Farming at Abu Hureyra. Oxford: Oxford University Press.

Moorey, P. R. S., 1994 Ancient Mesopotamian Materials and Industries: The Archaeological Evidence. Oxford: Clarendon Press.

Muscarella, Oscar W., 1989 King Midas of Phrygia and the Greeks. *In* Anatolia and the Ancient Near East. Kutlu Emre, Machteld Mellink, Barthel Hrouda and Nimet Özgüç, eds. pp. 333–344. Ankara: Türk Tarih Kurumu Basımevi.

Neve, Peter, 1996 Hattuša – Stadt der Götter und Tempel. Mainz: Philipp von Zabern.

Nissen, Hans J., 1998 Geschichte Alt-Vorderasiens. Munich: Oldenbourg.

Nissen, Hans, 2001 Cultural and Political Networks in the Ancient Near East during the

Fourth and Third Millennia B.C. *In* Uruk Mesopotamia & Its Neighbors: Cross-Cultural Interactions in the Era of State Formation. Mitchell Rothman, ed. pp. 149–179. Santa Fe: School of American Research.

Oates, David, and Joan Oates, 1976 Early Irrigation Agriculture in Mesopotamia. *In* Problems in Economic and Social Archaeology. G. de Sieveking, Ian Longworth, and K. Wilson, eds. pp. 109–135. London: Duckworth.

Oded, Bustenay, 1979 Mass Deportations and Deportees in the Neo-Assyrian Empire. Wiesbaden: Dr. Ludwig Reichert.

Özdoğan, Aslı, 1999 Çayönü. *In* Neolithic Turkey. The Cradle of Civilization. New Discoveries. Mehmet Özdoğan and Nezih Başgelen, eds. pp. 35–63. Istanbul: Arkeoloji ve Sanat Yayınları.

Özgüç, Tahsin, 1963 An Assyrian Trading Outpost. Scientific American 208:96–106.

Panaino, Antonio, 2000 The Mesopotamian Heritage of Achaemenian Kingship. *In* The Heirs of Assyria. Sanna Aro and Robert M. Whiting, eds. pp. 35–50. Helsinki: The Neo-Assyrian Text Corpus Project.

Parker, Bradley, 2001 The Mechanics of Empire. Helsinki: The Neo-Assyrian Text Corpus Project.

Parr, Peter, ed. 2003 Excavations at Arjoune, Syria. Oxford: BAR International Series 1134.

Pollock, Susan, 1989 Power Politics in the Susa A Period. *In* Upon This Foundation – The Ubaid Reconsidered. Elizabeth Henrickson and Ingolf Thuesen, eds. pp. 281–292. Carsten Niebuhr Institute Publications 10. Copenhagen: Museum Tusculanum.

Pollock, Susan, 1999 Ancient Mesopotamia: The Eden that Never Was. Cambridge: Cambridge University Press.

Postgate, J. Nicholas, 1992 Early Mesopotamia: Society and Economy at the Dawn of History. London: Routledge.

Potts, Daniel T., 1989 Gundeshapur and the Gondeisos. Iranica Antiqua 24:323–335.

Potts, Daniel T., 1999 The Archaeology of Elam: Formation and Transformation of an Ancient Iranian State. Cambridge: Cambridge University Press.

Potts, Timothy, 1994 Mesopotamia and the East: An Archaeological and Historical Study of Foreign Relations c. 3400–2000 B.C. Monograph 37. Oxford: Oxford University Committee for Archaeology.

Reade, Julian, 1980 The Architectural Context of Assyrian Sculpture. Baghdader Mitteilungen 11:75–87.

Roaf, Michael, 1983 Sculptures and Sculptors at Persepolis. Iran 21.

Root, Margaret C., 1979 King and Kingship in Achaemenid Art. Leiden: E. J. Brill.

Rothman, Mitchell, ed., 2001 Uruk Mesopotamia & Its Neighbors: Cross-Cultural Interactions in the Era of State Formation. Santa Fe: School of American Research.

Safrai, Ze'ev, 1994 The Economy of Roman Palestine. London: Routledge.

Salvini, Mirjo, 1995 Geschichte und Kultur der Urartäer. Darmstadt: Wissenschaftliche Buchgesellschaft.

Sanlaville, Paul, 1989 Considérations sur l'évolution de la Basse Mésopotamie au cours des derniers millénaires. Paléorient 15(2):5–27.

Sauer, James, 1986 Transjordan in the Bronze and Iron Ages: A Critique of Glueck's Synthesis. Bulletin of the American Schools of Oriental Research 263:1–26.

Scham, Sandra, 2002 Legacy of the Crusades. Archaeology September/October 2002:24–31.

Schick, Robert, 1998 Luxuriant Legacy. Palestine in the Early Islamic Period. Biblical Archaeologist 61(2):74–108.

Schippmann, Klaus, 1980 Grundzüge der parthischen Geschichte. Darmstadt: Wissenschaftliche Buchgesellschaft.

Schippmann, Klaus, 1990 Grundzüge der Geschichte des sasanidischen Reiches. Darmstadt: Wissenschaftliche Buchgesellschaft.

Schmid, Hans J., 1995 Der Tempelturm Etemenanki in Babylon. Mainz: Philipp von Zabern.

Schmidt, Klaus, 2000 Göbekli Tepe, Southeastern Turkey: A Preliminary Report on the 1995–1999 Excavations. Paléorient 26(1):45–54.

Schwartz, Glenn, 1994 Rural Economic Specialization and Early Urbanization in the Khabur Valley, Syria. *In* Archaeological Views from the Countryside: Village Communities in Early Complex Societies. Glenn Schwartz and Steven Falconer, eds. pp. 19–36. Washington: Smithsonian Institution Press.

Seeher, Jürgen, 2002 Heiligtümer – Kultstätten und multifunktionale Wirtschaftsbetriebe. *In* Die Hethiter und ihr Reich. Das Volk der 1000 Götter. Anonymus, ed. pp. 134–139. Stuttgart: Konrad Theiss.

Sherwin-White, Susan M., and Amélie Kuhrt, 1993 From Samarkand to Sardis. A New Approach to the Seleucid Empire. London: Duckworth.

Silberman, Neil Asher, 1995 Power, Politics, and the Past: the Social Construction of Antiquity in the Holy Land. *In* The Archaeology of Society in the Holy Land. Thomas E. Levy, ed. pp. 9–23. New York: Facts on File.

Simpson, St John, 2003 From Mesopotamia to Merv: Reconstructing Patterns of Consumption in Sasanian Households. *In* Culture through Objects. Ancient Near Eastern Studies in Honour of P. R. S. Moorey. Timothy Potts, Michael Roaf, and Diana Stein, eds. pp. 347–376. Oxford: Griffith Institute Publications.

Smail, R. C., 1995 Crusading Warfare (1097–1193). A Contribution to Medieval Military History. Second edition. Cambridge: Cambridge University Press.

Smallwood, E. Mary, 1976 The Jews under Roman Rule. From Pompey to Diocletian. Leiden: E. J. Brill.

Smith, Adam T., 2000 Rendering the Political Aesthetic: Political Legitimacy in Urartian Representations of the Built Environment. Journal of Anthropological Archaeology 19:131–163.

Smith, Adam T., 2003 The Political Landscape. Constellations of Authority in Early Complex Polities. Berkeley: University of California Press.

Sommerfeld, Walter, 1995 The Kassites of Ancient Mesopotamia: Origins, Politics, and Culture. *In* Civilizations of the Ancient Near East. Jack Sasson, John Baines, Gary Beckman, and Karen Rubinson, eds. pp. 917–930. New York: Charles Scribner's & Son.

Spek, Robartus J. van der, 1993 Assyriology and History. A Comparative Study of War and Empire in Assyria, Athens and Rome. *In* The Tablet and the Scroll. Mark E. Cohen, Daniel C. Snell, David B. Weisberg, eds. Bethesda: CDL Press.

Stein, Gil, 1994 Economy, Ritual, and Power in 'Ubaid Mesopotamia. *In* Chiefdoms and Early States in the Near East: The Organizational Dynamics of Complexity. Gil Stein and Mitchell Rothman, eds. pp. 35–46. Madison: Prehistory Press.

Stein, Gil, 1999 Rethinking World Systems: Diasporas, Colonies, and Interactions in Uruk Mesopotamia. Tucson: University of Arizona Press.

Sundermann, Werner, 1986 Studien zur kirchengeschichtlichen Literatur der iranischen Manichäer II. Altorientalische Forschungen 13:239–317.

Tsumura, David T., 1999 Kings and Cults in Ancient Ugarit. *In* Priests and Officials in the Ancient Near East. Kazuko Watanabe, ed. pp. 215–238. Heidelberg: Springer-Verlag.

Ussishkin, David, 1982 The Conquest of Lachish by Sennacherib. Tel Aviv: Tel Aviv University Press.

Ussishkin, David, 2003 Symbols of Conquest in Sennacherib's Reliefs of Lachish: Impaled Prisoners and Booty. *In* Culture through Objects. Ancient Near Eastern Studies in Honour of P. R. S. Moorey. Timothy Potts, Michael Roaf, and Diana Stein, eds. pp. 207–218. Oxford: Griffith Institute Publications.

Veenhof, Klaas, 1995 Kanesh: An Assyrian Colony in Anatolia. *In* Civilizations of the Ancient Near East. Jack Sasson, John Baines, Gary Beckman, and Karen Rubinson, eds. pp. 859–871. New York: Charles Scribner's Sons.

Vernant, Jean-Pierre, 2000 Writing and Civil Religion in Greece. *In* Ancestors of the West. Teresa Fagan, trans. Jean Bottéro, Clarisse Herrenschmidt, and Jean-Pierre Vernant. pp. 149–176. Chicago: University of Chicago Press.

Villard, Pierre, 1988 Les structures du récit et les relations entre texte et image dans le bas-relief Néo-assyrien. Word and Image 4(1):422–429.

Von der Way, T., 1987 Tell el-Fara'in, Buto. 2. Bericht. Mitteilungen des Deutschen Archäologischen Instituts Abteilung Kairo 43:250–257.

Walser, Gerold, 1966 Die Völkerschaften auf den Reliefs von Persepolis. Historische Studien über den sogenannten Tributzug an der Apadanatreppe. Berlin: Gebrüder Mann.

Watson, Patty Jo, 1983 The Halafian: A Review and Synthesis. *In* The Hilly Flanks and Beyond: Essays on the Archaeology of Southwest Asia. T. Cuyler Young, Philip E. L. Smith and Peder Mortensen, eds. pp. 231–249. Studies in Ancient Oriental Civilization No. 36. Chicago: Oriental Institute.

Weinstein, James M., 1981 The Egyptian Empire in Palestine: A Reassessment. Bulletin of the American Schools of Oriental Research 241:1–28.

Weiss, Harvey, ed., 1986 The Origins of Cities in Dry-Farming Syria and Mesopotamia in the Third Millennium B.C. Guilford, CT: Four Quarters Publishing.

Wenke, Robert J., 1987 Western Iran in the Partho-Sasanian Period: the Imperial Transformation. *In* The Archaeology of Western Iran. Frank Hole, ed. pp. 251–282. Washington: Smithsonian Institution Press.

Whitby, Michael, 1994 The Persian King at War. *In* The Roman and Byzantine Army in the East. Edward Dabrowa, ed. pp. 227–263. Krakow: Uniwersytet Jagiellonski Instytut Historii.

Whitcomb, Donald, 1995 Islam and the Socio-Cultural Transition of Palestine – Early Islamic Period (638–1099 C.E.). *In* The Archaeology of Society in the Holy Land. Thomas E. Levy, ed. pp. 488–501. New York: Facts on File.

Whiting, Robert, 1995 Amorite Tribes and Nations of Second-Millennium Western Asia. *In* Civilizations of the Ancient Near East. Jack M. Sasson, John Baines, Gary M. Beckman, and Karen S. Rubinson, eds. pp. 1231–1242. New York: Charles Scribner's Sons.

Wiesehöfer, Josef, 1996 Ancient Persia. Azizeh Azodi, trans. London: I. B. Tauris.

Wilhelm, Gernot, 1982 Grundzüge der Geschichte und Kultur der Hurriter. Darmstadt: Wissenschaftliche Buchgesellschaft.

Wilkinson, Tony J., 2003 Archaeological Landscapes of the Near East. Tucson: University of Arizona Press.

Wilkinson, Tony J., and Eleanor Barbanes, 2000 Settlement Patterns in the Syrian Jazirah during the Iron Age. *In* Essays on Syria in the Iron Age. Guy Bunnens, ed. pp. 397–422. Louvain: Peeters.

Winter, Irene, 1981 Royal Rhetoric and the Development of Historical Narrative in Neo-Assyrian Reliefs. Studies in Visual Communication 7:2–38.

Winter, Irene, 1982 Art as Evidence for Intercultural Relations Between the Assyrian Empire and North Syria. *In* Mesopotamien und seine Nachbarn. Hans J. Nissen and Johannes Renger, eds. Vol. 1, pp. 355–382. Berlin: Reimer.

Wright, Henry T., 1994[1983] Prestate Political Formations. *In* Chiefdoms and Early States in the Near East: The Organizational Dynamics of Complexity. Gil Stein and Mitchell Rothman, eds. pp. 67–84. Madison: Prehistory Press.

Wright, Henry T., 2001 Cultural Action in the Uruk World. *In* Uruk Mesopotamia & Its Neighbors: Cross-Cultural Interactions in the Era of State Formation. Mitchell Rothman, ed. pp. 123–147. Santa Fe: School of American Research.

Yoffee, Norman, 1981 Explaining Trade in Ancient Western Asia. Malibu: Undena Publications.

Young, Rodney S., 1981 Three Great Early Tumuli. The Gordion Excavations Final Reports, Vol. 1. Philadelphia: University of Pennsylvania Museum.

Young, T. Cuyler, 1980 480/479 B.C. – A Persian Perspective. Iranica Antiqua 15:213–239.

Zangenberg, Jürgen, 2003 Qumran und Archäologie. Überlegungen zu einer umstrittenen Ortslage. *In* Zeichen aus Text und Stein. Stefan Alkier and Jürgen Zangenberg, eds. pp. 262–307. Tübingen: Francke Verlag.

Zeder, Melinda, 1994 After the Revolution: Post-Neolithic Subsistence in Northern Mesopotamia. American Anthropologist 96:97–126.

Zimansky, Paul, 1995 Urartian Material Culture as State Assemblage: An Anomaly in the Archaeology of Empire. Bulletin of the American Schools of Oriental Research 299/300:103–115.

Zimansky, Paul, 2002 The "Hittites" at Ain Dara. *In* Recent Developments in Hittite Archaeology and History. K. Aslihan Yener and Harry A. Hoffner, eds. pp. 177–192. Winona Lake: Eisenbrauns.

Part I

Producing and Disseminating Knowledge About the Ancient Near East

Reinhard Bernbeck → backup?
and Susan Pollock → (it)

This set of four papers addresses a series of fundamental issues in Near Eastern archaeology. They include the variability of archaeological products, the multiple ways in which such products are created, the relationships between past and present, and the wider context in which archaeological praxis takes place.

There is no unified concept of or agreement on what the prototypical product of archaeological work is. None of the authors in this section denies the importance of the most obvious: material objects, such as artifacts, installations, and remnants of buildings. Material remains take on highly politicized meanings when exhibited in Western museums as a show of imperial power (Steele). Their value can also reside in capitalist profiteering (Pollock) or in subsistence acquired through looting (Yahya).

Archaeological products are not, however, limited to objects. Archaeologists spend a lot of time analyzing and presenting results of their work to a professional audience, that is, producing "knowledge" about the Near Eastern past. Of course, this process is fraught with problems related to the ideological, social, and political positioning of authors, and also of those people who "consume" or rework archaeological products (Bernbeck, Pollock). Our narratives are disputed within the discipline, but they also stand in a dialectical relation to other, non-archaeological accounts. Acknowledgment of this situation leads to critique of non-archaeologists' interpretations of our findings as well as a willingness to learn from them.

A third kind of archaeological product discussed in the following chapters is identity. The authors are mostly concerned with identity in the present, with only one case oriented towards the past (Bernbeck). Strong connections are drawn between archaeological remains as elements of group identity and human rights issues (Steele); in a similar vein, the past has an immense import for territorial disputes among groups, where political claims are often directly derived from contested archaeological interpretations (Yahya, Finkelstein). However, Pollock cautions that archaeological knowledge serves as only one of many elements in the construction of present identities, and we should not overestimate its influence.

The creation of archaeological products is a complex and multifarious process. Archaeologists oscillate between a naive belief in "objective data," the attempt to be explicit about the predispositions which influence their work, and unintentional manipulation of interpretations. One way in which the Near Eastern past was and continues to be manipulated is through the dissection of continuous phenomena into clear-cut entities. This can be observed in museums (Steele), in the construction of historical narratives (Bernbeck), and in a wider media discourse on archaeology (Pollock). These manipulations may often remain enshrined in the unrecognized circumstances of one's lifeworld and thus below the surface of discursive consciousness, whether of archaeologists or those who use their results. What the authors highlight is the need for research that uncovers problems of categorization in Near Eastern archaeology, whether in the field (cf. Gero 1996; Hodder 1999), during analysis, or in synthetic writing. Reflections in Near Eastern archaeology along the lines of Foucault's (1972) early work on history would be valuable contributions.

Silencing (Trouillot 1995) is an even more problematic part of the archaeological production process. The omission of certain sources in the representation of a past is always necessarily accompanied by emphasizing others (Ben-Yehuda 1995). Yahya describes silencing as a praxis in field archaeology from the level of project planning to conservation, and also in looting, where certain periods are excluded, destroyed, or neglected, depending on the political-ideological authority under which such activities take place. Interestingly, he advocates a more objective – less politicized – approach to archaeology than many of his Western colleagues. His description of a non-exclusive archaeology is of fundamental importance to any praxis in conflict-ridden – and other! – regions. Bernbeck discusses silencing as an unavoidable element of standard narrative production and suggests that archaeological texts need to be written in new and different ways. Narrating from multiple points of view avoids the silencing that comes with the single perspective of traditional academic writing.

A third theme that pervades all of the papers is the relationship between past and present. The authors take – to different degrees – a constructivist position, arguing that the ancient Near East is always seen from a particular viewpoint in the present. Crucial to renderings of the ancient Near East are concepts of time. Pollock shows how different anachronisms create a sense of distance or nearness to the past, depending on the desired interpretation. Entire time periods may even be blocked out of memory in the service of political domination (Steele, Yahya). On a comparative level, the intensity and chronological depth of whole research traditions can be an important factor in unequal potentialities for the creation of identities. The most blatant case in Near Eastern archaeology is disinterest in and neglect of Islamic periods. An additional layer of complexity is added if one considers that any narrative about the ancient Near East should take into consideration temporal conceptions of the past people one wants to speak about (Bernbeck, Charvát).

Another thread that runs through these contributions is the malleability of the ancient Near East for the present interpreter. Pollock's discussion of Gulf Wars I and II reveals how much archaeological interpretations are at the whim of non-specialists' readings, as does Bernbeck's account of novels whose writers construct the past either as a foil for the present or as an exotic other. Is there or should there be a limit to such multivocality? On the level of fieldwork, both Yahya and Steele strongly advocate a remedial praxis of close collaboration with local communities, identifying and retooling research in accordance with local needs and interests. Steele also warns against politically blind cooperation with governmental authorities in cases where archaeological research contributes to social problems, as in dam-building schemes. Her proposal to change from a representation of "what was saved" to "what was lost" has deep political implications that go well beyond a simple semantic adjustment.

Archaeologists have little power over the appropriation of their products by a wider public, especially by people who rework the results in their own ways. As long as archaeologists are unable themselves to capture the imagination of a larger public, they will be dependent on mediators such as journalists, filmmakers, or novelists to do so (Pollock, Bernbeck). Archaeology in the present world is firmly anchored in specialization and divisions of labor (Shanks and McGuire 1996). Why, however, should we leave to non-specialists the task of making our interpretations more widely accessible? Is the gulf between archaeology as professional praxis and a wider public so wide that it can only be bridged by simplifiers and producers of fiction? And if so, is there a need to limit somehow the potential damage that results from simplifying and thus misrepresenting our work? The discussions here suggest several responses. It is essential to analyze how our research is presented to a larger world by others, especially journalists and reporters (Pollock). In the process, we may be able to learn from non-archaeological ways of representation (Bernbeck). A greater focus on our own styles of writing is desirable: good writing (understandable, with a minimum of jargon, and still in accordance with the complexities of a subject) is not part of archaeological education. Creativity is underestimated, and the dry or esoteric languages of academia cut us off from the public. We are getting used to multiple ways of representing our work, so why not make the effort to contribute to narratives that reach out to a larger public?

While these papers address many problems inherent in the current praxis of fieldwork as well as accounts of the results, two important issues remain unresolved. On the level of production of "knowledge" and its representation, the focus on textual forms barely touches on the burgeoning field of electronic media, with its nearly limitless capacity for pictorial illustrations and non-linear forms of representation. The attendant problem of reversal of the relationship between material culture and its representations – where simulation takes precedence over reality – needs more attention.

Historically and politically more pressing is the fundamentally colonialist and paternalistic nature of Near Eastern archaeology. At the most basic level, even community projects that are financed and (co-)directed by Western archaeologists do not eschew this very basic power differential. Would a Near Eastern archaeology

entirely in the hands of archaeologists from the Middle East provide the solution?
We do not think so, at least not as long as the practitioners are educated principally in Western institutions. Such a "subaltern archaeology" would risk veiling the
continuation of the old colonial enterprise of searching for the roots of Western civilization in the ancient Near East, but with different personnel conducting the task.
Can a process of globalizing archaeological interpretation offer a solution? Hodder
(1999, 2002) argues that the availability of data on the internet widens access to
archaeological knowledge and allows participation not only of archaeologists from
all venues, but of multiple external interest groups, thus reducing the effects of past
colonialist praxis. His insistence that all such interest groups, from the local community to metropolitan artists, be treated equally is well taken but nevertheless
overly idealistic, since economic limitations to access (whether educational and linguistic background, available time, or travel resources) are neglected.

Even in a globalizing world, location still matters. One of the most striking
aspects of the praxis of Near Eastern archaeology is that no one expects Middle
Eastern archaeologists to work outside their own country or region, whereas
Western archaeologists consider it a matter of course to conduct research anywhere
in the world. This long-standing colonialist, economic, and political imbalance
could be resolved if archaeologists who want to work in the Middle East had to
find a counterpart, someone who would do a field project in their own country. The
resulting mix of interests, with field projects in the U.S. or Sweden run by professionals from Turkey, Jordan, or Iran would undoubtedly provide surprising new
insights into the archaeology of those countries. This would entail much wider political and economic consequences, such as better provisioning Middle Eastern universities with the means for research, including everything from books to financial
support. After 150 years of archaeological exploitation of the ancient Near East by
Western countries, it is time to come to terms with past, and continuing, injustice.

REFERENCES

Ben-Yehuda, Nachman, 1995 The Masada Myth. Madison: University of Wisconsin Press.
Foucault, Michel, 1972 The Archaeology of Knowledge. A. M. Sheridan Smith, trans.
        London: Tavistock.
Gero, Joan, 1996 Archaeological Practice and Gendered Encounters with Field Data. *In*
        Gender and Archaeology. Rita Wright, ed. pp. 251–280. Philadelphia: University of
        Pennsylvania Press.
Hodder, Ian, 1999 The Archaeological Process. Oxford: Blackwell.
Hodder, Ian, 2002 Ethics and Archaeology: the Attempt at Çatalhöyük. Near Eastern
        Archaeology 65:174–181.
Shanks, Michael, and Randall McGuire, 1996 The Craft of Archaeology. American An-
        tiquity 61:75–88.
Trouillot, Michel-Rolph, 1995 Silencing the Past. Boston: Beacon Press.

3

Who Has Not Eaten Cherries with the Devil? Archaeology under Challenge

Caroline Steele

For over 200 years people from the West have viewed the Middle East as a rich resource for the materials of antiquity from which they could obtain personal prestige, national glory, and historical antecedents. The results of their work contributed to the construction of a timeline of historical heritage that goes beyond Rome and Greece to the Biblical and earlier societies that rocked in the Cradle of Civilization. Though the methods of archaeological endeavors have been improved, and thoughts and views have been systematized into a profession whose members may hesitate to take simplistic linear views of the past, there remain distinct continuities of praxis between archaeology of the 19th century and that of the present. Difficulties in obtaining funding and the stipulations and obligations that accompany it, interactions between archaeologists and the inhabitants living near or on archaeological sites, and relations with local and national governments remain to this day problematic and challenging elements in the pursuit of Middle Eastern archaeology. Archaeologists continue to be identified as experts who discover buildings and objects from the past that provide legitimate information for the production – by themselves and others – of history(s) that can be used for political and social ends. Although the themes and particulars change, the practice of archaeology has always been and remains firmly embedded in wider social and political contexts.

While challenges occasioned by archaeology's connections to contemporary political and social issues are not recent developments, there is a marked increase in published discussion of them in the past two decades (e.g., Trigger 1989; Pollock and Lutz 1994; Kohl and Fawcett 1995; Meskell 1998). Reflections on archaeological praxis arise when the motives and actions of people, states, and institutions are open to question and interpretation, especially by those who are not included or do not participate in the dominant paradigms. I begin my reflections on archaeological praxis with a bit of historical perspective, pointing out some of the ethical issues that have long confronted archaeologists working in the Middle East. I then examine several specific examples of contemporary challenges facing archaeologists working in the Middle East that have not been the subject of sustained (published) reflection or debate. Finally, I draw out a series of general issues that have arisen in these and related social and political contexts, particularly the rise of globalization and the human rights movement, and consider the discipline's relationship to them.

I base my discussion on my experiences and conversations of the past 20 years during which I have worked in various Middle Eastern countries on British and American excavations, funded by both government and private agencies. I participated in excavations in Iraq during five years in the 1980s at the time of the Iran–Iraq War. After the Gulf War, I began working in Turkey where I was involved in a five-year dam rescue excavation and several years of site survey work. My other Middle Eastern experience includes working at the British Institute of Archaeology in Ankara and two seasons of excavation in Syria.

The following discussion cannot be a comprehensive review, nor can I offer clear-cut solutions. However, I do hope by pointing out the persistence of some issues and the emergence of others that pertinent problems in archaeological praxis will be illuminated and reflection on them encouraged.

Continuities and Legacies of Archaeological Praxis

When Austin Layard began excavations at Nimrud in 1845, his initial funding came from Sir Stratford Canning, who was gambling that the site would prove "fruitful" and thus further his political ambitions by associating him with the discovery of magnificent antiquities. The link between Canning's political ambitions and antiquities was the nascent British Museum. The acquisition of fabulous ancient objects would fulfill the British goal of filling the national museum with the "most prestigious and glorious accumulation of art from the entire history of mankind" (Larsen 1996:68). In addition, the acquisitions would keep the British competitive with the French who were busily backing excavations at Khorsabad to supply Assyrian antiquities for the Louvre. When Layard established that Nimrud was indeed a site with important potential – with a significant quantity of items defined as suitable for British Museum display – work was postponed while he waited for official permission to arrive from the Ottoman court and further funding from the British Museum. Finally, when he thought all was in order, he discovered that the British government had failed to allocate any funds to the British Museum for the continuation of his work (Larsen 1996:100).

Layard's travails in excavating Nimrud, which did not end once the financial backing from the British Museum came through, have a certain resonance today. Archaeologists are still dependent for funding on public, private, or both types of organizations. These resources all operate within larger contexts than that of the immediate archaeological research needs of applicants. Thus support of archaeological research continues to be contingent on personal, political, and economic factors (these factors are not just specific to the West). Pertinent considerations can be the applicants' previous success in receiving grants, their academic position, whether their research design addresses current hot academic topics or national political agendas and whether a site has "potential." Decisions as to whether a project will provide economic advantage through enhancing tourism or will fulfill legal prerequisites for construction projects can also be part of funding considerations. For archaeologists, acquiring funding can, or should, include questions about whether to accept money from individuals and institutions known to have collections that include stolen antiquities (Wilkie 2000:10), or whether to apply for funding or accept employment from institutions responsible for development projects (e.g., UNESCO), the policies of which are suspect in terms of whom they benefit.

Museums and Colonialism

Layard's tribulations also illuminate another awkward issue: the relationship between museums and archaeology. The relationship continues to be an ambivalent one revolving around the acquisition and curation of archaeological material (Brodie and Tubb 2002; Barker 2003). While it is no longer usual for museums to sponsor archaeological expeditions to other countries with the goal of obtaining items to fill their own display cases, as was once done by large institutions such as the British Museum or the Louvre, museums continue to fund overseas expeditions in order to enhance their reputations. They continue to be the major repositories for excavated materials and also to have a role in national agendas, parts of which include the prestige of having the biggest, most extensive, most exotic, and most valuable collections of objects. These collections are considered national treasures of the holding country rather than the country of origin. Few of the prominent national and private museums are prepared to return donated plunder or objects obtained by archaeologists in the 19th century to the nations where the items originated (Greenfield 1996; Robertson 2002:157–158). To justify their continued possession of such materials when their return is requested, museums attempt to legitimate their position by claiming a legal right to the material by citing their compliance with the 1970 UNESCO Convention on the Means of Prohibiting the Illicit Import, Export, and Transfer of Ownership of Cultural Property. However, the convention conveniently restricts the return of cultural property to materials *proven* to be stolen from public museums or monuments in the country of origin. Even more importantly, this convention, and the more recent Unidroit Convention (1995) concerning theft, are not retroactive, and only enter into effect the day of official ratification by a particular national signatory.

The trade in stolen and illicitly excavated antiquities is an ongoing crisis for archaeology, causing the destruction of archaeological contexts and information (Renfrew 2000; Brodie and Tubb 2002). While making an apparent show of concern with regards to stolen antiquities, museums are only dealing with combating future illicit "property" and denying any responsibility about artifacts they obtained before treaty ratification. Museums, being among the major holders of items of dubious provenance, lend a legitimizing weight to other collectors who acquire objects of doubtful origin. Archaeologists who work for and with museums can be seen as representing the museum's interests rather than those of the peoples and countries from which objects have come and where the archaeologists work.

There have, of course, been some changes in the roles of museums and the acquisition of archaeological objects since the 19th century. One significant change is that now Middle Eastern museums are the repositories for most of the archaeological objects that are legally excavated within their countries. In addition, Middle Eastern museums and antiquities departments control work through granting of permissions to excavate and conduct museum-based research. The earlier losses of archaeological material to foreign countries often occurred under permission-granting agencies headed by directors who were citizens of former colonial powers, for example, Gertrude Bell in Iraq and Henri Seyrig in Syria. In other instances, there was no antiquity regulatory agency at all but rather a monopoly for all excavations was given to a particular country, as was the case with the French in Afghanistan. Regulation of excavation by government authorization was born out of the realization of national power by former colonial or weak governments, such as the late Ottoman Empire, and was able to rectify archaeologists' previous practice of taking much of the excavated material back to their own countries.

Western projects that are permitted to work are funded and directed by Westerners, and the funding, both up front as well as institutional support services, is usually more generous than Middle Eastern countries can afford for their own projects. In that inequity, the structures of colonialism continue. And although today the artifacts remain in the country of origin, final site reports and attendant information are seldom published in the host country's language. Reports published by local archaeologists in Turkish or Arabic are seldom read by Westerners, most of whom do not have a reading knowledge of these languages (a notable solution to this problem are reports on the Carchemish and Ilısu dam salvage projects, which are published bilingually [Tuna and Öztürk 1999; Tuna et al. 2001; Tuna and Velibeyoğlu 2002]). Thus, the majority of archaeological information continues to be located in the West and not in the country in which the sites lie. Potential solutions to the continuing inequities could be Western financial and technical support to build museums and an archaeological infrastructure in Middle Eastern countries. Permanent loans of material to Western institutions would open up the possibilities for widening Western understanding, and the publication of Western excavation reports by Middle Eastern publishers in local languages would do the same for the Middle East.

Self-reflection in Archaeology

While archaeologists over the decades may have reflected on some of these issues, little of their thinking on these subjects has appeared in print until relatively recently (e.g., Trigger 1989; Kohl and Fawcett 1995; Shaw 2003). To date, much of the published discussion has centered on the relationship between archaeology and nationalism (Layton 1989; Makiya 1989; Shennan 1989; Díaz-Andreu and Champion 1996; Arnold 2002). Archaeological information is particularly susceptible to the designs of nationalist ideologies since it can be used to build national solidarity by constructing a common past. A particular past can also be used to justify present practices: for example, a lynchpin of the ideology of apartheid was that white settlers and Bantus spread inland from the Cape of Good Hope at the same time, implying that their claims of nationhood were chronologically the same (Hall 1999:64). One of the early and often cited works on nationalism and archaeology is Kohl and Fawcett's 1995 edited volume, but as the editors noted in the introduction there were no contributions from scholars who worked in the Middle East. This lack of representation was rectified in 1998 with the publication of Meskell's edited book. The main topic of concern in this literature is how the results of archaeological fieldwork have been or can be used as an instrument of oppression, justification, and aggrandizement by nationalist ideologues and governments. Some attention has also been directed to instances of archaeology used to openly construct new identities, such as Dietler's (1994) discussion of the use of the Gauls to fashion a Celtic identity for a unified Europe. Another topic that is beginning to be considered concerns the archaeologies of disenfranchised peoples and groups. They are usually thought inappropriate for "serious" scholarly consideration and funding and are consequently denied legitimacy and voice in Middle Eastern archaeology (Scham 2001).

The growth of reflection on ethics and the continuing role of archaeology in nationalist strategies and human rights are seen in issues of *World Archaeology* and in the introduction of new journals, *Journal of Social Archaeology* and *Public Archaeology*. Unfortunately, most prominent archaeological journals fail to address questions and topics directly related to the politics of archaeology. Many archaeologists working in the Middle East continue to maintain implicitly that they are solely cultural historians and as such are apolitical. The expression of this belief became particularly clear in the aftermath of the looting of the Iraq Museum and sites in Iraq. Humanitarian and political concerns were treated by some archaeologists as secondary to archaeological concerns, using rationalizing masks such as "loss of universal heritage." However, the critical work that has been done clearly demonstrates that archaeology is almost by necessity put to uses and abuses beyond value-free scholasticism. Archaeologists must be conscious of these issues and accept the necessity and responsibility of political engagement.

The growth of critical awareness about the many uses of archaeology combats its image as "an esoteric discipline that has no relevance for the needs or concerns of the present" (Trigger 1989:3), and clearly illuminates the need for continued critical consciousness of how it can be exploited by others as well as by archaeologists themselves (Ben-Yehuda 2002). I turn now to three examples of issues facing archaeologists who work at present in the Middle East. Each represents a case where most, if not all, of us succumb to "eating cherries with the devil." I consider the problematic elements of each example as well as alternatives that some archaeologists have chosen or might choose to explore.

For instance: asymmetric relations

Interpersonal relationships on excavations are almost always asymmetric. Practically all excavations in the Middle East employ local villagers as laborers, and they all have a representative from the national antiquities organization. They may also include students from various countries including the host country. In the upper portion of an excavation project's hierarchy a variety of interests is represented: the director, usually an academic; the representative, a government employee who sometimes has little formal archaeological training; site supervisors; students with varying levels of education, nationalities, and international travel experience. These people are all usually from the middle class with an urban background. In addition, there are landowners and local authorities who have vested interests in the excavation, from ownership of the land, granting permission to excavate, hiring and compensation of laborers, and the laborers (usually villagers) themselves. How does one juggle needs that revolve around a group of educated members of the middle class who generally do not earn a wage, less educated local inhabitants who are employed as wage laborers, local landowners' expectations, and national bureaucracies, to come up with fair compensation drawn from limited resources?

Even today, laborers usually continue to be completely alienated from the excavation. They are paid a wage that is either set by the local authorities or negotiated with the director of the excavation. The wage is always substantially below the level at which laborers would be paid in the West, but funding agencies would never fund an application that budgets for Western wage rates – and moreover there is the easy rationale that most Westerners on the excavation also receive very low payments, if any at all. The costs of living locally and the disparities that would exist between the wages of excavation laborers and other locals must also be considered. In some countries such as Turkey the wage is set by the government – in some cases, under IMF restrictions – and varies from area to area based on local wage differences. But in other situations such as in Iraq and Syria, each director personally negotiates with the laborers or local headman with regard to payment. Having to negotiate sets up a conflict between limited funding, which includes the assumption of paying low wages, local laborers who are vulnerable because of their need for money and endemic high rate of joblessness, and ethical responsibilities to pay a fair wage. The end result is that laborers usually end up with very low wages that do nothing to make them feel engaged with the project or with the visiting Westerners.

Laborers are usually seen as unskilled wage earners in need of constant supervision by the skilled non-local supervisor, a relationship that is colonial in nature (Berggren and Hodder 2003:422). This relationship is maintained even when the laborers have accumulated knowledge by working on the site for numerous seasons, whereas supervisors often change from year to year. The entire enterprise continues to be similar to archaeology 100 years ago when a small elite arrived in a community, employed a number of local inhabitants, got the material they wanted and/or used up their funds, and then left, never to be seen again by any local. Today the material that workmen excavate is rarely available to them after the project is over. They do not go to museums, which are usually not situated nearby and are not part of the workers' cultural life. Local inhabitants' interest in or understanding of the past and its material remains are rarely investigated or addressed. On the other hand, the educated members of the excavation, particularly the Westerners involved, gain professional experience, and they may use the data and even stories they hear from workmen to further their careers.

How can we change these ongoing colonialist inequities of wage and status? Unfortunately, there is a dearth of studies about the interactions between various groups on Middle Eastern excavations and how excavations impact the lives and opinions of local inhabitants (although there are some reports from Çatal Höyük: Shankland 1996, 2000). However, there is currently a group of archaeologists who are developing an archaeological approach that considers these issues and seeks to rectify them by including local inhabitants as partners, not as "labor." Community archaeology is a "distinctive set of practices within a wider discipline . . . the most important distinguishing characteristic is the relinquishing of at least partial control to a project to the local community" (Marshall 2002:211).

There is a need to establish inclusive policies such as those of community archaeology in Middle Eastern archaeology. While most of the community archaeology projects to date have involved indigenous peoples living in countries dominated by people of European descent (Spector 1993; Field et al. 2000; Arden 2002; Crosby 2002), the project of S. Moser et al. (2002) in Egypt provides an example of the possibilities for community archaeology in the Middle East (see also Yahya, this volume). By establishing a collaborative framework, archaeologists, who are gaining intellectual and career benefits from another society's heritage, are at the same time providing that society with an equal opportunity to benefit from the endeavor. Moser and team have included the inhabitants of Quseir al Qadim in a project to excavate the Roman and Mamluk harbor that was located there. Inclusion started with the original planning of the excavation, followed through with the training and employment of the local inhabitants, the creation of a heritage center that functions as a place where historical and cultural information about the community itself will be presented, and eventually the establishment of a tourist destination. While the heritage center does represent the interests of foreigners in having a tourist destination, the goal is to structure it so that the local community and economy benefits. The heritage center was a primary objective of the project; displays and temporary exhibits were designed from the onset of the excavation to generate interest and ensure that community members would be informed of the excavation's progress. The center provides educational opportunities as well as a forum for feedback between locals and foreign members of the team. Interviews with local people about their heritage were also considered a central component of the project. Interviews provided insights into how people respond to archaeological discoveries and provided diverse cultural interpretations about the complete life history of the site. However, at present the interviews are one-sided, being initiated by Westerners.

For a community such as Quseir, the role of the excavation in tourist development must be considered, in that tourism is a major industry in Egypt. Rather than reproducing the stereotypical Pharaonic representations, the community project initiated a program to produce goods inspired by finds from the site. These objects as well as books and guides will be available for sale at the community center, contributing to its becoming a self-sustaining entity (Moser et al. 2002).

The final part of this project is Western excavators' understanding and commitment to the site for a very long period of time, well past the excavation and even report publication. The community archaeology project's involvement in the community from its inception to establishing a self-sustaining center that can continue after their departure is notable. Generally, we are not really aware of the impact that our presence has on the lives of the local inhabitants, who are usually the rural poor. We certainly know a lot about how excavations impact research goals, careers, and museum acquisitions, but we need to find and pursue different ways to practice excavation, ones that will necessarily be more expensive and are done less quickly because they address needs of local partnership.

For instance: dam construction

My second example is enacted on a larger scale than the immediate relations between archaeologists and local communities. Turkey is in the middle of a giant dam building project called the Southeastern Anatolian Project (GAP) (Iraq, before 2003, and Syria are also undertaking dam-building projects). The goal of the project is to establish a series of dams on the Tigris and Euphrates Rivers in order to bring electricity and provide irrigation to an area of ca. 30,000 square miles, larger than the combined area of Belgium, Luxemburg, and the Netherlands. If GAP is completed according to plan, it will include 22 dams, 19 hydroelectric plants and 1.7 million hectares of irrigated land (Martz 1995; Özdoğan 2000:60). Three major dams, the Ataturk, Keban, and Birecik, as well as many smaller ones have been completed. The Turkish government claims that the resulting irrigation will enable farmers to grow a wider range of crops besides the grain that has been grown in the area and will allow Turkey to supply much of the food for the Middle East (Martz 1995). Officially, the dams will increase Turkish hydroelectric capacity and thereby contribute to industrial growth and an increase in the standard of living. However, most of the people affected and displaced by the dam projects are Kurds, people with whom the Turkish government has been in direct conflict, in some cases amounting to war, since 1984. Unofficially, the dams will do nothing to right the tensions between the Kurdish urban populations and the central Turkish government. Their construction will only add to the already large population of displaced and underserved Kurds in urban areas. People and groups who criticize government policies are considered by the government to be Kurdish Nationalists (as opposed to Turkish Nationalists) and prosecuted. Additionally, the population displacement caused by the dams has been used to dislocate the rural Kurdish resistance movement. Further important consequences of the project include the appearance of malaria and leishmaniosis (Bosshard 1999) and the widespread and adverse affect of planned irrigation systems on local ecology and farming practices, for example, effecting a change from subsistence and grain crops to cash crop farming with its attendant dependence on a market economy. Finally, these dams on the Tigris and Euphrates drastically decrease the volume of water that flows downstream to Syria and Iraq. The Turkish government continues to follow President Demirel's 1992 statement that water is a Turkish natural resource and that they do not tell oil-producing countries what to do with their oil (Martz 1995; Bosshard 2000; Arabicnews.com 2000). This attitude to water rights is cause for concern in a part of the world where water has always been important but now is essential to support growing populations in countries downstream of Turkey (Armagan 1992; Demirsar 1994; Jehl 2002).

It is generally acknowledged that the resettlement program for the 150,000–200,000 people impacted by the filling of the Ataturk Dam (completed in 1992) did not meet international standards of compensation (Yildiz 2001). It has been reported that at least 80 percent of the people affected received no compensation, and the resettlement resulted in major social problems when small communities were relocated to urban areas (Yildiz 2001). An archaeological site survey and program of excavations were associated with the construction project. Although many archaeological sites were flooded by the dam reservoir, their loss received little attention other than in Ph.D. dissertations and papers by archaeologists working on dam "rescue" projects.

The recent completion of the Birecik Dam also did not receive much international attention until the flooding of the site of Zeugma. The loss of the Roman mosaics there was the subject of much press coverage that usually included discussion about the loss to world heritage (Başgelen and Ergeç 2000). Indeed, the amount of international attention to the flooding of an important site was unprecedented for the whole GAP project (even though more sites were impacted by the Ataturk dam). But how many times did one read about the 30,000 people who were displaced? The case of Zeugma, with coverage in the Western press generating great interest in the site's stunningly preserved remains, contributes to increased international awareness of archaeological sites lost through dam building. But the press never gave sustained coverage to local inhabitants' loss of livelihoods and homes.

The next major component of the GAP project is to be the Ilısu dam. When completed, the Ilısu dam will affect the lives of between 36,000 (Ilısu Dam Campaign) and 78,000 (Yildiz 2001) people. ICOMOS describes the project as "a social, cultural, and environmental disaster" (Bumbaru et al. 2000:179). Archaeologists are concerned that the area to be flooded is a portion of the upper Tigris basin that has been occupied since at least the Middle Paleolithic, yet as of 2001 only one-fifth of the area has been surveyed for archaeological sites (Kitchen and Ronayne 2001). Among the cultural and social consequences of the dam is the scheduled flooding of the town of Hasankeyf. This Kurdish regional center has cultural remains dating back at least 10,000 years, including occupations by various historic peoples from the Assyrians through the Ottomans. It continues today as an important center for the surrounding villagers, with up to 30,000 pilgrims coming to visit the holy site of the tomb of Imam Abdullah each year (Ilısu Dam Campaign).

In part as a result of the flooding of Zeugma, a growing number of NGOs are organizing protests around the Ilısu dam. They likely increase their chances of catching public attention by referring to the rich archaeology and heritage of Hasankeyf, thus reminding people of the "loss" of Zeugma. Working with NGOs is an opportunity for archaeologists to contribute their particular expertise about the value of archaeological sites and thus broaden the range of protests and increase the strength of national and international appeals against dams. One way to do this is to join forces with organizations that emphasize these issues, such as the World Commission on Dams or the International Council on Monuments and Sites (ICOMOS), both of which have addressed the Ilısu Dam crisis (Brandt and Hassan 2000; Bumbaru et al. 2000). While the major strength of archaeology's voice is through its field of recognized expertise, there is no reason why archaeologists should not also discuss the toll on living people who are displaced as well as the damage to sites. Is that not indeed part of embracing an inclusive community approach to archaeology? The various campaigns against the Ilısu dam illustrate ways that archaeologists can contribute their expertise and lend authority to a larger campaign aimed at preventing a disastrous project.

Some archaeologists have done just that. Kitchen and Ronayne write that preventing the construction of the Ilısu dam is the only realistic archaeological strategy, but, more importantly to my mind, they add, "this is particularly the case since archaeologists increasingly recognize the rights of indigenous, ethnic minority and other local communities to play an equal part in the decision making about investigations of cultural heritage" (Kitchen and Ronayne 2001:38). The World Archaeological Congress sent a public letter to Prime Minster Blair condemning the Ilısu Dam not only for the loss of archaeological sites but also for the inadequate consultation with "affected communities in the area regarding cultural heritage and [the fact that there was] no serious attempt to involve them on an equal basis" (Hall 2001). In the case of the Ilısu dam, archaeological and human rights issues have been explicitly connected by some archaeologists who have spoken out and mentioned both losses of sites and those incurred by modern inhabitants.

The Ilısu Dam has come under a widespread and effective anti-dam campaign, not because it is necessarily the "worst" dam ever but because of circumstances of timing. Throughout the past ten years, the growing public awareness of issues of globalism, human rights, and the environment has contributed to a rising level of concern on the part of some about the impacts of dam building throughout the world, e.g., in China (Three Gorges Dam), India (Narmada River Valley), Mexico (proposed dams on the Usumacinta), as well as Turkey. Webpages, publicity, and letter-writing campaigns voicing concerns about the impact of the Ilısu dam have been undertaken by various Inter-Governmental Organizations (IGOs) and NGOs including the Council of Europe, Kurdish Human Rights Project, World Commission on Dams, Friends of the Earth, Ilısu Dam Campaign, and World Archaeological Congress. As a result of this campaign, the British government backed down from its support of the construction firm Balfour Beatty, which in turn led to a successful effort to get Balfour Beatty to withdraw its participation in the construction of the Ilısu Dam. The firm's withdrawal has not stopped the dam construction, but it is an indication that public pressure can on occasion have a significant effect. Other participants, such as the Swiss Bank UBS and the Italian firm Impregilo, have also withdrawn from the project because of pressure from these and other groups.

Should one do salvage work in the context of a controversial dam project such as GAP? By participating in rescue archaeology that has been incorporated into dam projects to meet the often token requirement for funding from outside sources, is one contributing to an endeavor that should be opposed if judged in terms of the human rights of those directly affected? Such rights include those of livelihood in the case of devastating water restrictions for people downstream, or the loss of homes, social networks, and employment for those displaced, especially given that they may already be at risk from previous government policies. Archaeological surveys and excavations associated with dam construction are usually termed rescue, or salvage, projects. But archaeologists seldom, if ever, recover all information even in ideal circumstances. A beneficial approach would be for archaeologists to draw attention to what is lost rather than the usual notion of "saving" or "salvaging" as much as possible. The data that archaeologists document should include not only sites as they view them, but also the ways local inhabitants view those sites and the wider implications of their loss.

On a more general level, do archaeologists living in developed countries have a right to protest that less developed countries undertake projects that are conceived to provide people with a better economy and living conditions? In 1986 the UN adopted the Declaration of the Right of Development which represented a change from its earlier position by declaring that development was not just economic growth but also some combination (albeit vague) of cultural, social, and political rights including self-reliance (Stohl et al. 1989:215). Unfortunately, many countries continue to hold the traditional position that economic rights (i.e., economic growth) subsume all other rights. What value have human rights and fundamental freedoms if there are no jobs or food? On the other hand, food without freedom and jobs without justice would be negations of human dignity (Saksena 1989:xii).

For instance: working in countries with repressive regimes

Virtually everywhere today there are different degrees of repression of political, ethnic, economic, and religious practices. While certainly no archaeologist can expect to go into a country and effect major policy changes, is it unethical to work in a country ruled by a repressive government? Or is it perhaps more to the point that moral irresponsibility occurs when one goes there and ignores the wrongs being done? Regrettably, archaeologists often tend to focus solely on sites rather than also on living populations, thus decontextualizing themselves from "sites of praxis."

For example, despite all the evidence that Iraq was guilty of flagrant human rights violations in the 1980s, archaeologists from the West continued to work there up to the first Gulf War, and some have continued to do so up to the present. During the 1980s Western governments were in full support of Iraq, supplying goods and arms, and certainly not decrying the extensive violations of civil and political rights committed by the Baathist regime. Should archaeologists have been more vocal at home or even in Iraq about the realities of life in that country? Were they not aware of local conditions because of the cultural gulf between themselves and their workmen? Would providing testimony to human rights organizations have been helpful or trying to publish information about the difficulties experienced by Iraqis at that time? Or is it more important to keep one's local contacts intact on the principle of "think global, act local," even if that means keeping quiet(er) at a broader level?

Since the end of the first Gulf War, because it has served the political interest of the West, there has been a great deal written about the injustices of the Iraqi regime (Cockburn and Cockburn 1999; Hamza 2000; Coughlin 2002; Mackey 2002). Enormous hardships – indeed violations of human rights – have also occurred due to Western sanctions. Some archaeologists returned to work in Iraq during that time. What were they doing apart from excavating? Did they help Iraqis they came in contact with feel less isolated from the rest of the world? Does doing so mitigate an attitude that otherwise seems to suggest that ancient sites are more important than the destroyed lives of modern inhabitants? How pressing is cultural heritage – even if it is "world heritage" – when Iraq is in ruins? In political contexts that are ever increasingly global (what country can claim not to be linked to repressive regimes?), with human rights violations occurring in every country, where does one draw a line and decide that working in one country is no longer acceptable while working in another is?

Oppressive regimes occur everywhere although Iraq under Saddam Hussein represents a particularly egregious case. Unfortunately, archaeologists often hesitate to pass judgment on the political regimes of the countries in which they are working and also are reluctant to be involved in activism associated with criticizing these regimes. However, this reluctance is often due not to ignorance or even politesse to host governments: at the heart of the matter is often little but self-interest. The process of deciding whether or not to speak up or to work in a particular country is easily corrupted by self-legitimizing defenses based on one's own interests, which include not only intellectual passion, but job security. It is easy to rationalize a decision by saying, wherever I work I will encounter problems, or adopting a cultural relativist stance ("who am I to judge another culture?").

I would suggest, at the risk of eating cherries with the devil, that one could ethically work in a country that is governed by a repressive regime if one also combines the decision with activism, both in the country where one is working and at home. Abroad, one could develop an inclusive project, whether along the lines of community archaeology mentioned above or some other type of local partnership. If local inclusion is not allowed, or the state controls all aspects of the excavation (i.e., you are actually working for that oppressive state), these are instances that define an ethical line one should not cross – one should not work in that country. At home, activism can include involvement with various organizations and speaking out (and writing) about issues related to the country in which one is working, or in cross-over activism, for example, people who work in Egypt speaking out about Syria and those working in Iran about Turkey. There one must take a risk: by bearing witness to what one has seen and experienced (both good and bad), one may be denied funding or permission to return to work in that country. And there is always the consideration that one's own country is supporting not only oppressive regimes but tyrannical ones guilty of heinous crimes (such as Western support of Iraq during the Iran–Iraq war). There are ample grounds for activism with regards to Western national policies that support oppression at home and abroad. And yet, when faced with the decision whether to work in a country with clearly documented humanitarian crimes on a dreadful scale, surely one should look elsewhere for a place to conduct archaeological research, while at the same time not dismissing the crimes and their victims by failing to protest against them and act for change.

Archaeology and Human Rights

As the previous examples illustrate, there are numerous competing interests and structures that contribute to the ethically challenging situations in which archaeology and archaeologists find themselves. Various institutions, from governmental to NGOs and IGOs, as well as legal agreements, including UN conventions and those of other international organizations, provide a structural framework that is meant both to confine the actions of interested parties and offer them some room to maneuver. Interest groups are themselves multiple, including local people in the countries where archaeologists work, Middle Eastern governments, Western funding agencies and educational institutions that employ archaeologists, and, of course, archaeologists themselves.

As archaeologists, we often work and spend an important part of our lives among those who do not have such basic human rights as clean water, economic self-sufficiency, or self-determination, and people who are affected by national or international projects such as dam construction or tourism. This means that we cannot pretend to be specialized professionals who explore only the past, whose expertise is generally conceived outside the profession (and sometimes within it as well) to be limited to matters that deal directly with archaeological materials and cultural heritage issues. In what follows, I consider some of the additional problems that we as archaeologists of the Middle East face if we take the sociopolitical and economic context of our work seriously.

The current world context can be characterized as one that includes greater globalization, numerous instances of genocide, ecological destruction, and pandemics. Western states have become rhetorically associated with the liberal ideology that personal rights matter, that the vulnerable and marginalized should be accorded special attention, public authority should respect personal autonomy and preferences, reason should prevail over emotionalism, and progress is possible (Forsythe

2000:31). These are worthy ideals, and human rights claims have become tools and weapons for people who are striving to achieve better lives, but they also can be used as tool of oppression, such as when they are employed in nationalist rhetoric (Ishay and Goldfisher 1997).

An important tenet of liberal ideology is the concept of global norms centered on human rights, and fundamental human rights are understood as transcending cultural differences. However, the doctrine of transcendent human rights is seen by some as just another example of the conceptual, cultural, and philosophical Western imperialism over non-European peoples and traditions (Matua 2002:155). Cultural relativism has been invoked as a useful tool in the fight against cultural imperialism. Relativism embraces the view that there are throughout the world a great diversity of morals, values, and histories. Differences in attitudes and practices are seen as part of a diverse world, and the traditions of a group, whether ethnic, national, or other, as essential to the well-being and survival of that group. However, practicing relativism makes it difficult to respond to outstanding acts of political and ethnic violence that are currently so prevalent (Hinton 2002:2). Holding the belief that one can work for the cessation of political and social violence puts one in the position of endorsing the ideology of global human rights, but being sensitive to issues of cultural domination requires one to consider how these issues can be approached in a culturally appropriate manner.

Everywhere there are instances of oppression and lack of self-determination, and the concept of human rights is very much a part of the current international social and political context. How are archaeologists responding? In many cases, by burying their heads in the sand and claiming that their research is apolitical. In other cases, archaeologists are emerging as participants in the discourse on human rights – at least tangentially – through their identification as experts on cultural heritage. Archaeology has been used in international cultural heritage identification by human rights activists who are fighting for political and economic rights for minority peoples such as the Kurds (Yildiz 2001). This is a sometimes conflicted position in that archaeologists raise their voices over the loss of archaeological sites while remaining silent on the destruction of homes and livelihoods of inhabitants on and around sites (for an exception, see Kitchen and Ronayne 2001), and only rarely consider inequities in their own working relations with local people.

As archaeologists we are already intrinsically involved in human rights debates because rights to cultural heritage are included in the United Nations International Covenant on Economic, Social and Cultural Rights (Ishay 1997). Often the right to a cultural heritage is used by those trying to gain wider economic or political power (for example, Yildiz 2001). Here archaeologists find themselves in yet another potentially contradictory situation. On the one hand their role as arbitrators of archaeological cultural heritage leads to their work being incorporated into large human rights campaigns, often international in name but actually Western dominated. On the other hand, they work within local communities and should be familiar with the particular needs and desires of the inhabitants living near archaeological sites. For example, the reports of the World Commission on Dams, which include a substantial contribution by archaeologists (Brandt and Hassan 2000), details the impacts of dam building. Documenting shoddy economics, huge social costs, and violations of human rights, they advocate more rigorous standards for planning future projects, including prior informed consent of affected peoples. But it has been pointed out that the Commission avoids addressing the fact "that dams are the very antithesis of development for the poor because they enable the expropriation of the resources of the river valley, placing the livelihood of the people who depend on rivers at the disposal of those who have the power to exploit them" (Williams and McCully 2000). Archaeologists work locally and can provide significant insights of their own and of the rural populations with whom they interact. When they return to the West it is important not to be co-opted into ignoring the urgency of local concerns in the face of grand-scale international cultural heritage campaigns, comprised of various organizations with overlapping, but not identical agendas.

There are a great variety of laws, local and national, as well as international treaties and conventions that define what kinds of items form part of international "cultural heritage." On the international level the UNESCO Convention for the Protection of World Cultural and National Heritage (1972) gives broad definitions that have provided a basis for many of the laws regarding cultural heritage. This UNESCO Convention states that "monuments, groups of buildings, and sites with historical, aesthetic, archaeological, scientific, ethnological or anthropological value" *could* be part of cultural heritage. To be identified and recognized as a World Heritage Site, the items must have "outstanding universal value from the point of view of history, art or science." Needless to say, who does the defining is crucial to the identification of outstanding universal value. Unfortunately, while indigenous peoples have histories and objects of historical value, these are often not recognized by law unless they are endorsed by someone who is regarded as legitimate (powerful) by local, national, or international establishments. Archaeologists, along with historians and anthropologists, are recognized by the UN, courts of law, funding institutions, and governments as legitimate experts on cultural matters. But how different is the dynamic between archaeologists and institutions that defer to their expertise on the definition of "real" history (termed cultural heritage) from that of the British Museum curators in the 19th century who set up a collection of sculptures called the "Chain of Art" in order to establish for the public which art was (and by implication, which was not) significant (Jenkins quoted in Larsen 1996:68)?

While today other histories are known and written, the West continues to hold the imprimatur of their legitimacy: the UN's role in identifying and legislating cultural heritage is a case in point. Western archaeologists and museums have not always considered that the ease with which their expert opinions are accepted is due to their being members of dominant national or international communities rather than the absolute value of what they are saying.

It does sometimes appear as though the past has been narrowed down and limited to the degree that only "legitimate" groups can claim a "cultural heritage," which is often synonymous with national identification. Thus, in order to garner rights of self-determination and all they entail in terms of group social and political rights, one must have a legitimate cultural heritage. Whether it is the so-called international community claiming that a site is part of world heritage, a nation-state asserting national heritage, or a particular group affirming its own heritage, cultural heritage has become a powerful ideological tool. Unfortunately, there is an inherent circularity, in that a group must be legitimate in order to assert its cultural heritage but also needs that heritage to claim legitimacy. This no-win situation is further complicated by the fact that group identity is a construct with a political function and is constantly in flux.

By embracing the identity of world citizens working for world heritage, Western archaeologists in the Middle East today can justify and explain themselves and their profession when accused of being exploitative or imperialist. Who are the mourners when an archaeological site is destroyed, and what are the relative degrees of legitimacy attributed to their voices? Are they the villagers who watch their homes and fields disappearing beneath rising dam waters or the far away "world citizens" who may wish to visit the area as tourists or excavate there to enhance an academic career? Legitimacy remains within the domain of those with political and economic power and not necessarily with those who have the most to lose.

Ultimately, there is the question of priorities: are the living people or the artifacts and sites of those long dead more important? Do food, shelter, and rights to self-determination take precedence over preserving material remains of (someone's) cultural heritage, or the other way around? I suspect that many archaeologists would claim that these priorities can be finessed by relocating people to "better homes" and by excavating a site so that villagers' cultural heritage is "enriched." These are nothing more than self-serving arguments, however, as it is seldom possible to avoid giving precedence to either the local inhabitants' needs or archaeologists' desire to excavate. Nor can archaeologists invoke world citizenship and its attendant claim of contributing to world heritage as justification when a site they wish to "save" is part of a project that relocates thousands of people without compensating them for the loss of their homes and livelihoods (for example, Zeugma: Başgelen and Ergeç 2000). However, it is not just issues associated with dam building but all of the problems of archaeological work discussed above that can no longer be brushed aside as pertinent to the domain of human rights rather than archaeology.

While private transnational groups, such as Human Rights Watch and Amnesty International, and international laws about human rights are growing in number, the most powerful key for increasing the number of people who have basic rights remains locked up with national policies that express national interests. It is states that approve human rights legislation, and it is states that manipulate foreign assistance in relation to the rhetoric of human rights. But states work for their own self-interests, and these interests do not necessarily match those of human rights organizations. States do not exist to report the truth about human conditions; they exist to exercise power in the national interest as the governing elites define it. The most that NGOs can do is pressure states and corporations by publicizing what they identify as wrongdoing in hopes that they will respond to subsequent public embarrassment by changing the targeted policies.

NGOs do not have large or concentrated memberships that can threaten electoral punishment, nor do they have budgets that are capable of making or withholding significant financial contributions to political parties (although for many, contributing would be unethical). NGOs, and here I include archaeological associations, publish information in the hopes of long-term education and short-term dissemination to influence policy. Most members of archaeological associations would not see themselves as capable of individually influencing foreign or national policy, nor would they consider their professional organizations to be the same as "expert" human rights NGOs such as Amnesty International or Human Rights Watch. But organizations do have a voice, presented as the sum of their members' voices. Archaeology is in a position to use its authority with regards to the value that ancient objects and places can have in the present in order to widen arguments for human rights. Archaeological organizations have already begun to speak out and join with other organizations, particularly with regards to dam construction. The World Archaeological Congress wrote to Tony Blair about Zeugma, and its members have joined with environmentalists and others at the World Commission on Dams to publish reports and working papers on the cultural and environmental damage that occurs with dam construction (Brandt and Hassan 2000). Working within large organizations does risk co-option and the silencing of some positions. And there remain many other instances, such as the recent 2003 invasion of Iraq, where archaeologists generally have not raised their voices to protest anything other than the destruction of sites and theft of antiquities.

Conclusion

With growing self-reflection in archaeology, multiple practices of the discipline in the past and present have become, at least in some circles, subject to explicit discussion. Clearly, archaeologists practice a profession that ought to engage with larger social and political contexts. While one may question whether the concept of global human rights is truly international or one that denies the diversity of human cultures, it is certainly an endeavor in which archaeology is emerging as a legitimizing voice. As such, archaeologists need to become much more involved with human rights issues and therefore with debates about their validity. Archaeology of the Middle East is still largely at the receiving end of the relationship between human rights and archaeology, but it is conceivable that scholars could contribute to the solution of humanitarian problems, even if their contributions are incremental (for example, through the World Archaeological Congress). By excavating the past and living in or alongside communities that are threatened in the present, archaeologists have within their remit both a tool for change and obligations to the people they work with. Archaeologists are participants in a social and political praxis that goes far beyond that of many other academics.

Whether on the level of personal conscience, in deciding whether or not to work under an oppressive regime, or at a community level, establishing ethical and fair relations with the people who live next to archaeological sites, or participating in international campaigns that are far removed from immediate archaeological issues revolving around the local community, the praxis of archaeology challenges us to be self-reflexive but to resist turning that reflection into a career tool. A starting point must be the local communities within which we work, both at home and abroad, and considered decisions that respect the rights of people to strive to achieve a better life economically, politically, and culturally.

REFERENCES

Arabicnews.com, 2000 Turkey and Waters to Syria and Iraq. Regional, Economics, February 23. http://www.arabicnews.com.

Arden, Traci, 2002 Conversations about the Production of Archaeological Knowledge and Community Museums at Chunchumil and Kochol, Yucatán, Mexico. World Archaeology 34:379–400.

Armagan, Haldun, 1992 A Few Too Many Flags on the Tigris and Euphrates, Turkish Hydroelectric Plans Worry Iraq, Syria. World Paper, October:13.

Arnold, Bettina, 2002 Justifying Genocide: Archaeology and the Construction of Difference. In Annihilating Difference: The Anthropology of Genocide. Alexander Laban Hinton, ed. pp. 95–116. Berkeley: University of California Press.

Barker, Alex W., 2003 Archaeological Ethics: Museums and Collections. In Ethical Issues in Archaeology. Larry J. Zimmerman, Karen D. Vitelli, and Julie Hollowell-Zimmer, eds. pp. 71–83. Walnut Creek, CA: Altamira Press.

Başgelen, Nezih, and Rifat Ergeç, 2000 Belkis/Zeugma • Halfeti • Rumkale: A Last Look at History. Istanbul: Archaeology and Art Publications.

Ben-Yehuda, Nachman, 2002 Sacrificing Truth: Archaeology and the Myth of Masada. Amherst, NY: Humanity Books.

Berggren, Åsa, and Ian Hodder, 2003 Social Practice, Method and Some Problems of Field Archaeology. American Antiquity 68:421–434.

Bosshard, Peter, 1999 A Case Study of the Ilısu Hydropower Project (Turkey). Bern Declaration (March 1999). http://wwwfinance@evb.ch, www.evb.ch.

Bosshard, Peter, 2000 An NGO Perspective on the Ilısu Dam: Vested Interests and Politics. International Water Power and Dam Construction (April 2000). www.ilisu.org.uk/debate1.html.

Brandt, Steven, and Fekri Hassan, eds., 2000 World Commission on Dams Working Paper on Cultural Heritage Management. World Archaeological Congress. http://www.dams.org/thematic.

Brodie, Neil, and Kathryn Walker Tubb, 2002 Illicit Antiquities: The Theft of Culture and the Extinction of Archaeology. New York: Routledge.

Bumbaru, Dinu, Sheridan Burke, Michael Petzet, Marilyn Truscott, and John Ziesemer, eds., 2000 Heritage at Risk: ICOMOS World Report 2000 on Monuments and Sites in Danger. Munich: K. G. Saur.

Cockburn, Andrew, and Patrick Cockburn, 1999 Out of the Ashes: The Resurrection of Saddam Hussein. New York: HarperCollins.

Coughlin, Con, 2002 Saddam King of Terror. New York: HarperCollins.

Crosby, Andrew, 2002 Archaeology and Vanua Development in Fiji. World Archaeology 34:363–378.

Demirsar, Metin, 1994 Syria Urges Water-Sharing Pact over Euphrates. Reuters World Service, February 5.

Díaz-Andreu, Margarita and Timothy Champion, eds., 1996 Nationalism and Archaeology in Europe. London: University College London Press.

Dietler, Michael, 1994 "Our Ancestors the Gauls": Archaeology, Ethnic Nationalism, and the Manipulation of Celtic Identity in Modern Europe. American Anthropologist 96:584–605.

Field, J., R. Barker, E. Coffey, L. Coffey, E. Crawford, L. Darcy, T. Fields, G. Lord, B. Steadman, and S. Colley, 2000 Coming Back: Aborigines and Archaeologists at Cuddie Springs. Public Archaeology 1:35–48.

Forsythe, David, 2000 Human Rights in International Relations. Cambridge: Cambridge University Press.

Greenfield, Jeanette, 1996 The Return of Cultural Treasures. Second edition. Cambridge: Cambridge University Press.

Hall, Martin, 1999 Legacy of Racism. Archaeology 52/3:64–65.

Hall, Martin, 2001 Letter to Tony Blair. January 16, 2001. www.ilisu.org.uk.

Hamza, Khidir, with Jeff Stein, 2000 Saddam's Bombmaker: The Terrifying Story of Iraqi Nuclear and Biological Weapons Agenda. New York: Scribner.

Hinton, Alexander Laban, ed., 2002 Annihilating Difference: The Anthropology of Genocide. Berkeley: University of California Press.

Ilısu Dam Campaign, The Archaeological Impacts of the Ilısu Dam. http://www.ilisu.org.uk/archaeol.html. Accessed October 2002.

Ishay, Micheline, ed., 1997 The Human Rights Reader: Major Political Essays, Speeches, and Documents from the Bible to the Present. New York: Routledge.

Ishay, Micheline, and David Goldfischer, 1997 Human Rights and National Security: A False Dichotomy. In The Human Rights Reader: Major Political Essays, Speeches, and Documents from the Bible to the Present. Micheline Ishay, ed. pp. 377–402. New York: Routledge.

Jehl, Douglas, 2002 In Race to Tap the Euphrates, the Upper Hand is Upstream. New York Times, August 25:1, 9.

Kitchen, Willy, and Maggie Ronayne, 2001 The Ilısu Dam in Southeast Turkey: Archaeology at Risk. Antiquity 75:37–38.

Kohl, Philip L., and Clare Fawcett, eds., 1995 Nationalism, Politics, and the Practice of Archaeology. Cambridge: Cambridge University Press.

Larsen, Mogens Trolle, 1996 The Conquest of Assyria: Excavations in an Antique Land 1840–1860. New York: Routledge.

Layton, Robert, ed., 1989 Conflict in the Archaeology of Living Traditions. One World Archaeology Series. London: Unwin Hyman.

Mackey, Sandra, 2002 The Reckoning: Iraq and the Legacy of Saddam Hussein. New York: W. W. Norton.

Makiya, Kanan, 1989 The Republic of Fear: The Politics of Modern Iraq. Berkeley: University of California Press.

Marshall, Yvonne, 2002 What is Community Archaeology? World Archaeology 24/2:211–219.

Martz, Nathan, 1995 Ataturk Dam in Turkey and its Economic and Environmental Characteristics in a Politicized Arena. TED Case Studies, Volume 4(1), January 1995. http://www.american.edu/TED/class/all.htm.

Matua, Makau, 2002 Human Rights: A Political and Cultural Critique. Philadelphia: University of Pennsylvania Press.

Meskell, Lynn, ed., 1998 Archaeology Under Fire: Nationalism, Politics and Heritage in the Eastern Mediterranean and Middle East. New York: Routledge.

Moser, Sylvia, Darren Glazier, James E. Phillips, Lamya Nasser el Nemr, Mohammed Saleh Mousa, Rascha Nasr Aiesh, Susan Richardson, Andrew Conner, and Michael Seymour, 2002 Transforming Archaeology Through Practice: Strategies for Collaborative Archaeology and the Community Archaeology Project at Quseir, Egypt. World Archaeology 24:220–248.

Özdoğan, Mehmet, 2000 Cultural Heritage and Dam Projects in Turkey: An Overview. *In* World Commission on Dams Working Paper on Cultural Heritage Management. Steven Brandt and Fekri Hassan, eds. pp. 58–61. World Archaeological Congress. http://www.dams.org/thematic.

Pollock, Susan, and Catherine Lutz, 1994 Archaeology Deployed for the Gulf War. Critique of Anthropology 14:263–284.

Renfrew, Colin, 2000 Loot, Legitimacy, and Ownership: The Ethical Crisis in Archaeology. London: Duckworth.

Robertson, Geoffrey, 2002 Crimes Against Humanity: The Struggle for Global Justice. New York: The New Press.

Saksena, K., 1989 Human Rights and Development: An Asian Perspective. *In* Human Rights and Development. David Forsythe, ed. pp. ix–xii. Basingstoke: Macmillan.

Scham, Sandra Arnold, 2001 The Archaeology of the Disenfranchised. Journal of Archaeological Method and Theory 8:183–213.

Shankland, David, 1996 Çatalhöyük: The Anthropology of an Archaeological Presence. *In* On the Surface: Çatalhöyük 1993–1995. Ian Hodder, ed. pp. 349–358. Cambridge: McDonald Institute for Archaeological Research and the British Institute of Archaeology at Ankara.

Shankland, David, 2000 Villagers and the Distant Past: Three Seasons' Work at Küçükköy, Çatalhöyük. *In* Toward Reflexive Method in Archaeology: The Example at Çatal Höyük. Ian Hodder, ed. pp. 167–176. Cambridge: McDonald Institute for Archaeological Research and the British Institute of Archaeology at Ankara.

Shaw, Wendy M. K., 2003 Possessors and Possessed, Museums, Archaeology, and the Visualization of History in the Late Ottoman Empire. Berkeley: University of California Press.

Shennan, Stephen J., ed., 1989 Archaeological Approaches to Cultural Identity. One World Archaeology Series. London: Unwin Hyman.

Spector, Janet, 1993 What This Awl Means: Feminist Archaeology at a Wahpeton Dakota Village. St. Paul: Minnesota Historical Society Press.

Stohl, Michael, David Carlton, Mark Gibney, and Geoffrey Martin, 1989 U.S. Foreign Policy, Human Rights and Multilateral Assistance. *In* Human Rights and Development. David Forsythe, ed. pp. 196–234. Basingstoke: Macmillan.

Trigger, Bruce, 1989 A History of Archaeological Thought. Cambridge: Cambridge University Press.

Tuna, Numan, and Jean Öztürk, eds., 1999 Salvage Project of the Archaeological Heritage of the Ilısu and Carchemish Dam Reservoirs. Activities in 1998. Ankara: Middle East Technical University.

Tuna, Numan, Jean Öztürk, and Jale Velibeyoğlu, eds., 2001 Salvage Project of the Archaeological Heritage of the Ilisu and Carchemish Dam Reservoirs. Activities in 1999. Ankara: Middle East Technical University.

Tuna, Numan, and Jale Velibeyoğlu, eds., 2002 Salvage Project of the Archaeological Heritage of the Ilisu and Carchemish Dam Reservoirs. Activities in 2000. Ankara: Middle East Technical University.

Wilkie, Nancy C., 2000 Moynihan's Mischief: Aiding Unethical Antiquities Dealers. Archae-
    ology 53/6:10.
Williams, Phil, and Patrick McCully, 2000 Lies, Dam Lies. The Guardian, November 22.
    http://website.lineone.net/jon.simmons/roy/lie0011.htm.
Yildiz, Kerim, 2001 The Human Rights Impact of the Ilısu Dam, Southeast Turkey and the
    Current Impossibility of Proper Consultation in Turkey. http://www.publiceyeon-
    davos.ch/archiv/ky_26_01_01.htm.

4

Archaeology and Nationalism in the Holy Land

Adel H. Yahya

Introduction

Political and religious interests in the Holy Land have resulted in the greatest density of archaeological excavations anywhere in the Middle East, if not world-wide. Contrary to common belief, however, those interests seem to have done more harm than good to the science of archaeology in the Holy Land and the Middle East as a whole. It has been said that the introduction of the Bible into the realm of Middle Eastern archaeology is primarily due to the efforts of the Palestine Explo-ration Fund (PEF), which was established in 1865 by a group of British church-men and biblical scholars. These individuals sought to use archaeology to restore faith in the Bible, which was being eroded by Darwinism (Lipman 1988). But the bond between the Bible and the Middle East goes back far beyond the 19th century. Religious attachments of Jews, Christians, and Moslems to the holy places have long been a primary motivation for the exploration of the Holy Land and its an-tiquities. In addition to the visits of millions of pilgrims who have frequented the country from the fourth century C.E. on, early excavations here were undertaken by private individuals seeking religious relics and ancient works of art (Silberman 1993). This bond between archaeology and religion was further illustrated in modern times by the establishment of more Western archaeological societies includ-ing the Deutsche Palästina Verein in 1878, the École Biblique et Archéologique of the French Dominican order in 1890, and the American Schools of Oriental Research in 1900.

Basic to biblical archaeology as a discipline and field of study is a strong belief in the historicity of the Bible. For many biblical archaeologists, the field is geared primarily towards proving the accuracy of the biblical narratives. Biblical archaeol-ogists have concentrated their efforts exclusively on biblical sites – Iron Age through Roman period – and even on specific layers dating to this period. This has been the case in Palestine as well as in neighboring countries such as Jordan, Lebanon, Syria, and even Egypt. Byzantine, Islamic, Crusader, and even prehistoric sites and layers have been excluded from archaeological investigations and from presentation(s) to the public. Biblical archaeologists represent an extreme example of the bias towards literary sources, namely the Bible, while archaeologists in general are traditionally biased towards material culture. It is not uncommon for biblical archaeologists to argue that when the evidence from an archaeological excavation does not fit that from the Bible, one may conclude that the archaeological evidence is either incomplete or incorrectly interpreted (Pritchard 1962:22). Biblical passages are taken literally as guides to the location, identification, and interpretation of archaeological sites and finds, as Kenyon indicates explicitly in her Jericho excavation report. She concludes, however, that "in attempting to reconcile literary and archaeological evidence, biblical records cannot be taken literally" (Kenyon 1957:258).

Archaeologists have recently been questioning the validity and motivations behind the use of biblical narratives in archaeology and even the foundations of biblical archaeology as a discipline (see Finkelstein, this volume). This paper is devoted to investigating the impact of politics and religion on the archaeology of the Middle East in general and of the Holy Land in particular. It will focus on the role of archaeology in the current Middle Eastern conflicts, which have troubled the region and the world over the past century. The concentration here will be on the most recent developments in Palestinian/Israeli archaeology rather than the distant past.

Archaeology and Nationalism

Archaeology has often been used in different parts of the world to support nationalist, colonialist, and imperialist claims, with horrifying results (Trigger 1984; Bernbeck and Pollock 1996). There does not seem to be a way to exclude religion and politics from archaeology, which is after all a social science and hence political and partial. Politicization, however, can be a blinding factor in archaeology when it is exaggerated and used irrationally, as has in fact been the case in the Holy Land. There seems to be no place in the world where archaeology has been given such immediacy and has been so much manipulated as a political and ideological tool as in the Holy Land. Archaeology here has obvious religious and political connotations and has been used to serve modern political goals, including laying claims to the land and denying the claims and narratives of the other side. Archaeology has thus far added to the competing claims of the two modern peoples, the Palestinian Arabs and Israeli Jews.

Israeli state ideology bases its claims to the Holy Land on biblical narratives dating back to the Iron Age. It asserts that religious and linguistic continuity supports their claims, citing the survival of the Hebrew language and Jewish religion as proof. These points are taken as compelling arguments in the face of Arab and Moslem assertions of their continuous presence in the country over the past 1,400 years. The Israeli side tends to deny the multicultural character of the Holy Land, fearing that an admission of that would eradicate the Jewish nature of the present state of Israel.

The Palestinian Arabs on the other hand cite more recent events, especially the domination of Islam in Palestine during the past 14 centuries. More and more Palestinians today argue, in response to Israeli claims, that their presence in the land dates from the Bronze and Early Iron Ages. The Palestinian president Yasser Arafat is renowned for his famous slogan, "*inna fiha qawman jabbarin*," referring to the biblical passage (Numbers 13:23) in which the scouts of Moses warned against attacking the Canaanites who were a great people with very strong, walled cities. From this point of view, the Palestinian Arabs of today are the direct descendants of the Canaanites of the Bronze Age, whose presence in the country preceded that of the Israelites. Other Palestinians express their claims to the land in terms of cultural continuity and point out that modern Palestinian towns and villages display a remarkable cultural continuity from the Bronze and Iron Ages into the modern period. Those towns and villages often have names that reflect those listed in ancient records. Furthermore, their traditional agro-pastoralist village subsistence strategies are believed to have ancient origins (Nashef 2000:25). Palestinians in general refuse to recognize Jewish heritage in Palestine, fearing that this recognition will lead to the appropriation of their land by the modern state of Israel.

Biblical archaeology has so far served to complicate the work of archaeologists in the Holy Land and elsewhere in the Middle East. The Arab-Israeli conflict is not fought by machine guns and fighter jets alone, but also by shovels, in pits, school curricula, and on computer screens. War zone archaeology has attained the status of a new discipline in the archaeology of the country, perhaps as a legitimate successor to biblical, Palestinian, or Israeli archaeology.

The founding of the state of Israel in 1948 was partially predicated on the biblical history of the region, particularly the stories of the kingdoms of David and Solomon. Ever since 1948, the work of most Israeli archaeologists has been primarily geared towards promoting Jewish claims and establishing a Jewish national identity (Glock 1985; Rosen 1998). That is probably why biblical sites in Israel and even in the occupied Palestinian territories receive far more attention from Israeli archaeologists than prehistoric or Islamic sites in Israel itself. This partiality also holds true for official Israeli bodies, including the Israeli national parks authority, the Israeli department of antiquity, and the departments of antiquity of the Israeli civil administrations of the occupied West Bank and Gaza. Despite their abundance, Islamic sites – many of which are large and important cities in Israel itself, such as Ramla, Jaffa, and Akko – have been neglected and left to decay, while smaller, less significant, and less attractive biblical sites, such as Masada and even Qumran and Herodion in the West Bank, have been nicely restored and presented to the public. This explicit selection of contexts in the archaeological record to be disregarded or even destroyed is equivalent to erasure of memory and selective historiography.

Israeli involvement in the management of Palestinian cultural heritage, especially since 1967, and the occupation of the West Bank and Gaza by Israel have created much alienation, if not enmity, between Palestinians and their cultural heritage.

This has found its expression in the widespread phenomenon of illegal digging at ancient sites, what is locally known as grave digging. This illegal activity is feeding a legal, but badly regulated Israeli antiquities market and through it an aggressive international antiquities trade. Previously excavated, mostly biblical sites, are being targeted by what may be called subsistence looting, because of widespread knowledge that biblical period finds sell better to Israeli antiquities dealers as well as to Christian and Jewish collectors worldwide. Biblical sites and objects have become in this context a kind of negative heritage (Meskell 2002).

The other excuse for targeting biblical sites that is often cited by illegal Palestinian excavators and antiquities dealers is that they were excavated by foreign or Israeli archaeologists and are thus serving Israeli rather than Palestinian purposes. This category of dealers is in fact making a deliberate choice of which sites to vandalize and which to leave alone. Some of those dealers would go so far as to accuse archaeologists and conservationists, including Palestinians, of serving the enemy if they were to oppose illegal digging of ancient sites or make any effort to preserve biblical sites in the occupied Palestinian lands. They point out that the presence of such sites in the Palestinian areas was used by Israeli settlers to justify confiscating Palestinian land and building settlements on it. This view is further illustrated by the Israeli civil administration's policy of denying building permits to Palestinians if antiquities are found in or around their land. This policy, which pays no regard to legitimate Palestinian needs, has contributed to the enmity between Palestinians and their cultural heritage and has rendered the work of archaeologists and conservationists much more difficult.

Even when Israel handed over six major cities in the West Bank and most of the Gaza Strip to the Palestinian authority in 1996 as part of the Oslo accords, it refused to turn over most archaeological sites, although many of them lie within populated Palestinian areas. The Israeli military authorities insisted on maintaining full control over those sites under the pretext that most of them are holy to Jews, and thus Palestinians, who are overwhelmingly Moslem, cannot be trusted to look after them. Such sites as Sebastia and Joseph's Tomb near Nablus, Herodion near Bethlehem, Tel Al Nasba, Gibeon, and Bethel near Ramallah, just to name a few, remained in Israeli hands. But the Israeli military authorities have, unsurprisingly, done nothing to upgrade or protect them, while at the same time they have effectively prevented the Palestinian authorities from doing so themselves. Many sites have literally become isolated and neglected Israeli islands in the midst of a sea of Palestinian inhabitants.

The current uprising (*intifada*) which began in October 2000 resulted in rapid erosion of the economic base of the Holy Land, including both the Palestinian areas and Israel. Even though the latter economy is undoubtedly much larger and more immune, the new situation caused a huge setback for archaeology in both countries. Not only did archaeological activities decline, and in the case of the Palestinian areas ceased almost entirely, but the situation in previously excavated sites, most of which are biblical sites, has deteriorated to an unprecedented level. Furthermore, due to the decline of the tourism sector and decreasing revenues in the past couple of years, the Israeli and Palestinian authorities are no longer willing or

able to pay for the maintenance and upkeep of historical sites. The once flourishing tourist industries such as ceramics, olive-wood carving, embroidery, and traditional glass are on the verge of collapse. As a result, popular interest in tourist
attractions including ancient sites, biblical and otherwise, has declined remarkably.
The Palestinian authority is presently not in any position to protect or maintain
cultural heritage sites in the West Bank and Gaza, let alone biblical sites. Understandably, the situation of protected archaeological sites, particularly biblical sites,
in Israel and even in some parts of the West Bank is less dreadful than their counterparts in the rest of the West Bank and Gaza, but that is far from saying that
ancient sites in Israel are in a healthy situation. In fact even the most important
tourist attractions in Israel itself, such as the old cities of Akko and Jaffa, and even
Jerusalem, are in bad shape. They are abandoned and deserted as a consequence
of the *intifada*.

The rate of unemployment amongst Palestinians during the current *intifada* has
reached unprecedented levels, 60% according to the most conservative estimates of
the Palestinian Bureau of Statistics. More than half of the Palestinian population
of the West Bank and Gaza are living below the poverty line of two US dollars per
person per day, according to the World Bank. That represents an almost fourfold
decline in the daily revenues of more than seven dollars, or $2,600 per capita annual
income, before the *intifada*. In these circumstances many Palestinians, especially in
rural areas, have resorted to the most desperate and destructive practice of van-
dalizing archaeological sites to sell finds to whomever will buy them. Most objects
find their way into Israel, while others go abroad to worldwide collectors who come
to the country as tourists seeking "holy objects" of all kinds.

The other form of Israeli involvement in Palestinian cultural heritage, which has
contributed to the alienation of Palestinians from their cultural heritage, is the
Israeli settlement policy. Most settlements in the West Bank and Gaza, such as
Ghanim, Shilo, Bethel, Michmas, Kiriat Arba', etc., have been given biblical names
regardless of their historical or religious significance. It is true that some settlers,
especially the ultra-orthodox, are ideologically motivated to live in the occupied
West Bank and Gaza, but one should not infer from this that Israeli settlers go to
the West Bank to preserve biblical or Jewish heritage. The overwhelming majority
of Israeli settlers in the Palestinian occupied territories are in fact driven there by
political and economic, rather than religious or historical motivations. Houses in
the settlements are simply much cheaper than houses in Israel, and settlers receive
generous subsidies from the state, at the expense of the Israeli and American tax-
payers. I very much doubt if any settler would stay in the West Bank or Gaza if it
were not for the incentives offered by the government in the form of cheap housing
and generous subsidies.

That many settlements such as Bethel, Gibeon, Michmas, Atarot, Anatot, Beit
Horon, and Kiriat Arba' are removed from archaeological sites attests to the fact
that the settlement movement is fundamentally about colonizing Palestinian land
rather than preserving Jewish heritage. Most archaeological sites in the West Bank
and Gaza Strip could not be included within settlements because they are occupied by modern Palestinian villages or towns. In fact, settlers living nearby rarely

visit these sites, and I would argue that very much like the Palestinian villagers, most of them hardly know where those sites are and are ignorant of their historical and religious significance. Furthermore, most of the more than 200 large and small Israeli settlements in the West Bank and Gaza Strip have no historical significance whatsoever from a biblical viewpoint. The Gaza Strip settlements, for example, are hard to justify, as Gaza is not known to be significant in Jewish traditions, nor is Jericho, which is a cursed city from a Jewish point of view, not to mention the tens of small and isolated hilltop settlements in the West Bank.

Palestinian archaeologists accuse biblical scholars of neglecting Islamic sites and overlooking Islamic layers not only because they lack interest, but also because they lack knowledge of Islamic civilization and culture (Abu Khalaf 1987). The fact that we know so little about Islamic history and have more evidence for Bronze and Iron Age Palestine than for the Islamic period, which has dominated the landscape of the country and the Middle East as a whole over the past 1,400 years, is quite troubling for Palestinian archaeologists today. It is equally troubling that most handbooks on the archaeology of Palestine end with either the Persian or Roman periods. What little has been published of the Islamic period is limited to monumental architecture, chiefly in Jerusalem. This means that the Islamic period is not an important connection with the past for biblical scholars and their intended Western audiences, according to Albert Glock, who concludes that "the history of archaeology in Palestine has failed to portray the intellectual context which would validate it" (Glock 1987:5). The history of ancient Palestine has been ignored and silenced by biblical scholars because its object of interest has been an ancient Israel conceived and presented as the taproot of Western civilization (Whitelam 1996:1).

A Step Forward

It was not until recently that some archaeologists of the Holy Land, including some Israeli archaeologists, realized the need to insulate their studies from political and religious influences (Finkelstein 1991; Rosen 1998). These archaeologists repudiate discrimination against sites and occupations on the basis of their period, political, or religious connotations. They employ scientific methodologies and pursue the same questions as archaeologists in other countries, for example, studies of settlement patterns, trade, and economy of ancient civilizations. These archaeologists often run into conflicts with religious authorities, especially Jewish leaders, over excavations of sites containing human remains, and with nationalist leaders over their interpretations of archaeological evidence. This does not mean, however, that Israeli and other biblical archaeologists are about to abandon biblical sites; on the contrary, the biggest excavations currently under way in Israel are still conducted at famous biblical sites such as Ashkelon/Askalan in the south and Megiddo/Tell al-Mutasallim in the north.

There are some other positive developments including the emergence of a new generation of Palestinian archaeologists, most of whom are trained at Western universities in Europe and the US. This coincides with the materialization of several

public Palestinian institutions to deal with Palestinian antiquities and cultural heritage, including the Palestinian Authority's Departments of Archaeology in Gaza and
the West Bank, the Palestinian Association for Cultural Exchange (PACE), the
Center for Architectural Conservation (RIWAQ), and others, all of which were
made possible after the coming of the Palestinian Authority to the West Bank and
the Gaza Strip in 1996. It is still premature to talk of a well defined Palestinian
school of archaeology, but Palestinians archaeologists are certainly trying to develop
a sense of their past. Some of them are launching excavations in Gaza and the West
Bank in cooperation with international colleagues, while others are trying to inject
their own interpretations of previous archaeological work in the country (Yahya et
al. 1999).

It should be remembered here that although archaeology constitutes some kind
of national obsession in Israel, or a second religion as some say, until very recently
this discipline was totally neglected by Palestinian academics and institutions. The
Israelis have more than a century of biblical scholarship and half a century of Israeli
scholarship on their side, while the Palestinians are just beginning to introduce their
reading of the history of the country in an effort to establish their own national
identity (Ju'beh 2003). Palestinian archaeologists, like their Israeli counterparts, are
wrestling with the issues of how and how much religion and politics should be
allowed to influence their work. The issue is still far from being resolved, and it
seems that a lot of ink and, regrettably, more blood too will be spilled before this
issue is resolved satisfactorily.

It appears that Palestinians in the past were content for others to authenticate
what appeared to them to be self-evident – their rights to the land (Tamari 1987).
But since those who investigate an arena of knowledge tend to bring to the investigation their own ideological preferences and priorities, it is biblical archaeology
and its Israeli-Zionist offshoots that have reigned supreme so far. It is quite indicative in this regard that the first serious program of archaeology at a Palestinian academic institution did not start until the late 1980s. Its founding was due for the
most part to the efforts of Albert Glock (1925–92), an American professor of
archaeology affiliated with the Albright Institute of Archaeological Research in
Jerusalem from 1970–80. In 1976 Glock became affiliated with Birzeit University,
and his sincere efforts culminated in the establishment of the first Palestinian Institute of Archaeology at that university in 1988 (Kapitan 1999). It was not until the
1990s that a few other programs of archaeology were established at two other Palestinian academic institutions, namely the Higher Institute of Islamic Archaeology at
al-Quds University in 1992, and the departments of archaeology at the same university in 2000 and at al-Najah University, Nablus in 1993. It is most regrettable
that the first Palestinian Institute of Archaeology at Birzeit never recovered from
the tragic assassination of Prof. Glock in 1992, and it was closed down in 2003
because of financial problems.

There are still many obstacles that need to be overcome before one can start
thinking of a proper policy to safeguard archaeological sites in the Holy Land, not
least of which is facilitating access to sites, abandonment of the policies of segre-
gation and closures, as well as the modernization of antiquities laws, including

toughening laws governing the antiquities market if not banning trade in antiquities altogether. To achieve that goal, all concerned official bodies in the Palestinian areas and in Israel, including the departments of antiquities, national parks authorities, and the ministries of culture, tourism, and environment ought to act immediately. It is not enough that those official bodies be functional. They ought to be efficient and cooperative, too, to ensure a proper protection scheme for the antiquities of the Holy Land as a whole.

The Holy Land and the West Bank of the Jordan River in particular encompass some of the most important world cultural heritage sites. It is the land of the earliest known human settlements and the world's holiest cities: Jerusalem, Jericho, Hebron, and Nablus, among others. Whatever the political solution for the Palestinian-Israeli conflict may be, the Holy Land is and always will be one unit from a cultural point of view, if not a splinter of a larger cultural sphere which includes the entire Middle East and beyond. And from an economic point of view, it is one tourist destination, or actually part of a larger tourist destination that includes at least Jordan, Syria, Lebanon, and Egypt.

There should be no doubt that maintaining archaeological sites and the protection of the Holy Land's cultural heritage can play a vital role in the economic revival of the country and the region as a whole. Economic viability will be one of the most crucial issues facing Palestine, Israel, and indeed the entire region in peacetime, and archaeologists have an important role to play in this regard. They can and should help in promoting reconciliation between the peoples of the region and the world at large by creating a framework to maximize the enjoyment of the country's and region's heritage for its people and for visitors from abroad. This will require them to render more neutral the study of history and archaeology, reevaluating periods and constellations within them, and encouraging the dissemination of knowledge and provision of educational materials, as well as facilitating access to all sites of interest to the world – prehistoric, biblical, Byzantine, Islamic, Crusader, and others. Palestinian, Israeli, and foreign archaeologists working in the Holy Land should commit themselves to the rich history, diversity, and resources of the country, and therefore to supporting an agenda that both protects heritage and promotes change. This will facilitate the mutual understanding of the past, something that biblical archaeologists in the past did not consider at all. Reconciliation may not inevitably lead to a "shared" version of our pasts – that may not in fact be possible or desirable – but the interaction of our differing views and narratives will give vitality to our dialogue and present a challenge we seldom encounter in our work as archaeologists.

Negotiating the Past

During the Oslo process most Israeli and Palestinian politicians argued, and tried hard to convince their publics, that talking about the past and confronting the difficult issues in the Arab-Israeli conflict would only complicate the negotiating process between the Palestinians and Israelis. The process itself and subsequent events in the region including the present *intifada* suggest that this view was ill-con-sidered. It is clear now that dealing with the past and confronting the difficult issues is a prerequisite for achieving peace in the troubled region. Or, as the late Edward Said rightly put it, "there can be no possible reconciliation and no possi-ble solution unless these two communities – the Arabs and the Jews, Israelis and Palestinians – confront the experience of each in the light of the other" (Said 1999:20).

More and more scholars today, Palestinian, Israeli, and foreign archaeologists working in Palestine/Israel, are realizing that archaeology cannot and should not be used for the purposes of exclusion. They are practicing archaeology to further coex-istence between societies whose adjacency requires a great deal of tolerance and reconciliation. This kind of talk may sound naive and overly optimistic in today's inflamed atmosphere, but the reversion to past practices is certainly no alternative. It is true that overcoming the present difficulties and filling the vacuum created by the absence or indifference of the official bodies is going to be difficult. But the good will of individual Palestinian, Israeli, and foreign archaeologists can make a big difference. It will create the necessary conditions for peace and revitalize the country and the region as a whole.

Archaeology for the Future

Believing that practicing archaeology is not a fantasy but rather an essential tool to better the lives of present and future generations, a group of Palestinian archaeol-ogists and conservationists aided by international colleagues and agencies have been working since 1996 to develop a proper strategy to maintain and rehabilitate en-dangered world cultural heritage in the Palestinian areas. They formed the Pales-tinian Association for Cultural Exchange (PACE) to protect archaeological sites, through public education, public awareness, rehabilitation work, and research. PACE believes that archaeologists have a role to play in the cultural and economic revival of the country and the region as a whole and works to satisfy the demands of the general public, local and international tourists, conservationists, and researchers. And perhaps most crucially, it tries to tackle religious and political sen-sitivities in the region.

The organization has made its work relevant by engaging local communities in protecting endangered heritage, especially in rural areas. To ensure public integra-tion in protection and preservation of historical sites, it concentrates its efforts on the youth, women, and educators as well as local authorities. It coordinates its efforts with the local communities and forms "Local Committees to Protect Cul-tural Heritage" in every village and region. The committees are usually constituted of members representing the different local community organizations: village coun-cils, youth clubs, women's groups, churches, mosques, and so on. Regular monthly meetings are held between the organization's staff and those committees to plan and organize activities. Furthermore, PACE makes relentless efforts to expose its work to the outside world through publicity and exchange visits to ensure a proper evaluation of the work and continued flow of ideas and thoughts. It should be said here that PACE is one of several organizations in this field, and I cite its work here, rather than any other, because I have first-hand knowledge of it in my capacity as director of the organization for several years. The activities of the organization can be summarized as follows:

1   Organizing intensive public awareness campaigns in the various regions of the West Bank, and particularly in rural areas, to encourage local communities to safeguard world cultural heritage sites and the environment in their regions as a future asset for the community and the world at large. Archaeological sites are protected regardless of their period, religious, or national connotation. The public awareness campaigns usually include a series of lectures, slide shows, films, town meetings, and tours led by members of the organization and experts in the field of cultural heritage, preservation, and conservation. They cover a wide range of topics and periods as well as all kinds of sites including prehistoric ones such as Shuqba (Wadi Natuf) and Jericho; biblical sites such as Beitin/Bethel, Tel al-Tal/Ai, al-Jib/Gibeon, Tel Balta/Shechem; Roman and Byzantine sites including Jifna/Gophna, Atara, and Aboud; as well as Islamic sites such as Nabi Musa, Beit Rima, and Deir Ghassaneh.

2   Rehabilitating and vitalizing endangered historical and environmental sites, especially in the villages, to serve local communities rather than burden them. Some sites have been transformed into public parks or playgrounds to serve the immediate needs of the local communities, as in the case of the Ottoman Maqam of Sheikh Khaled in Deir Ghasaneh, Ramallah, which was transformed into a public park, the Byzantine pool of Beitin (Bethel) which was transformed into a playground for the village youth, and the 19th-century building of the Taha family in Beit Rima that was turned into a cultural center and public garden. Most of these projects were carried out in cooperation with other Palestinian NGOs including RIWAQ, the Palestinian Hydrology Group (PHG), PARC, and local village councils.

3   Producing literature on the sites and villages in the form of brochures, tour guide books and booklets, and other promotional materials in different languages. The production of this literature is seen by the organization as means to empower the local communities and a necessary step to promote the sites as possible tourist destinations for local and international tourists. The organization also installs identification marks on the sites to attract the attention of the local communities and encourage them to preserve those important archaeological places. One of PACE's proud achievements has been the production of the first Palestinian tour guidebook of the West Bank and Gaza Strip, the first ever of its kind by Palestinians. The book has been published in Arabic, English, and Italian, and plans are underway to publish it in German, French, and Hebrew.

4   PACE has also provided and continues to provide short-term job opportunities for the men and women of the villages on the archaeological sites in an effort

to ease the alienation between the people and their heritage, reduce the rate of unemployment among Palestinians in rural areas, and thus protect archaeological sites from vandalism. The people of the villages are hired to clean the sites, build stone terraces around them for protection, while others are employed to collect oral data in the form of in-depth interviews with the elders of the villages to be used in the research and for archival purposes.

5 PACE promotes traditional Palestinian handicrafts, especially hand-made ceramics and embroidery. The later is an exclusively female artistic tradition. We encourage women to use their ancient designs in an effort to preserve a precious heritage and at the same time support those women who embroider articles for sale to make a living.

PACE's projects are usually made possible thanks to generous financial contributions from different American and European non-governmental and governmental agencies. Although the organization has experienced tremendous difficulties in its efforts, it is safe to say that its overall efforts have been successful. Unstable political conditions in the country during the current *intifada*, which has just entered its fourth year, has literally crippled the organization and confined us to our immediate surroundings, the Ramallah area. Conflicts of interest with the Palestinian department of antiquities, the Israeli military authorities, and aggressive illegal excavators has exhausted much of our time and energy. Despite that, PACE's efforts resulted in a remarkable decline in the rate of illegal digging at all sites where the organization has been active. The situation of those sites has either improved or at least stabilized.

Conclusion

One of the most affirmative characteristics of the work of archaeologists today is a growing awareness of the relevance of archaeology for present and future generations. To really make a difference, archaeologists and conservationists should transform their role into that of facilitators for community-based education and action. This methodology has proved itself in the particularly impossible case of Palestine. The work of the Palestinian Association of Cultural Exchange, small as it is, has succeeded in ensuring genuine public interest in cultural heritage and helped reduce the harm wrought by the nationalist practices attributable to traditional archaeology. It has strengthened local communities' abilities to generate income and at the same time protect their heritage and environment even in times of war and total distress, as persist in the Holy Land these days.

Acknowledgments

I'm grateful to my colleagues Susan Pollock and Reinhard Bernbeck for the invitation to participate in this book, and for reviewing the manuscript of this chapter and suggesting important comments for its improvement. I would also like to thank my colleagues Sandra Scham and Ann Killebrew for their enthusiastic support of PACE's work, which stands at the heart of this article.

REFERENCES

Abu Khalaf, Marwan, 1987 Archaeological Excavations of Islamic Sites in Palestine. Birzeit Research Review 4:66–94.

Bernbeck, Reinhard, and Susan Pollock, 1996 Ayodhya, Archaeology, and Identity. Current Anthropology 37S:S138–142.

Finkelstein, Israel, 1991 The Emergence of Israel in Canaan: Consensus, Mainstream and Dispute. Scandinavian Journal of the Old Testament 2:47–49.

Glock, Albert, 1985 Tradition and Change in Two Archaeologies. American Antiquity 50:464–477.

Glock, Albert, 1987 Prolegomena to Archaeological Theory. Birzeit Research Review 4:4–39.

Ju'beh, Nazmi, 2003 al-Mashad al-Hadari fi Filistin (The Cultural Scene in Palestine). Higher Council of Education and Culture – PLO (in Arabic).

Kapitan, Thomas, ed., 1999 Archaeology, History and Culture in Palestine and the Near East: Essays in Memory of Albert E. Glock. Alberta, GA: Scholars Press.

Kenyon, Kathleen, 1957 Digging up Jericho. London: Ernest Benn.

Lipman, Vivian, 1988 The Origins of the Palestine Exploration Fund. Palestine Exploration Quarterly 120:45–54.

Meskell, Lynn, 2002 Negative Heritage and Past Mastering in Archaeology. Anthropological Quarterly 75:557–574.

Nashef, Khaled, 2000 'Khirbet Birzeit' 1996, 1998–1999: Preliminary Results. Journal of Palestinian Archaeology 1/1:25–27.

Pritchard, James, 1962 Gibeon, Where the Sun Stood Still. Princeton: Princeton University Press.

Rosen, Steven, 1998 Is Archaeological Education in Israel Stagnating? In One Hundred Years After Petrie: Essays in Honor of Walker I. Ackerman. Haim Marautz, ed. pp. 219–229. Beer-Sheva: Ben-Gurion University Press.

Said, Edward, 1999 Palestine: Memory, Invention and Space. In The Landscape of Palestine: Equivocal Poetry. Lila Abu-Lughod, R. Heacock, and Khaled Nashef, eds. pp. 3–20. Birzeit-Palestine: Birzeit University Publications.

Silberman, Neil Asher, 1993 The New Encyclopedia of Archaeological Excavations in the Holy Land. Jerusalem: Israel Exploration Society.

Tamari, Salim, 1987 A Weak Spot. Birzeit Research Review 4:1–3.

Trigger, Bruce, 1984 Alternative Archaeologies: Nationalist, Colonialist, Imperialist. Man n.s. 19:355–370.

Whitelam, Keith, 1996 The Invention of Ancient Israel. New York: Routledge.

Yahya, Adel, Muin Sadeq, and Hana Abdel Nour, 1999 PACE Tour Guide of the West Bank and Gaza Strip. Ramallah: Palestinian Association for Cultural Exchange.

5

Archaeology Goes to War at the Newsstand

Susan Pollock

Stories about archaeology feature with surprising frequency in the news.[1] Apart from a passing curiosity, one might reasonably ask why students and practitioners of archaeology should pay attention to the reporting of archaeology in the mainstream news media. It is all too tempting to dismiss such reports as factually flawed or highly simplistic. Ignoring the reporting of archaeology in the news (and other forms of media) is, however, a mistake. The news and other media products are the primary ways in which non-archaeologists learn and form opinions about archaeology. As such, the media shape the public's overall view of what archaeology is, what archaeologists do, and whether and why archaeology has any social value. These media-shaped perceptions of archaeology are, in turn, key to people's ideas about how archaeological evidence can be interpreted and hence how it may be used (as well as abused). To the extent that archaeologists neglect the media's representations of archaeology, we indirectly abdicate responsibility for the ways in which our work is used: we are drawn, albeit often unwittingly and unwillingly, into the political agendas of others. The apparent innocuousness of many reports on archaeology – their appeals to the "disinterested curiosity" of the reader or viewer or the communication of what seems to be a "common sense" message – makes their ideological impact all the greater.

In this chapter, I draw on the work of a number of media analysts for general insights into news production and consumption before turning to some of the specific features of archaeology as a newsworthy topic.[2] I suggest that archaeology's apparent power to legitimize present-day collective identities, through particular constructions of temporality and notions of ownership, is a central reason why it is often drawn upon for contemporary political agendas. These ideas are examined and elaborated in two case studies of recent violent events in which archaeology figured prominently in the news – in Iraq, in the context of two Gulf wars (1991 and 2003), and in Afghanistan, with the destruction of the Bamiyan Buddhas, followed by the U.S.-led war in 2001. On the basis of these examples, I argue that

Middle Eastern archaeology has been used to promote a view of the modern Middle East and our relations to it that furthers U.S. government policies in times of war and diplomatic crises in the region.

Our Mediated World

Media are arguably our major source of information about the world and the principal means by which culture is disseminated; they have "colonized culture" (Kellner 1995:35). To put it in the starker terms used by the philosopher Günther Anders, when we wish to know what is going on in the world, we go home and turn on the television or radio; instead of going to witness events, events visit us in our homes through the media (Anders 2002[1956]:110). Anders contends that we no longer live *in* the world, but rather simply consume, and what we primarily consume are images. As a result, we inhabit a world that is more phantom-like than real, in which there is no longer a distinction between reality and its representation (see also Baudrillard 1976:110–117; Debord 1977; Appadurai 1991).

The media "function to amuse, entertain, and inform," but also to impart beliefs and values that help to integrate people into social structures (Herman and Chomsky 1988:1). They produce the raw materials people use to construct identities and help create what Benedict Anderson (1991) has called "imagined communities": those communities which are neither formed nor held together principally through face-to-face interactions.

Herman and Chomsky (1988) have developed a "propaganda model" of news production. They contend that propaganda is the way in which democracies try to control people, since they may not do so (outrightly) by force. They identify a set of filters that shape the production of news. The first of these filters is the size, wealth, and concentration of ownership of the dominant media. Most news producers are profit-making enterprises that base their decisions about how to produce the news to a substantial degree on the programs' and products' money-making potential. Over the course of the past couple of decades, American media producers have been increasingly bought up by large corporate entities in whose interests they tend to operate. These include entertainment conglomerates as well as corporations that have substantial defense contracts (Bagdikian 2000; McChesney 2002:372–374).

A second filter results from the role played by advertising as a principal source of income for news media. Media seldom air or publish reports that might produce conflict with the interests of their owners or their major advertisers – interests that include big business and the state (McChesney 2002:375).

A third filter identified by Herman and Chomsky is the heavy reliance on "expert sources" as the basis for the news. The reliance on experts – especially on the same ones over and over – is one of the ways in which media avoid the expenses of investigative reporting (Borjesson 2002:13; Hendrix 2002:171). The "experts" used by the major news media come predominantly from government and big business, once again ensuring that their interests will be served (see also Gans 1979).

Together, these filters and others result in the marginalization, if not elimination, of dissenting voices in the news that reaches most people.[3]

Some analysts have contested the view that the dominant media are principally producers of propaganda. Kellner (1995:59) contends that the media help to "establish the hegemony of specific political groups and projects," but they are not principally propaganda instruments for the state. He suggests that the media do not present their readers, viewers, and listeners with a single, coherent ideological position. Rather, as profit-driven money machines, they constantly seek to enlarge their audiences, and to do so they try to provide "something for everyone" (Kellner 1995:93, 212–213).

The production of a news story is a multi-layered process that involves more than one person as well as a variety of interests. Reporters pursue leads, interview people, search for "experts," and write the text of a story. But decisions about what to publish or broadcast are usually made by editors, who may direct a reporter to a story or pull him or her off one, modify the tone of a report and thereby its force and intent, or "kill" a story altogether (Hendrix 2002:171). Editors, in turn, are subject to control by media owners whose agendas and financial interests may lead to rejection or substantial alteration of particular stories.

The consumption or reception of media products is inextricably linked to their production (Lutz and Collins 1993; Kellner 1995; Thompson 1995). In his study of American public television, Dornfeld found that producers consider their audiences to be relatively predictable and spend much "time and energy predicting, invoking, and strategizing about how to hold the[ir] attention" (Dornfeld 2002:254). Kellner claims that audiences may resist meanings conveyed by the media and instead rework them to form their own (Kellner 1995:3), a view that contrasts pointedly with Anders's argument that media so dominate our understanding and perception of the world that we simply cannot think outside them. Although Kellner does not deny that media manipulate the public, he maintains that people also rework media products to "produce their own meanings and pleasures out of this material" (Kellner 1995:108; see also Enzensberger 1970).

I return in the concluding section of this chapter to the debate on the extent to which the media expound a single ideological position. But regardless of the position one adopts, a key point in these as well as other critical approaches is that media products, like all representations, are invariably *mis*representations, not because they are "wrong," but rather because they are always partial. No news story, regardless of the best intentions of its creator, can escape this partiality. A call for critical analyses of media products is a recognition of the ever-present need to critically interrogate all representations, thereby engaging in a critique of ideology.

Why Does the Past Matter?

A key question must be posed before analyzing representations of archaeology in the news: how is the past, as it is investigated through archaeology, presented to the public in order to make it seem to matter in the midst of myriad contemporary issues? In other words, if the portrayal of archaeology in the news amounts to more than merely stimulating or satisfying curiosity, for what reasons do news producers and the news-consuming public see archaeology as relevant to their lives?

One of the most salient reasons is that the past is widely thought to be key to collective identities in the present, a means through which identities can be formed and reinforced (for example, Lowenthal 1985; Härke 1993; Abu el-Haj 2001). Having a precedent is seen as giving a group the right to exist, a point that has figured prominently in discussions of nations and nationalism (Anderson 1991). Identities are not constructed in a vacuum but rather in a context of other, already existing identities; their establishment and maintenance form an arena of potential struggle (Friedman 1992b; Bernbeck and Pollock 1996). The assertion of an identity acquires meaning in relation to others: boundaries and differences are the very stuff through which identities are defined (Barth 1969). The key role of the past in identity formation means that control of the past and its interpretation is a source of power in the present.

One of the central means by which the connections between past and present are configured and used to create meaning from archaeological remains is through the representation of spatiotemporal relationships. Invariably, the ways we construct and narrate understandings of the past carry with them particular conceptualizations of time. Time is neither an absolute nor a neutral measure, but rather it is subject to a variety of "manipulations" that bear a host of possible meanings (see Charvát, this volume).[4] Temporal constructions have particularly powerful political implications because they are multiple and open to strategic use. Linear time is a way in which we define the content of relations between ourselves and others; we construe others in terms of their spatial and temporal distance from us (Fabian 1983).

Time, in particular the past, may be a "means of *representing a difference*" (de Certeau 1988:85), but it may also be used to emphasize similarity. This is a matter of nearness and distance but also of the extent to which continuity or discontinuity between past and present is emphasized. For present purposes, these distinctions result in a four-part scheme.

1 *Verbiederung*/Familiarization: In his searing critique of the effects of media culture on contemporary social relations, Günther Anders emphasizes the familiarization of past events that makes them seem similar to what we know in the present (Anders 2002:117–126). He contends that the omnipresence of media products serves to make the whole world, including the past, seem familiar in a cheap sort of a way, what he terms *Verbiederung*. People from the past are spoken about as though they were our neighbors, with the present thereby becoming a direct and "natural" continuation of the past. In this way the past is effectively done away with, because everything is made to seem near and thereby similar to us.

2 Alienation: Related to the notion of familiarization is the phenomenon of alienation (*Verfremdung*), from which, according to Anders, *Verbiederung* comes. Alienation makes what is close and familiar in the present appear distant and

strange. Another version of alienation portrays past events as close in time but with a distinct discontinuity to the present. This latter form of alienation is commonly found in colonial contexts, with the history of colonial subjects delegitimized by denying a connection between them and the history of the land they inhabit.

3   Ascending anachronisms: The past may also be made to seem familiar by using a quite different temporal device. An event may be pushed back in time – made distant – but at the same time emphasizing continuity with the present. In this way, legitimacy is conferred upon contemporary practices by establishing a long tradition and precedent that extend deep into the past. Such a use of time, referred to as an ascending anachronism by the historian Alain Delivré (1974:177–183), presents the past as distant, yet at the same time it draws on the notion of familiarity by establishing a connection between a past practice and one known in the present.

4   Past as other: In other cases where the distance between past and present is accentuated, discontinuity with the present may underscore the strangeness, otherness, and radical difference of the past: it becomes a "foreign country" (Lowenthal 1985). An emphasis on distance may promote a perception of the past as exotic and romantic, or it can contribute to its denigration (Fabian 1983:23–24). This temporal construct is often a version of alienation.

In these varied ways narratives about the past – whether in the news media or in academic accounts – make connections to the present in terms that bear a host of connotations. It is precisely these sorts of unstated implications of what seems to be a neutral measure – time – that help to "naturalize" identity claims that rest on understandings of the past.

The importance of the past to present-day concerns does not by itself explain why archaeology is – or in some cases is not – seen by people other than archaeologists as an important and valid source of knowledge about the past. While archaeology is a suspect enterprise for some people (many Native Americans, for example) and of little import for others, the weight it brings to bear in many appeals to the past rests on its materiality. Trouillot (1995:29) has remarked that "history begins with bodies and artifacts" (see also Verdery 1999), with the physical traces left behind that impose some limits on historical narratives. For many Westerners, material remains impart an impression of objectivity; unlike words, they do not (seem to) lie (Härke 1993).

The materiality of archaeological evidence offers a tangible indication of past events and practices, and physical existence of archaeological remains is not easily disputed. Materiality is a facet of archaeology that is often alluring to non-archaeologists. It is what draws people to museum exhibits even in this "age of mechanical reproduction" – the perception that old objects that were not industrially produced have an "aura" or authenticity (Benjamin 1968[1936]). Despite this nostalgic allure, archaeological objects are regularly drawn into commoditized transactions in art and antiquities markets.

News of the Ancient Near East

I turn now to two case studies in which I examine reporting on archaeology of the Middle East in the print news media. I concentrate principally upon U.S. media, supplemented by some materials from other English-language sources. I will consider the ways in which archaeology is drawn upon, through appeals to notions of identity, temporality, and ownership, in the context of reporting on and shaping public opinion about contemporary world events. My analysis focuses on readings of the articles themselves.

War and archaeology in Iraq

The first case centers on reporting about archaeology in the contexts of Gulf War I (1991) and II (2003).[5] In both wartime situations, there was a marked increase in reports about the archaeology of Iraq in comparison to their frequency at other times.[6] Why did the print media devote so much attention to archaeology in war time? The sheer fact of its emphasis in the context of major political and military conflict is a signal that archaeology was employed to help support political agendas. Otherwise, one would expect it to be evoked just as often to promote constructive, peacetime goals.

Close readings of newspaper articles on archaeology in Iraq show that four positions were taken with regard to the past and its relationship to the present. In the first of these, the antiquity of Iraq's past and its continuity with the *Western* world today were foregrounded, an approach that used ascending anachronisms. The second position relied on a form of alienation in which modern Iraqis were divorced from their past in an implied devolution from greatness to barbarity. A third version considered Iraqis, as embodied in the person of Saddam Hussein, to follow closely in the footsteps of the Mesopotamian past, but solely in terms of the most negative features of that history. Finally, in the wake of undeniable damage to ancient monuments, sites, and artifacts after the first Gulf War but especially in the aftermath of the second one, reporters were confronted with a conundrum that many seem to have had difficulty resolving. In some cases, this produced a combination of confusion and denial; in others, anger and critique edged to the fore.

Newspaper reports on the archaeology of Iraq in the context of the two Gulf Wars made the case that it was very important. A crucial reason for its salience that appeared repeatedly in the news was that Iraq's ancient past is related to American identity: Mesopotamia – more or less the area of present-day Iraq – is understood as the "cradle of [Western] civilization."

In an approach made explicit in archaeology by V. Gordon Childe (1928), but one with much deeper historical roots, Western civilization is viewed as the historical and cultural heir of the "great civilizations" of the ancient Near East. Zainab Bahrani (1998) has recently argued that a particular, constructed Mesopotamian identity has been historically a part of – indeed, almost a requirement for – Western narratives about the progress of civilization (see also Van de Mieroop 1997). To bolster this purported connection, which transcends substantial distances in time and space, requires a true sleight-of-hand. The Mesopotamian past is familiarized by accentuating continuity – demonstrating that that past contains the antecedents of much of what we today prize in Western civilization – and also, in another sense, distanced by being shown to be very old. These ancient roots contribute to the greatness and legitimacy of "our modern civilization," in a phenomenon referred to by Bruce Trigger (1984) as "imperialist archaeology."

In newspaper accounts connections between the Iraqi past and us were asserted in a variety of ways. A common means was by identifying Mesopotamia as "the cradle of civilization." Sometimes the connection to the West was made even more specific: "While President Bush describes Iraq as the 'axis of evil' and the lair of a defiant Saddam Hussein, young American military cadets are learning that it is also the cradle of *Western* civilization" (Miniclier 2003:E1, emphasis added).

This strategy was made explicit through appeals to "firsts," those inventions credited to ancient Mesopotamia and also judged basic to our modern civilization: "the place where man first took the step from village culture to high civilization in about 4000 B.C." (Honan 1991:Arts Sec., 13). "The Mesopotamians were the first to record their thoughts in writing, the first to divide the day into 24 hours, the first to eat off ceramic plates" (Solomon 2003:Sec.6, 15).

Biblical connections were also emphasized. Ur was described as "the legendary birthplace of Abraham" (Longworth 1991:9), and mention was made of "an oil refinery at Basra, [that] now occupies a purported site of the Garden of Eden" (Ringle 1991:C1). Sometimes biblical referents were linked to more secular ones: "Troops that invaded from the south crossed territory called the cradle of civilization and traditionally considered the site of the Garden of Eden" (Witham 2003).

In these ways, readers were encouraged to recall, or form, a sense of identification with the ancient past of Iraq. From there, it was only a short step to developing ideas about ownership of that past. In the context of the first Gulf War, in particular, the remains of ancient civilizations in Iraq were to be understood as possessions of "humanity" at least as much as of the inhabitants of present-day Iraq (Petit 1991:A8; MacLeod 2003).[7] In this respect, archaeology in Iraq is depicted in much the same way as oil, the other resource commonly associated with that country in the West – as assets that have international owners and interests. Just as oil is crucial to the operation of American civilization, so, too, is the archaeology of Iraq to be understood as part of American heritage (Pollock and Lutz 1994:269–270). A key difference is that oil and the profits it generates are the genuine interest of powerful businesses and the U.S. government, whereas archaeology is wielded principally as an ideological tool used to support actions that sustain these oil (and other) interests.

In some accounts modern Iraqis were implied to have descended to barbarous depths in comparison to their glorious ancestors. Surely, therefore, *they* could not be the rightful heirs of this past. A *New York Times* editorial proclaimed, "The Cradle,

Ironically, of Civilization" (Editorial 1991:A30), whereas a slightly more subtle version appeared in a description of the site of Ur: "The tales of death and destruction contrasted sharply with the quiet dignity and grace of the ancient ruins of Ur, . . . It was a cultured Euphrates River port then, in 4000 B.C." (Drogin 1991:A10).

Newspaper accounts occasionally constructed another relationship between past and present in which modern-day Iraqis are the heirs of ancient Mesopotamia, but of the barbaric and aggressive aspects rather than of the great achievements. It is therefore no surprise that modern Iraqis act so badly: "Many of the ancient sites are ruins today because of past wars. Their construction and their destruction are proof that neither warfare nor egomania are new in the region" (Longworth 1991:9).

Although each of these approaches highlighted a different set of relationships between past and present, they are not necessarily mutually exclusive. A construct that emphasizes Western inheritance of the glories of ancient Mesopotamia does not rule out the possibility that Iraqis inherited the brutal aspects of that past. However, at certain times it became difficult for journalists to maintain these constructs without producing a contradictory discourse.

Overall, newspaper accounts at the times of both Gulf Wars relied to a significant extent on equations of the ancient Mesopotamian past with a heritage that is part of contemporary Western civilization. While this approach made clear why readers should care about Iraq's past, it also posed a potential conundrum: if that past was really such an important part of our heritage, how were we to reconcile that fact with U.S. bombing and invasion of the country, which posed risks to its material remains? As one journalist wrote, "What does it mean that, if war breaks out, we're almost certain to bomb it [Basra, supposed location of the Garden of Eden]?" (Ringle 1991:C1). Although some critical questions were raised, most reports sought to answer them in ways that did not detract from support of the American-led wars.

At the time of the 1991 Gulf War, journalists tended to adopt the position that because Iraqi heritage is ancestral to Western civilization, it was incumbent upon us to ensure its preservation. In the face of Saddam's willingness to jeopardize this heritage – most commonly asserted by claims that Iraqi military installations were located near important sites and museums (Pollock and Lutz 1994:278–279) – U.S. military damage would be either unavoidable or the lesser evil. Some journalists referred to U.S. military officials' claims that they were doing their best to minimize "collateral damage" to archaeological sites, although the same reports often noted that archaeologists evinced skepticism (Cooke 1991). Articles that appeared in the aftermath of the war frequently contained statements by archaeologists that military damage seemed to have been minimal, but that the main harm was caused by looting and agricultural projects that took place after the war. A few reports went on to suggest that the U.N.-imposed economic sanctions were at least partly responsible for creating the conditions in which looting flourished and massive new irrigation works were necessary (Saltus 1992).

Journalists' approaches differed in some notable respects in the second Gulf War. The relatively small number of articles on the archaeology of Iraq in U.S. newspapers in the months preceding and especially during the first weeks of the invasion implies a reluctance on the part of newspaper journalists or editors to raise the issue of archaeology in the "cradle of civilization." Perhaps this was a reflection of the very limited international support for the U.S. government's position, along with considerable domestic opposition to a war: invoking an issue that could easily become a double-edged sword – a war that might damage "our" heritage, as many archaeologists argued vocally in the months prior to the invasion – may have seemed too risky. The newly created policy of "embedding" reporters in military units was an explicit attempt to ensure that they would feel themselves "part of the team" and may well have curtailed certain kinds of reports, whether due to lack of opportunity to investigate particular kinds of stories or an unwillingness to broach touchy subjects (Andersen 2003). The fact that archaeological remains had suffered from Gulf War I, even if indirectly, may have lessened editors' and journalists' appetite for engaging with archaeology a second time in a war-time context. Some of the reports that did appear in the U.S. press were decidedly ambivalent, mentioning damages incurred as a result of Gulf War I (Solomon 2003; Wilford 2003) as well as the provisions of the Hague conventions for protection of cultural property during war (Cotter 2003; Neuffer 2003). One such report mentioned Mesopotamia's purported legacy of aggression, while also pointing to the contradictions posed by invading such a country: "[F]reshmen cadets at the U.S. Air Force Academy in Colorado Springs are receiving a thought-provoking lecture from their history teacher: 'President Bush speaks of the need to "defend civilization,"' Lt. Col. Dave Kirkham tells his students. 'Then I point out the irony of defending civilization against the cradle of civilization,' adds Kirkham" (Miniclier 2003:E1).

Other stories emphasized promises by U.S. military officials to do their best to avoid damage to sites and monuments (Witham 2003) or claimed that any destruction that resulted would be Saddam's fault (Glick 2003).

With the looting of the Iraq Museum in the second week of April, however, reports on archaeological topics skyrocketed into headlines around the world. Journalists were confronted with the specter of American complicity in the wholesale destruction of what they – and many archaeologists – had long construed as a part of their own past (Pollock 2003). The story of the Iraq Museum was told in a variety of ways, ranging from outright anger to disbelief and denial. No longer was there an easy or obvious way to reconcile the presumed good intentions of U.S. military and political leaders with a concern for the material remains of "our" past. Perhaps unsurprisingly, it was at this time that a significant number of articles appeared in which the archaeology of Iraq was deemed to be principally the heritage of modern Iraqis – so we were not destroying *our* past after all. It is still too soon to tell how journalists will ultimately seek to deal with this dilemma.

I turn now to a second case in which archaeology has appeared prominently in the print news media in recent times: Afghanistan. As we will see, the themes emphasized and the ways archaeology was constructed as newsworthy are distinct in a number of ways from those highlighted in the Iraqi case.

The Buddhas of Bamiyan and the U.S.-led war in Afghanistan

In March 2001, following several weeks of threats and international attention, the Taliban government of Afghanistan ordered that two monumental statues of Buddha in the remote Bamiyan Valley be blown up. The incident, as well as the destruction of anthropomorphic artifacts in the National Museum in Kabul, provoked an international outcry that was echoed for weeks in the news media. Afghanistan surged once again into the headlines following the September 11 attacks in New York and Washington and remained front-page news through the remainder of the year, as the U.S. prepared and carried out a war to depose the Taliban government and attempt to rid the country of members of Al-Qaeda.

Stories about archaeology in Afghanistan proliferated during these periods, first when the Taliban government carried out its threat to destroy the two monumental statues of the Buddha. A second peak occurred during the U.S.-led war that resulted in the toppling of the Taliban government.[8]

Already before the destruction of the Buddhas, the U.S. was heading on a collision course with the Taliban. Similarly to Saddam Hussein, the Taliban had previously enjoyed substantial, if tacit, U.S. government support (Rashid 2000: 157–182). As a result, turning them into a despised and illegitimate government required a case to be made that they should be (re)construed as the archenemy.[9] Once again, archaeology was mobilized in the press in a variety of ways to support this process.

In the case of archaeology in Afghanistan, however, reporters faced a problem that had not confronted them in the Iraqi case. Whereas Mesopotamia was almost instantly recognizable as "the cradle of civilization" and appeals to biblical referents made the connections even clearer, for most members of the Western public – and apparently for journalists as well – Central Asia was unfamiliar territory and lacked obvious connections to the West. Indeed, most Westerners had probably never heard of the Buddhas in the Bamiyan Valley prior to their final destruction, an act which the Taliban deliberately broadcast widely (Colwell-Chanthaphonh 2003:93). There were no convenient biblical and only a few other links that reporters could easily draw upon to promote a feeling of identification among an American reading public. As a result, the strategies used to try to make the archaeology of Afghanistan newsworthy – if it was not connected to us, why should we care? – were different from those employed in the two Gulf wars.

One approach emphasized the exoticness of the Afghan past, using, where possible, referents that could be expected to evoke some degree of familiarity. Mentions of Alexander the Great and the Silk Road were frequent. Some reports focused on Afghanistan as a crossroads between "high cultures" to the West (Greek and Roman) and East (Indian and Chinese), thereby partaking of their greatness but also subtly implying that Afghanistan had no cultural existence of its own (cf. Flood 2002:653): "The two Buddhas were hewn with the classical features of all subcontinental Buddhas, but the figures were draped in Greek robes. The combination represented the unique fusion of classical Indian and Central Asian art with Hellenism, introduced by the armies of Alexander the Great" (Squitieri 2002).

A second approach involved a variety of strategies that used archaeology and ancient monuments to cast the Taliban in a bad light. Some reports contrasted the ostensible peacefulness and calm of Buddhism – represented by the two monumental statues that were demolished – with the supposed belligerence of Islam. The religious stereotypes implied by such a contrast were not articulated directly but kept rather at the level of insinuation: "'Central Asia then was an example of tolerance,' says Angelina Drushina . . . 'It was only later that tolerance was destroyed.' Like the Taliban who came after them, the Arab invaders who swept through Tajikistan and Afghanistan would accept no deviation from their own brand of religion" (Toronto Star 2001:Business, 1).

Most newspaper accounts included some statement about whose cultural heritage was being destroyed or should be preserved. The number of articles portraying the cultural heritage of Afghanistan as belonging to Afghans was approximately equal to the number that claimed it to be the property of all humanity. A small minority of reports suggested that Afghanistan's archaeological remains belonged to both Afghans and the rest of the world or proposed that it was the heritage of the inhabitants of the Bamiyan Valley (in the specific case of the Buddhas), Eurasia, Greece, or the region around Afghanistan. Most narratives that constructed the cultural heritage as specifically Afghan appeared around the time of the destruction of the Bamiyan Buddhas. Stories either pitted the Taliban against "real" Afghans – the former ready to destroy the heritage of the latter – or lumped all Afghans together as a group that did not know enough to preserve the heritage of a portion of its population: "Afghanistan's fundamentalist Taliban movement . . . is waging war on the country's cultural heritage, blowing up treasured statues from Afghanistan's pre-Islamic past" (Editorial 2001). In this way the Taliban were depicted as barbaric, in that they willfully destroyed the country's heritage and in so doing sought to create a distinct break between (a part of) the past and the present.

During the U.S.-led war, most reports treated artifacts and monuments from Afghanistan as humanity's heritage. At a time when nearly the whole world was supposed to be at war against the Taliban government, newspaper readers were encouraged to unite around a concern for a heritage that belonged to all humanity. As in the Gulf Wars, this strategy had the potential to backfire, if U.S. forces were seen to have damaged humanity's heritage. In anticipation of such possible claims, reports assigned very different motivations for the destruction of monuments and artifacts depending upon the party that caused it. When attributable to the Taliban, destruction was regularly portrayed as willful (compare the Iraqi case in which Saddam and his associates are claimed to have endangered archaeological remains out of callous disinterest). In contrast, damage resulting from the U.S.-led war was described as accidental, a form of regrettable but unavoidable "collateral damage," and as less destructive than that wrought by the Taliban: "Archaeologists say they are concerned that intensive bombing could destroy a mosque or other site in one of the cities. But nothing, they said, could compare to the damage already done by people in the country" (Cook 2001:C1). In either case, whether heritage was claimed to be Afghan or humanity's, the resulting narrative served to portray the barbarity of the Taliban who intentionally demolished it.

The theme of cultural heritage and the ramifications of destruction, looting, and sale of antiquities on the preservation of that heritage pervaded many newspaper reports on archaeology in Afghanistan. With rare exceptions, the reports treated cultural heritage as specifically material – artifacts and monuments – thus disappearing if the material items themselves were destroyed:[10] "[S]ince 1979, when the Soviets invaded, fighting and looting across the country has been erasing world history, entire chapters at a time" (Cook 2001:C1).

This nearly exclusive equation of heritage with material objects is not borne out in standard usages of the term. Dictionary definitions mention property but also "something transmitted by or acquired from a predecessor: inheritance, legacy" as well as "tradition" (Webster's Third New International Dictionary). International agreements concerning the treatment of cultural heritage give considerable weight to material remains but are not limited solely to tangible items. Articles 1 and 2 of the 1970 UNESCO convention on prevention of illicit transfer of cultural property, for example, discuss cultural property, a part of cultural heritage, as that which "is specifically designated by each State as being of importance for archaeology, prehistory, history, literature, art or science . . . ," a list that extends well beyond material items.

By tacitly equating heritage with (ancient) artifacts and monuments, newspaper reports turn the discussion of damage to Afghanistan's past into a matter of tangible property and ownership.[11] The material remains stand in contrast to intangibles, which are often thought to be barred from possession or not subject to exclusive ownership, a characterization more typical of Mesopotamia in its guise as the "cradle of civilization." By framing stories in terms of property and ownership, the unfamiliar – archaeology of Afghanistan – was placed in the familiar territory of commodities and capitalism.

When cultural heritage is treated as consisting of material objects and material objects are understood as things that can be owned, it is an easy step to view heritage as a commodity like any other that can be bought and sold. However, acquiescing to the implicit equation of artifacts with commodities meant that reporters could not easily condemn the sale of antiquities, an enterprise of dubious legality at best. Although news reports did not directly condone the sale of antiquities, few gave it the harsh treatment reserved for reports of the destruction of antiquities: "The destruction of the Buddhas was the most vivid strike of the Taliban's jihad against Afghanistan's textured culture and history" (Squitieri 2002:10D). It might be concluded that while the sale of cultural heritage is not really a crime, the destruction of it – so that it can never be sold or possessed – is.

The tacit acceptance of archaeological objects as commodities contrasts with reporters' tendency to personify the artifacts and monuments they discussed: "The destruction of the Buddhas of Bamiyan was as spectacular as it was devastating. First, soldiers sprayed bullets at the statues – one of which, at 178 feet tall, stood higher than any other Buddha in the world. Mortally but not fatally wounded, the statues hung on" (Buckholtz 2001:E1).

Material remains were written about as if they had emotions and could be hurt, reminiscent of reporters' use of a metaphor of rape in the context of the Iraqi invasion of Kuwait (Pollock and Lutz 1994:279). By attributing emotional qualities to objects, journalists effectively treated them as aura-bearing (Benjamin 1968), an oddly paradoxic stance toward objects that were also accepted as commodities. Implied in the personifications is that these were not merely inanimate objects – it was emphatically not that "All we are breaking are stones" as a speaker for Mullah Omar is reported to have declared (Moore 2001:A1) – but rather animate beings with feelings that were sometimes portrayed as more meaningful than those of Afghan people themselves. The depiction of the destruction of "objects with emotions" becomes one more way of constructing and reinforcing notions of the barbarity of the Taliban, in distinct contrast to the beauty and peace described as radiating from the Buddhas.

Conclusions

News reports about archaeology are affected by many of the same factors that shape the production of other news stories in contemporary U.S. society. Although the reasons that reports on archaeology of the Middle East appear in the news are not limited solely to the connections that can be made to contemporary politics, it is striking that such stories proliferate at times of political crisis. At those times, when U.S. national interests are perceived to be at stake, the mainstream media regularly contribute to the mobilization of public opinion, almost always in support of government causes (see above; also Herman and Chomsky 1988; Kellner 1992; Chomsky and Barsamian 2001:47–50). Archaeology is one of the many domains through which public opinion about the wisdom of interventions in foreign countries is molded. Of course, in the broader scheme of things, reports about archaeology were just one small part of the total coverage of Iraq or Afghanistan in the context of mobilization for the Gulf Wars and the invasion of Afghanistan. These wars would undoubtedly have happened even if no mention had ever been made in the press of ancient civilizations and biblical connections of sites in Iraq or the destruction of the Buddhas in the Bamiyan Valley. Yet, stories about archaeology contributed to the overall efforts to construct U.S. public opinion in favor of war.

Appeals to the importance of archaeological remains are not triggered automatically in any situation in which they are endangered, but rather specifically where powerful interests are perceived to be directly at stake. During the Iran–Iraq war (1980–88), not a single article that concerned itself with possible war-related damage to archaeological remains in either country appeared in the *Washington Post* or *New York Times*,[12] newspapers that frequently reported on archaeology in the Middle East during the Gulf and Afghan wars.

To serve political agendas, regardless of whose, news reports featuring archaeology must draw connections between an apparently esoteric study of the past and current affairs. As we have seen, temporal and spatial metaphors are important in this endeavor, helping to shape our understandings of and relationships to the past. They were employed in the examples considered here in a variety of ways. The notion that Western civilization as well as "Western" religions (Christianity and Judaism) are rooted in the ancient Near East runs deeply in the minds of most educated people in the West.[13] This underlying belief made it easy for reporters to link the archaeology of Iraq to contemporary political issues and identities, whether by claiming the great achievements of the Mesopotamian past as our legacy or connecting the modern government of Iraq to the most aggressive and unappealing aspects of that past. Either way, military intervention in Iraq was thereby "justified" in order to preserve the material remains of "our" heritage and wrest humanity's (read, the West's) legacy from the hands of tyrants who would misuse or jeopardize its preservation.

Journalists seem to have found it more difficult to construct direct ancestral ties between the Afghan past and the contemporary West. This may have been in large part because the prominent, historically attested religions in Afghanistan have been Buddhism and Islam rather than Christianity or Judaism. For the most part journalists highlighted the exoticness and difference of Afghanistan's past and its status as a crossroads of other, more familiar "great civilizations." That past was often cast as part of world heritage, offering a reason for the U.S. to intervene to preserve its material remains. In other instances, its destruction was treated as principally a problem for Afghans, whose history and culture were to be understood as decimated by the barbarity of their own people, the Taliban.

Despite the variety of different rhetorical strategies used in the news articles, they nearly all worked to support the same hegemonic position – demonization of the declared enemy (Saddam, the Taliban) and therefore justification for a U.S.-led war. The *appearance* of diversity in the stories could lull readers into thinking that they were reading diverse perspectives when in fact the underlying message was the same. One means by which this is accomplished is by pitting "experts" against each other in collections of quotes (or in talk shows), but ensuring that the disagreements among them are actually trivial. It could be argued that Kellner's (1995:93) contention that the media do not present a single, consistent ideological position is rather an obfuscation, another filter in Herman and Chomsky's set of mechanisms that shape the news as propaganda.

As archaeologists what positions or actions might we take in response to the way our discipline is presented for public consumption in the media? An important consideration here is the use of the past in general and archaeology in particular to create and reinforce identities and identification with a particular past. References to archaeology in news stories frequently draw on connections between material remains of the past and identities in the present. Over the past few decades, archaeologists have also reengaged with questions of identity, often taking the position that archaeological evidence should be used – invariably selectively – to bolster identity-based interests of indigenous and other disenfranchised groups. But archaeological evidence marshaled in support of identity claims can also be employed to engender support for political agendas that many archaeologists may not wish to embrace, as these analyses of archaeology in the news have shown.

Identity claims need not invariably support the status quo. The past can be used to demonstrate continuity and precedent but also, in a more liberatory fashion, to imagine possibilities for change and a different future (Härke 1993; Sommer 1993; Scham 2001; cf. Meskell 1998). Nonetheless, using identity as a basis for a vision of change often carries with it problems of essentialism and the static assumptions that lie at the heart of many concepts of identity (Bernbeck and Pollock 1996). Identity claims are necessarily selective and partial, and from an "objectivist" position they can be critiqued and deconstructed (Friedman 1992a, 1992b). Friedman warns us, however, that practices of identity are part of the basic fabric through which people constitute their senses of self; in that respect, they are no trivial matters to be lightly demolished with the wave of an academic hand. Can we find ways to counteract the pernicious uses of the past for contemporary identity building while at the same time not retreating into an academic impasse in which our principal "achievement" is to explode the "myths" of identity by which others live (cf. Shepherd 2002)?

Sommer (2000:138) has proposed that we should seek to emphasize "the strangeness of the past, the wonder and the horror" of it. Such a proposal may go some way to avoiding identification with the past, but it also runs the risk of turning past peoples into foils for contemporary stereotypes and bigotries. An alternative is for archaeologists to focus on exposing the interests that are served by the selective uses of the past in contemporary identity building, including in media portrayals. Such an approach would point up the partiality of these depictions, highlighting how particular interests structure specific uses of the past. By exposing interests, one does not attack a collectivity's existential basis but rather lays open the grounds on which a group claims to be distinctive and, in many cases, privileged.

Reports about the archaeology of the Middle East are likely to evoke for most non-specialist readers the daily images of the contemporary Middle East which flood the news media, a place that is regularly portrayed as one of violent and persistent conflict, of virulent hatreds and rampant anti-Americanism. A reporter or editor working on a story on the ancient Near East may draw, implicitly or explicitly, on these prevalent images as a way to create relevance and hence newsworthiness for his or her story, or she or he may seek to mark a clear division between past and present. Either way, no story about archaeology in the ancient Near East will escape comparison to contemporary events, attitudes, and politics. Archaeology is never innocent, and its evocation in the news is always part of a larger story and a larger agenda with which archaeologists would do well to engage.

Acknowledgments

I would like to thank Reinhard Bernbeck, Maria das Dores Cruz, and Norman Yoffee for their careful, critical readings of previous drafts of this chapter. They helped greatly to sharpen and clarify my arguments.

NOTES

1 As an example: in a one-year period from March 2002 to February 2003, over 100 articles dealing in some way with archaeology appeared in the *New York Times* and more than 50 in the *Los Angeles Times*.

2 The media includes far more than news. My focus in this paper is, however, on those media products that can be labeled news – recognizing that the distinction between news and entertainment has become increasingly blurred – and specifically print news. A detailed consideration of archaeology in television broadcasts would provide an important supplement to this focus on the print media, but it is beyond the scope of this paper.

3 Herman and Chomsky (1988:26–31) identify two additional filters which I do not discuss here.

4 These "manipulations" of time are in one sense unavoidable: anyone engaged in writing history must, for example, choose a (necessarily arbitrary) beginning point, which will exert a profound effect on the resulting narrative (Said 1978:15–25; de Certeau 1988:11).

5 This expands upon work I began with Catherine Lutz on the 1991 Gulf War (Pollock and Lutz 1994).

6 A keyword-based search of the Lexis-Nexis database of major newspapers for the eight-month period from August 2, 1990 (the date of the Iraqi invasion of Kuwait) to March 31, 1991 (shortly after the official end of the war) yielded 49 articles in U.S. newspapers dealing with the archaeology of Iraq. Most of these appeared in the months of January through March 1991 when the war took place. In contrast, during the eight-month period preceding the invasion of Kuwait (December 1989 though July 1990), only nine stories about archaeology in Iraq were published in the same sample of newspapers. A similar, but not identical, pattern is evident for Gulf War II: the number of articles rose noticeably in the two months prior to the war's beginning (January and February 2003) although it remained relatively small, but declined during the first few weeks of the war, only to reach an unprecedented peak after the looting of the Iraq Museum (Pollock 2003).

7 The focus on "humanity" may have been a diplomatic attempt to avoid the appearance of claiming a direct connection with the U.S.

8 A Lexis-Nexis search for news articles in the English-language print media for the period from January 1, 1995 (the year in which the Taliban began moving into Afghanistan) through September 13, 2002 (just after the first anniversary of 9/11) yielded maximally four per year from 1995 to 2000. In March of 2001 alone, 16 articles appeared – almost all to do with the destruction of the Buddha statues. In October through December of that year, during the U.S.-led war, 10 articles concerned with archaeological topics appeared in these papers.

9 The situations were dissimilar insofar as the U.S. government had been moving for some time toward a new position on the Taliban, whereas the estrangement from Saddam occurred abruptly after the August 1990 invasion of Kuwait.

10 On conflicting notions of cultural heritage on the parts of Westerners and the Taliban, see Bernbeck (2003).

11 The notion and implications of ownership are important areas for further study (cf. Moustakas 1989; Napier 2002).

12 This is based on a Lexis-Nexis search for articles on the archaeology of these countries during this time period.

13   By making this statement in this way, I do not wish to deny that there *are* connections
     between the ancient Near East and the contemporary Western tradition. Rather, the
     issues are twofold: that there are also connections between people living in the Middle
     East today and that past and that our history must be understood as tied to much of
     the rest of the world as well, whether we wish to acknowledge those links or not.

REFERENCES

Abu el-Haj, Nadia, 2001 Facts on the Ground: Archaeological Practice and Territorial Self-
     Fashioning in Israeli Society. Chicago: University of Chicago Press.
Anders, Günther, 2002[1956] Die Antiquiertheit des Menschen. Band I. Über die Seele im
     Zeitalter der zweiten industriellen Revolution. München: C. H. Beck.
Andersen, Robin, 2003 That's Militainment! The Pentagon's Media-Friendly "Reality" War.
     Extra! 16(3):6–9.
Anderson, Benedict, 1991 Imagined Communities: Reflections on the Origin and Spread of
     Nationalism. Revised edition. London: Verso.
Appadurai, Arjun, 1991 Global Ethnoscapes: Notes and Queries for a Transnational Anthro-
     pology. *In* Recapturing Anthropology: Working in the Present. Richard G. Fox, ed. pp.
     191–210. Santa Fe: School of American Research.
Bagdikian, Ben, 2000 The Media Monopoly. Sixth edition. Boston: Beacon.
Bahrani, Zainab, 1998 Conjuring Mesopotamia: Imaginative Geography and a World Past.
     In Archaeology under Fire: Nationalism, Politics and Heritage in the Eastern Mediter-
     ranean and the Middle East. Lynn Meskell, ed. pp. 159–174. London: Routledge.
Barth, Fredrik, 1969 Introduction. *In* Ethnic Groups and Boundaries: The Social Organisa-
     tion of Cultural Difference. Fredrik Barth, ed. pp. 9–38. Oslo: Universitetsforlaget.
Baudrillard, Jean, 1976 L'Échange symbolique et la mort. Paris: Éditions Gallimard.
Benjamin, Walter, 1968[1936] The Work of Art in the Age of Mechanical Reproduction. *In*
     Illuminations. Hannah Arendt, ed. Translated by Harry Zohn. pp. 217–251. New York:
     Schocken Books.
Bernbeck, Reinhard, 2003 Krieg, Imperialismus und Archäologie: Zur Zukunft der Vergan-
     genheit Afghanistans. Das Altertum 48:279–312.
Bernbeck, Reinhard, and Susan Pollock, 1996 Ayodhya, Archaeology, and Identity. Current
     Anthropology 37S:S138–142.
Borjesson, Kristina, 2002 Editor's Introduction. *In* Into the Buzzsaw: Leading Journalists
     Expose the Myth of a Free Press. Kristina Borjesson, ed. pp. 11–14. Amherst, NY:
     Prometheus Books.
Buckholtz, Alison, 2001 Casualties of War. Washington Post, October 28:E1.
Certeau, Michel de, 1988[1975] The Writing of History. Translated by Tom Conley. New
     York: Columbia University Press.
Childe, V. Gordon, 1928 The Most Ancient East: The Oriental Prelude to European Pre-
     history. London: Kegan Paul.
Chomsky, Noam, and David Barsamian, 2001 Propaganda and the Public Mind: Conver-
     sations with Noam Chomsky. Cambridge, MA: South End Press.
Colwell-Chanthaphonh, Chip, 2003 Dismembering/Disremembering the Buddhas: Render-
     ings on the Internet during the Afghan Purge of the Past. Journal of Social Archaeol-
     ogy 3:75–398.
Cook, Gareth, 2001 Land of the Lost in Afghanistan. Boston Globe, October 30:C1.

Cooke, Robert, 1991 Bombing Worries Archaeologists. Newsday, January 22.

Cotter, Holland, 2003 Oldest Human History Is at Risk. New York Times, February 25:E1, 5.

Debord, Guy, 1977 Society of the Spectacle. Detroit: Black & Red.

Delivré, Alain, 1974 L'Histoire des rois d'Imerina: Interprétation d'une tradition orale. Paris: Klincksieck.

Dornfeld, Barry, 2002 Putting American Public Television Documentary in Its Place. In Media Worlds: Anthropology on New Terrain. Faye Ginsburg, Lila Abu-Lughod, and Brian Larkin, eds. pp. 247–263. Berkeley: University of California Press.

Drogin, Bob, 1991 Dignity of Ancient City of Ur is Marred by Indignity of War. Los Angeles Times, March 28:A10–11.

Editorial, 1991 The Cradle, Ironically, of Civilization. New York Times, January 18:A30.

Editorial, 2001 Obliterating History in Afghanistan. New York Times, March 3:A12.

Enzensberger, Hans Magnus, 1970 Constituents of a Theory of the Media. New Left Review 64:13–36.

Fabian, Johannes, 1983 Time and the Other: How Anthropology Makes its Object. New York: Columbia University Press.

Flood, Finbarr Barry, 2002 Between Cult and Culture: Bamiyan, Islamic Iconoclasm, and the Museum. Art Bulletin 84:641–659.

Friedman, Jonathan, 1992a Myth, History, and Political Identity. Cultural Anthropology 7:194–210.

Friedman, Jonathan, 1992b The Past in the Future: History and the Politics of Identity. American Anthropologist 94:837–859.

Gans, Herbert, 1979 Deciding What's News: A Study of CBS Evening News, NBC Nightly News, Newsweek, and Time. New York: Random House.

Glick, Caroline, 2003 In the Fray – Ruinous Strategy: Saddam Holds Antiquities Hostage. Wall Street Journal, March 27:D7.

Härke, Heinrich, 1993 Vergangenheit und Gegenwart. In Macht der Vergangenheit – Wer macht Vergangenheit? Sabine Wolfram and Ulrike Sommer, eds. pp. 3–11. Wilkau-Hasslau: Beier and Beran.

Hendrix, David, 2002 Coal Mine Canaries. In Into the Buzzsaw: Leading Journalists Expose the Myth of a Free Press. Kristina Borjesson, ed. pp. 151–173. Amherst, NY: Prometheus Books.

Herman, Edward, and Noam Chomsky, 1988 Manufacturing Consent: The Political Economy of the Mass Media. New York: Pantheon.

Honan, William, 1991 Attacks on Iraq Worry and Divide Archeologists. New York Times, February 9:Arts section, 13, 17.

Kellner, Douglas, 1992 The Persian Gulf TV War. Boulder: Westview.

Kellner, Douglas, 1995 Media Culture: Cultural Studies, Identity and Politics Between the Modern and the Postmodern. London: Routledge.

Longworth, R. C., 1991 Bombing Threatens Iraqi Archeological Riches. Chicago Tribune, January 23:9.

Lowenthal, David, 1985 The Past is a Foreign Country. Cambridge: Cambridge University Press.

Lutz, Catherine, and Jane Collins, 1993 Reading National Geographic. Chicago: University of Chicago Press.

MacLeod, Donald, 2003 Blown Away. The Guardian, March 25:10.

McChesney, Robert, 2002 The Rise and Fall of Professional Journalism. In Into the Buzzsaw: Leading Journalists Expose the Myth of a Free Press. Kristina Borjesson, ed. pp. 363–381. Amherst, NY: Prometheus Books.

Meskell, Lynn, 1998 Twin Peaks: The Archaeologies of Çatalhöyük. *In* Ancient Goddesses: The Myths and the Evidence. Lucy Goodison and Christine Morris, eds. pp. 46–62. London: British Museum Press.

Miniclier, Kit, 2003 The Cradle of Civilization. Denver Post, January 26:E1.

Moore, Molly, 2001 Afghanistan's Antiquities Under Assault. Washington Post, March 2:A1.

Moustakas, John, 1989 Group Rights in Cultural Property: Justifying Strict Inalienability. Cornell Law Review 74:1179–1227.

Napier, A. David, 2002 Our Own Way: On Anthropology and Intellectual Property. *In* Exotic No More: Anthropology on the Front Lines. Jeremy MacClancy, ed. pp. 287–318. Chicago: University of Chicago Press.

Neuffer, Elizabeth, 2003 Confronting Iraq. Boston Globe, January 24:A1.

Petit, Charles, 1991 Gulf War Imperils Major Artifacts of Civilization. San Francisco Chronicle, January 19:A8.

Pollock, Susan, 2003 The Looting of the Iraq Museum: Thoughts on Archaeology in a Time of Crisis. Public Archaeology 3:117–124.

Pollock, Susan, and Catherine Lutz, 1994 Archaeology Deployed for the Gulf War. Critique of Anthropology 14:263–284.

Rashid, Ahmed, 2000 Taliban: Militant Islam, Oil and Fundamentalism in Central Asia. New Haven: Yale University Press.

Ringle, Ken, 1991 Babylon Revisited: Iraq in an Ancient Past. Washington Post, January 15:C1, C4.

Said, Edward, 1978 Orientalism. New York: Vintage.

Saltus, Richard, 1992 Plowshares Threaten Ancient Iraqi Sites. Boston Globe, February 7:2.

Scham, Sandra, 2001 The Archaeology of the Disenfranchised. Journal of Archaeological Method and Theory 8:183–213.

Shepherd, Nick, 2002 Heading South, Looking North. Archaeological Dialogues 9:74–82.

Solomon, Deborah, 2003 Iraq's Cultural Capital. New York Times, January 5:Sec.6, 15.

Sommer, Ulrike, 1993 Der ruhmreiche Krieg der Geschichte gegen die Zeit. *In* Macht der Vergangenheit – Wer macht Vergangenheit? Sabine Wolfram and Ulrike Sommer, eds. pp. 13–18. Wilkau-Hasslau: Beier and Beran.

Sommer, Ulrike, 2000 Archaeology and Regional Identity in Saxony. Public Archaeology 1:125–142.

Squitieri, Tom, 2002 Afghanistan's Monumental Destruction. USA Today, March 14:10D.

Thompson, John, 1995 The Media and Modernity: A Social Theory of the Media. Stanford: Stanford University Press.

Toronto Star, 2001 The Hidden Buddha. Toronto Star, November 22:Business, 1.

Trigger, Bruce, 1984 Alternative Archaeologies: Nationalist, Colonialist, Imperialist. Man n.s. 19:355–370.

Trouillot, Michel-Rolph, 1995 Silencing the Past: Power and the Production of History. Boston: Beacon.

Van de Mieroop, Marc, 1997 On Writing a History of the Ancient Near East. Bibliotheca Orientalis 54:285–305.

Verdery, Katherine, 1999 The Political Lives of Dead Bodies: Reburial and Postsocialist Change. New York: Columbia University Press.

Wilford, John Noble, 2003 War in Iraq Would Halt All Digs in Region. New York Times, February 25:E1, 5.

Witham, Larry, 2003 Allied Troops Bypass Holy Sites. Washington Times, March 27:A1.

6

The Past as Fact and Fiction: From Historical Novels to Novel Histories

Reinhard Bernbeck

Once upon a time, when king Nimrod had all newborn children in his kingdom slain, Abraham was born in a roomy cave on the steep slope of the rocky mountain below Nimrod's castle near Harran. Abraham's mother hid the boy, but Nimrod the hunter found the infant in his cradle. He tore the baby from his mother's hands, went up to the castle and, by means of two columns erected on the fortress, catapulted the small body into a hot furnace at the foot of the abyss. At this moment, God saved Abraham. He transformed the blazing fire into cool, clear water and the burning embers into carp. King Nimrod's daughter Zelikha jumped after Abraham from the walls of the castle, and God let her land in a basin with a gushing spring.

Residents of Urfa in southeastern Turkey relate stories such as this one about the mountain in their town, the castle on top, the cave, columns, and carp ponds in the city center. The fish and the cave are sacred places. Three mosques have been built in the vicinity and pilgrims come from afar to pray in this "city of prophets."

Archaeologists have found that a spring already attracted groups in the aceramic Neolithic when a "Pre-pottery Neolithic B" settlement existed nearby, with dense deposits of lithic blades and traces of fireplaces. The two columns with Corinthian capitals on the mountain were erected during the reign of the Roman emperor Gordian III between 240 and 242 C.E. In the ninth century C.E., the fortress walls were built, and in the early 13th century, the Khalil ur-Rahman mosque was constructed at the edge of the spring.

In the Urfa story, human imagination has turned extant natural phenomena such as the cave and spring as well as cultural monuments from the past into a dramatic, internally consistent story. The bad in the person of Nimrod attempts to triumph over virtue, but celestial power saves the good – in the person of Abraham – at the last moment. Fire turns into water, wood into lively carp. The patriarch Abraham overcomes the heathen Nimrod. Ethical contrasts are woven into a story about

well-known personalities and sensually experienced environment. The rising narrative tension up to its "happy end" never fails to excite its audience.

Archaeology offers only an alienated, impersonal history. The dissecting gaze and
the analytic sharpness cut off the possibility for a zestful narration: the PPNB lithic
blades sticking out of a profile in the city center only inspire archaeologists.
Not much is to be seen, and one must go to the museum in order to acquire
the necessary contextual archaeological knowledge. For Urfa's residents, neither
the museum nor information about the castle's building phases are points of
reference.

Despite their scientific character, archaeological interpretations are by no means
close to "reality." If, for instance, we talk about the Neolithic as a time of "revolutionary" innovations, this hardly matches the self-understanding of Neolithic
people, although their views should be included in any history that pretends to be
realistic. Our interpretations are based on knowledge of thousands of years of later
development, which were beyond the horizon of PPNB people in the Urfa region.

Archaeological discourse and local fables are formally not so distinct as they may
seem at first sight. Both are characterized by a mixture of facticity and fictitious
elements. But where do the differences lie, and should we as archaeologists insist
on their importance? In order to address such problems, I examine a Western literary category located at the intersection of these two styles of narration, historical
novels. I want to pursue two questions. What can we learn about our own ways of
producing narratives by considering how authors of fiction conceive of the past?
Furthermore, could insights from analysis of historical fiction help us to conceptualize archaeological narratives in new ways? I begin with a discussion of the relationship between archaeology, the past, prehistory, and history.

Creating Meaning

All forms of representation of the past, from catalogs to interpretive articles and
historical syntheses, contain "data," isolated pieces from a past that do not, however,
carry "history" within themselves. It is the relations archaeologists and historians
create between data that produce meaning. As archaeologists or historians, we separate past phenomena, objects and texts alike, and rejoin them according to specific preferences (Koselleck 1979:204; Trouillot 1995:26, 48). The result is a
discourse about elapsed time, recounted from a particular viewpoint: a linear narrative. Archaeologists may use visual aids in the presentation of their narratives, but
the core of their works remains linear and textual. Therefore, I use the more encom-
passing notions "historian" and "history" when I speak of the problems both archaeologists and historians face in their representations of the past.

By now, it is probably clear that I advocate a breakdown of boundaries between
archaeology and history. I understand history and archaeology as activities whose
most general goal is to give an aggregation of sources from the past meaning it did
not possess. History as *res gestae* has neither meaning, purpose, causality, nor coherence (Lessing 1983[1919]). The latter are all created by historians, based on their

own interests and prejudices (Koselleck 1997:87–88). It is irrelevant whether we deal with sources from "prehistoric" or "historical" times. Periods from which we have texts do not produce different kinds of meanings than those without texts (Certeau 1988:65). The only distinction in the presence of texts is the greater quantity and variability of "data" that have to be woven together into a meaningful narrative. The amount of data may become difficult for a single researcher to handle and lead to specializations within historical research, such as the division into archaeology and philology.

In the creation of meaning, the loading of constructed facticity with fictitious elements remains a contentious subject (Rüsen 1994:20–21). Should we minimize the fictitious portion of history, and if so, how? Can the production of a meaningful narrative be anchored in an explicit methodology? These problems have led to two fundamentally divergent solutions in archaeology. In North American archaeology of the 1960s, analogies between the "ethnographic present" and an archaeological past were seen as a methodologically sound means to elucidate relations between fragmentary "data" of the past. Material remains were compared with material culture in present societies, and from similarities between past remnants and present objects, conclusions were drawn about unpreserved aspects of the past (Verhoeven, this volume). Systematization of this approach led to a specialized branch of research, ethnoarchaeology (David and Kramer 2001). Two problems with the reliance on analogical reasoning are the categorization of "similar" (past and present) societies as static and the implication that both are different from the – usually Western – society of the interpreter. From this perspective, analogies are an "alienating mode of creating meaning." The past is envisioned as half-empty pigeon-holes to be filled by analogies from similarly exotic, present-day, non-Western cases. By necessity, such a past becomes different from "us," and the sterile categorizations produce a picture of "people without history."

Another way to create historical meaning is derived from hermeneutics and originated in a continental European context. The concept builds on the idea that the fundamental experience of being human allows the historian access to any past. There is an "original agreement between [searching, R.B.] subject and [investigated, R.B.] object" (Humboldt 1967[1821]). Instead of a quintessential otherness of the past, hermeneutics assumes a timeless similarity of human life. This "identifying mode of creating meaning" tends to deduce the present from an explored past and at the same time projects the present into that past, thus denying alterity to history.

Both ways of creating meaning are restrictive. Analogies are limiting because the past receives its significance only from comparison with present non-Western societies. The possibility of an unknown *past* alterity is excluded. Hermeneutics fails to envision such alterity because of its reliance on human experience, which can only be the outcome of the historian's lifeworld. Such issues of historical method are only one dimension of the problem. Inextricably linked to fictional content in histories is their form. In order to fully understand fictional elements in our writings, we need to be aware of how we construct narratives. I focus on ways in which pasts are narrated by analyzing three novels about the ancient Near East. I am concerned with several formal aspects of these novels that influence their content: the lives of the authors, their use of language and the construction of narrators, times of narration, the role of imagination and of reflexivity. All of these issues are pertinent to the creation of historical narratives, to which I will refer sporadically. At the end of this paper, I will draw the various critiques together and suggest new ways of narrating the past.

The Ancient Near East and Historical Novels

A search for high quality literary works[1] about pre-Hellenistic Mesopotamia brings little to light. Apparently the ancient cultures between the Euphrates and Tigris are regarded by writers as so strange that creative involvement with them appears impossible. A preference for the "lands of the Bible" is based on familiarity that is primarily an imagined one. The "exotic other" of Orientalism (cf. Said 1978) is rescaled: historical novels of the ancient Near East create a stark contrast between Biblical "roots of Western civilization" and past "pagan" cultures.

The three novels I selected – Thomas Mann's *Joseph and his Brothers* tetralogy, Lion Feuchtwanger's *Flavius Josephus* trilogy, and Stefan Heym's *King David Report* – all treat periods in the history of Palestine. I begin with a précis of each novel.

Thomas Mann's Joseph and his Brothers

Mann planned this novel during journeys to Egypt in the years 1925 and 1930. It turned into an *opus magnum* of four volumes, each subdivided into seven chapters. The first volume appeared in 1933, after the Nazi seizure of power in Germany; the last volume was printed in 1943 in Stockholm by a publisher of exile literature. Work on the story accompanied Mann's loss of German citizenship.

The first volume, *The Stories of Jacob*, contains a long philosophical discussion about whether the deep past was different from the present. Myth as the repetition of "typical situations," the central tenet of the whole novel, is associated with a cyclic conception of time. What was, arises again; no event is unique in mythical history. The Fall, fratricide, and the flood had occurred at many places and times. The remainder of the first volume contains a discussion between Joseph and Jacob, which then turns into a lengthy review of the stories of the Biblical patriarchs.

In the second volume, *Young Joseph*, the first three chapters portray Joseph's education as a scribe and intellectual by the servant Eliezer. Mann takes this as an occasion for a detailed discussion of myths in general. The remaining chapters treat the infuriatingly egoistic dreams of Joseph, which provoke his brothers to throw him into a well. Taking inspiration from the Book of Job, Mann turns Jacob into a figure who struggles over the existence of God when he hears of the alleged death of his favorite son.

The epic length of the volumes increases with *Joseph in Egypt*, based on Genesis 39. Mann discusses the tensions between what he calls the "above" (rationality,

mind, intelligence) and the "below" (desire, life, fertility): Joseph in the service of
the eunuch Potiphar whose wife wants to entice Joseph in sexual intercourse.
Attracted and repulsed, he flees but lands in prison. The last volume begins with a
debate among angels, who gloat over the fate of humanity and of Joseph in particular. However, Joseph is able to escape his bad luck. In prison, he interprets the
dreams of prominent servants in Pharaoh's palace and of the Pharaoh himself, after
which he lands in a high political position in Egypt. At this point, his brothers appear
at his office in search of support because of a drought in Palestine. He finally makes
his identity known to them, and the novel comes to an end with Jacob's death.

Lion Feuchtwanger's Flavius Josephus

Feuchtwanger was a prolific writer of historical novels. The one with which I am
concerned here was written between 1931 and 1940 and retraces the life of the
Jewish historian Flavius Josephus who lived in the late first century C.E.

The Jewish War is the most eventful of the novel's three volumes. After a lengthy
journey to Rome, Flavius Josephus returns to Palestine to become a leader in the
Jewish rebellion against Roman occupation in 69 C.E. During the siege at the castle
of Jotapata, fellow combatants choose death deliberately over captivity, while Flavius
Josephus manages to be taken prisoner and predicts to the Roman general Vespasian
that he will become emperor. With the fulfillment of the prophecy, Flavius Josephus
receives Roman citizenship. The first volume of Feuchtwanger's work ends with the
destruction of the Second Temple in Jerusalem under Vespasian's son Titus.

The Jew of Rome, the second volume of the series, revolves again around struggles over Jewish identity, but on a more personal level. Feuchtwanger discusses Jew-
ishness through the conflict-ridden relationship of Flavius Josephus with his wives,
one a Jew and the other of Greek Alexandrian origin. This volume also relates the
composition of *De Bello Judaico* by the protagonist, an historical work by the real
Flavius Josephus (Michel and Bauernfeind 1959).

In the last volume, another work of the actual Flavius Josephus, *Antiquitates*, is
referred to. In Feuchtwanger's account, Flavius Josephus goes through internal
struggles in the writing of this universal history which he originally wants to be
"objective." However, in the increasingly repressive climate under the Roman
emperor Domitian he decides to politicize his history, and recites it in public. After
a reflexive turn, the aging Flavius Josephus travels back to Palestine, takes part in
another revolt against the Romans and is dragged to death by a military unit under
the orders of his own son.

Stefan Heym's King David Report

Stefan Heym's novel focuses on one of the most famous persons of the Old Testament, King David. Heym, an East German citizen, published this novel in West
Germany in 1972, since he was at the time denied publication rights in the GDR.

The work had been written, like most of his other books since his years in the U.S., first in English and then translated by the author into German (Zachau 1982:12). It treats the Biblical events of kings Saul and David (ca. 10th century B.C.E.) from the chronological perspective of David's successor, Solomon.

According to Heym's plot, Solomon establishes a commission to monitor the production of "the one and only true report" about his father King David's deeds. The historian assigned the task of composing the history is Ethan the Esrahite, who – according to the Old Testament – is the author of the 89th Psalm. The entire novel is a parody of the official historiography of the GDR, and Heym himself is to be identified with the central figure Ethan. Instead of smoothing the events into a narrative well adapted to the dominant ideology, Ethan attempts to insert contradictions and problems into his work. At the end of his task, he falls from grace and is exiled from Jerusalem, impoverished and condemned to erasure from collective memory.

Narratives as Social Products

Social relations of production in all literary works are inextricably interwoven with their content and form (Eagleton 1976:59–83). The three novels reveal unexpected parallels in the historical conditions of their composition. All three authors were of German upbringing, escaped Nazi persecution, lived in exile in the U.S., and had severe problems in the McCarthy era (Zachau 1982:16–17; Sternburg 1984:306; Heilbut 1997:365–370). Feuchtwanger and Heym were Jews; Mann's wife was of Jewish descent. This brought all three into risky, sometimes life-threatening situations during Nazi times.

Feuchtwanger, a well-known author by the beginning of the 1930s, was in North America on a visit at the time of Hitler's seizure of power. He attacked Hitler publicly from abroad. Two months later, Feuchtwanger's house in Berlin was demolished, and the manuscript of the second volume of *Flavius Josephus* destroyed; one year of work was lost. On May 10, 1933, his (and other intellectuals') books were publicly burnt (Hans 1976:240). On August 23, his name was published with 33 others on the first "deprivation of citizenship" list.

Feuchtwanger was lucky throughout this misfortune. On his lecture tour in the U.S. in 1932–33, he met Eleanor Roosevelt, the wife of the future president, an event that became crucial for his escape from Europe. The writer lived for several years in Sanary-sur-Mer, a center for German exile writers in France. With the beginning of the Second World War, Feuchtwanger was interned, then released, and only barely reached the American consulate in Marseille. From there, he crossed the Atlantic and began a new life in Pacific Palisades (California). Because of a large Anglophone readership for his novels, Feuchtwanger had no material problems in exile.

Feuchtwanger rewrote the second volume of *Flavius Josephus* in France and added a third one. In these books, the protagonist Flavius Josephus experiences drastic turns in his life. These changes are a reflection of the sharp reversal of

Feuchtwanger's own fortunes. The first volume ended with Flavius Josephus reject-ing armed resistance. The second volume echoes the experiences of Feuchtwanger's initial years in exile and his commitment to a movement of literati with a strong Marxist "popular front" element. The last volume provides a stark contrast to the principles illustrated in the first volume. Written in the precarious situation of half-imprisonment in the American consulate in Marseille, parallels between the emperor Domitian and Hitler are unambiguous. The Flavius Josephus of the novel adheres to a radical position, endorsing openly the armed fight against dictatorship.

Despite his opposition to fascism, Thomas Mann was courted to a degree by the Nazis who wanted to keep this recipient of the Nobel prize for literature in the country. However, in July 1933, Heydrich, one of the Nazis' bloodiest butchers, announced an arrest warrant for the writer and seized his fortune (Kurzke 1993:136–137). Mann moved via Switzerland and Sanary-sur-Mer to the U.S., where he became an American citizen in 1941. Work on the Joseph novels turned during volatile, dark times into a source of continuity for him. Mann was so well known abroad that he had to face fewer dangers than other exile writers. However, despite his fame as a Nobel laureate and bourgeois author, the FBI established a file on Mann in which he was accused of communist leanings (Kurzke 1993:172–173). Disappointed, he left the U.S. in 1952 (Heilbut 1997:310–311).

In Mann's account of Joseph, his own living conditions become apparent, though less clearly than in Feuchtwanger's case. Joseph's exile in Egypt is only a superfi-cial parallel to Mann's life. The background of Mann's Joseph story is his intellec-tual fascination with Nietzsche's works, particularly the *The Birth of the Tragedy* (1968[1872]). Nietzsche's reinterpretation of Greek myths turned the humanism, rationality, and formal perfection of Greek art on its head. Greek myth was re-read as orgy, lust, and aggression, as a path to the Übermensch, a concept that was only a step away from such fascist pseudo-theories as Alfred Rosenberg's "new myth." Mann – following the Marxist philosopher Ernst Bloch – attempted to "turn myth into the humane" again (Mann 1999:201). At the same time, he tried to show that the origin of such humanity lay in the Orient, in Jewish culture.

Stefan Heym was considerably younger than the two other writers. A student of journalism in Berlin, he was supposed to be arrested the day after the burning of the German parliament, staged by the Nazis themselves in 1933. He got word of the threat and fled to Prague. Heym's literary career began in U.S. exile, where he wrote for the German socialist weekly *Volksecho* in New York. During the Second World War, he served in the U.S. army in a department of psychological warfare. In the McCarthy era, Heym ran into troubles and requested asylum in the GDR. He returned his U.S. war medals, and emigrated a second time. In the GDR, he soon landed in the ranks of the opposition. The government would probably gladly have let him go to West Germany, but Heym stubbornly stayed. With the fall of the Berlin wall in the year 1989, Heym's personal life took a final surprising turn. He remained faithful to his socialist convictions and was elected as representative of the Party of Democratic Socialism in the German Bundestag. Once again a stranger

in his own country, he encountered hostility from the West German political establishment (Heym 1992).

Heym's works show an interest in the role of the writer in society, and *The King
David Report* is no exception. This fundamentally political novel uses Old Testament events as an allegory that vividly describes how the GDR regime dealt with
undesirable intellectuals, people who knew "too much." At the same time, the book
shows that writers can always succeed in inserting some subversive elements into
their texts. Interpreters from the capitalist West have tried to read into the novel a
criticism of "totalitarianism," a critique that equates the repression of intellectuals
in fascist and socialist systems (Böll 1972; Reich-Ranicki 1974). Judging by Heym's
own life, nothing could be further from the truth.

What are the connections between this account of the conditions of production
of historical novels and our roles as archaeologists and historians? Just as the details
of authors' lives influence their novels, academic narratives about the past never
eschew the highly variable relations of scholarly production. It is a mistake to
measure the narratives of American, Middle Eastern, or European archaeologists
with the same yardstick. A unified academic standard for peer-reviewed journal articles or books is based on the largely fictive values of the ivory tower of Western academic life, presupposing a personal environment without economic or political
problems. Texts by scholars with easy access to resources are judged by the same
criteria as works from those who have to struggle to consult even basic literature.
Economic realities of academic production are not acknowledged by the establishment despite the conditions in some Middle Eastern countries where university
professors have to have a second job to survive materially.

The examples of these historical novels show that writing is not an activity isolated from social conditions. Some academic narratives about the ancient Near East
are colored by the unreal concerns of people for whom social security, health insur-
ance, and material wealth are unquestioned givens, leading to interests in ethereal
topics such as domestication of the self, phenomenology of landscapes, or feasting
as politics. The luxury of engaging in such intellectual fashions is accompanied by
the devaluation of more down-to-earth interests that archaeologists from non-
Western walks of life may find more relevant.

Some decisions in the lives of the three writers discussed above would probably
be viewed with incredulity by many scholars. Heym requested asylum in the GDR
after fleeing the U.S., and Mann turned away with horror from the U.S. in the
McCarthy era. Such moves mean voluntarily giving up one's habitual lifeworld for
a new one, going (back) to another world without prospects for a "career," in order
to live in less repressive conditions.

We might ask ourselves whether and when the moment arrives at which we ought
to leave a familiar professional and social environment for political reasons. A drift
from a democratic to an authoritarian system of government is not limited to such
extreme cases as fascist Germany.[2] As long as political repression occurs sporadically and hurts scholars rarely and randomly, verbal protest may seem sufficient. In
such a climate, a primarily politically motivated emigration would be ridiculed
as a hysterical reaction – as was the case in academic circles in Nazi Germany.

Independent authors may leave repressive systems more easily than academically based scholars because the former are not integrated into institutions. But financial security and professional networks should not lead to the automatic refusal of the risks that invariably accompany radical changes of one's lifeworld.

Problems of Narration and Language[3]

Formal analysis of any narrative, whether novels or histories, reveals that authors willingly or unwillingly create a narrator who recounts a story. When explicitly conceptualized, as in most literary works, narrators are more than a mere means of representation. The dialectical relationship between narrator and content is sometimes skillfully employed to give the content an additional dimension. In academic narratives, the construction of narrators remains largely unrecognized, and the connections with issues of content remain underexplored.

Language is not an unproblematic means of representations of a past. Historical novels are steeped with the search for an adequate vocabulary. An obvious preference would seem to be the language of the novel's subjects, which is difficult for the cases discussed here, since these languages are dead and rarely at the disposal of novelists or readers.

Heym found an elegant solution in *The King David Report*. He used the language of Luther's Bible translation which is still the best-known Bible version in German and understandable despite its archaisms. This anachronistic language serves as a persiflage for the equally unnatural language of the SED (Socialist Unity Party of the GDR). In addition, by inserting "real-socialist" German terms, for instance "non-person" (*Unperson*), "infiltration," "work of fomenting" (*Wühlarbeit*), "literary high treason," and the "backdirt heap of history" (Trotsky's creation; cf. Attar 2001:282), the author establishes a dialectic relationship between past and present.

Heym's novel is less a narrative of adventures than an adventure in narrating. Ethan, the fictive author of David's biography, is inhibited by social and political constraints whose insights into the actual events are broadened by a variety of witnesses (Eisele 1984:1). Ethan's sources consist of interviews with court personnel, the presentations of a bard, verbal reports of a brutal army leader, and a reading by a prophet. Apart from these informants, Heym includes – invented – archives of cuneiform tablets. On a formal level, the novel establishes a dialectic relation between fictitious historical sources and a real book, the Bible. With the inclusion of multiple contradictory sources, the Bible is exposed as a fictitious pastiche of past events.

Feuchtwanger's *Flavius Josephus* is less complexly constructed. The novel is related in the third person singular, from the perspective of an omniscient narrator. Its form remains firmly in the bourgeois tradition of 19th-century novels (Köpke 1983:51). Feuchtwanger employs different types of language. The basic idiom is colloquial German, with conventional adjectives. The description of personalities relies on highly repetitive descriptors, turning them into stereotyped characters. Street language is employed to attribute class origins to particular people.

Efforts to insert linguistic properties from antiquity appear only in the case of the priests of the Jerusalem temple. Here, an antiquated German is used to imitate ancient Hebrew. Feuchtwanger underlines the contemporaneity of the problems addressed by the novel through a consistently modern choice of language, reducing the exoticness of historical alterity (Köpke 1989:137). In line with this functionalist language use is the simple narrative style through which the work becomes easily accessible to a wider public and open to the reproach of writing at the edge of triviality (Vietor-Engländer 1989:321, 328).

Mann's novel about Joseph is so complex in its formal structure that only a few important characteristics can be mentioned. He connects the narrative structure with the main topic of the novel, the myth. The narrator is most evident in sections related in the first person plural, where he displays a distance to the world of the novel's figures. This narrative situation often changes abruptly to a narrator with an internal perspective (of one of the characters) or to the views of a "pseudo-scholarly critic" of Biblical tradition (Heftrich 1990:14–15).

In his representation of a "multicultural" Egypt, Mann employs English and French loanwords (in German) to characterize the influence of foreign languages of the time on Egyptian. In contrast to Feuchtwanger's contemporary use of language, Mann includes ancient Egyptian words. For the reader, this strengthens the fiction of being in the past and in the place of the narrated events and reduces the linguistically induced familiarity with the story that inevitably comes through the use of German (Hamburger 1945:32–33). Mann must have immersed himself in basic principles of ancient Near Eastern languages, since he embroiders the novels' syntax with stylistic elements fashionable in ancient Hebrew and Akkadian, such as the *parallelismus membrorum* ("measure and beauty, love and grace") or the *figura etymologica* ("dreamer of dreams"; cf. Fischer 2002:144–147).

It is instructive to compare these formal aspects of novels to historical and archaeological narratives. Do the latter follow their own, specific rules of representation, or can we learn from the use of language and narrators of historical fiction? Historians have argued over the best ways of representing the past since Aristotle, and the dispute has re-emerged with White's (1973, 1987) critiques of historical narration and a European form of "historical anthropology" (Dülmen 2000; cf. Rüsen 1987). With the appearance of *Writing Culture* (Clifford and Marcus 1986), cultural anthropologists problematized their forms of textual representation. This has led to a much wider rethinking of the field's identity (Benson 1993). In archaeological theory, reflections on textual forms and implications for power relationships emerged some time ago with poststructuralism and feminist archaeology (Hodder 1989; Bapty and Yates 1990; Tringham 1991; Spector 1993). More recent work (see below) broadens these concerns.

In my opinion, such reflections on narrative structures have rarely had an effect on Near Eastern archaeology. In order to demonstrate this, I chose arbitrarily the 1987 volume of the journal *Iraq*. Nearly all articles in this issue employ a passive, neutral voice. But scattered throughout these texts are judgmental remarks which unintentionally illuminate the character of narrators. In a paper on the site of Tello, Crawford (1987:71) writes that "a group of copper foundation figures was found," only to continue: "Sadly, they are not inscribed." An excavation report about a pre-historic site, written in an impersonal style, uses a first person plural narrator where the interpretation of a building's function is questionable: "We do not believe that it was a 'ritual' structure" (Merpert and Munchaev 1987:21). This is followed by, "Its most likely purpose . . ." The contrast between collective denial and emphatic impersonal, omniscient affirmation creates a sharp narrative boundary between two alternatives of interpretation.

Roaf and Killick's contribution (1987) in the same volume is radically different in form. The authors' reference to Agatha Christie and detective Hercule Poirot is a skillful trick to produce tension in a paper with the extremely dry topic of stratigraphic comparisons. Quotations from Christie's book *The Mysterious Affair at Styles* insert (fictitious) persons and dialogues into this piece of otherwise perfectly "scientific" literature, a creative change from the usual dull academic writing style.

Common to all articles in the volume is an implicit narrator. My example is only meant to indicate the need for a systematic, much wider re-reading and critique of archaeological (and historical) styles of narration, taking into account different kinds of texts such as books, articles, or reviews. While writers of fiction must always consider the perspective from which they tell a story – the relationship between what is narrated and the mode of narrating is a dialectical one – most archaeologists uncritically regard language as a linear, unproblematic means of representation that does not affect content. Positivism, rejected by many authors, creeps in through the back door of language use. The 19th-century assumption prevails that language is capable of representing the world faithfully. Against this naive representational view, Cassirer (1955) argued that language is rather a means to *shape* reality. In order to change writing habits, a primary necessity is a wide-ranging critical analysis of narrative styles of the past, both in general and of the ancient Near East (e.g., Hackett and Dennell 2003).

Narrated Time and Time of Narration

Narrated time and time of narration are related in multiple ways. In Feuchtwanger's *Flavius Josephus* and Heym's *The King David Report*, the past serves as foil for the present, a "distant mirror." In Heym's novel the parallel to the GDR is so obvious that it could not be ignored by the regime's censorship. For Feuchtwanger, who wrote theoretical treatises about historical novels (1963, 1985), the "distant mirror" was the only real legitimation for this literary form, a stylistic means to represent contemporary burning political and social issues in "costume." The distancing and exoticization of present issues through their placement in the past deepens the appreciation of our own world. As Feuchtwanger put it (1985:155), "one recognizes the silhouettes of a mountain chain better from a distance than in the middle of them."

The Flavius Josephus novel underscores his theory in two regards. First, Feuchtwanger uses Josephus to describe the problematic position of a writer who lives in a diaspora where he meets hostility from the foreign community and other expatriates. Clearly, we encounter the author's own problems located in the past. Secondly, the novel contrasts nationalism and global citizenship, a question of great concern to European Jews in times of rising fascism (Nyssen 1974:158).

In Mann's novel, the relationship between past and present is differently conceptualized. At the very beginning of the novel, in the chapter "Descent into Hell," Mann rejects the teleological story of the Bible as well as modern linear notions of history and time. The author interweaves the principal subject, the myth, with the novel's form. He uses a cyclical concept of time, characteristic of myths, for his own narration. To this end, Mann exploits C.G. Jung's theses of archetypes and archetypical situations, implying the return of figures and events. For instance, Abraham claimed twice, when under distress, that his wife Sarah was his sister, as did his son Isaac. Mann interprets these cross-generational repetitions as imitations that need not even have taken place in praxis. For Isaac, they may have stayed completely in the realm of rhetoric and fancy. In mythical thinking, it is unnecessary "to clearly differentiate between being and meaning" (Mann 1999:22; cf. Nolte 1996). Similarly, there is no clear boundary between this life and a netherworld or between past and future.

Mann set himself the task of pressing the cyclicity of events into a linear narrative. The narrator repeatedly mulls over this problem (e.g. Mann 1978:81–82). Persons return several times in different incarnations. Joseph himself is an archetype with the characteristics of Sumerian Tammuz, Greek Dionysos, and Egyptian Osiris (Berger 1971:54–57).

However, Mann's depiction of myth serves also as a "distant mirror" on a metalevel. The concern with myth in the world of Joseph reflects the dominant interest in myths among the bourgeoisie of early 20th-century Germany (Nipperdey 1990:512–516). Nietzsche's philosophy, Wagner's Germanocentric operas, and Freud's psychology are all centrally concerned with myths.

Lukács (1962:288–290) has pointed out that parallels across periods of time, such as the "distant mirror," imply historical stasis. Therefore, historical novels with contemporary concerns would display an ahistorical quality, giving them popular appeal because it seems as if past people had grievances and joys identical to those of the present (Settis 1986:147). This accusation could also be applied to many theoretically informed archaeological writings that have a present agenda as a basis. If Lukács's idea is accepted, archaeological works of feminist or Marxist persuasion would tend to be particularly ahistorical due to their focus on contemporary concerns. However, Lukács's argument is problematic since preservation of the status quo, likewise a program anchored in the present, is often implicitly included in historical novels. Aware of this, Lukács (1962:337) adds that historical novels must show the path from a past situation to the present. All historical works must focus on historical change in order to escape the "freezing" view of a distant mirror. Feminist historians have promoted similar views (Scott 1986).

Another possibility is to abandon the linearity of Western historical narratives entirely, pursuing Mann's ideas further. Historians sometimes address temporal cyclicity on a theoretical level (Röttgers 1998). The integration of these concepts in historical narratives would be particularly apposite for many societies of the ancient Near East that held cyclical views of time (Maul 1994). A hermeneutically conscientious historiography would have to find new narrative forms to express the dialectical tension between the linearity of the time of narration and the cyclical nature of narrated time.

Mimesis and Imagination

Aristotle's conviction that historiography is an art and not a science, but an art different from poetry, still affects the relationship of literature and history. According to Aristotle, historical mimesis imitates the details of (past) reality in a narrative, whereas poetry uses mimesis as an imitation of possible and likely events by focusing on general, recursive patterns of reality (Burke 1997:77).

Historical novels include both kinds of mimetic elements to various degrees. Here, I am interested in the role of historical mimesis, in the inclusion of external "sources" in the creation of the three novels. Heym simply relied on discussions with the historian of religion Beltz, who assured him that there were no secondary sources for the history of King David outside the Bible. Heym's project had, as he tells us, the "huge advantage" of avoiding lengthy investigations. He could concentrate exclusively on analysis of the Biblical text and its inconsistencies in order to derive a story about the way it was composed (Heym 1988:761–764). Heym knew that the Biblical texts about David had been compiled after King Solomon's life (Finkelstein, this volume), but preferred to set the commissioning of the history in Solomon's time to describe him as an usurper striving for legitimation (Hutchinson 1992:152–153).

Feuchtwanger (1985:157) opts openly for "lies that promote imagination" rather than historical mimesis severely restrained by reliance on evidence. In one of his novels, he asks, "Was it important whether Jesus of Nazareth had actually lived? An image of him existed which was intelligible to the world. Through this image, and only through this image, truth came into being." The historical effect of fiction is immeasurably greater than any academic history. Feuchtwanger's over-estimation of his own literary power finds its echo in his Flavius Josephus.

Despite his contempt for factual history, Feuchtwanger created entire scenes based on descriptions of archaeological monuments. The plundering of the temple in Jerusalem is derived from the relief on the Arch of Titus in Rome (Feuchtwanger 1932:439). The author had examined this building during a journey to Italy (Jeske and Zahn 1984:47). The rendering of Vespasian's physiognomy correlates in detail with the emperor's busts (Feuchtwanger 1932:170–172). In such descriptions Feuchtwanger follows a double strategy. He remains entirely in the realm of fiction for individuals or places that are not central to his novel. But for major characters and locations, he adheres strictly, wherever possible, to specific archaeological monuments, portraying physical traits by referring to a statue of the person in question and to buildings on the basis of their preserved remains.

Mann pursues an approach less hampered by chronological details, individual identity of statues, or the experience of place. This does not imply a lack of knowledge, since his letters suggest intense research (Mann 1999). Mann

picked freely from his readings those elements that corresponded most closely
to his plans for the novel. At the center of attention in his choice of readings are
works by the historian of religion Alfred Jeremias, one of the "pan-babylonists"
under the influence of the anti-Semitic orientalist Hugo Winckler. Additional inspiration came from "pan-mythological" theories of Bachofen, C. G. Jung and
Mereschkowski, who contended that myths in all pre-modern societies were structurally similar.

While Mann read a large amount of academic and "fringe" literature on the
history of religion, he had no ambitions to remain faithful to culture-historical
sources. The model for one description of Joseph was a statue of Hermes by
Lysippos (Mann 1999:86). Elsewhere, Joseph is fashioned after the painter Paul
Ehrenberg with whom the young Mann had a homoerotic relationship, and in yet
another place after a relief of Cha-em-het, the chief of the grain barns under
Pharaoh Amenhotep III (Kurzke 1993:64–67). Hence, the protagonist is merged
from several highly divergent sources. Multiplicity of prototypes also applies to Mut-
em-enet who appears in the Bible only as the "wife of Potiphar." Mann literally
pulls her out of the darkness of anonymity by providing her with the highly sug-
gestive name "Mut in the desert valley." For the description of Egyptian personalities, statues serve as a foil. However, Mann did not agonize over such "banalities"
as chronology. While he placed his story in the late second millennium B.C.E., he
knowingly used a statue of the first century B.C.E. for the description of the reac-
tionary priest Beknechons (Fischer 2002:596–597). Not surprisingly, Mann spoke
of the "droll exactness" of archaeology (cited in Mieth 1976:39).

Despite such a cavalier attitude, Mann insists on the scientific aspects of his
novel, particularly in its historical-religious and archaeological facets (Hamburger
1945:34). If the author cared about his sources, why was he so inconsistent in the
use of archaeological materials? The answer lies again in Mann's central concern
with myth. Mythical thinking implies the condition where words such as "once"
can be applied to past and future similarly, where a person memorizes actions as
his or her own which are deeply anchored patterns of recursive praxis. They are
part of what Lévi-Bruhl called *participation mystique*: a lack of distinction between
object and subject, a conception of the self not as an ego with clear boundaries
between self and world but as a more or less active identification with (human and
other) predecessors. As Eliezer is the servant of generations of patriarchs, the figure
of Beknechons is a *Wiedergänger*, a re-occurring archetype with "transpersonal psychology." Consequently, historical accuracy is not just unimportant but *detrimental*
for Mann's novel, which aims at unveiling a mythical worldview completely alien
to modern historical thinking.

The comparison of these novels reveals a general similarity in the treatment of
historical mimesis: it is enfolded in poetic mimesis which facilitates the focus on
individual lives. However, there is considerable variability in the importance of historical detail. A commitment to a high degree of historical mimesis may, as in
Feuchtwanger, be accompanied by programmatic statement to the contrary. On the
surface, Mann seems to abstain from any attempt at imitation of reality. However,
his goal is historical mimesis on a deeper level of past worldviews.

Any historical-archaeological narrative is likely to be built on a reverse relationship between historical and poetic mimesis. The world of the possible is subordinated to a narrative that imitates "reality." The extent to which the inclusion of poetic mimesis may be beneficial to historical mimesis itself, as shown in Mann's novel, remains largely unexplored in theoretical discussions of history and archaeology (Bernbeck and Pollock 2002).

Narrative Reflexivity

All three works discussed here stand out by their high degree of reflexivity. In Feuchtwanger and Heym, reflexivity is realized through a protagonist-writer whose occupation plays a predominant role in the narrative. In order to problematize the act of writing, Feuchtwanger avails himself of a challenger for Flavius Josephus in the person of Justus of Tiberias. Feuchtwanger repeatedly employs the confrontation of these authors to demonstrate how the same "historical material" may lead to diametrically opposed historical narratives. Flavius Josephus produces a seven-volume account of the "Jewish War," full of compromises and concessions. Justus argues with statistics and numbers in a slim book, "sharp, clear, polished and ineffective" (Feuchtwanger 1936:9). Reason stands against passion and truth against dramatic effect (Köpke 1989:140). In a clever fashion, Feuchtwanger discusses his views about historiography: legend-like narratives are more effective than dry facts (Sternburg 1984:239).

In Heym's *The King David Report*, the historian Ethan is at the mercy of a commission. Heym shows less the prejudices of Ethan than those of the committee members. Heym seems to believe in the possibility of an impartial historiography when he has Ethan state that "you cannot entirely divorce history from truth" (Heym 1997:244). However, he also puts cynical words in the mouth of his protagonist (Heym 1997:39): "Blessed be the name of the Lord our God, whose truth is like a field arrayed with flowers of many colours, for each man to pick the one striking his fancy." Whole sections of Heym's novel are a collage of invented contradictory historical sources that lead readers to reflect on the general reliability of historical material. The novel also creatively addresses the necessity of selectivity and silencing in storytelling in order to provide coherence and closure to a narrative (cf. Wesseling 1991:119–127).

Mann's novel situates reflexivity not – as in Feuchtwanger's and Heym's cases – on an epistemological but on an ontological level of historiography: the narrator of the novel problematizes the creation of entire worlds instead of questioning the methods of narration such as source selection. In the process, the narrator relativizes his own created world as one among many possibilities. This is emphasized where the narrator's ironical advice stands in opposition to what is going to be reported. Additionally, a connection between form and content is constructed as the protagonist Joseph goes through a process of increasing reflexivity in the novel, and Mann creates a parallel movement of a narrator who increasingly reflects on his ways of telling the story (Nolte 1996:142).

This dialectic relationship of narrator and story is complicated by the changing point of view of the narrator who propagates on the one hand "life as it recounts itself" as the historical original, declaring that he represents events in accordance with their truthful reality. On the other hand, narration of the long gone past is for him an entreaty and a "taste of death," built on traditions about the past that are skimpy and sparse (Mann 1978:32–34). The narrator of the Joseph story is a dubious, unstable figure. A reflecting subject, critical towards history as well as self-critical, he forces readers to stay distant from the story. Then suddenly, the narrator accompanies the story directly and empathetically in its own development. At such a point, he openly requests the readers' sympathy with the actors. Mann himself argued that such contradictory ways of narrating follow a "principle of indecision," an attitude he preferred over determination and clarity. The inclusion of internal reproach does not have Joseph's "real" history as its main focus but the "pure possibility of narrating" (Petersen 1991:147, 152–153).

The political effect of Mann's mode of narration is far less obvious than in Heym's or Feuchtwanger's works. The characters in their novels emphasize falsifications in historiography caused by imbalances of power and subjective perception. In Mann's figures, this epistemological ability to critique is missing since their mode of thinking is mythical. Thus, only the narrator can be critical. However, since Mann's narrator can neither be located clearly in space nor time, and since this narrator explicitly relativizes his own account, he does not acquire a capacity of political criticism. Mann's narrator remains encapsulated in the bourgeois ideology of *l'art pour l'art*.

Academic discourse is much more geared towards reflexivity, both in history and archaeology, than literary works. Droysen introduced reflexivity in his 19th-century "historics" (cf. White 1987:88–93), and reflexivity has recently become a focus in postprocessual methodologies (Hodder 2000). Such reflexivity largely remains epistemological, problematizing the ways of representing the past, but not addressing ontological questions of narration and "pastness."

Toward the Future of Historical Narratives

In this last section, I address the implications of a consideration of historical novels for our own work as historians and archaeologists. I am concerned with three main issues, politics of narration, agents of narration, and facticity.

Politics of narration

Politics of narration includes the author's relations of production and the construction of a relational past. The conditions in which authors work merit more consideration than we as historian-archaeologists are willing to admit. Issues of class, religion, nationality, language, connections to publishers, and affiliations with institutions all help to structure a highly unequal field of discourse. Unfortunately, professional ideologies produce the impression of a level field. The ultimate irony is that we often research social inequality while denying its existence in our own realm. Silencing is not just a matter of discourse *about* "the past," but also of its multiple constructions which are not all given a chance in a particular present locale (but see Hodder 1999). Multivocality in archaeology remains for the most part an utterly normative concept, where "voices" are treated as coherent units whose connections to a material world and relations of power are not problematized. Worse, some "voices" are folded into mainstream discourse as a means to domesticate them, as has happened with some strands of feminist archaeology.

Historical novels reveal another element of fundamental importance for the politics of narration: narratives are based on their own negation, the conflicting versions that never make it into a written history. History's most basic error is to assume that "sources have the right of veto" (Koselleck 1979:206), that they can unequivocally constrain interpretations of the past. As Heym shows so well, remains that survive to serve as sources are the result of power struggles *in the past*. Textual or archaeological preservation are not based on socio-politically neutral acts of a stream of "tradition" or "agency" (Barrett 1994; Pauketat 2000). Rather, past curation, mutilation, recycling, and outright destruction are political acts. What we need is a political taphonomy (cf. Bernbeck 2003), investigations into how any "document of civilization . . . is at the same time a document of barbarism" (Benjamin 1992:248).

Any narrative about the past is diachronically relational since it establishes a link between a past and a specific present. In the three novels, power relations between narrated time and time of narration explore this theme. The metaphor of a "distant mirror" is employed by authors and literary critics alike to characterize writings that emphasize similarities between past and present. On the other hand, an explicit rift may be created in order to preserve the past's alterity. Academic history diverges from these possibilities in that pasts are at best shattered distant mirrors or fragments of alterities. But the political implications are comparable. Archaeologists opt implicitly for one or the other of these links. Constructions of past world systems (e.g., Algaze 1993) are a clear case of mirroring, as is a recent book on women in the ancient Near East (Bahrani 2001). Currently relevant issues serve as the foreground for an interpretation of the past. Feuchtwanger's powerful defense of such an approach (1985) and his emphasis on free imagination are more convincing than much of the theoretical archaeological literature that tries to legitimize the authority of such narratives by arguing for facticity where fictionality prevails.

The construction of alterities originally may have been the goal of anthropological Near Eastern archaeology. In Lukács's (1962) and Rüsen's (1989:121–135) views, alterities have the important potential to show a way out of a present that has lost its utopian imagination. However, the teleology of the anthropological focus on social evolution renders that path useless in this regard. The present is conceived as inherently "better" because more complex than the past. A remedy would be the construction of non-directional, truly historical alterities. This entails the development of a "hermeneutics of the unfamiliar" (Jauß 1991:70–71).

The relation between past and present is neither dialectical nor a dialogue, but one of inequality (but see Joyce 2002:10–14). We inflict narrative constructions on a past, sometimes creating the voices with which we wish to have a dialogue, and these discourses, not the past itself, reassure or haunt us and generations to come. This political element of narrating the past plays an essential role in all three novels. While it has recently been addressed in archaeology, it remains a separate meta-discourse – such as this paper – rather than an integrated element of archaeological narratives.

Agents of narration

Archaeology has not been preoccupied with the construction of narratives. Apart from occasional references to the literary turn in cultural anthropology, remarks about Hayden White's analyses of history prevail (cf. Pluciennik 1999; Joyce 2002:13–16). This focus on (thought-provoking) ideas of a single author does not do justice to the diversity of historiographical issues. White (1973; 1987) concentrates on tropes, emplotment, and their ideological implications to the exclusion of most other aspects of narratives and combines them into an overly rigid typological scheme (White 1973:29; cf. Stückrath 1997).

One formal element of narratives that plays no role in White's theories is the agent of narration. Narrators are necessary constructs in any linear account of the past but are unconsciously suppressed in archaeological texts or remain confused mediators between what is narrated and the author's product. As noted, novelists have taken ingenious steps to weave the narrator(s) into their stories. Today, novels with an omniscient narrator are considered anachronistic (Lukács 1962:19–29), whereas this is still the dominant style in academic writing about the past.

As historians, we would profit from an explicit discussion about narrators in our writings. Time as a cultural construct of narratives could be creatively relativized by conceptualizing it as rhythmic in the perspective of a specific narrator, rather than as physical-objective. On a more general level, the reflexive conceptualizing of narrators would help us to reflect critically on the form of our texts and gain some distance to our renderings of the past, thereby seeing them as stories told by an intermediary agent. It would also force us to divest emotionally from an overly close commitment to a particular construction of the past, a position perceptible in many archaeological texts heavily concerned with relevance and an ideology of facticity.

Facticity and fiction

Isn't striving for factual knowledge and interpretation based on such knowledge fundamentally different from poetry and literary writing? Fiction writers may consciously produce ideology, whereas most historians still try to limit such influence on their work. In my introduction, I pointed out that past realities are not

identical to historical reality. Historians construct meaningfulness by arbitrarily dissecting past residues into clearly delimited items, documents, and contexts – sources
– only to merge the disjointed fragments into a new continuum. However, the new
entity has a profoundly different character from the originally encountered resid-
ual: it is linked in a linear textual narrative.

History needs to be seen as cultural and historical praxis that occurs in specific
social relations of production. Like the standard novel, what we know as standard
history is a textual product typical for an emerging 19th-century capitalist bourgeoisie (Barthes 1968:33–34). Does this mean, as some historians claim (Jenkins
1999:202–206), that we should abandon the pursuit of narratives about the past
altogether? I do not think so. However, there is a need to continually rethink their
form. Historical and archaeological narratives are ideological in that they generally
claim facticity, at least of sources. As already argued, the production of relations
among sources in the "rejoining" process of historiography involves fiction. A future
task must be to analyze the dialectical relation between the construction of datasets
and the creation of an interpretive narrative from them. This process is a social
praxis that cannot simply be seen as creative ingenuity or academically rigorous
method. It is driven by conventions, which in turn are recreated by the act of narrative production.

Future narratives of the past: aspectival historiography

Most of the problems raised in this discussion of historical novels involve the form
of narratives. The present use of linear textual accounts in much of Near Eastern
archaeology, with (suppressed) omniscient narrators and an unreflective use of language, is in need of change unless we accept the implications for content that come
with this particular narrative form. Conventions that we use for our accounts of the
past reproduce coherent worlds. Yet postmodern conditions do not have a place for
know-it-all historical narrators who skillfully weave autonomous "data" into meaningful wholes. Such narratives may be the result of a yearning for a reliable, closed
world, however cruel and conflict-ridden the content may be. When reflecting on
narrative form, authors often refer to the erroneous belief that comprehensibility of
a story is reduced when multiple perspectives are considered. Indeed, our notion
of perspective itself is a historical product. "Perspective," or "looking through," has
its origin in the individualistic gaze that originated in Renaissance art and can be
compared to strict points of view in literature (cf. Jay 1993:51–53, 171–210). This
fundamental concept began to disintegrate in the early 20th century with Freud,
in art with cubism, and has reached new lows with postmodern architecture and
philosophy.

History and archaeology have remained impervious to the end of perspectivism
because its demise weakens the rarely questioned fundamentals of professions concerned with the past. Particularly in hermeneutic approaches, a single-narrator perspective leads by necessity to an unrealistic representation of the past. It conceals
conflicts by telling a story from one angle. An historical account should rather

integrate divergent standpoints that do not add up to a harmonious whole. Following Brunner-Traut's (1992:7–40) terminology, such a historiography can be called "aspectival."[4]

Any past topic, whether a political system, gender relations, or a period as a whole, was certainly seen by diverse people *in the past* in multiple ways. If we wish to depict the past not as a wishful dream but as an unknowable world inhabited and acted upon by people with different interests, we should recount it from several different perspectives at the same time and abandon the harmonious bourgeois perspective of the individual onlooker.

How can such an aspectival history be told concretely without turning the historical text into an incomprehensible narrative? The aspectival historical text must include several viewpoints and therefore several narrators. However, a history that employs frequent switches of perspective and narrator, close to the ideas of the *nouveau roman* in French literature (Morrissette 1963), seems impractical because the reader's effort to follow the form would inhibit comprehension of content. A preferable solution might be to create several fictitious narrators who recount, one after the other, alternative histories of the same period or theme. Put differently, an aspectival history should consist of several (perspectival) histories. Invented narrators would draw on the same past residues, classifying them variably and according to individual preferences into particular sets of sources, silencing some, and putting the remainder together in a specific way.[5] Not only would a reader be confronted with alternative accounts of a past but also with the – more or less reflexive – creation of building blocks of the historical narrative. Where identical sources are used, variable evaluations would introduce differences in historical reconstructions and relativize simplified and harmonious narratives.

It may sound as if I propose to recreate an edited book by inventing narrators of single chapters. Rather, I suggest that in order to illuminate the underestimated political and social importance of the act of narrating, motivations and restrictions of narrators of different histories should be discussed in fictitious frame stories. They would reveal each historical construction as the result of a specific relationship between today's social relations of production and a past.

Each individual narrative thereby keeps its internal coherence, and would even appear as "hyper-coherent" in its harmony of narrator, his or her life circumstances and interests, and the history created. However, the juxtaposition with other, thematically identical histories produces an aspectival, broken structure. Different social conditions in the present lead to divergent representations of one and the same "past." The aspectival historical discourse is not just broken by references to disparate source selection and construction of relations between sources. The past would not only be a (more or less distant) mirror, but the invented frame stories would act as a second mirror which the present – in terms of the historiographic form – holds up for the past. Different world views and perspectives of historians, influenced by power relations and general socioeconomic conditions, echo multiple viewpoints by people in the past.

Perspectives originate in aesthetic considerations. A perspective implies a basic social agreement between the producer of an object and a public that takes this point of view as unquestioned and often unquestionable. This ideology reached its zenith with the 19th-century bourgeois era. Reality has long since overhauled such a "view of things." In a world characterized by the contemporaneity of the non-contemporaneous, and the dissolution of physical space as a center of life, perspective in historical narratives is an anachronism.

Prospects

At the beginning of this paper, I juxtaposed a popular and an academic account of Urfa's past. The discussion of historical novels and their comparison with archaeological narratives leads me to conclude that academic renderings of the past are formally quite close to popular stories. Following a present fashion in archaeology and inserting "living people" into the past would be equal to succumbing to the desire for a historically unrealistic closure and harmony. If the goal of "peopling" our narratives is to reach out to non-specialist readers, we would do better to insert present-day figures who conceive of the past in different ways and thereby cast doubt on both the myth of unilinear development from early agriculturalists to Roman civilization and Nimrod's atrocities. Narratives of the past are always in need of critique.

Acknowledgments

I thank Eskandar Abadi and Svend Hansen for awakening my interest in the analysis of historical novels. Maria das Dores Cruz, Geoff Emberling, and Susan Pollock provided important critique and insightful comments on earlier versions of the paper.

NOTES

1   I follow Horkheimer and Adorno (1991[1944]:130–131) in separating high quality art from low quality culture industry on the basis that the latter relies on "substitute identity." The core of products of the culture industry is imitation of other works and their supposed similarity to reality, rather than transcendence of that reality.
2   The post-September 11 intellectual and political environment in the U.S. exhibits this erosion of democratic rights and values.
3   In the following section, I use the linguistic male form when referring to narrators because all narrators of the three novels are conceptualized as male.
4   I do not agree with Brunner-Traut's primitivist interpretation of the aspective.
5   To reach such goals, clear and creative writing would need to be stressed in academic education. Good writing skills are neither a mysterious "gift" nor an ability that can be learned mechanically.

REFERENCES

Algaze, Guillermo, 1993 The Uruk World System. Chicago: University of Chicago Press.
Attar, K. E., 2001 Stefan Heym's 'King David Report': a Microcosmic Precursor. Neophilologus 85: 273–286.
Bahrani, Zainab, 2001 Women of Babylon. London: Routledge.
Bapty, Ian, and Timothy Yates, eds., 1990 Archaeology after Structuralism. London: Routledge.
Barrett, John C., 1994 Fragments from Antiquity. Oxford: Blackwell.
Barthes, Roland, 1968 Writing Degree Zero. Annette Lavers and Colin Smith, trans. New York: Hill and Wang.
Benjamin, Walter, 1992 Illuminations. Harry Zohn, trans. London: Fontana.
Berger, Willy, 1971 Die mythologischen Motive in Thomas Manns Roman 'Joseph und seine Brüder'. Köln: Böhlau.
Benson, Paul, ed., 1993 Anthropology and Literature. Urbana: University of Illinois Press.
Bernbeck, Reinhard, 2003 Der grüne Punkt im Alten Orient. In Müll. Facetten von der Steinzeit bis zum Gelben Sack. Mamoun Fansa and Sabine Wolfram, eds. pp. 35–46. Mainz: Philipp von Zabern.
Bernbeck, Reinhard, and Susan Pollock, 2002 Reflections on the Historiography of Fourth Millennium Mesopotamia. In Material Culture and Mental Spheres. Arnulf Hausleiter, Susanne Kerner, and Bernd Müller-Neuhoff, eds. pp. 171–204. Münster: Ugarit-Verlag.
Böll, Heinrich, 1972 Der Lorbeer ist immer noch bitter. Der Spiegel, September 18:158–159.
Brunner-Traut, Emma, 1992 Frühformen des Erkennens. 2nd edition. Darmstadt: Wissenschaftliche Buchgesellschaft.
Burke, Peter, 1997 Die Metageschichte von 'Metahistory'. In Metageschichte. Hayden White und Paul Ricoeur. Jörn Stückrath and Jürg Zbinden, eds. pp. 73–85. Baden-Baden: Nomos.
Cassirer, Ernst, 1955 The Philosophy of Symbolic Forms. Ralph Manheim, trans. New Haven: Yale University Press.
Certeau, Michel de, 1988 The Writing of History. Tom Conley, trans. New York: Columbia University Press.
Clifford, James, and George E. Marcus, 1986 Writing Culture. Berkeley: University of California Press.
Crawford, Harriet, 1987 The 'Construction Inférieure' at Tello. A Reassessment. Iraq 49:71–76.
David, Nicholas, and Carol Kramer, 2001 Ethnoarchaeology in Action. Cambridge: Cambridge University Press.
Dülmen, Richard van, 2000 Historische Anthropologie. Bonn: Böhlau.
Eagleton, Terry, 1976 Marxism and Literary Criticism. Berkeley: University of California Press.
Eisele, Ulf, 1984 Die Struktur des modernen deutschen Romans. Tübingen: Niemeyer.
Feuchtwanger, Lion, 1932 Josephus. Willa and Edwin Muir, trans. New York: Viking.
Feuchtwanger, Lion, 1936 The Jew of Rome. Willa and Edwin Muir, trans. New York: Viking.
Feuchtwanger, Lion, 1942 The Day Will Come. Caroline Oram, trans. New York: Viking.
Feuchtwanger, Lion, 1963 The House of Desdemona. Detroit: Wayne State University Press.

Feuchtwanger, Lion, 1985 Vom Sinn und Unsinn des historischen Romans. *In* Lion Feuchtwanger: '. . . für die Vernunft, gegen Dummheit und Gewalt'. Walter Huder, Friedrich
Knilli, Herrmann Haarmann, and Klaus Siebenhaar, eds. pp. 154–159. Berlin: Publica.

Fischer, Bernd-Jürgen, 2002 Handbuch zu Thomas Manns 'Josephsromanen'. Tübingen:
Francke.

Hackett, Abigail, and Robin Dennell, 2003 Neanderthals as Fiction in Archaeological Narrative. Antiquity 77:816–827.

Hamburger, Käte, 1945 Thomas Manns Roman 'Joseph und seine Brüder'. Stockholm:
Bermann-Fischer Verlag.

Hans, Jan, 1976 Historische Skizze zum Exilroman. *In* Der deutsche Roman im 20.
Jahrhundert, vol. 1. Manfred Brauneck, ed. pp. 240–259. Bamberg: C. C. Buchners.

Heftrich, Eckhard, 1990 Höhere Stimmigkeit. *In* Romane von gestern – heute gelesen. Band
3: 1933–1945. Marcel Reich-Ranicki, ed. pp. 11–17. Frankfurt a.M.: S. Fischer.

Heilbut, Anthony, 1997 Exiled in Paradise. 2nd edition. Berkeley: University of California
Press.

Heym, Stefan, 1988 Nachruf. Frankfurt a.M.: Fischer.

Heym, Stefan, 1992 Filz. Munich: Bertelsmann.

Heym, Stefan, 1997 The King David Report. Evanston, IL: Northwestern University Press.

Hodder, Ian, 1989 Writing Archaeology: Site Reports in Context. Antiquity 63: 268–274.

Hodder, Ian, 1999 The Archaeological Process. Oxford: Blackwell.

Hodder, Ian, ed., 2000 Towards a Reflexive Method in Archaeology. The Example at
Çatalhöyük. Cambridge: McDonald Institute for Archaeological Research.

Horkheimer, Max, and Theodor W. Adorno, 1991 Dialectic of Enlightenment. John
Cumming, trans. New York: Continuum.

Humboldt, Wilhelm von, 1967[1821] On the Historian's Task. Wilma Iggers, trans. History
and Theory 6: 57–71.

Hutchinson, Peter, 1992 Stefan Heym. The Perpetual Dissident. Cambridge: Cambridge
University Press.

Jauß, Hans-Robert, 1991 Die Paradigmatik der Geisteswissenschaften im Dialog der
Disziplinen. *In* Geisteswissenschaften Heute. Eine Denkschrift. Wolfgang Frühwald,
et al., eds. pp. 45–72. Frankfurt a.M.: Suhrkamp.

Jay, Martin, 1993 Downcast Eyes. Berkeley: University of California Press.

Jenkins, Keith, 1999 Why History? Ethics and Postmodernity. London: Routledge.

Jeske, Wolfgang and Peter Zahn, 1984 Lion Feuchtwanger oder Der arge Weg der
Erkenntnis. Stuttgart: J. B. Metzler.

Joyce, Rosemary A., 2002 The Languages of Archaeology. Oxford: Blackwell.

Köpke, Wulf, 1983 Lion Feuchtwanger. Munich: C. H. Beck.

Köpke, Wulf, 1989 Lion Feuchtwangers 'Josephus'. Ost und West. *In* Lion Feuchtwanger.
Materialien zu Leben und Werk. Wilhelm von Sternburg, ed. pp. 134–150. Frankfurt
a.M.: Fischer.

Koselleck, Reinhart, 1979 Vergangene Zukunft. Frankfurt a.M.: Suhrkamp.

Koselleck, Reinhart, 1997 Vom Sinn und Unsinn der Geschichte. *In* Historische
Sinnbildung. Klaus E. Müller and Jörn Rüsen, eds. pp. 79–97. Hamburg: Rowohlt.

Kurzke, Hermann, 1993 Mondwanderungen. Wegweiser durch Thomas Manns Joseph-
Roman. Frankfurt a.M.: Fischer.

Lessing, Theodor, 1983[1919] Geschichte als Sinngebung des Sinnlosen. Munich: C. H.
Beck.

Lukács, Georg, 1962 The Historical Novel. Hannah and Stanley Mitchell, trans. Atlantic
Highlands: Humanities Press.

Mann, Thomas, 1978 Joseph and his Brothers. Helene Lowe-Porter, trans. Harmondsworth: Penguin.

Mann, Thomas, 1999 Selbstkommentare: Joseph und seine Brüder. Edited by Hans Wysling. Frankfurt a.M.: Fischer.

Maul, Stefan, 1994 Zukunftsbewältigung. Mainz: Philipp von Zabern.

Merpert, Nikolai Ya., and R. M. Munchaev, 1987 The Earliest Levels at Yarim Tepe I and Yarim Tepe II in Northern Iraq. Iraq 49:1–36.

Michel, Otto, and Otto Bauernfeind, 1959 Einleitung. In Flavius Josephus. De Bello Judaico. Otto Michel and Otto Bauernfeind, eds. pp. XI–XXXVI. Darmstadt: Wissenschaftliche Buchgesellschaft.

Mieth, Dietmar, 1976 Epik und Ethik. Tübingen: Niemeyer.

Morrissette, Bruce, 1963 Les romans de Robbe-Grillet. Paris: Éditions de Minuit.

Nietzsche, Friedrich, 1968[1872] The Birth of the Tragedy. In Basic Writings of Nietzsche. Walter Kaufman, trans. and ed. New York: Modern Library.

Nipperdey, Thomas, 1990 Deutsche Geschichte 1866–1918, vol. I. Arbeitswelt und Bürgergeist. Munich: C. H. Beck.

Nolte, Charlotte, 1996 Being and Meaning in Thomas Mann's 'Joseph' Novels. London: W. S. Maney & Son Ltd.

Nyssen, Elke, 1974 Geschichtsbewußtsein und Emigration. Munich: Wilhelm Fink.

Pauketat, Timothy, 2000 The Tragedy of the Commoners. In Agency in Archaeology. Marcia-Anne Dobres and John Robb, eds. pp. 113–129. London: Routledge.

Petersen, Jürgen H., 1991 Der deutsche Roman der Moderne. Stuttgart: Metzler.

Pluciennik, Mark, 1999 Archaeological Narratives and Other Ways of Telling. Current Anthropology 40:653–678.

Reich-Ranicki, Marcel, 1974 Zur Literatur der DDR. Munich: Piper.

Roaf, Michael, and Robert Killick, 1987 A Mysterious Affair of Styles: The Ninevite 5 Pottery of Northern Mesopotamia. Iraq 49:199–230.

Röttgers, Kurt, 1998 Die Lineatur der Geschichte. Amsterdam: Editions Rodopi.

Rüsen, Jörn, 1987 Narrativität und Modernität in den Geschichtswissenschaften. In Theorie der modernen Geschichtsschreibung. Pietro Rossi, ed. pp. 230–237. Frankfurt a.M.: Suhrkamp.

Rüsen, Jörn, 1989 Lebendige Geschichte. Göttingen: Vandenhoeck & Ruprecht.

Rüsen, Jörn, 1994 Historische Orientierung. Bonn: Böhlau.

Said, Edward, 1978 Orientalism. New York: Vintage Books.

Scott, Joan, 1986 Gender: A Useful Category of Historical Analysis. American Historical Review 91:1053–1075.

Settis, Salvatore, 1986 Die Zeitmaschine. Über den Umgang mit Geschichte. In Vom Umschreiben der Geschichte. Ulrich Raulff, ed. pp. 147–153. Berlin: Wagenbach.

Spector, Janet, 1993 What this Awl Means. St. Paul: Minnesota Historical Society Press.

Sternburg, Wilhelm von, 1984 Lion Feuchtwanger. Königstein: Athenäum.

Stückrath, Jörn, 1997 Typologie statt Theorie? Zur Rekonstruktion und Kritik von Hayden Whites Begrifflichkeit in 'Metahistory'. In Metageschichte. Hayden White und Paul Ricoeur. Jörn Stückrath and Jürg Zbinden, eds. pp. 86–103. Baden-Baden: Nomos-Verlag.

Tringham, Ruth E., 1991 Households with Faces: the Challenge of Gender in Prehistoric Architectural Remains. In Engendering Archaeology: Women and Prehistory. Joan Gero and Margaret W. Conkey, eds. pp. 93–131. Oxford: Blackwell.

Trouillot, Michel-Rolph, 1995 Silencing the Past. Boston: Beacon Press.

Vietor-Engländer, Deborah, 1989 Wetcheeks Welterfolg. Kritischer Forschungbericht. In

Lion Feuchtwanger. Materialien zu Leben und Werk. Wilhelm von Sternburg, ed. pp. 312–335. Frankfurt a.M.: Fischer.

Wesseling, Elisabeth, 1991 Writing History as a Prophet. Postmodernist Innovations of the Historical Novel. Amsterdam: John Benjamins.

White, Hayden, 1973 Metahistory. Baltimore: Johns Hopkins University Press.

White, Hayden, 1987 The Content of the Form. Baltimore: Johns Hopkins University Press.

Zachau, Reinhard K., 1982 Stefan Heym. München: C. H. Beck.

PART II

Reassessing Evolutionary "Firsts"

Reinhard Bernbeck
and Susan Pollock

Ever since the writings of V. G. Childe, the ancient Near East has been known as a region of evolutionary "firsts." Research on the relation between Neandertals and modern humans has a long tradition in the Levant. The Near East is famous for the earliest transition from hunting and gathering to herding and agricultural communities, often referred to as the "Neolithic Revolution." The same is true for urbanization, and, many would claim, for the development of the state as a political form of organization. Finally, empires appear very early in ancient Mesopotamia. The papers in this section discuss facets of these fundamental changes, providing new ideas about their timing, internal processes, and past people's own perceptions of them. Topics that occur repeatedly are power disparities, means of communication, social cohesion, demography and reflections on relations between past and present.

   This series of papers exhibits a shift in basic conceptions that parallel major chronological periods. Thus, for research on the Palaeolithic, biological evolution plays an important, if not dominant, role (Shea). With the "Neolithic revolution," changes in social, economic, and political structures become the predominant concern (Kujit and Chesson; Forest). Anthropological strands of Near Eastern archaeology have investigated all these issues intensely. However, anthropological interest in the ancient Near East usually stops abruptly with the beginnings of what has traditionally been conceived as "historical times," when large numbers of written documents – principally clay tablets – become available. Texts reveal intricate connections among religious ideas, state administration, and economic transactions. Could it be that the fast pace of historical change and the complex web of evidence is too burdensome for highly abstract anthropological models and paradigms? Ever since the abandonment of a culture-historical framework in the early 1960s, anthropological archaeology of processual and various postprocessual persuasions has had an unfortunate tendency towards theoretical generalization that made it difficult to integrate multifarious and often discrepant historical knowledge into a coherent account. Historical times, in turn, are the preferred fields of European-style Near Eastern archaeology, with a focus on the connections between texts and material culture derived from an understanding of change as historical rather than evolutionary. Though often dismissed, the Old Testament is part of this textual tradition, and its importance as a foundation for three major world religions in the present has resulted in a heavy emphasis on archaeological research of the relevant time periods (Finkelstein).

One of the themes that runs through these chapters is the importance of demographic change. The possibility of acquiring archaeological evidence of demographic change rather than simply assuming it is a result in large part of the introduction of regional surveys into Near Eastern archaeology by Adams (1965, 1981; Adams and Nissen 1972). All of the papers rely heavily on demographic estimates, from reflections about the probability of Neandertal extinction in the Levant (Shea) to deforestation and its connections to a concurrent overpopulation in the late Pre-Pottery Neolithic (Kujit and Chesson); from the "evolutionary dead-end" of city-states as densely populated centers that cannot solve their conflictual relations until a hegemonic state appears (Forest) to the comparison of two textually well-known polities in early Biblical times (Finkelstein) and imperialist deportations that decimated these and other peripheries (Liverani). In this connection, it is interesting to note that demographic change as a background factor is recognized and relied upon, but that methods of assessing it (estimation of population per hectare of settlement, change in settlement patterns through time, etc.) have not developed at the same pace as the complex interpretations based upon it.

Demographic processes go hand-in-hand with changing political and social circumstances. Authors in these chapters use different terminologies that imply fundamentally different concepts and values of historical change. Notions such as resistance, contest, and negotiation give archaeological interpretations a specific, implicitly judgmental character. Whereas Shea represents Palaeolithic humans as strategizing individuals, in Kujit and Chesson's Levantine Neolithic we encounter unspecified groups in negotiation over positions, for which they employ material items. For historical periods, arguments are more complex. Forest discusses theories about state emergence and their applicability for the ancient Near East. He finds conflict models and associated ideas about aggrandizing and strategizing elites wanting and sees in the Mesopotamian development towards the state a realization of Hobbes's idea of the social contract that serves the interests of all. His views differ substantially from those of mainstream researchers in the ways he conceptualizes states. As a consequence, he argues that states emerged much later in the ancient Near East than the archaeological orthodoxy maintains. Finkelstein discusses political conditions in times of state emergence in the Levant. In his account, resistance by small-scale polities against major empires has detrimental effects, whereas collaboration creates a situation that is in the interest of all – the empire as well as its periphery. According to Finkelstein, ethical and political values promulgated by prophets such as Amos or Micah – oppositional voices of the ancient Near East (Bloch 1959:1541) – are at best misguided, if not invented after the fact. Liverani's account diverges from such a sympathetic view of bowing to the powers that be, through his ironic rendering of the imperial perspective that can only see in imperial expansion the beneficial results of saving peripheries from chaos.

Reflections on ways of communicating tie this section together. Forest gives new meaning to the worn-out idea of "complexity," which is traditionally understood as vertically differentiated units (hierarchy) plus horizontal differentiation (division of labor; Flannery 1972). He suggests that it is not simply the number of separate units that is historically important, but rather the social distance between such units, producing variable patterns of communication that lead, in the case of increasing distance, to greater anonymity. Forced breakdown of communication is a typical imperial strategy, as implied in the Roman *divide et impera* notion, which is well exemplified in Liverani's account of sophisticated strategies of ancient Near Eastern deportation schemes. Even more fundamental is the problem Shea tackles: could different sub-species in the Middle Palaeolithic communicate, and if so, how? Were both Neandertals and modern humans able to speak as we are? And did they have general capacities for symbolic behavior? Shea advances the idea that Neandertals were not able to invest an exterior world with meaning – even though they may have been able to speak – whereas modern humans developed a symbolizing capability that went beyond interactions with each other to the assignment of meaning to a material environment.

Related to communication is the topic of social cohesion, or in systems theory parlance, integration. In Finkelstein's account of King Josiah's time, in whose reign the Old Testament took its definitive shape, he argues that (religious) ideology is responsible for social cohesion. Finkelstein reads the Bible as an "invention of tradition" (Hobsbawm and Ranger 1983), and his central question is the moment of this invention and its accompanying power constellations, rather than the tradition's content. Archaeology, through its ability to analyze social structures and ancient landscapes, becomes in Finkelstein's hands a means to investigate the genesis of a text. He points out that ideologies inherent in the Biblical tradition are at the core of expansionist tendencies, an argument further elaborated by Liverani. According to Liverani, empires are not characterized by social cohesion but by a multitude of ethnic groups that all have their specific interests. Therefore, royal ideologies are largely self-indoctrination for courtiers rather than means to intimidate foreign visitors. Kujit and Chesson, despite some hesitation and critique of functionalist arguments, connect the development of ritual items such as figurines to social stress. Their interpretation of changing characteristics of figurines as deliberate under-scores in a broader sense the "invented traditions" concept; however, in their case it does not serve to consolidate an elite. Forest's position partly dispenses with the notion of cohesion as a "problem" by relegating it to the habitual realm, with an emphasis on consensus that is to be understood as a matter of course. He histori-cizes this position by proposing that consensual development ended with the emer-gence of hegemonies, which as a result needed to produce integrating traditions. In this respect his argument stands in contrast to Kujit and Chesson's ideas who see the need for integration as already a problem in Neolithic times. In Paleolithic periods in the Middle East, social cohesion arises on the level of sub-species com-munication and contact. Shea questions the possibilities for social contact between

Neandertals and modern humans who inhabited the Levant in the Middle Paleolithic.

The relationship between past and present, a problem raised in the first section of this book reappears here in several papers. Liverani artfully interweaves his discussion of ancient Near Eastern empires with the imperialism of colonial and modern times. His insightful comments about the "descriptive" terminology for ancient Near Eastern empires mirrors Pollock's analysis of media discourse. His accounts of Assyrian and Achaemenid imperial policies have an uncannily familiar ring. Finkelstein leaves no doubt that texts reflect the ideologies of their composition rather than their content, but in his case, this plays out as a relationship between two past periods, the seventh century B.C.E. and earlier times of kings David and Solomon. His reflections parallel Bernbeck's discussion of historical novels. The implications of Liverani's and Finkelstein's arguments are far-reaching. Archaeologists tend to see all materials from one context as contemporaneous. However, they may be altered items and texts from earlier times, and such modified objects or texts may tell us less about their time of production than that of their alteration. Both of these papers provide abundant evidence that such processes are part of the history of archaeology itself and that we are ourselves agents of such manipulation.

Interpretations of the past necessarily stand in a dialectical relation to the present. It is interesting to note that all of the papers in this section – and of the volume as a whole – employ a modus of representing the past that is best described as "selective intentionality." The deliberate character of actions seems to be arbitrarily affirmed and/or rejected. Could Neandertals have attempted to stave off their own extinction? Is it likely that Neolithic people deliberately opted for ambiguity, as Kujit and Chesson argue – not without themselves expressing some doubts? Did the late kings of Judah have all the freedom for ideological and political maneuvering Finkelstein accords them? Could they decide themselves about their relationships to the "superpower" Assyria? And could it not be that decisions taken at the Assyrian court were to a certain extent dependent not only on power play and internal conflict, but on habitual practices? In these cases, intentionality and deliberateness emerge like islands out of an unaddressed sea of habitual practices. On the other hand, where the habitual is explicitly discussed, its presence or absence is simply asserted – as in Forest's claims that change in the Uruk period was slow, and that people were appreciating the growing polities as being in their own interest, no matter where they were positioned in society. Writing an account of the past is deeply influenced by our own deliberate or habitual ways of bestowing intentionality on some past people and withdrawing it from others, a subject that warrants much more explicit discussion in archaeology.

REFERENCES

Adams, Robert McCormick, 1965 Land Behind Baghdad. Chicago: University of Chicago Press.

Adams, Robert McCormick, 1981 Heartland of Cities. Chicago: University of Chicago Press.

Adams, Robert McCormick, and Hans Nissen, 1972 The Uruk Countryside. Chicago: University of Chicago Press.

Bloch, Ernst, 1959 Das Prinzip Hoffnung. Frankfurt a.M.: Suhrkamp.

Flannery, Kent, 1972 The Cultural Evolution of Civilizations. Annual Review of Ecology and Systematics 3:399–426.

Hobsbawm, Eric, and Terence Ranger, eds., 1983 The Invention of Tradition. Cambridge: Cambridge University Press.

7

Bleeding or Breeding: Neandertals vs. Early Modern Humans in the Middle Paleolithic Levant

John Shea

When Cro Magnon met Neanderthal, one or the other may occasionally have bled, but I think that they surely bred (if the sexes were properly assorted).

(Hooton 1946:338–339)

For much of the 20th century, evidence from the Middle Paleolithic period in the East Mediterranean Levant (47,000–240,000 B.P.) supported the hypothesis that modern humans evolved from Neandertal ancestors. Since the mid-1980s Neandertals' ancestral status has been challenged by fossil, genetic, and archaeological evidence. Today there is an emerging consensus that Neandertals were a distinct human species who competed with early modern humans for the same niche in the Later Pleistocene of Western Eurasia (Tattersall and Schwartz 2000; Hublin 2000; but for a dissenting view, see Wolpoff 1996). Although one might expect the exclusion of Neandertals from modern human ancestry to diminish scientific interest, it has not. If anything, Neandertal origins, their possible interactions with modern humans, and the mystery of their extinction are among the hottest research topics in paleoanthropology. This paper reviews the Middle Paleolithic archaeological record associated with Neandertals and early modern humans in the Levant and examines evidence bearing on these humans' possible interactions and their evolutionary relationships.

Neandertals originated in the late Middle Pleistocene (>130,000 B.P.) probably from *Homo heidelbergensis* populations of Europe (Hublin 2000). Neandertal fossils have been found at sites throughout much of Europe and western Asia dating to as recently as 30,000 B.P. In the East Mediterranean Levant (Syria, Lebanon, Israel, Jordan, and the Sinai Peninsula), Neandertal fossils have been found at Tabun, Kebara, Shukbah, Amud, and Dederiyeh caves (figure 7.1). Distinctively Neandertal cranial features include a suprainiac fossa (a ridge on the back of the skull), a retromolar space (a gap between the third molar and the ascending part

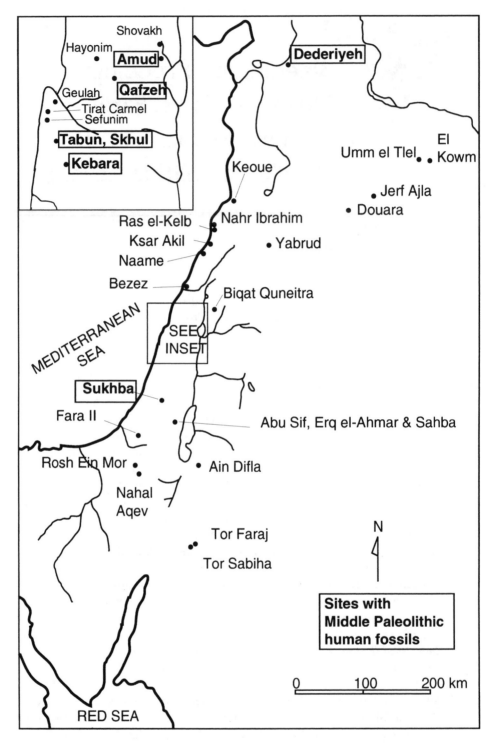

Figure 7.1 Map of the Levant showing the locations of principal Middle Paleolithic sites (author's original)

of the jaw), and midfacial prognathism (forward-flexed cheekbones and nasal bones) (Lieberman 1995). Thick deposits of cortical bone and enlarged joint surfaces indicate Neandertals were extremely powerful individuals who habitually exerted themselves at or beyond the peak levels of recent human populations (Trinkaus et al. 1998). Their postcranial remains feature the relatively short distal limb segments characteristic of populations that have adapted physiologically to life in cold climates (Holliday 2000). It has long been suspected that Neandertals had less capacity for speech production and language than modern humans, but this hypothesis remains controversial (Schepartz 1993).

The term "early modern humans" refers to the subset of modern-looking human fossils dating to before the Middle Paleolithic/Upper Paleolithic (hereafter MP/UP) Transition (>36,000–47,000 B.P.). Fossil evidence and numerous studies of genetic variation among living humans suggest early modern humans originated in Africa near the end of the Middle Pleistocene (>130,000–250,000 B.P.) (Klein 1999). Most such early modern human fossils occur in African contexts, but two sets of early modern human fossils have been found in the Levant at Skhul and Qafzeh caves. Like modern humans, the Skhul/Qafzeh fossils have relatively short, basicranially-flexed skulls with high frontal bones and prominent chins. The postcranial skeletal robusticity of the Skhul/Qafzeh humans is comparable to recent humans, and their relatively long distal limb segments suggest origins in a warm tropical climate (Holliday 2000).

In Europe, Neandertals are associated mainly with the Middle Paleolithic "Mousterian" industry and various MP/UP Transitional industries, such as the Chatelperronian. The earliest European modern humans are associated with Upper Paleolithic complexes, such as the Aurignacian. The chronological priority of research in Europe has resulted in debates about Neandertal and modern human evolutionary relationships usually being framed in terms of contrasts between the Middle vs. Upper Paleolithic. Upper Paleolithic assemblages differ from their Middle Paleolithic predecessors by preserving consistent evidence for the following innovations (Klein 1999:520–556):

- systematic production of prismatic blades,
- carved and decorated bone/antler/ivory and stone implements,
- representational and abstract art in a variety of media,
- regional and short-term chronological variation in artifact design choices ("style"),
- long-distance exchange networks in lithic and other raw materials,
- high-speed/low mass projectile weapons (spearthrower darts),
- functional differentiation of living space (storage pits, architecture).

Some of these behaviors are known from earlier periods and from contexts associated with Neandertals and other pre-modern humans (Mellars 1995; McBrearty and Brooks 2000), but they only become regular features of the archaeological record after 47,000 B.P. and in contexts associated with modern humans.

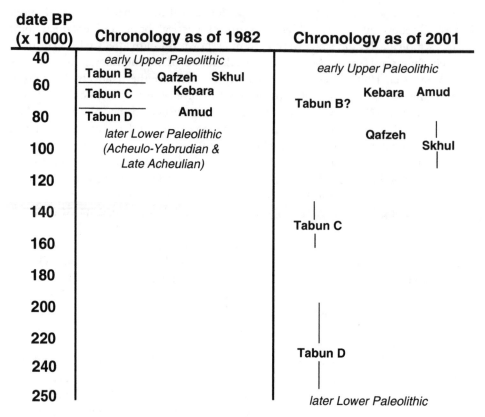

Figure 7.2 Changes in the chronology of Middle Paleolithic human fossil sites in the Levant 1982–2001. For references, see text (author's original)

Possible interactions between Neandertals and early modern humans in Europe are thought to have occurred over a relatively brief period, 8,000–10,000 years at the continental scale (28,000–36,000 B.P.), but probably closer to 2,000–4,000 years in any given region (Pettit 1999; Churchill and Smith 2000:106; Pilbeam and Bar-Yosef 2000). In Europe, the first appearance of modern humans practicing Upper Paleolithic adaptations typically coincides (within a few thousand years) with the last appearance (and presumed extinction) of local Neandertals.

In contrast, the Levant contains evidence for possible Neandertal-early modern human interactions for a much longer period (see figure 7.2). Fully 83,000 years (47,000–130,000 B.P.) separate the first appearance of modern humans in the Levant from the last appearance of Neandertals in that region (Bar-Yosef 1998; Grün and Stringer 2000). These humans' prolonged co-residence in the Levant is compelling evidence that the European MP/UP Transition records only one very late, and potentially atypical, episode in the long course of Neandertal and early modern human co-evolution.

Historical Background

The 1925 discovery of "Galilee Man" in Zuttiyeh Cave, near Tiberias (Turville-Petre 1927) was the first indication that the Levant possessed a rich paleoanthropological prologue to its Biblical heritage. Shortly thereafter, Dorothy Garrod's 1929–34 excavations in the Tabun, Skhul, and El Wad caves on Mount Carmel revealed a long sequence of occupations stretching from the Lower Paleolithic to the Epipaleolithic (Garrod and Bate 1937). The interpretation of Middle Paleolithic human remains from Tabun and Skhul have had a lasting influence on broader models of modern human origin and Neandertal extinction.

In Tabun Cave Levels B–C Garrod recovered one adult burial and numerous fragmentary human remains. This discovery replicated similar finds of Neandertal remains together with Mousterian tools then coming to light elsewhere in southern Europe. At Skhul Cave, a small collapsed rockshelter about a hundred meters east of Tabun, ten archaic-looking specimens of early modern humans were extracted from Middle Paleolithic levels that were heavily brecciated (i.e., mineralized into a concrete-like hardness). In describing the Tabun and Skhul fossils McCown and Keith (1939) grouped them together as a single fossil sample. Although they recognized that there were differences between the more "paleoanthropic" (Neandertal-like) Tabun fossils and the more "neoanthropic" (modern human-like) Skhul fossils, combining these samples seemed justified by several factors. The most important of these was Garrod's argument for the chronostratigraphic equivalence of Skhul Level B and Tabun Level C. But, it was also the case that some of the Skhul fossils exhibited primitive morphologies reminiscent of those seen among Neandertals. In the end, McCown and Keith interpreted the Tabun and Skhul fossils as a single population in the throes of an evolutionary transition.

In emphasizing variability within the "Mount Carmel Man" population, McCown and Keith anticipated interpretive trends that would not become common in paleoanthropology until after the 1950's "New Synthesis" in evolutionary biology. Other paleoanthropologists treated the Mount Carmel fossils as either a combination of separate Neandertal and early modern human samples or as the products of hybridization between Neandertals and early modern humans (e.g., Hooton 1946). As additional Neandertal and early modern human fossils were discovered during the 1950s and 1960s, McCown and Keith's views were more broadly adopted. By the 1960s, the Middle Paleolithic humans of southwest Asia were increasingly accepted as a population evolving from Neandertal ancestors into early modern humans (Howell 1959). The Middle Paleolithic archaeological record of the Levant was seen as documenting Neandertals' behavioral transformation into anatomically and behaviorally modern humans (Binford 1968; Jelinek 1982; Marks 1988).

Because the Middle Paleolithic in the Levant was largely beyond the effective range of radiocarbon dating, the weak point of this evolutionary model was its chronology. Until recently, most researchers supported a "short" chronology for the Middle Paleolithic. This chronology placed the origins of the Middle Paleolithic around 80,000–90,000 B.P., and postulated a Neandertal–modern human transition by around 40,000–50,000 B.P. (Farrand 1979; Jelinek 1982:99).

It was not until refinements of thermoluminescence (TL), electron-spin resonance (ESR), and uranium-series dating in the mid-1980s that the short chronology could be tested. The first application of TL dating to Neandertal contexts at Kebara Cave produced results congruent with the short chronology, 47,000–65,000 B.P. (Valladas et al. 1987). However, TL dates for the early modern human contexts at Qafzeh (Levels XVII–XXIV) averaged a surprising 92,500 B.P. (Valladas et al. 1988). These dates reversed the long-assumed chronological relationship between the Levantine Neandertal and early modern human fossils in the Levant. Further TL and ESR dating established that Skhul, too, was vastly older than expected, 80,000–130,000 B.P. (Mercier et al. 1993), while the Amud Neandertals were relatively recent, ca. 50,000–70,000 (Valladas et al. 1999). The inferred age of the Tabun fossils remains unclear owing to uncertainties about the stratigraphic provenance of these fossils within the complex stratigraphy of Tabun Cave (Bar-Yosef and Callendar 1999). A second set of problems concerns markedly divergent results of TL, ESR, and U-Series dating for Tabun (Grün et al. 1991; McDermott et al. 1993; Mercier et al. 1995; Grün and Stringer 2000). Nevertheless, at the very least, these new dates overturn any model in which Levantine Neandertals can be the ancestors of the Skhul/Qafzeh humans.

Human Demographic Discontinuity in the Pleistocene Levant

The complicated pattern of alternations between Neandertal and early modern human occupations of the Levantine caves revealed by the new "long chronology" raises questions about the assumption of human demographic continuity during the Middle Paleolithic period.

Paleoanthropologists routinely assume continuity between human fossil samples separated by thousands of kilometers and hundreds of millennia. This is a reasonable accommodation to small sample sizes and a patchy fossil record, but it also involves a tacit assumption that extinction is a rare occurrence among humans (Brace 1964). Our large population size, broad geographic distribution, and technological adaptations insulate recent humans from many of the forces that push other large mammals to extinction. However, we cannot necessarily extend these qualities to smaller, isolated, and non-agricultural Pleistocene societies. A wide variety of circumstances can force large terrestrial mammals with slow reproductive rates, like humans, below their minimum viable population size and into conditions from which demographic recovery is impossible (Gilpin and Soulé 1986). It seems reasonable to suspect that many human fossil samples are undoubtedly evolutionary "dead ends" and that human evolution in any particular region should have been marked by recurring demographic discontinuities. Assessing the risk of human population extinction requires knowledge about their distribution, size, and degree of geographic isolation.

The distribution of Middle Paleolithic sites within the Levant suggests that the core area of human settlement was the Mediterranean oak-pistachio woodland and its ecotone with the *Artemisia* steppe (Horowitz 1987). This association with the Mediterranean woodland is not arbitrary. Mediterranean woodlands contain more edible plant, small animal, and large game species per unit area than any other major ecozone in Western Eurasia (Blondel and Aronson 1999). The size of this core area undoubtedly varied widely through time. The highly restricted present-day distribution of woodland, roughly 80,000 sq. km provides a reasonable minimum estimate, while the polygon enclosing all known Middle Paleolithic sites in Lebanon, Syria, Jordan, and Israel provides a maximum estimate of 120,000 sq. km. This tight settlement focus on the Mediterranean woodland is an important way in which the Levantine Middle Paleolithic differs from the Upper Paleolithic and Epipaleolithic periods. It suggests that the size of Middle Paleolithic human populations was probably closely correlated with climate change and variability.

The Levant is not a large region, and the pre-agricultural populations of this ecozone can never have been very numerous. One can derive an estimate of overall Middle Paleolithic population size in the Levant from the population density figures for recent human hunter-gatherers living in broadly comparable temperate woodland habitats. Using Binford's (2001: 152) figure of eight persons per 100 sq. km yields a projected regional population of 6,400–9,600. These numbers are larger than Wobst's (1976) minimum viable human population of 475 individuals, but they are almost certainly an overestimate. Even though estimates of Neandertals' energy requirements are within the range of those for living humans (Sorenson and Leonard 2001), numerous zooarchaeological studies suggest Middle Paleolithic humans were less effective at collecting smaller game than recent human hunter-gatherers (Klein 1998; Stiner et al. 1999). If both these inferences are correct, then it seems reasonable to infer that Middle Paleolithic population densities were much lower than those of the recent human hunter-gatherers. These populations' risk of encountering minimum viable population thresholds would therefore have been significantly higher, particularly if they were isolated from other human populations.

The Levant is often described as a biogeographic "corridor," but during the Late Pleistocene it was often an island of woodland bounded by sea, desert, and mountains. Episodically, the coastal woodlands would have been isolated from southern latitudes by the northward expansion of those steppe and desert ecozones during warmer periods and the southward movement of montane vegetation during colder periods (Weinstein-Evron 1990). Southwest Asian steppe and desert habitats appear to have been settlement frontiers for Middle Paleolithic humans. The Lisan Lake, which filled the southern and central Jordan Rift Valley, would have separated human populations living in the coastal hill country of the southern Levant from those on the Transjordan Plateau for much of the Middle Paleolithic period (Malchus et al. 2000). To the south, the Nile Delta appears to have been a formidable barrier to faunal dispersals (Tchernov 1998:78–79).

Settlement pattern evidence, comparative demographic data from ethnographic hunter-gatherers, and paleoclimatic evidence support a model of Levantine Middle Paleolithic human populations numbering less than 10,000 people living along the Mediterranean coast and adjacent hill country. Large mammals with slow reproductive rates that are isolated in small populations living in circumscribed refugia are at an intrinsically higher risk of extinction than populations distributed over broader areas and more ecologically-diversified habitats (MacArthur and Wilson 1967). These risks of extinction would be compounded further if the population in question consisted of more than one distinct species (Gilpin and Soulé 1986). These basic ecogeographic considerations suggest reasons to question the popular assumption of human demographic continuity in the Middle Paleolithic Levant. In fact, a critical examination reveals problems with the human fossil and archaeological evidence that is often cited in support of continuity hypotheses.

The sample of relatively complete human fossils from the Levant is small. There are seven adult early modern humans from Skhul and Qafzeh and three adult Neandertals from Tabun, Kebara, and Amud. The seven adults and two juvenile Neandertals from Shanidar Cave, Iraq (Trinkaus 1984) are sometimes included in discussions of the Levantine fossil record. Several recent studies of these fossils' cranial and postcranial morphology have interpreted the absence of a clear morphological break between early modern human and Neandertal samples as evidence for gene flow and demographic continuity among Levantine Middle Paleolithic human populations (Wolpoff 1996; Simmons 1999; Kramer et al. 2001).

One of the problems with inferring gene flow from morphological similarities is that different species may share many features with each other because they have a recent common ancestor. Some morphological similarities between Neandertals and the Skhul/Qafzeh humans are ones shared broadly among Middle Pleistocene humans. Analysis of DNA from Neandertal fossils suggests their last common ancestor with living humans lived ca. 500,000 B.P. (Höss 2000). The unique morphological similarities between the Skhul/Qafzeh humans and the Levantine Neandertals may reflect these populations' having a common ancestor who lived more recently than 500,000 B.P. Unfortunately, no DNA has been successfully recovered from either the Levantine Neandertals or the Skhul/Qafzeh humans. Thus, we cannot directly estimate the antiquity of these fossils' last common ancestor. Nor can we test the hypothesis that the Skhul/Qafzeh humans are ancestral to human populations who lived in the Levant after 80,000 B.P. Even though they are frequently referred to as "early modern humans" or "Proto-Cromagnons," there is no direct genetic evidence that the Skhul/Qafzeh humans are ancestral to any subsequent human population. They may be an evolutionary "dead end." If so, then treating the Skhul/Qafzeh humans as ancestors of modern humans may lead to erroneous conclusions about the larger pattern of Neandertal–modern human evolutionary relationships.

Homoplasy is a second problem for continuity arguments based on the human fossil record. Homoplasy refers to morphological similarities resulting from convergent evolution among different species (i.e., similarities not shared with their last common ancestor). There are many possible mechanisms by which such similarities could arise among different human populations. Probably the best documented of these are Bergmann's and Allen's rules (the tendencies for mammals living in colder climates to evolve larger bodies and shorter appendages than their tropical counterparts). Inter-species competition for the same niche can also lead to "convergent character displacement" in morphological structures, particularly those related to food acquisition (Grant 1972). That Levantine Neandertals have essentially the same brachial index (the length of forearm relative to length of upper arm) as the Skhul/Qafzeh humans (Trinkaus 1984:269) and yet a markedly different one from European Neandertals may be evidence of such convergent evolution.

Viewed in isolation, morphological similarities between the Levantine Neandertal and Skhul/Qafzeh human fossils may seem compelling evidence for demographic continuity. But such arguments need to be contrasted with the numerous studies suggesting many behavioral differences between these fossil samples. These differences include habitual levels of exertion (Trinkaus et al. 1998; Pearson 2000), gripping positions and patterns of object manipulation (Churchill and Trinkaus 1990; Niewoehner 2001), degrees of social buffering of environmental stresses (Berger and Trinkaus 1995), locomotor patterns (Trinkaus 1992; Rak 1990), and adaptations to temperature regimes (Holliday 2000). The scale of these and other morphological differences between Neandertals and early modern humans is greater than that between interbreeding primate species (Schillaci and Froehlich 2001). That these differences persist in the Levant, western Asia, and Europe for tens of thousands of years suggests they have strong genetic components reinforced by reproductive isolation. We may never know if the Neandertals and early modern humans were truly different species, but these morphological differences seem ample justification for maintaining a taxonomic distinction between them (Schwartz 1999).

The argument that Neandertal and early modern human association with the same Levantine Mousterian industry is proof of demographic continuity (Wolpoff 1989:136; Clark 1992:194) reflects a questionable equation of Paleolithic industries and archaeologically-defined cultures. There is a crucial difference between these archaeological entities. Lower and Middle Paleolithic industries are defined wholly on the basis of lithic technology and typology. Archaeological cultures take lithic variation into account, but they also usually encompass variation in complementary lines of evidence, such as pottery, architecture, and mortuary rituals. Because lithic industries are based on fewer lines of evidence, it is possible that two independent populations facing similar needs for stone tools could independently create superficially similar lithic assemblages.

Traditionally, archaeologists seek information about the social affinities of prehistoric humans in patterns of morphological variation in artifact designs, or style. The search for stylistic variation in stone tools usually focuses on heavily modified tool types and complex technological processes, among which independent duplication of the same designs or procedures is less likely (Sackett 1982). Unfortunately, the Levantine Mousterian lacks many of the heavily modified artifact-types that are found in North African and West Asian Middle Paleolithic assemblages (e.g., foliate bifaces, handaxes, steep-edged scrapers). The scrapers, notches, den-

Table 7.1 Correlation of hominid fossils and core reduction strategies

	Qafzeh XVII–XXIV	Kebara levels IX–XII	Amud level B
Human remains	Early modern humans (Vandermeersch 1981)	Neandertals (Bar-Yosef et al. 1992)	Neandertals (Hovers et al. 1995)
Predominant core preparation strategy	radial/centripetal (Boutié 1989)	unidirectional-convergent (Meignen and Bar-Yosef 1992)	unidirectional-convergent (Hovers 1998)

ticulates, and other retouched tools in Levantine Mousterian assemblages are so minimally modified that they do not contain sufficient "imposed design" to tell archaeologists much about the cultural affinities of the human populations who made them.

Analysis of technological processes (*chaînes opératoires*) has recently augmented the more traditional object-oriented search for stylistic variation in the Levantine Mousterian (Meignen 1995). Levallois core reduction strategies are the most technologically complex aspect of Levantine Mousterian stone industry. Ancient flintknappers' choices among the range of possible core reduction strategies can be inferred from the orientation of dorsal scar patterns on Levallois flakes. Theoretically, these strategies are functionally equivalent. A competent flintknapper can use any one of them to obtain flakes of a desired size and shape. Flintknapping skills were probably acquired through imitative learning in much the same way as analogous skills are learned both by humans and by non-human primates (Byrne 2001). Accordingly, one would expect members of the same stone-tool-making population to exhibit similar choices among alternative core reduction strategies (Lemmonier 1992:1–2). In fact, at those three sites where core reduction strategies have been studied in detail (Qafzeh, Kebara, and Amud), early modern humans and Neandertals appear to have systematically chosen to use different core reduction strategies (see table 7.1). A radial/centripetal core reduction strategy dominates the Qafzeh XVII–XXIV assemblages (Boutié 1989), while an alternative, unidirectional-convergent, core reduction strategy dominates the assemblages from Kebara (Levels IX–XII) and Amud (Level B) (Meignen and Bar-Yosef 1992; Hovers 1998) (figure 7.3). These contrasting lithic *chaînes opératoires* are difficult to explain if early modern humans and Neandertals shared the same cultural identity.

Taken at face value, both the human fossil record and the lithic archaeological evidence are consistent with the hypothesis of human demographic discontinuity. Neandertals and early modern humans appear to have occupied the Levant separately, each occupying essentially the same ecological niche when they were present in the region.

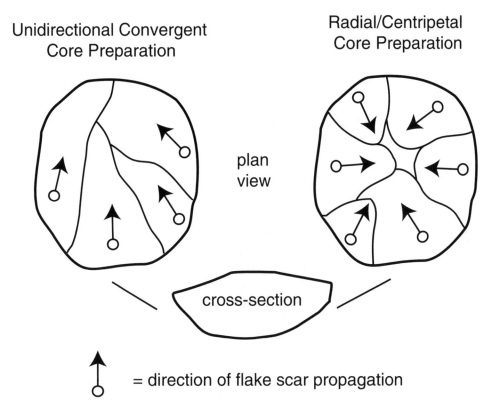

Figure 7.3 Contrasting unidirectional-convergent and radial/centripetal core preparation strategies. Either method can be used to create the same shape of flake (author's original)

An organism's niche is defined by the physical space it occupies, the resources it consumes, and its competitors for space and resources. In terms of these variables, Levantine Neandertals and the Skhul/Qafzeh humans had very similar niches. Sites containing Neandertal remains are somewhat more broadly distributed than finds of early modern humans, but both kinds of sites are most densely concentrated in the Mediterranean woodland "core area" of northern Israel, Lebanon, and western Syria. Stable isotope (Sr/Ca) evidence suggests similar Neandertal and early modern human diets contained similar proportions of plant and animal food sources (Schoeninger 1982). Both humans and Neandertals appear to have been about equally effective at competing with the larger Levantine carnivores (i.e., lion, leopard, wolf, crocuta, and hyena) for the carcasses of large mammals. Their faunal assemblages are dominated by the same small territorial species, such as gazelle, fallow deer, roe deer, ibex, and boar. Large migratory species, such as wild cattle, hartebeest, horse, zebra, and onager, are relatively rare (except at Skhul, where archaeological recovery techniques bias the sample) (Bar-Yosef 2000:120–121; Shea 2001a:Table 5).

Middle Paleolithic Human Strategic Variability

It is reasonable to expect different human species sharing a (geologically) recent last common ancestor to occupy similar niches in the Levant. However, if we accept the hypothesis that Neandertals and early modern humans migrated into the Levant from different continents, it would be surprising if the behavioral strategies they used to occupy this niche were also identical. At present, there is affirmative evidence for differences in Neandertals' and early modern humans' technological organization and seasonal mobility strategies. There is also plausible, if somewhat less conclusive, evidence for differences in symbolic behavior.

The term "technological organization" refers to the ways in which material culture is influenced by structural aspects (e.g., time-budgeting, frequency, risk) of human activities involving tool use (Torrence 1989). Stone spear point production appears to be one area in which Neandertal and early modern human technological strategies differ from each other. Most Levantine Mousterian assemblages contain thin and symmetric triangular flakes, or "Levallois points." Microwear analysis and morphometric comparisons with ethnographic hunting weapons suggest these triangular flakes were designed for use as spear points (Shea 1988). Recent human hunting populations who use spear points like those found in the Levantine Mousterian, do so primarily in the context of ambush or "intercept" hunting, predatory forays that are restricted in space and time and targeted on a specific kind of prey. Typically, such points are armatures for dispatch weapons (tools for killing an already immobilized animal) (Churchill 1993; Ellis 1997). Evidence consistent with such use of stone points during the Levantine Mousterian has been discovered at Umm el Tlel (Syria), where a fragmentary Levallois point is embedded in the cervical vertebra of an equid (Boëda et al. 1999).

The lithic assemblages associated with Levantine Neandertals contain far more Levallois points than those associated with the Skhul/Qafzeh humans (Shea 1998). The elevated levels of point production associated with Neandertals could suggest their hunting strategies placed greater emphasis on intercept hunting than those of early modern humans living in a similar environment (Shea 1998:S58–59). Analysis of the large mammal remains from Kebara confirms a pattern of ambush/intercept hunting by Neandertals (Speth and Tchernov 1998). Unfortunately, biased recovery at Skhul (Garrod and Bate 1937:94) and poor preservation at Qafzeh (Rabinovich and Tchernov 1995) make it difficult to evaluate early modern human hunting strategies with the zooarchaeological evidence.

Like most Mediterranean climates, the Levant experienced seasonal variation in rainfall, and therefore predictable shifts in the abundance and distribution of plant and animal food sources. Most human hunter-gatherers cope with seasonal resource fluctuations by a strategy of seasonal mobility, that is, by moving their residential sites between foraging patches with complementary sets of resources. Seasonality data suggest that while Neandertals and early modern humans used caves for similar purposes, they integrated these sites into their land-use strategies in different ways.

Cementum increments are among the most reliable seasonal indicators present in mammal remains (Lieberman 1994). Cementum is a continuously growing tissue that secures teeth in the mandibular corpus. Among ungulates whose diets shift from hard dry foods in the summer to soft wet foods in the winter (most bovids and cervids), seasonal variation in diet creates a pattern of alternating opaque and translucent cementum increments. The outermost of these increments provides an estimate of the season in which an animal died. Originally, these seasonal estimates were only able to identify either "dry" or "wet" seasons (i.e., summer vs. winter), but refinements of the method now allow increased precision (Lieberman 1998). Cementum increments from Skhul and those levels of Qafzeh associated with early modern humans preserve evidence for Winter/Spring and Fall occupations (respectively). Samples associated with Neandertal remains at Kebara and Tabun, in contrast, preserve evidence for multiseasonal occupation. It is not clear if this multiseasonal pattern results from numerous short-term occupations through-out the year or a prolonged and continuous occupation. Of these two scenarios, a series of short-term occupations is more likely. Few modern hunter-gatherer groups who live in the Temperate Zone remain at or near the same site throughout the year, except for those who depend heavily on marine resources (Kelly 1995:125).

This interpretation is consistent with a model of European Neandertal social organization and mobility strategies recently proposed by Gamble (1999:265–267). This model proposes that Neandertals did not move across the landscape as recent human hunter-gatherers do, as cohesive multifamily groups linked together in regional alliance networks. Rather, Gamble proposes that Neandertals made rela-tively short-distance movements, primarily as individuals, and that they formed coresident groups and effective social networks on a temporary, ad hoc, basis. In this model, multiseasonal occupations like those seen at Kebara and Tabun would reflect numerous short-term occupations of small groups and individuals taking advantage of these caves' sheltering properties and their proximity to habitual path-ways across the landscape. If Gamble's hypothesis about European Neandertal mobility strategies is correct, it may be significant that Levantine Neandertals also appear to be practicing this same mobility strategy, and not the seasonal mobility strategy of the Skhul/Qafzeh humans. This suggests that the organization of Nean-dertal society was fundamentally different from those of both the Skhul/Qafzeh humans and recent hunter-gatherers.

Subsistence and settlement pattern evidence suggests that Neandertals and the Skhul/Qafzeh humans occupied similar, or even identical, niches in the Levantine biological community. Neandertals and early modern humans seem to have adapted to this niche by employing different strategies of technological organization, and seasonal mobility. There probably were other adaptive differences, but these are the ones that have been detected so far. These strategic differences are subtle. They probably do not result from vast differences in cognitive abilities, so much as they do from differences in the energetic costs and benefits influencing each population's choice of strategies for coping with a particular set of challenges.

Neandertal–Early Modern Human Evolutionary Relationships

There is no direct evidence that Neandertals and early modern humans ever encountered each other in the Levant. Nevertheless, the region is so small and the Middle Paleolithic so long that most researchers take it for granted that such encounters must have occurred. What happened when Neandertals and early modern humans met? The principal hypotheses about Neandertal–early modern human coevolutionary relationships between 47,000–130,000 B.P. involve vicarism, niche partitioning, assimilation, and competitive exclusion.

Vicarism involves the geographic and chronological separation of two or more closely related populations (typically different species or subspecies). Vicarious taxa are ecologically redundant with each other, and their distribution across the landscape varies with distribution of the particular habitats to which each is best adapted. Rak (1993) has suggested such a vicarious relationship between Neandertals and early modern humans. He proposes that early modern humans inhabited the Levant during warmer phases, when the region was more closely linked to North Africa, and Neandertals inhabited the region when colder European climates prevailed. Each population either migrated out of the region or became extinct as the regional climate changed. The vicarism hypothesis is consistent with most of the geochronological evidence (Bar-Yosef 1998) and mammal biostratigraphic data (Tchernov 1998). The principal evidence against this hypothesis is that some radiometric dates suggest possible overlap between the ages of the Skhul fossils and some of the Levantine Neandertals (McDermott et al. 1993; Grün and Stringer 2000). Because these dates depend on accurately inferring the history of sample radiation dosage, which can introduce errors into comparisons involving different sites, they do not conclusively refute the vicarism hypothesis.

Niche partitioning involves two or more species altering their behavior so that neither competes with the other for the same suite of resources. Henry (1995:132) has proposed such a model, suggesting that early modern humans may have developed specialized adaptations to steppe habitats in the interior and southern Levant while Neandertals occupied the coastal woodlands. As noted earlier, the absence of human fossil remains from the southern and interior parts of the Levant makes this hypothesis difficult to test. However, the overall similarity of the large mammal assemblages from all Neandertal and early modern humans sites argues against significant or long-term niche partitioning by these humans (Rabinovich and Tchernov 1995).

Assimilation involves two populations interbreeding and forming a hybrid population between their "parent" populations. Several researchers have proposed this model for the Levant, based either on morphological similarities among the Levantine Neandertal and Skhul/Qafzeh fossil samples (Arensburg and Belfer-Cohen 1998; Simmons 1999; Kramer et al. 2001) or their archaeological associations (Kaufman 1999), or some combination of both (Clark 1992). It is not yet clear from fossil DNA evidence if there were genetic obstacles to hybridization between Neandertals and early modern humans (Schwartz 1999). That the archaeologically detectable behavioral differences between Levantine Neandertals and the Skhul/Qafzeh humans are broadly comparable in scale to behavioral differences among recent human hunter-gatherers living in similar habitats (e.g., Milton 1991; Kelly 1995; Binford 2001) suggests no obvious behavioral obstacle to such interbreeding. Nevertheless, the fact that hybrid offspring of closely related species can be sterile poses an additional obstacle for testing the assimilation hypothesis. To assess the long-term evolutionary significance of such hybridization, one would have to track specific genes from parent populations, through hybrids, and into subsequent generations. While most paleoanthropologists consider Neandertal–early modern human interbreeding a theoretical possibility, the consensus is that it has not been conclusively demonstrated (Tattersall and Schwartz 1999).

Competitive exclusion involves a population altering its ecological strategies in such a way as to earn a net reproductive gain at the expense of a rival population. Often invoked to explain Neandertals' extinction and the spread of the Upper Paleolithic to Europe, it has less often been invoked for the fate of the Skhul/Qafzeh humans around 65,000–80,000 B.P. (Shea 2001b:29). Between 47,000–65,000 B.P., more or less coincidental with the first major cold phase of the Last Glaciation, only Neandertal fossils are known from Levantine sites. Archaeological residues associated with these Neandertal fossils indicate a novel adaptive strategy combining an emphasis on intercept hunting of large game with multiseasonal occupation of the coastal cave sites. These behavioral patterns are thus far known only from the Levant, and only in association with Neandertals, which is what one would expect if they first emerged in the context of competition with early modern humans. Nothing in the paleoanthropological record conclusively refutes the competition hypothesis, but it does assume that our current knowledge about Levantine Neandertal and early modern human behavior adequately encapsulates the full range of their strategic variability.

Which of these scenarios of Neandertal–early modern human coevolutionary relationships is most likely correct? The niche partitioning and assimilation hypotheses both require assumptions about the evidence that are not in and of themselves independently verifiable. These assumptions include such seemingly irresoluble issues as the identities of toolmakers at sites without fossils, the possibility of Neandertal–early modern human interbreeding, the genetic basis for specific morphological similarities among human fossils, and the "cultural" nature of lithic industrial variability. While they are not parsimonious, the niche partitioning and assimilation hypotheses are not demonstrably wrong. The hypotheses of vicariance and competitive exclusion both fit well with Middle Paleolithic chronological and stratigraphic evidence. The sticking point between them is whether Neandertals and early modern humans were ever in the Levant at the same time. Geographic circumscription may have intensified competition between Neandertals and early modern humans to the point where any episodes of sympatry (both hominids being present in the same area at the same time) were so brief as to be archaeologically invisible. It is not clear if this issue can be resolved with the present array of sites and geochronometric techniques. The standard errors of TL, ESR, and U-Series dates from the Middle Paleolithic are so large that one could obtain "identical" dates for sites separated by thousands, or even tens of thousands of years.

Conclusion

In discussing models of human demographic continuity in the Middle Paleolithic Levant, this essay has brought to the foreground two issues that have been given short shrift in recent discussions of modern human origins. These issues are extinction and competition. Each is vitally important, not only for understanding human population dynamics in the Middle Paleolithic Levant, but also for understanding recent developments in human evolution as well.

Extinction stalks every species, including modern humans. Our large population size and our technological achievements insulate us from all but the most extreme extinction-causing events. Earlier human populations were buffered from extinction to varying degrees by their technological adaptations and social institutions, but it is probably a mistake to project any sort of "extinction immunity" to Pleistocene humans, including the Skhul/Qafzeh humans and the Levantine Neandertals. Both lived in small groups during periods when rapid climate change caused dramatic short-term changes in their habitats. Decades of middle-range research in conservation biology have identified small group size and rapid climate change as factors that elevate the risk of extinction among large mammals with slow reproductive rates. The common assumption of demographic continuity among Pleistocene human fossils flies in the face of what we have learned about extinction from firsthand observation. Countless human populations must have become extinct, and it is possible, indeed likely that both the Levantine Neandertals and the Skhul/Qafzeh humans are among these evolutionary "dead ends." The sentimental need (or narrative necessity, see Landau [1991]) to identify a "winner" among the evolutionary players in the Levant makes it difficult for us to accept the non-ancestral status of these fossils, but the Levant is a tough neighborhood. It is a region in which many species have been weighed and found wanting.

How do these considerations alter our understanding of the Middle Paleolithic of the Levant? The hypothesis that early modern humans were not successful in their first attempt to adapt to the Levant and adjacent parts of Europe and western Asia refocuses our attention on the differences between the Middle Paleolithic Upper Paleolithic modern human adaptations as clues to later humans' adaptive radiation. The Levant contains the oldest evidence for an indigenous transition to Upper Paleolithic adaptations (Bar-Yosef 2000). This is probably no accident. The presence of well-entrenched Neandertal populations in the Levant, effectively blocking the major land route out of Africa, may have been a major stimulus to the development of Upper Paleolithic adaptations by modern humans along the Northeast African "frontier." The first post-Middle Paleolithic modern human occupations of Eurasia, Australia, and the Americas all contain evidence for two novel behaviors, the use of high-speed/low mass projectile weapons and the establishment of extensive alliance/exchange networks reinforced by symbolic material culture.

The former suggest a devastating capability to attack a wide range of prey whose legacy can be seen in large mammal extinctions throughout these newly-colonized lands. The latter suggest a high degree of integration between language and material culture (in effect, exosomatic information storage) for which there is little or no prior evidence in human evolution. Most paleoanthropologists believe Neandertals possessed some form of spoken language (Schepartz 1993); but it is not clear that they were able to extend their linguistic abilities to exosomatic media in the same way as modern humans have done since early Upper Paleolithic times. As Wobst (1977) has noted, the principal advantage of investing symbolic meaning in material culture is that it encourages cooperation and altruism among individuals who would otherwise be divided from each other by kinship or linguistic differences.

One of the key differences between Neandertals and early Upper Paleolithic modern humans may lie not so much in possessing spoken language, but rather in modern humans' novel ability to invest meaning in material culture, and thereby to forge extensive alliance networks among otherwise small, isolated populations. It may be difficult for us to imagine living in a society in which material culture is not a medium for symbolic information. Yet, it appears that early modern humans and Neandertals lived this way for tens of thousands of years. In contrast, it is relatively easy to imagine how individuals living in such a society would be at an immediate and disproportionate evolutionary disadvantage in competition against individuals who belonged to such extensive social networks.

The appearance of these novel Upper Paleolithic adaptations marks a major change in modern humans' ability to displace rival human species. Throughout Western Eurasia, the appearance of modern humans together with Upper Paleolithic material culture precedes Neandertal extinction by only a few thousand years (Pettit 1999). Even in those parts of Western Europe where Neandertals adopted elements of Upper Paleolithic adaptations, doing so seems only to have bought them relatively little time and no detectable increase in their geographic range (Zilhao and d'Errico 1999). Those few instances in which Neandertal remains are associated with evidence for Upper Paleolithic behavior, such as the Chatelperronian, Uluzzian, Bachokirian "cultures," cluster both in space and in time. Spatially, they are located in southern Europe, which is, historically, a biogeographic refuge for Palearctic mammals. These are the places where one finds the last living representatives of populations dwindling to extinction. These symbolic behaviors also cluster chronologically in the millennia immediately preceding the last appearances of Neandertals in each region. Perhaps these were cases of "too little, too late," last desperate attempts by Neandertals to stave off extinction by adopting strategies analogous to their major ecological and evolutionary rivals. Unless there was some demographic catastrophe among European Neandertal populations that has left neither archaeological nor fossil evidence, the principal cause of Neandertal extinction appears likely to have been a change in modern human behavior. The most likely context for such a change is in the contest between Neandertals and early modern humans for the human niche in the Middle Paleolithic Levant.

Acknowledgments

I thank Curtis Marean, Daniel Kaufman, Patricia Crawford, and Yin Lam for their comments on earlier drafts of this paper. I alone am responsible for the views expressed here.

REFERENCES

Arensburg, Baruch, and Anna Belfer-Cohen, 1998 Sapiens and Neandertals: Rethinking the Levantine Middle Paleolithic Hominids. *In* Neandertals and Modern Humans in Western Asia. Takeru Akazawa, Kenichi Aoki, and Ofer Bar-Yosef, eds. pp. 311–322. New York: Plenum.

Bar-Yosef, Ofer, 1998 The Chronology of the Middle Paleolithic of the Levant. *In* Neandertals and Modern Humans in Western Asia. Takeru Akazawa, Kenichi Aoki, and Ofer Bar-Yosef, eds. pp. 39–56. New York: Plenum.

Bar-Yosef, Ofer, 2000 The Middle and Early Upper Paleolithic in Southwest Asia and Neighboring Regions. *In* The Geography of Neandertals and Modern Humans in Europe and the Greater Mediterranean. Ofer Bar-Yosef and David Pilbeam, eds. pp. 107–156. Cambridge, MA: Peabody Museum of Archaeology and Ethnology, Bulletin No. 8.

Bar-Yosef, Ofer, and Jane Callendar, 1999 The Woman from Tabun: Garrod's Doubts in Historical Perspective. Journal of Human Evolution 37:879–885.

Bar-Yosef, Ofer, Bernard Vandermeersch, Baruch Arensburg, Anna Belfer-Cohen, Paul Goldberg, Henri Laville, Liliane Meignen, Yoel Rak, John Speth, Eitan Tchernov, Anne-Marie Tillier, and Steve Weiner, 1992 The Excavations in Kebara Cave, Mt. Carmel. Current Anthropology 33:497–550.

Berger, Thomas, and Erik Trinkaus, 1995 Patterns of Trauma among the Neandertals. Journal of Archaeological Science 22:841–852.

Binford, Lewis, 2001 Constructing Frames of Reference: An Analytical Method for Archaeological Theory Building Using Hunter-Gatherer and Environmental Data Sets. Berkeley: University of California Press.

Binford, Sally, 1968 Early Upper Pleistocene Adaptations in the Levant. American Anthropologist 70:707–717.

Blondel, Jacques, and James Aronson, 1999 Biology and Wildlife of the Mediterranean Region. New York: Oxford University Press.

Boëda, Eric, J. Geneste, C. Griggo, N. Mercier, S. Muhesen, J. Reyss, A. Taha, and H. Valladas, 1999 A Levallois Point Embedded in the Vertebra of a Wild Ass (*Equus africanus*): Hafting, Projectiles and Mousterian Hunting Weapons. Antiquity 73:394–402.

Boutié, Paul, 1989 Étude technologique de l'industrie moustérienne de la grotte de Qafzeh (près de Nazareth, Israël). *In* Investigations in South Levantine Prehistory/Préhistoire du Sud-Levant. Ofer Bar-Yosef and Bernard Vandermeersch, eds. pp. 213–230. Oxford: British Archaeological Reports.

Brace, C. Loring, 1964 The Fate of the "Classic" Neandertals: A Consideration of Hominid Catastrophism. Current Anthropology 5:3–43.

Byrne, Richard, 2001 Social and Technical Forms of Primate Intelligence. *In* Tree of Origin: What Primate Behavior Can Tell Us about Human Social Evolution. Frans de Waal, ed. pp. 145–172. Cambridge, MA: Harvard University Press.

Churchill, Steven, 1993 Weapon Technology, Prey Size Selection, and Hunting Methods in Modern Hunter-gatherers: Implications for Hunting in the Palaeolithic and Mesolithic. *In* Hunting and Animal Exploitation in the Later Paleolithic and Mesolithic of Eurasia. Gail Peterkin, Harvey Bricker, and Paul Mellars, eds. pp. 11–24. Washington: American Anthropological Association.

Churchill, Steven, and Fred Smith, 2000 Makers of the Early Aurignacian of Europe. Yearbook of Physical Anthropology 43:61–115.

Churchill, Steven, and Erik Trinkaus, 1990 Neandertal Scapular Glenoid Morphology. American Journal of Physical Anthropology 83:147–160.

Clark, Geoffrey, 1992 Continuity or Replacement? Putting Modern Humans in an Evolutionary Context. *In* The Middle Paleolithic: Adaptation, Behavior and Variability. Harold Dibble and Paul Mellars, eds. pp. 183–206. Philadelphia: University of Pennsylvania Museum Press.

Ellis, Christopher, 1997 Factors Influencing the Use of Stone Projectile Tips: An Ethnographic Perspective. *In* Projectile Technology. Heidi Knecht, ed. pp. 37–78. New York: Plenum.

Farrand, William, 1979 Chronology and Paleoenvironment of Levantine Prehistoric Sites as Seen from Sediment Studies. Journal of Archaeological Science 6:369–392.

Gamble, Clive, 1999 The Palaeolithic Societies of Europe. New York: Cambridge University Press.

Garrod, Dorothy, and Dorothea Bate, eds., 1937 The Stone Age of Mount Carmel, vol. 1. Excavations in the Wady el-Mughara. Oxford: Clarendon Press.

Gilpin, Michael, and Michael Soulé, 1986 Minimim Viable Populations: Processes of Species Extinction. *In* Conservation Biology: The Science of Scarcity and Diversity. Michael Soulé, ed. pp. 19–34. Sunderland, MA: Sinauer Associates.

Grant, P., 1972 Convergent and Divergent Character Displacement. Biological Journal of the Linnaean Society 4:39–68.

Grün, Rainer, and Christopher Stringer, 2000 Tabun Revisited: Revised ESR Chronology and New ESR and U-series Analyzes of Dental Material from Tabun C1. Journal of Human Evolution 39: 601–612.

Grün, Rainer, Christopher Stringer, and Henry Schwarcz, 1991 ESR Dating of Teeth from Garrod's Tabun Cave Collection. Journal of Human Evolution 20:231–248.

Henry, Donald, 1995 Late Levantine Mousterian Patterns of Adaptation and Cognition. *In* Prehistoric Cultural Ecology and Evolution: Insights from Southern Jordan. Donald Henry, ed. pp. 107–132. New York: Plenum.

Holliday, Trenton, 2000 Evolution at the Crossroads: Modern Human Emergence in Western Asia. American Anthropologist 102:54–68.

Hooton, Earnest, 1946 Up from the Ape. Revised Edition. New York: MacMillan & Co.

Horowitz, Aaron, 1987 Subsurface Palynostratigraphy and Paleoclimates of the Quaternary Jordan Rift Valley Fill, Israel. Israel Journal of Earth Sciences 36:31–44.

Höss, Matthias, 2000 Neanderthal Population Genetics. Nature 404:453–454.

Hovers, Erella, 1998 The Lithic Assemblages of Amud Cave: Implications for Understanding the End of the Mousterian in the Levant. *In* Neandertals and Modern Humans in Western Asia. Takeru Akazawa, Kenichi Aoki, and Ofer Bar-Yosef, eds. pp. 143–164. New York: Plenum.

Hovers, Erella, Yoel Rak, Ron Lavi, and William H. Kimbel, 1995 Hominid Remains from Amud Cave in the Context of the Levantine Middle Paleolithic. Paléorient 21(2):47–61.

Howell, F. Clark, 1959 Upper Pleistocene Stratigraphy and Early Man in the Levant. Proceedings of the American Philosophical Society 103:1–65.

Hublin, Jean-Jacques, 2000 Modern-nonmodern Hominid Interactions: A Mediterranean Perspective. *In* The Geography of Neandertals and Modern Humans in Europe and the Greater Mediterranean. Ofer Bar-Yosef and David Pilbeam, eds. pp. 157–182. Cambridge: Peabody Museum of Archaeology and Ethnology, Bulletin No. 8.

Jelinek, Arthur, 1982 The Middle Paleolithic in the Southern Levant with Comments on the Appearance of Modern *Homo sapiens*. *In* The Transition from Lower to Middle Paleolithic and the Origins of Modern Man. Avraham Ronen, ed. pp. 57–104. Oxford: British Archaeological Reports.

Kaufman, Daniel, 1999 Archaeological Perspectives on the Origins of Modern Humans: A View from the Levant. Westport, CT: Bergin & Garvey.

Kelly, Robert, 1995 The Foraging Spectrum: Diversity in Hunter-Gatherer Lifeways. Washington: Smithsonian Institution Press.

Klein, Richard, 1998 Why Anatomically Modern People did not Disperse from Africa 100,000 Years Ago. *In* Neandertals and Modern Humans in Western Asia. Takeru Akazawa, Kenichi Aoki, and Ofer Bar-Yosef, eds. pp. 509–522. New York: Plenum.

Klein, Richard, 1999 The Human Career. 2nd edition. Chicago: University of Chicago Press.

Kramer, Andrew, Tracey Crummett, and Milford Wolpoff, 2001 Out of Africa and into the Levant: Replacement or Admixture in Western Asia. Quaternary International 75:51–63.

Landau, Misia L., 1991 Narratives of Human Evolution. New Haven: Yale University Press.

Lemmonier, Pierre, 1992 Elements for an Anthropology of Technology. Ann Arbor: University of Michigan Museum of Anthropology Anthropological Paper, 88.

Lieberman, Daniel, 1994 The Biological Basis for Seasonal Increments in Dental Cementum and their Application to Archaeological Research. Journal of Archaeological Science 21:525–539.

Lieberman, Daniel, 1995 Testing Hypotheses about Recent Human Evolution from Skulls: Integrating Morphology, Function, Development, and Phylogeny. Current Anthropology 36:159–198.

Lieberman, Daniel, 1998 Neandertal and Early Modern Human Mobility Patterns: Comparing Archaeological and Anatomical Evidence. *In* Neandertals and Modern Humans in Western Asia. Takeru Akazawa, Kenichi Aoki, and Ofer Bar-Yosef, eds. pp. 263–276. New York: Plenum.

MacArthur, Robert, and Edward Wilson, 1967 The Theory of Island Biogeography. Princeton: Princeton University Press.

Malchus, Malka, Yehouda Enzel, Steven Goldstein, Shmuel Marco, and Mordechai Stein, 2000 Reconstructing Low Lake Levels of Lake Lisan by Correlating Fan-delta and Lacustrine Deposits. Quaternary International 73/74:137–144.

Marks, Anthony, 1988 The Middle to Upper Paleolithic Transition in the Southern Levant: Technological Change as an Adaptation to Increasing Mobility. In La Mutation, Janusz Kozlowski, ed. pp. 109–124. Liège: ERAUL Université de Liège.

McBrearty, Sally, and Alison Brooks, 2000 The Revolution that Wasn't: A New Interpretation of the Origin of Modern Human Behavior. Journal of Human Evolution 39:453–563.

McCown, Theodore, and Arthur Keith, 1939 The Stone Age of Mt. Carmel, vol. 2. The Fossil Human Remains from the Levalloiso-Mousterian. Oxford: Clarendon Press.

McDermott, F., Rainer Grün, Christopher Stringer, and C. Hawkesworth, 1993 Mass-spectrometric U-series Dates for Israeli Neanderthal/Early Modern Hominid Sites. Nature 363:252–255.

Meignen, Lilliane, 1995 Levallois Lithic Production Systems in the Middle Paleolithic of the Near East: The Case of the Unidirectional Method. *In* The Definition and Interpretation of Levallois Technology. Harold Dibble and Ofer Bar-Yosef, eds. pp. 361–380. Madison, WI: Prehistory Press.

Meignen, Lilliane, and Ofer Bar-Yosef, 1992 Middle Paleolithic Lithic Variability in Kebara Cave, Mount Carmel, Israel. *In* The Evolution and Dispersal of Modern Humans in Asia. Takeru Akazawa, Kenichi Aoki, and Tasuku Kimura, eds. pp. 129–148. Tokyo: Hokusen-sha.

Mellars, Paul, 1995 The Neanderthal Legacy: An Archaeological Perspective from Western Europe. Princeton: Princeton University Press.

Mercier, N., H. Valladas, Ofer Bar-Yosef, Bernard Vandermeersch, Christopher Stringer, and J. Joron, 1993 Thermoluminescence Date for the Mousterian Burial Site of Es Skhul, Mt. Carmel. Journal of Archaeological Science 20:169–174.

Mercier, N., H. Valladas, G. Valladas, and J. Reyss, 1995 TL dates of Burnt Flints from Jelinek's Excavations at Tabun and Their Implications. Journal of Archaeological Science 22:495–509.

Milton, Katherine, 1991 Comparative Aspects of Diet in Amazonian Forest-dwellers. Philosophical Transactions of the Royal Society of London, Section B 334:253–263.

Niewoehner, Wesley, 2001 Behavioral Inferences from the Skhul/Qafzeh Early Modern Human Hand Remains. Proceedings of the National Academy of Sciences 98: 2979–2984.

Pearson, Osbjorn, 2000 Activity, Climate, and Postcranial Robusticity: Implications for Modern Human Origins and Scenarios of Adaptive Change. Current Anthropology 41:569–608.

Pettit, Paul, 1999 Disappearing from the World: An Archaeological Perspective on Neanderthal Extinction. Oxford Journal of Archaeology 18:217–240.

Pilbeam, David, and Ofer Bar-Yosef, 2000 Afterword. *In* The Geography of Neandertals and Modern Humans in Europe and the Greater Mediterranean. Ofer Bar-Yosef and David Pilbeam, eds. pp. 183–188. Cambridge: Peabody Museum of Archaeology and Ethnology, Bulletin No. 8.

Rabinovich, Rivka, and Eitan Tchernov, 1995 Chronological, Paleoecological, and Taphonomical Aspects of the Middle Paleolithic Site of Qafzeh, Israel. In Archaeozoology in the Near East II. Hijlke Buitenhuis and Hans-Peter Uerpmann, pp. 5–44. Leiden: Backhuys Publishers.

Rak, Yoel, 1990 On the Differences Between Two Pelvises of Mousterian Context from Qafzeh and Kebara Caves, Israel. American Journal of Physical Anthropology 81:323–332.

Rak, Yoel, 1993 Morphological Variation in Homo neanderthalensis and Homo sapiens in the Levant: A Biogeographic Model. *In* Species, Species Concepts, and Primate Evolution. William Kimbel and Lawrence Martin, eds. pp. 523–536. New York: Plenum.

Sackett, James, 1982 Approaches to Style in Lithic Archaeology. Journal of Anthropological Archaeology 1:59–112.

Schepartz, Lynn, 1993 Language and Modern Human Origins. Yearbook of Physical Anthropology 36:91–126.

Schillaci, Michael, and Jeffery Froehlich, 2001 Nonhuman Primate Hybridization and the Taxonomic Status of Neanderthals. American Journal of Physical Anthropology 115:157–166.

Schoeninger, Margaret, 1982 Diet and Evolution of Modern Human Form in the Middle East. American Journal of Physical Anthropology 58:37–52.

Schwartz, Jeffrey, 1999 Can We Really Identify Species, Living or Extinct? Anthropologie 37:211–220.

Shea, John, 1988 Spear Points from the Middle Paleolithic of the Levant. Journal of Field Archaeology 15:441–450.

Shea, John, 1998 Neandertal and Early Modern Human Behavioral Variability: A Regional-scale Approach to the Lithic Evidence for Hunting in the Levantine Mousterian. Current Anthropology 39:S45–S78.

Shea, John, 2001a The Middle Paleolithic: Neandertals and Early Modern Humans in the Levant. Near Eastern Archaeology 63:38–64.

Shea, John, 2001b Modern Human Origins and Neanderthal Extinction: New Evidence from the East Mediterranean Levant. Athena Review 4:21–32.

Simmons, Tal, 1999 Migration and Contact Zones in Modern Human Origins: Baboon Models for Hybridization and Species Recognition. Anthropologie 37:101–109.

Sorenson, Mark, and William Leonard, 2001 Neandertal Energetics and Foraging Efficiency. Journal of Human Evolution, 40:483–495.

Speth, John, and Eitan Tchernov, 1998 The Role of Hunting and Scavenging in Neandertal Procurement Strategies: New Evidence from Kebara Cave (Israel). In Neandertals and Modern Humans in Western Asia. Takeru Akazawa, Kenichi Aoki, and Ofer Bar-Yosef, eds. pp. 223–240. New York: Plenum.

Stiner, Mary, Natalie Munro, Todd Surovell, Eitan Tchernov, and Ofer Bar-Yosef, 1999 Paleolithic Population Growth Pulses Evidenced by Small Animal Exploitation. Science 283:190–194.

Tattersall, Ian, and Jeffrey Schwartz, 1999 Hominids and Hybrids: The Place of Neanderthals in Human Evolution. Proceedings of the National Academy of Sciences 96:7117–7119.

Tattersall, Ian, and Jeffrey Schwartz, 2000 Extinct Humans. Boulder, CO: Westview Press.

Tchernov, Eitan, 1998 The Faunal Sequences of the Southwest Asian Middle Paleolithic in Relation to Hominid Dispersal Events. In Neandertals and Modern Humans in Western Asia. Takeru Akazawa, Kenichi Aoki, and Ofer Bar-Yosef, eds. pp. 77–90. New York: Plenum.

Torrence, Robin, 1989 Re-tooling: Towards a Behavioral Theory of Stone Tools. In Time, Energy, and Stone Tools. Robin Torrence, ed. pp. 57–66. Cambridge: Cambridge University Press.

Trinkaus, Erik, 1984 Western Asia. In The Origins of Modern Humans. Fred Smith and Frank Spencer, eds. pp. 251–293. New York: Alan R. Liss.

Trinkaus, Erik, 1992 Morphological Contrasts Between the Near Eastern Qafzeh-Skhul and Late Archaic Human Samples: Grounds for a Behavioral Difference. In The Evolution and Dispersal of Modern Humans in Asia. Takeru Akazawa, Kenichi Aoki, and Tasuku Kimura, eds. pp. 277–294. Tokyo: Hokusen-Sha.

Trinkaus, Erik, Chris Ruff, and Steven Churchill, 1998 Upper Limb Versus Lower Limb Loading Patterns among Near Eastern Middle Paleolithic Hominids. In Neandertals and Modern Humans in Western Asia. Takeru Akazawa, Kenichi Aoki, and Ofer Bar-Yosef, eds. pp. 391–404. New York: Plenum.

Turville-Petre, Francis, ed., 1927 Researches in Prehistoric Galilee: 1925–1926. London: British School of Archaeology in Jerusalem.

Valladas, H., J. Joron, G. Valladas, B. Arensburg, Ofer Bar-Yosef, Anna Belfer-Cohen, Paul Goldberg, H. Laville, Lilliane Meignen, Yoel Rak, Eitan Tchernov, A. M. Tillier, and Bernard Vandermeersch, 1987 Thermoluminescence Dates for the Neanderthal Burial Site at Kebara in Israel. Nature 330:159–160.

Valladas, H., N. Mercier, L. Froget, E. Hovers, J. Joron, W. Kimbel, and Yoel Rak, 1999 TL Dates for the Neanderthal site of the Amud Cave, Israel. Journal of Archaeological Science 26:259–268.

Valladas, H., J. Reyss, J. Joron, G. Valladas, Ofer Bar-Yosef, and Bernard Vandermeersch, 1988 Thermoluminescence Dating of Mousterian 'Proto-Cro-Magnon' Remains from Israel and the Origin of Modern Man. Nature 331:614–615.

Weinstein-Evron, Mina, 1990 Palynological History of the Last Pleniglacial in the Levant. *In* Les industries à pointes foliacées du Paléolithique supérieur européen. Janusz Kozlowski, ed. pp. 9–25. Liège: ERAUL Université de Liège.

Wobst, H. Martin, 1976 Locational Relationships in Paleolithic Society. Journal of Human Evolution 5:49–58.

Wobst, H. Martin, 1977 Stylistic Behavior and Information Exchange. *In* For the Director, Research Essays in Honor of James B. Griffin. Charles Cleland, ed. pp. 317–342. Anthropological Paper 61. Ann Arbor: Museum of Anthropology, University of Michigan.

Wolpoff, Milford, 1989 The Place of Neanderthals in Human Evolution. *In* The Emergence of Modern Humans. Erik Trinkaus, ed. pp. 97–141. New York: Cambridge University Press.

Wolpoff, Milford, 1996 Human Evolution (1996–1997 Edition). New York: McGraw-Hill.

Zilhao, João, and Francesco d'Errico, 1999 The Chronology and Taphonomy of the Earliest Aurignacian and its Implications for the Understanding of Neandertal Extinction. Journal of World Prehistory 13:1–68.

8

Lumps of Clay and Pieces of Stone: Ambiguity, Bodies, and Identity as Portrayed in Neolithic Figurines

Ian Kuijt and
Meredith S. Chesson

The human body is always treated as an image of society and . . . there can be no natural way of considering the body that does not involve at the same time a social dimension.

Douglas (1982:70)

Introduction

The Neolithic of the Near East encompassed some of the most profound and fundamental innovations in human lifeways in our species' history. Approximately 11,500 years ago, people in certain regions of the southern Levant established the earliest sedentary villages in the world, settling down in food-producing communities relying on domesticated plants and animals for subsistence. This transition involved tremendous changes in lifeways, with a move from a mobile hunting and gathering lifestyle to one of year-round sedentism and food production of cereals. The establishment of viable farming communities may have required several generations, but from an archaeological standpoint this shift appears to be fairly rapid in certain areas. However, there is ample evidence to demonstrate that these early farmers continued to hunt animals and gather plants, as well as trading domesticated cereals for plants and animals hunted and gathered by people in the nearby upland areas, especially east of the Jordan River.

From the perspective of many archaeologists, as well as the general public, one of the most interesting aspects of the ancient Near Eastern Neolithic is the assemblage of exotic anthropomorphic statues, animal and human figurines, and plastered and painted human skulls, all potentially representing powerful, idealized forces of nature, fertility, and society's struggle to control and contain shifting structures of economy and lifeways (see Verhoeven, this volume). The representation of humans in Neolithic communities is a topic that has received a great deal of attention as a crucial element of several researchers' interpretive frameworks for understanding Levantine early agricultural society. At the foundation of this literature are two deceptively simple questions: "What do figurines do?" and "What do figurines mean?" To address these questions, researchers have utilized diverse theoretical perspectives from a broad spectrum of disciplines, especially art history, religious studies, ancient history and literature, sociocultural anthropology, and archaeology. They have, moreover, usually explored these questions by examining Neolithic figurines from a broad geographic and temporal scope. While drawing upon this foundation, this chapter differs from most previous treatments in two ways. First, we approach these questions as anthropological archaeologists, with a strong focus on the spatial and temporal contexts of these objects on micro- and macro-level scales. Secondly, we limit our analysis to all published objects from the Pre-Pottery Neolithic of the southern Levant, restricting the geographic and temporal scope in order to focus on the use of figural representation in a defined space and time. This chapter discusses three-dimensional representations of humans, animals or geometric shapes in the form of figurines, statues, masks, or human skulls from southern Levantine Pre-Pottery Neolithic (PPN) sites (figure 8.1).

We argue that the attention to context forces us to change research questions about figurine function and significance, contextualizing peoples' manufacture, use, and discard of these objects within the social, economic, and political frameworks of their communities. Thus, this chapter explores how researchers can investigate the potential meanings and functions of figurines to PPN peoples. In this period people established the first agricultural communities in the world, essentially creating a new way of life that focused on sedentism, agriculture, and animal herding. Throughout the PPN period, we witness the tremendous growth and eventual abandonment of these earliest agricultural communities. Interestingly, the nature and scale of manufacture and use of figural representations of humans, animals, and geometric shapes shift in these communities over time, often changing with documented transitions in economic and social practices. Our focus, then, rests on understanding how we can explore the relationships between social and economic behavioral changes and figurine use in these communities, and more specifically, how the representation of human forms may reflect changing understandings of what it meant for people to live in these communities as individuals and members of collective groups.

Figurines, Bodies, and Identity

Analysis and interpretation of the social and symbolic context of prehistoric anthropomorphic figurines has produced an extensive series of debates and discussions. Researchers have generated a substantial body of literature which explores questions of why people make figurines, what figurines "do," what figurines mean, and what we can learn about a society from its figurines. This historical context and

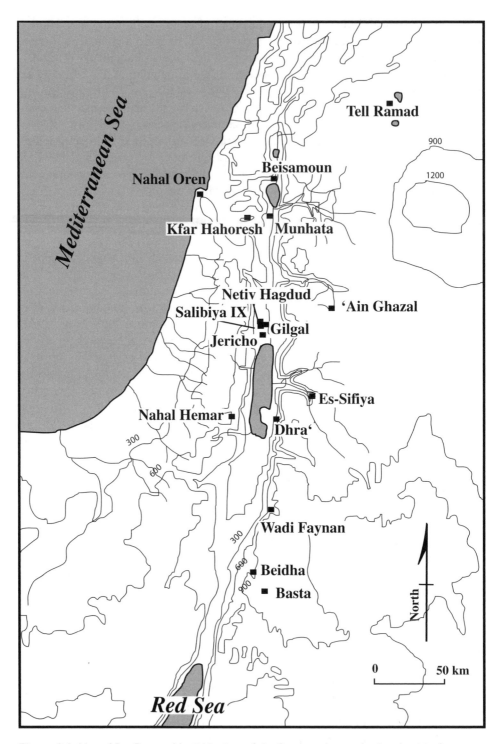

Figure 8.1 Map of Pre-Pottery Neolithic sites of the Southern Levant (authors' original)

overview of the practice and theory of figurine studies has been widely discussed in several surveys (in particular the *Cambridge Archaeological Journal* feature "Can We Interpret Figurines?" [Bailey 1996; Haaland and Haaland 1996; Hamilton 1996; Marcus 1996; Ucko 1996]; Knapp and Meskell 1997; Lesure 2002). These authors note that figurines represent a unique form of human representation with a complex array of meanings, simultaneously obvious and nuanced, that may change throughout their life history as the makers and/or users of the figurines negotiate their own lives and relationships. The figurine may change hands several times over its life history, be used in many different and differently charged contexts, and embody multiple significances to different people (Joyce 1993; Bailey 1996).

Figurines involve the creation of the human image in a three-dimensional, durable, and tangible format that extends beyond gesture, voice, and language in portraying some aspect of humanness (Bailey 1996). While many figurines may not have been designed to be strictly realistic representations of a human form, nevertheless they do depict recognizably human elements. What is often interesting is the nature of this representation, namely which elements are emphasized and which are de-emphasized or even omitted (Joyce 1993). Joyce argues that details of human images are not random; rather they are deliberate and reflect stereotyping of mental constructs by the makers and users of them. Thus, emphases and omissions in figurines potentially represent a series of naturalized features that are important elements in how a particular society understands the materiality of human bodies and social identities. Douglas (1982) notes this close and inseparable relationship between peoples' physical bodies and social bodies. In outlining the connections between the personal and social body, Douglas (1982:63) discusses the interesting implications for how societal structures can be expressed on the body, arguing that, "The social body constrains the way the physical body is perceived. The physical experience of the body, always modified by the social categories through which it is known, sustains a particular view of society." We believe that the figural representation of humans potentially intensified this relationship between the personal and social. In representing the human form in a durable material good, people created an enduring representation of the personal and social body, focusing attention on the key elements of what it meant to be a person and exist in a human body in a particular society.

Many researchers have recognized this connection and interpreted this relationship as a potential venue for expressing concepts of identity, particularly sex and gender, in a society (Martin 1987; Butler 1990, 1993; Lacqueur 1990; Lock 1993), prompting archaeologists to think about identity in the archaeological past (Conkey and Gero 1997, and references therein; Gilchrist 1999; Meskell 1999; Joyce 2000). While the vast majority of archaeological studies of gender successfully de-couple the concept of gender from sex and recognize gender as a social construct, they do not similarly problematize the notion of sex (Knapp and Meskell 1997). Lacqueur (1990) and Butler (1990, 1993) have demonstrated the constructed nature of sex and gender, that people's understandings of their biological, material bodies are just as socially constructed as understandings of their own gender identities. Therefore there can be multiple ways of understanding the materiality of human bodies that may differ across space and time. How does this affect our study of anthropomorphic figurines? If researchers do not question the binary categories of male and female and conflate categories of sex and gender, then their approach to human figurines by default assumes the presence of only these two categories. They approach the figurine assemblage looking for signs of maleness (penis) and femaleness (breasts, hips, buttocks) that are associated with secondary sexual characteristics. They may also categorize figurines according to other traits, such as costume, hair, or even find context, that may be interpreted as indicating male or female characteristics. If figurines do not display any of these markings then they are often placed in an "Other" category that may or may not enter researchers' discussions of normative ideas about sex and gender in a society. This constrained approach fails to consider the social construction of sex or gender, or the complexity of figural representation of human bodies.

In this paper we discuss how integrating theories of the social construction of sex and gender with the analysis of anthropomorphic figurines from the PPN period of the Southern Levant allows researchers to explore the possible meanings and social context of figurine use in early agricultural villages. Specifically, we focus upon two major themes in this reexamination of Neolithic figurine use, meaning, and interpretation. First, rather than accepting the traditional view of two naturalized sexes, we instead investigate the spectrum of representation and explicate the nature of marked, unmarked, and ambiguous representations. We argue that for some periods of the Neolithic the traditional search by researchers for two naturalized sexes is misleading and inappropriate, as the vast majority of PPN figurines are unmarked, and thus the emphasis on males and females as key binary features of identity is inaccurate. In this way, we hope to gain a greater understanding of how the PPN people understood what it meant to be human, and how they linked their bodies, and portrayals of human bodies, to the expression of identities. Second, we emphasize the importance of context in analyzing figurines (Joyce 1993; Bailey 1996; Haaland and Haaland 1996; Marcus 1996; Knapp and Meskell 1997; Soffer et al. 2000; Voigt 2000). Since meaning is contextual, and often spatially organized, these objects can hold multiple significances. Therefore it is imperative to pay close attention to the context of the objects in any analysis of figurines. In initially exploring the nature of PPN representation, as well as the context of each figurine, we ask several general questions to document and explore issues of bodily representation and potential meanings:

- What elements of the human body are represented? Are representations restricted to portions of bodies (e.g., head, penis), or is the entire human form included?
- What bodily elements are omitted (e.g., feet, hands, legs, secondary sexual characteristics)?
- Are there any indications of marking or emphasizing certain bodily elements (e.g., head, eyes, buttocks, penis)?
- Where was this object found? What other material culture or structural elements were associated with this figurine?

- What is the overall nature of economic organization, political structure and social organization of the site in which this figurine was found?

These serve as a foundation for exploring the social and political context of figurines from different phases of the Neolithic (cf. Lesure 2002). We now turn to a brief introduction to the major social, economic, and political structures of the Pre-Pottery Neolithic periods in the southern Levant.

Zoomorphic and Anthropomorphic Figurines in the Southern Levantine Neolithic

There is no question that archaeological field research in the southern Levant provides researchers with our most detailed understanding of the technological background, temporal and spatial distribution of the use and manufacture of zoomorphic and anthropomorphic figurines, as well as clay geometrics, within any single region of the Near East (Bar-Yosef 1997) (figure 8.1). Research in other geographic areas, specifically at the settlements of Çatal Höyük, Hajji Firuz, and Gritille Höyük (Mellaart 1967; Ucko 1968; Voigt 1983, 1985, 2000; Forest 1994; Hamilton 1996), provide important insights into figurine use from surrounding areas. When considering figurine use in the southern Levant, it is clear that changes in both style and frequency of different types of figurines are seen in all of the major phases of the Pre-Pottery Neolithic period, including the first sedentary collector-agricultural villages in the Pre-Pottery Neolithic A (PPNA), the formation of established agricultural villages of the Middle Pre-Pottery Neolithic B (MPPNB) and the eventual emergence of large aggregate villages of the Late Pre-Pottery Neolithic B period/Pre-Pottery Neolithic C (LPPNB/PPNC). Each phase of the PPN involves a specific combination of settlement patterns, socio-economic structures, and community types (Bar-Yosef and Meadow 1995) (table 8.1).

PPNA

The PPNA period represents the first period of the Neolithic of the Near East. It is characterized by relatively small forager-farmer communities whose architecture is primarily composed of oval-circular stone structures. There are seven anthropomorphic figurines dated to PPNA contexts from several sites and all are carved in the round from limestone or formed of baked clay (figure 8.2; tables 8.2, 8.3, 8.4). One figurine has also been found at el-Khiam and identified as anthropomorphic, but we have characterized it as unknown or unidentifiable due to the lack of any overt human features (figure 8.2d). All but the el-Khiam figurine are stylized representations of portions or all of a human body, and each involves a unique combination of marked features or omissions. For example, excavators at Dhra' and Netiv Hagdud have argued that two figurines represent female bodies, based on their identification of secondary sexual characteristics (breasts, hips), and overall shape of the figures (figure 8.2e–g) (Bar-Yosef and Gopher 1997; Kuijt and

Table 8.1 Summary of Pre-Pottery Neolithic settlement systems and figurines

Time period	Calibrated C14	Settlement types	Settlement scale[b]	Economic practices[c]	Stresses on the community	Figurines
PPNA	11,700–10,500 B.P.	Camps Hamlets	10–100 people	Hunting foraging farming	Shift from foraging to food production; establishing sedentary communities	Fairly equal proportions of unmarked human figurines, figurines with breasts and hips (female), and phalli (male); no geometric or zoomorphic figurines
EPPNB[a]	Unresolved	Unresolved	Unresolved	Unresolved	Unresolved	None
MPPNB	10,500–9,500 B.P.	Camps Hamlets Villages	10–750+	Hunting foraging farming herding	Population aggregation and growth; increasing scale and size of communities and of stable economic/social/political structures	Majority figurines zoomorphic; human figurines, statues, masks, and skulls mostly unmarked (few statues with breasts marked)
LPPNB/ PPNC	9,500–8,700 B.P.	Camps Hamlets Villages	50–750+	Hunting foraging farming herding	Increasing crowding and population density in large communities; stress from resource depletion, scale of food production necessary to support large communities	Majority of figurines zoomorphic and geometric; most human figurines unmarked (few with breasts and hips, possible phalli reported)

[a] See Goring-Morris and Belfer-Cohen 1998 and Kuijt 1997 for alternative views on the development and foundation of the EPPNB in the southern Levant.
[b] See Bar-Yosef and Meadow 1995 and Kuijt 2000b for estimates for site size and population growth through different phases of the Neolithic.
[c] See Bar-Yosef and Meadow 1995 and Goring-Morris and Belfer-Cohen 1998 for overviews of Pre-Pottery Neolithic economic practices.

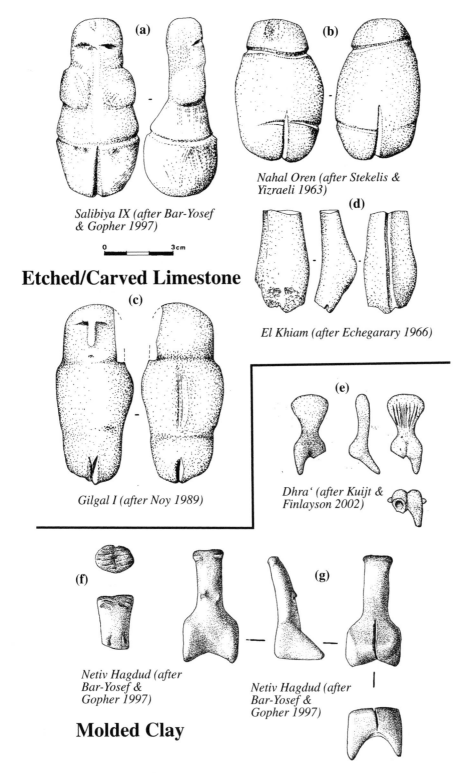

(a)

Salibiya IX (after Bar-Yosef & Gopher 1997)

0 3cm

Etched/Carved Limestone

(b)

Nahal Oren (after Stekelis & Yizraeli 1963)

(d)

El Khiam (after Echegarary 1966)

(c)

Gilgal I (after Noy 1989)

(e)

Dhra' (after Kuijt & Finlayson 2002)

(f)

Netiv Hagdud (after Bar-Yosef & Gopher 1997)

(g)

Netiv Hagdud (after Bar-Yosef & Gopher 1997)

Molded Clay

Figure 8.2 Pre-Pottery Neolithic A period figurines (*sources*: a–d: Cauvin 1994: Figure 6; e: Kuijt and Finlayson 2002; f–g: Bar-Yosef and Gopher 1997: Figure 6-1.2; reproduced by permission)

Table 8.2 Sites with figurines from the southern Levantine Pre-Pottery Neolithic

Objects	PPNA	MPPNB	LPPNB/PPNC	Sources
Human figurines and phalli	WF-16 (1); Salibiya IX (1); Dhra' (2); Gilgal I (1); Nahal Oren (1); Netiv Hagdud (1)	'Ain Ghazal (40), Nahal Hemar (3); Munhata (1); Beidha (1)	Basta (1); 'Ain Ghazal (8)	Bar-Yosef and Alon 1988; Bar-Yosef and Gopher 1997; Finlayson, pers. comm. 2001; Kirkbride 1968; Kuijt and Finlayson 2002; Noy 1991; Perrot 1966; Rollefson 2000; Schmandt-Besserat 1998b; Stekelis and Yizraeli 1963
Statues, busts and heads	–	Jericho (1); 'Ain Ghazal (32)	–	Garstang and Garstang 1940; Rollefson 1986, 2000; Schmandt-Besserat 1998a
Plastered and painted skulls and masks	–	'Ain Ghazal (8); Beisamoun (2); Jericho (7); Kfar Hahoresh (2); Nahal Hemar (6)	Basta (1); Ramad (2)	Arensburg and Hershkovitz 1989; Bar-Yosef and Alon 1988; de Contenson 1967; Ferembach and Lechevallier 1973; Goren et al. 2001; Goren et al. 1993; Goring-Morris 2000; Griffin et al. Rollefson 1998; Rollefson 1986, 2000; Rollefson et al. 1985; Rollefson et al. 1999; Schmandt-Besserat 1998a; Strouhal 1973; Yakar and Hershkovitz 1990
Zoomorphic figurines	–	'Ain Ghazal (151)	Es-Sifiya (215); Basta (5); 'Ain Ghazal (2+)	Hermansen 1997; Kafafi and Rollefson 1995; Mahasneh and Bienert 1999; Mahasneh and Gebel 1999; Nissen et al. 1991; Rollefson and Kafafi 1996
Geometric figurines	–	–	Es-Sifiya (102); Basta (>1); 'Ain Ghazal (3)	Hermansen 1997; Kafafi and Rollefson 1995; Mahasneh and Bienert 1999; Mahasneh and Gebel 1999; Nissen et al. 1991; Rollefson and Kafafi 1996
Amorphous/ unknown/ undescribed	El Khiam (1)	–	'Ain Ghazal (121); Basta (small numbers)	Echegarary 1966; Kafafi and Rollefson 1995; Nissen et al. 1991; Rollefson and Kafafi 1996
Totals	N = 8	N = 254	N = 464	

Table 8.3 Summaries of figurine data by period

Period	Human figurines	Statues, busts, and heads	Plastered and painted human skulls and masks	Zoomorphic figurines	Geometric figurines	Amorphous or unknown	Totals
PPNA	7 (87.50%)	0 (0.00%)	0 (0.00%)	0 (0.00%)	0 (0.00%)	1 (12.50%)	8
MPPNB	45 (17.72%)	33 (12.99%)	25 (9.84%)	151 (59.45%)	0 (0.00%)	0 (0.00%)	254
LPPNB/ PPNC	9 (1.94%)	0 (0.00%)	3 (0.65%)	225 (48.49%)	106 (22.84%)	121 (26.08%)	464
Totals	61 (8.40%)	33 (4.55%)	28 (3.86%)	376 (51.79%)	106 (14.60%)	122 (16.80%)	726

Finlayson 2002). Similarly, recent excavations at WF-16 and Dhra' have recovered two carved phalli (one at each site) (Finlayson 2001, personal communication). It should be noted, however, that four of the eight PPNA anthropomorphic figurines can be interpreted as ambiguous, without any specific markers of sex or gender (Bar-Yosef 1997; Cauvin 2000a). In the three cases where find context was noted, figurines were recovered in trash deposits (Bar-Yosef and Gopher 1997; Kuijt and Finlayson 2002). No clearly identified zoomorphic figurines are known from the PPNA.

PPNB

The PPNB is commonly divided into three main phases: Early PPNB (EPPNB), Middle PPNB (MPPNB), and Late PPNB/PPNC (LPPNB/PPNC). The collective PPNB assemblage contains at least 718 published zoomorphic, anthropomorphic, and geometric figurines. This figure must be viewed as an approximation given the vagaries of published data, and lack of detail in some preliminary reports (tables 8.2, 8.3, and 8.4). We briefly review the data from these three sub-periods.

EPPNB

The EPPNB is traditionally viewed as a transitional cultural phase between PPNA and MPPNB (e.g., Goring-Morris and Belfer-Cohen 1998), but remains poorly understood by researchers. As discussed elsewhere (Kuijt 1998), serious questions have been raised about the validity of this cultural-historical phase. Regardless of one's acceptance of the EPPNB as a cultural-historical unit, there are no published examples of anthropomorphic or zoomorphic figurines from any of the archaeological sites dating to this period.

Table 8.4 PPN figurines with published contextual information

Site	Period	Material culture	Context type	References
Dhra'	PPNA	1 human figurine, 1 phallus	Trash deposit	Kuijt and Finlayson 2002
Hagdud	PPNA	1 human figurine	Trash deposit	Bar-Yosef and Gopher 1997
'Ain Ghazal	MPPNB	36 human figurines	Trash deposit	Schmandt-Besserat 1998b
Nahal Hemar	MPPNB	4 plastered skulls	Cave	Yakar and Hershkovitz 1990; Arensburg and Hershkovitz 1989
Nahal Hemar	MPPNB	2 limestone masks	Cave	Arensburg and Hershkovitz 1989
'Ain Ghazal	MPPNB	33 anthropomorphic statues	Caches in extramural locations	Rollefson 2000; Schmandt-Besserat 1998a
'Ain Ghazal	MPPNB	8 painted and/or plastered skulls	Caches in extramural locations	Rollefson 2000; Schmandt-Besserat 1998a
'Ain Ghazal	MPPNB	150 zoomorphic figurines	Trash deposits, including cache of 23 figurines	Rollefson 2000; Schmandt-Besserat 1997, 1998b
'Ain Ghazal	MPPNB	1 cattle figurine	Plaster storage bin, figurine below 3 Bos metacarpals	Rollefson 2000; Schmandt-Besserat 1997, 1998b
Beisamoun	MPPNB	2 plastered skulls	Caches	Goren et al. 2001
Jericho	MPPNB	7 plastered skulls	Caches	Kenyon 1981; Goren et al. 2001; Strouhal 1973
Kfar Hahoresh	MPPNB	2 plastered skulls	Caches	Goren et al. 2001; Goring-Morris 2000
'Ain Ghazal	LPPNB/PPNC	1 human figurine (identified as female)	Found on stone walkway between two buildings	Rollefson 2000; Schmandt-Besserat 1998b
es-Sifiya	LPPNB/PPNC	101 geometric figurines and 215 zoomorphic figurines	Found in single context: Unit C11, Locus 9, described as a "production context," and interpreted as a workshop	Mahasneh and Gebel 1999; Mahasneh and Bienert 1999
Basta	LPPNB/PPNC	4 zoomorphic figurines	All found in single cache	Hermansen 1997

MPPNB

The MPPNB period is characterized by the appearance of developed agricultural villages characterized by free-standing rectangular residential buildings, domesticated plants and animals, and new developments in lithic technology. Perhaps the most dramatic aspect to representational practice in the MPPNB lies in the appearance of many new forms of anthropomorphic representations. These include large, full body anthropomorphic statues, large busts with painted faces, face masks made of clay and stone, plastered/painted and cached skulls and masks, and small anthropomorphic figurines made of baked clay or carved in stone (figures 8.3, 8.4, 8.5, and 12.1). In addition, zoomorphic representations appear in the MPPNB for the first time, including significant numbers of cattle figurines made of baked clay recovered from multiple settlements (Bar-Yosef 1997). In contrast to the limited number of figurines recovered from PPNA sites, there is a remarkable abundance of these objects in the MPPNB (figures 8.3, 8.4, and 8.5; tables 8.2, 8.3, and 8.4). These objects have been recovered from a wide variety of contexts, including public caches, trash deposits, fills, and residential spaces.

LPPNB/PPNC

The LPPNB/PPNC period reflects continuity in general architectural and settlement practices from the MPPNB period. Villages are characterized by rectangular architecture with one and two-story buildings constructed against each other. While there are some important elements of continuity in the manufacture and use of figurines from MPPNB to LPPNB, there are also some clear differences. Elements of continuity include the use of zoomorphic figurines made of baked clay (figures 8.4, 8.6; tables 8.2, 8.3, and 8.4). With the exceptions of one stone human figurine depicting a head and a fragment of a stone mask from Basta, and eight human figurines from 'Ain Ghazal, the LPPNB/PPNC people did not represent humans widely in any medium. Twenty-three figurines from es-Sifiya have been characterized by Mahasneh, Gebel and Bienert as anthropomorphic male (Mahasneh and Bienert 1999; Mahasneh and Gebel 1999). Based on the published examples of the seven classes of human figurines proposed by Mahasneh and Bienert (1999), we disagree with these researchers and categorize these objects as geometric figurines (although we might also entertain their categorization as "Unknown" or "Unidentifiable"). There are no clear indications of human features (much less "male" characteristics), even highly stylized ones, and thus we argue that these figurines are not demonstrably anthropomorphic representations. While we see a remarkable decline of human representations in the LPPNB/PPNC, we witness a marked increase in the number of geometric figurines found at several LPPNB/PPNC sites. Furthermore, while zoomorphic figurines continue to be used in these communities, the number of these is much smaller compared to the MPPNB period.

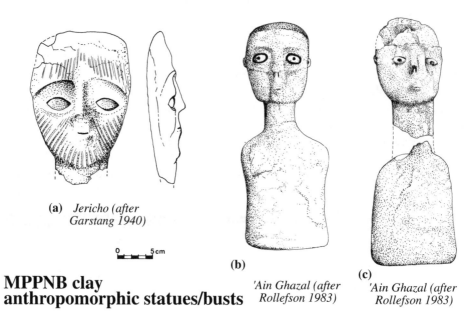

(a) *Jericho (after Garstang 1940)*

0 ____ 5 cm

(b)

MPPNB clay anthropomorphic statues/busts

'Ain Ghazal (after Rollefson 1983)

(c)

'Ain Ghazal (after Rollefson 1983)

0   10   50 cm

'Ain Ghazal (after Rollefson 1983)

MPPNB cache of clay anthropomorphic statues/busts from 'Ain Ghazal

Figure 8.3 Middle Pre-Pottery Neolithic B period anthropomorphic busts and statues, and cache from 'Ain Ghazal, Jordan (*source*: Cauvin 1994: Figures 39–40; reproduced by permission)

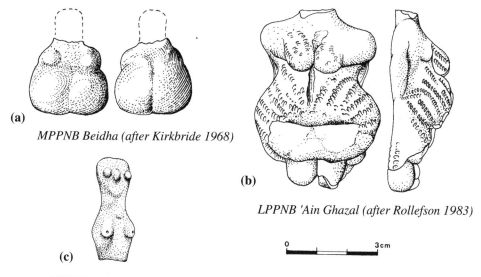

(a)

MPPNB Beidha (after Kirkbride 1968)

(b)

LPPNB 'Ain Ghazal (after Rollefson 1983)

0   3cm

(c)

MPPNB Munhata (after Perrot 1966)

Baked clay anthropomorphic figurines

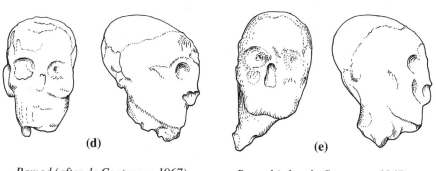

(d)

Ramad (after de Contenson 1967)

(e)

Ramad (after de Contenson 1967)

LPPNB Skulls plastered with clay

Figure 8.4 Middle and Late Pre-Pottery Neolithic B period anthropomorphic figurines and plastered skulls (*source*: Cauvin 1994: Figures 36 and 41; reproduced by permission)

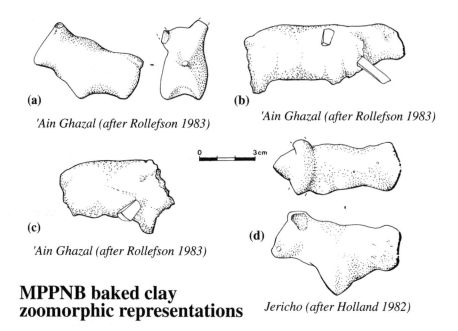

(a)

'Ain Ghazal (after Rollefson 1983)

(b)

'Ain Ghazal (after Rollefson 1983)

0   3 cm

(c)

'Ain Ghazal (after Rollefson 1983)

(d)

MPPNB baked clay zoomorphic representations

Jericho (after Holland 1982)

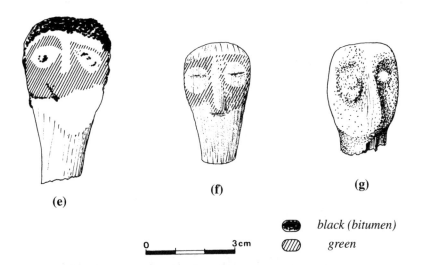

(e)

(f)

(g)

● black (bitumen)

▨ *green*

0   3 cm

MPPNB Nahal Hemar anthropomorphic / facial representations on bone

(after Bar-Yosef and Alon 1988)

Figure 8.5 Middle Pre-Pottery Neolithic B period zoomorphic figurines and facial representations (*source:* Cauvin 1994: Figures 37–38; reproduced by permission)

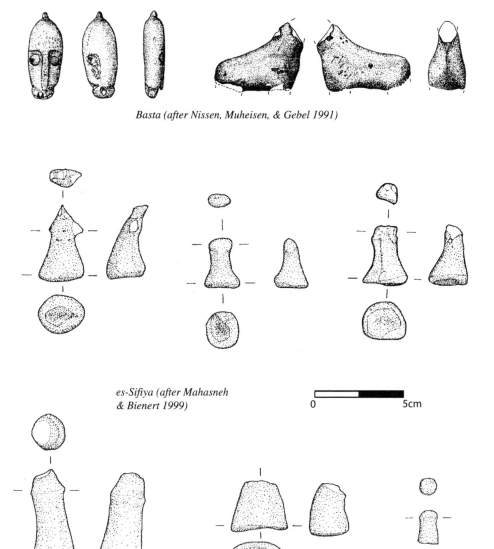

Basta (after Nissen, Muheisen, & Gebel 1991)

es-Sifiya (after Mahasneh
& Bienert 1999)

0   5cm

LPPNB Clay and Stone Figurines

Figure 8.6 Late Pre-Pottery Neolithic B/Pre-Pottery Neolithic C zoomorphic and geometric figurines (*sources*: Nissen et al. 1991: Figure 6, reproduced courtesy of the Basta Joint Archaeological
Project; Mahasneh and Bienert 1999: Figures 4–7, reproduced by permission)

Meaning and Current Interpretations of Neolithic Figurines

With this brief outline of the shifts in frequencies of the manufacture and use of anthropomorphic, zoomorphic, and geometric figurines in the southern Levant, we now turn to a discussion of how these patterns have been interpreted by researchers. Moving beyond the realm of primarily descriptive reports, the studies of two researchers, Denise Schmandt-Besserat (1997, 1998a, 1998b) and Jacques Cauvin (1994, 2000a, 2000b), have understandably received considerable attention from prehistorians, professional archaeologists, and the general public. Focusing upon archaeological data from 'Ain Ghazal in Jordan, Schmandt-Besserat has published a series of reports that are among the most detailed descriptive treatments of Neolithic anthropomorphic and zoomorphic figurines from the southern Levant. On the basis of these descriptive foundations, Schmandt-Besserat has developed an interpretive framework for analyzing the materials from 'Ain Ghazal, and by extension, arguments for the meanings and ritual use of similar figurines from other Near Eastern Neolithic settlements. Adopting a similar approach, Cauvin (1994, 2000a, 2000b) draws together archaeological data from different periods and places of the Neolithic and attempts to develop a structuralist argument for meaning and symbolism for the entire Near East. Collectively, these works serve as our most detailed considerations of materials from an individual archaeological settlement and an attempt to situate these data and others into a regional context.

Schmandt-Besserat: figurines from 'Ain Ghazal

Schmandt-Besserat's research provides our most detailed treatment of the manufacture, use and meanings of zoomorphic and anthropomorphic representations of MPPNB and LPPNB communities. As described earlier, the MPPNB people represented humans in several media, including statuary, masks, small figurines, and cached painted, plastered and undecorated human skulls (Bar-Yosef 1997; Cauvin 2000a; Rollefson 2000, 2001a; Kuijt 2001). Even more numerous and common are the clay zoomorphic figurines. The majority of these zoomorphic figurines come from the MPPNB occupation of 'Ain Ghazal. As outlined by Schmandt-Besserat (1997), zoomorphic objects are remarkably uniform, with the quadrupeds represented as standing, and varying in size from 3 to 15 cm in length. These animals are portrayed with horns, recovered from caches, and are widely interpreted as being bovine. Many of the animals were beheaded, and in the case of a few (the exact number remains unreported), apparently stabbed with several small pieces of flint.

Schmandt-Besserat (1997) envisions the continued appearance of animal depictions as part of an age-old Near Eastern art tradition from the Paleolithic period to the third millennium B.C. Like Cauvin (1994), Schmandt-Besserat accepts that the frequency and endurance of these motifs is linked to a symbolic tradition that reflects ancient Near Eastern thought and meaning. Drawing upon historical accounts of third millennium B.C. Mesopotamia, she argues that there are a number of shared elements between the historical accounts and the figurines recovered from 'Ain Ghazal and concludes that these are a by-product of magic practices.

As with small solid clay anthropomorphic figurines, the appearance in the MPPNB of large statues has been widely discussed by researchers as a major symbolic development within Neolithic villages. With regards to 'Ain Ghazal, Schmandt-Besserat (1998a:9) agrees with Rollefson's (2001a) suggestions that the large jump in size of human figures from the PPNA to the PPNB illustrates the appearance of public ritual use of the figurines. Specifically, she suggests that the small PPNA figurines were designed for use in homes, while the large statues were presented in public contexts, and that the statues are unlikely to be related to ancestor worship (1998b:11). Instead, her interpretation stresses that the significance of the figures is seen in the magnitude of the statues and the transition from domestic figurines of the PPNA to the use of large statues to be seen by the entire PPNB community. As with the development of clay zoomorphic figurines, she sees the monumental figures as powerful symbols that help foster community cohesion, a largely functionalist explanation.

In exploring the predominance of clay anthropomorphic figurines in the MPPNB and a rare stone statue from the PPNC period, Schmandt-Besserat (1998b:111) argues that both types depict females, but there are qualitative differences between the stone and clay figurines. For example, she notes (1998b:111–112) that the stone figurine is executed with careful planning and that the rarity of stone figurines highlights the importance of work in this medium. In contrast, the clay figurines were made of a common material, required little time investment, were discarded with other refuse, and were therefore probably related to magic-making activities in brief periods of domestic use. Thus, the stone statues' material, rarity, and aesthetic composition denote a valued artifact destined for a formal public function (see also Foster 1993:33).

Although separated by several thousand years, Schmandt-Besserat (1998b) argues that the antecedents for the PPNC stone statue are found in the earlier Natufian and PPNA period stone figurines. Drawing upon the ideas of Gopher and Orelle (1996), she finds that most stone carvings in the PPNA were sexually ambiguous or even dual-gendered representations that can alternatively be viewed as representations of male genitalia (she argues that these objects appear to be stylized phalli, from another viewpoint a stylized human female). From her perspective these stone images belong to a pan-Near Eastern Neolithic phenomenon, linked to earlier Natufian and PPNA figurines focused on sexuality or reproduction and appear to reflect pregnancy rather than conception (Schmandt-Besserat 1998b).

Jacques Cauvin: symbolism, models, and interpretations

In what is unquestionably the most provocative consideration of Neolithic figurines in the Near East, Cauvin (2000a, 2000b) has written several articles and books exploring the potential links between the origins of agriculture and ritual/religious changes. From the perspective of archaeological data his interpretations and reconstruction of the birth of gods in the Neolithic are centered almost entirely upon changes in figurines, and more specifically zoomorphic and anthropomorphic figurines. With the exception of some limited material from the site of Mureybet for the PPNA, Cauvin's interpretation of symbolism and its relation to the origins of agriculture is based on figurine data from the southern Levant, examining changes between the PPNA and PPNB.

Developing arguments for the first phase of his interpretation of the revolution of Neolithic symbols, Cauvin contrasts the PPNA period with the Natufian of the southern Levant, arguing that Natufian art was essentially zoomorphic (Cauvin 2000a:25). Unfortunately, Cauvin provides a highly generalized treatment of these materials, failing to recognize that some Natufian art is anthropomorphic, including carved human heads, and in one case, a couple engaged in intimate physical contact, often interpreted as representing sexual intercourse (Perrot 1966; Noy 1991; Weinstein-Evron and Belfer-Cohen 1993; Bar-Yosef 1997). Focusing on the Levantine Khiamian, viewed by Cauvin as a sub-phase of the PPNA period predating the Sultanian, he argues that there was a revolution of symbols (i.e., figurines) that predates the origins of agriculture. Cauvin suggests that it is at this time that we see the emergence of two dominant symbolic figures: the woman and the bull. He argues, moreover, that female figurines are representations of a Goddess, found in PPNA sites in the southern Levant as well as at Mureybet. The Bull, representative of a male God, is indicated by skulls of aurochs buried complete with horns in houses at Mureybet. While Bull symbolism is not found in the southern Levant, he suggests that the Goddess and the Bull form a separate, yet related, symbolic system for the Khiamian.

Having described these two lines of symbolism, Cauvin (2000a:29) argues that these objects represent material culture associated with a new religion. Interestingly, he does not directly address the nature of this religion in the Khiamian; rather he describes it through the perspective of archaeological materials from Çatal Höyük, occupied some 2,000 years later and situated in central Turkey. Guided by the Çatal Höyük analogy, Cauvin (2000a:32) argues that a form of Neolithic female monotheism existed in PPNA. His treatment of this religion is, however, brief and presented in a way in which one has to ask how such perspectives were developed.

For the southern Levantine PPNB period, Cauvin argues that we see a full-fledged emphasis and important shift from female figurines as representations of goddesses to bull figurines, representing a masculine God (Cauvin 2000a:124). While baked and stone figurines viewed as female (due to secondary sexual characteristics, including breasts, large buttocks and abdomen) continue to appear, Cauvin sees bull figurines in the PPNB as complementing and even overtaking the authority and power of female figurines. Their increased importance, moreover, is reflected in their high frequency. Interestingly, Cauvin also views the plastered MPPNB statues from Jericho and 'Ain Ghazal as males, although there is no clear indication that these representations are anything but ambiguous and unmarked bodies. In the case of the Jericho example (figure 8.3a), he accepts Garstang and Garstang's (1940) interpretation that the painted lines on the face represent a bearded rather than a tattooed or painted face. Considering the statues cached at

'Ain Ghazal, he accepts that one of them is female but states, "The absence of sexual distinctions could have been intended to make the representations either asexual, or as is more probable, masculine by default" (Cauvin 2000a:111). As with Schmandt-Besserat, Cauvin's approach to figurine interpretation leans heavily upon materials from later periods and from a broad geographic area, decontextualizing materials and weakening his interpretive framework.

Decontextualization and the use of texts and illustrations to understand the Neolithic

Beyond some of the specific concerns raised above, several additional questions should be raised about the approaches that Cauvin and Schmandt-Besserat have adopted in their analysis of Neolithic figurines. Interestingly, despite the very different focus and intent of these two authors, both share a remarkably similar approach to interpreting the meaning and importance of figurines to communities in the past. Their interpretive approach is founded on the assumption that analogies from later cultures can be read onto the Neolithic on the basis of historical symbols from highly complex societies from thousands of years later and across significant geographic distances. Cauvin provides his readers with no rationale for this; rather he appears to assume that such an approach can be adopted with no consideration of potential weaknesses (Hodder 2001; Rollefson 2001b). Schmandt-Besserat (1997) does directly explore why such an approach can be adopted. She notes that the foundation for her approach is centered on the earlier work of Postgate (1994), arguing that our understanding of the third to first millennia B.C. (through textual accounts) allows researchers to project into the past. Moreover, she accepts van Dijk et al.'s (1985:1) assumption that later texts were transcriptions of a long-lived oral tradition that had its roots in prehistory. While this may be correct, it seems remarkably premature to accept her argument that magic is universal, and as implied in her work, that the repetitive and formal nature of ritual and magic mean that the practice and meaning were largely unchanged from the 13th to the third millennium. While recognizing the important contribution of her descriptive work, Schmandt-Besserat's (1997, 1998a, 1998b) social interpretations of Neolithic anthropomorphic and zoomorphic figurines are undermined by considerable interpretive decontextualization and a version of orientalism in which the nature of the ancient Near East is unchanged.

Both of these researchers are heavily influenced by a structuralist or structural functionalist perspective; both ask what figurines "do" in these Neolithic communities and how figurines reflect the underlying social, ritual, and economic structures of Neolithic society. Schmandt-Besserat sees figurines as tools in magic activities. She argues (Schmandt-Besserat 1998b:111–112) that the find context of the PPNC stone figurine (lying face down on a stone-paved walkway between two buildings, which she interprets as a "deliberately formal" context) and the material (stone) suggest that this figurine had been displayed in a special location, "destined for a formal, public function." In considering the potential uses and meanings of this figurine, she states that it can be understood (now and in the past) as a metaphor for creation, as a reflection of how the 'Ain Ghazal community members understood the nature of their origins, the birth of their people.

In many ways Cauvin interprets the meaning and function of Near Eastern Neolithic figures from a structuralist perspective, particularly Lévi-Strauss's ideas about duality and societal structures. In his model of figurines reflecting a dual religious system focusing on the Goddess and the Bull, Cauvin "reads" the figurine data from southern Levantine sites as indicating a system of opposing female and male structures. The assumption of an essentialized duality of males and females, and relating these structures to Neolithic peoples' concepts of nature and culture, finds only tenuous support from the figurine data. Neolithic people may have understood their lives and cosmologies in terms of a dual system of essentialized maleness and femaleness, but Cauvin is approaching the data with this assumption as the foundation for his argument, rather than demonstrating the presence of this belief system.

While in many societies a structuralist or structural functionalist paradigm may provide accurate insights into why people behave in certain ways and how they understand the world, we believe that imposing a dual set of structures onto Neolithic cosmologies is an approach that does not resonate well with the data. Instead, we suggest that researchers approach the question of what Neolithic figurines mean, and how people used them, by integrating questions of function with those of the nature of representation and their context. Most archaeologists, and indeed most anthropologists, are interested in questions of function in any society. Archaeologists in particular use functional questions about material culture as a foundation for examining questions of social, economic, and political organization. As outlined by Voigt (2000), questions of function must always be concerned with context, and interpretation of one without the other is extremely limiting and problematic.

Neolithic Figurines: Analysis, Methods, and Interpretation

In her detailed treatment of context and Neolithic figurines, Voigt (2000) draws upon ethnographic literature to consider how patterned distributional data and figurine form and breakage from Hajji Firuz and Gritille Höyük aid researchers in interpreting figurines. Her integration of contextual reconstruction (focusing closely on disposal patterns), combined with ethnographic insights, provides a productive means of evaluating alternative interpretations of the possible uses and social contexts of figurines in Neolithic communities. Echoing her arguments, one of the major methodological concerns we have with current interpretive approaches centers on the issue of archaeological context. Any interpretation of the social and ritual context of figurines from any stage of the Neolithic requires archaeologists to work backwards in time from the spatial and depositional context of the object, through consideration of the possible use of the figurines in the past, to the methods of construction, and broader social meaning(s) behind these objects. Of these stages it is only the locus of manufacture and/or eventual discard that archaeologists are able to directly reconstruct. Our ability to accomplish this goal, however, is often undermined by the limited contextual and associational information recorded and published by archaeologists. In other cases, moreover, these associations are largely assumed rather than demonstrated in a systematic manner.

Compilation of published figurine, statue, skull, or mask data with contextual information (table 8.4) illustrates the limited nature of this assemblage. Clearly, the most commonly reported objects are those associated with "special" contexts, such as a dedicatory cache, while the provenance of figurines from fills, refuse, or other contexts are not mentioned. In this way, certain objects are given more interpretive weight, though the meanings attached to items found in "less-than-special" contexts might have been as powerful as those objects found in caches. Without attention to all figurines, found in all types of contexts, we will never be able to understand in a broad sense how people used figurines in Neolithic communities.

A second concern focuses on the necessity for researchers to conceptually de-couple anthropomorphic and zoomorphic figurines in their interpretations. Beyond the descriptive treatments of these materials, it is often assumed that Neolithic fig-urine manufacture and use was static through time, with unchanged meanings, and that different types of figurines can be treated as components of a single interpre-tive analysis (Cauvin 2000a). For example, Cauvin (2000b) treats zoomorphic and anthropomorphic figurines as being integrated and part of some larger pan-Near East cosmological system. While systems of MPPNB and LPPNB anthropomor-phic figurines may have been interrelated in meaning, organization, and expression, it is likely that different figurine forms were conceptualized by Neolithic commu-nity members as being symbolic manifestations of different social and ritual realms. Research by Voigt (2000) and Ucko (1968) indirectly raises this issue when they highlight that ethnographic use of figurines and their life histories are remarkably varied and often include conceptual divisions of cult figures, vehicles of magic, teaching figurines, and toys (Voigt 2000: Table 2). From this perspective, it is pos-sible that different types of figurines, such as clay cattle and anthropomorphic figurines from 'Ain Ghazal, were material and symbolic manifestations of very different realms (e.g., hunting magic or toys vs. seated female figurines employed in birth rituals).

Frequency and symbolic ambiguity in figurines

The incorporation of new perspectives on Neolithic figurine use forces us to con-front several important issues that have largely been avoided by researchers. One of these is the question of why there was relatively little use of certain types of figurines. For instance, why are there so few anthropomorphic figurines in the MPPNB? Secondly, why did people use other figurines more frequently? Bar-Yosef (1997) raises the same issue for earlier periods. Considering this general question, he provides a functionalist explanation for the relative paucity of symbolic art, and argues that imagery is related to ritual; in the case of rock art, the absence of Natufian parietal art may be linked to differences in social structure and variation in subsistence resources (Bar-Yosef 1997:176). Addressing the possible meanings and symbolic uses of Neolithic art and figurines, Bar-Yosef defers to Cauvin's (2000a) interpretation of the emergence of female figurines as being related to issues of human reproduction and soil fertility. On the question of why there are so few artistic representations from the LPPNB and early Pottery Neolithic, Bar-Yosef suggests that increased use of anthropomorphic and zoomorphic figurines may have been related to the emergence of complex symbolic behaviors for enhancing group cohesion and resolving inter-group conflicts.

While in general agreement with Bar-Yosef, we feel that there are other dimensions that need to be considered to gain insights into how Neolithic social systems were organized. First, we believe that in the process of developing broader interpretations of Neolithic figurine use, researchers have not addressed how the frequency of these objects might be related to their use. It is important to consider how few anthropomorphic and zoomorphic figurines have been recovered from the PPNA and to address the implications for this paucity vis-à-vis current interpretive models. There are a number of possible explanations, including the low population density at these settlements and the social contexts of use. Reconstruction of population levels (site size, number of human burials, total roofed floor area) (Kuijt 2000b) compared to the number of figurines illustrates that figurine frequency is not a function of population growth, and by extension, suggests that the frequency of figurines is probably related to the social context of use.

The relative scarcity of PPNA figurines in Neolithic villages also highlights another possibility: that figurines served very different social roles in different phases of the Neolithic. Both their low frequency and, perhaps more importantly, the fact that there is no evidence to suggest that southern Levantine PPNA figurines were cached or buried in ritual or dedicatory contexts, supports the argument that figurines served a very different social role in the PPNA compared to the MPPNB/LPPNB. At Netiv Hagdud and Dhra', the only PPNA settlements with relatively convincing female figurines, these figurines were found as single objects and in extramural midden deposits. The frequency and burial context of MPPNB and LPPNB figurines, plastered and painted skulls, and statues illustrate a very different phenomenon. Large anthropomorphic figurines and statues were found in spatially discrete caches while smaller figurines were found in trash deposits and discrete caches.[1] In some cases, like es-Sifiya, several hundred clay figurines were found in a single context. At other settlements, such as Jericho and 'Ain Ghazal, community members buried large anthropomorphic statues in caches. The depositional context of these figures, the placement of these caches in public contexts, and the frequency of objects buried suggest that they were important material and symbolic expressions of the views and beliefs of members of Neolithic communities.

A third question centers on why people in the past deliberately marked or obscured the gender and/or sex of human representations when constructing figurines. In light of the frequency of these objects in the MPPNB and their apparent burial in public contexts, it is surprising that most, but not all, of the large anthropomorphic statues have no clearly marked secondary sexual characteristics. The recovery of some large anthropomorphic figurines with breasts and enlarged buttocks illustrates that Neolithic artists sometimes chose to represent morphological differences of humans in clay. Thus, we have to ask why they depicted female secondary sexual characteristics on a minority of large anthropomorphic statues while deliberately constructing the majority of these statues as ambiguous with limited, if any, indications of sexed or gendered identities?

Ambiguity and mortuary practices

While the answer to this question will never be fully known, it is interesting to note that the patterning of deliberate ambiguity is also seen in mortuary practices in the MPPNB and LPPNB periods, and that similarities in these practices may reflect deliberate attempts to mask or control differences at the individual, household, and community level. As illustrated in several recent syntheses of MPPNB mortuary practices (Goring-Morris 2000; Kuijt 2000a, 2001), burials were organized in such a way that deceased males and females of any age above approximately 12 were treated in the same manner: skulls of adults were removed sometime after the primary burial, and no grave goods were placed with the bodies (Bonogofsky 2001). Interestingly, all but one of the small human figurines found at 'Ain Ghazal were found with their heads removed (Rollefson 2001a, pers. comm.). Rollefson has suggested that this decapitation of human figurines mirrors the practice of skull removal in mortuary practices (Rollefson 2001a). Rollefson (2001b) and Kuijt (2001) have both suggested that the MPPNB and LPPNB secondary mortuary practices of skull removal, plastering, painting and caching may be related to some ritual structure of ancestor veneration.

Following several ethnographic studies (Hertz 1960; Kan 1989; Schiller 1997), we envision secondary mortuary practices in MPPNB communities as reflecting two interrelated, yet distinct, social dimensions: (a) the recognition of the individuality of the deceased; and (b) the idealization of links between the living, the deceased, and collective ancestors. While recognizing that variation is likely to exist within communities and through different regions, we believe that overall the acts of homogenous grave preparation, burial of individual dead, and absence of mortuary goods can best be interpreted as reflecting a means of controlling/limiting displays of identity, privilege, or wealth within these communities. The widespread use of secondary mortuary practices in the PPN probably served as community events in which memories of collective and individual ancestries were actively negotiated and defined. We suggest, moreover, that the efficacy and power of these practices physically and symbolically relied on the creation of social memory by ritual practitioners, who employed a shared set of symbols understood by community members.

We believe that this creation of social memories in mortuary practices offers a potential analog for understanding the use of figurines in the PPN period, particu-

larly in the MPPNB. The homogeneity of mortuary practices appears to emphasize
the deconstruction or masking of individual differences and focus on collective
identities. Furthermore, the removal of heads of human figurines and the stylized
representation of the human features may suggest that the people of 'Ain Ghazal
understood the relationship between the physical and the social body very differently than we do. The ambiguity, in choosing to not mark sexual differences in
human representations, fits this same pattern, with the vast number of anthropomorphic objects unmarked by secondary sexual characteristics. The deliberate
manner in which the majority of large anthropomorphic statues and figurines from
'Ain Ghazal were crafted provides no indication of sex or gender, masking any sense
of individuality, with most statues conforming to a stylized set of features (enlarged
heads with marked facial features, especially eyes; frequent omission or diminution
of legs and arms). In masking differences, the MPPNB people stressed a collective,
community identity, and emphasized egalitarian values and limited social differentiation within the community, just as we see in mortuary practices and in the built
environment (Kuijt 2001).

Future considerations

In considering the general trajectory of figural representations of humans over the
PPNA and PPNB, there is an interesting shift in marking or not marking secondary
sexual characteristics on figurines, or representing portions or entire bodies. While
clearly in need of further research and subject to revision, we offer these observations as preliminary interpretations. First, while the numbers of human figurines in
the PPNA and LPPNB/PPNC are small in comparison to zoomorphic and geometric figurines from the PPNB, some intriguing patterns seem to be emerging.
During the PPNA, figurines are very rare, and there is a relatively even proportion
of marked female figurines (displaying breasts and enlarged hips), unmarked human
figurines, and figurines of phalli; interestingly, there are no zoomorphic or geometric figurines. In the MPPNB, by contrast, the vast majority of human figurines or
statues are unmarked. A few of the statues from 'Ain Ghazal display breasts, but
there are no "corresponding" representations of male genitalia or phalli. Moreover,
the majority of MPPNB figurines are zoomorphic. Finally in the LPPNB/PPNC,
the overwhelming majority of figurines are zoomorphic or geometric, but in the
human figurines found we see once again the representation of breasts and hips on
full body representations of females or female gendered figurines and a rare example
of a phallus from Basta (which has been interpreted by the excavators as deliberately ambiguous, displaying a phallus or a ram's head). From this list of general
characteristics by period, several patterns beg to be investigated. For example, representations of female bodies, with hips and breasts, are complemented by the representation of male phalli in only a few rare cases. So why are males not represented
in full-bodied form? Why do the proportions of human, zoomorphic, and geometric figurines shift through time, with the PPNA and LPPNB/PPNC more similar

to each other and markedly different from the MPPNB corpus? The vast majority of MPPNB figurines do not mark secondary sexual characteristics: why this emphasis on ambiguity?

Aside from the representation of secondary sexual characteristics, there are some omissions, emphases and deliberate alterations of human representations that also raise some interesting issues. In the MPPNB in particular, the statuary often omits legs and arms or portrays them in smaller proportion than the torso and head. The heads of these figures are enlarged and emphasized in the depiction of facial features, particularly the eyes. Additionally, the deliberate removal of heads from human figurines at MPPNB and LPPNB/PPNC 'Ain Ghazal coincides with the practice of skull removal in mortuary practices: what could be the relationship and significance of these symbolically similar behaviors? Finally, what does it mean that we find the vast majority of all figurine types in trash deposits?

Drawing upon the broader social, economic, and political context of PPNA, MPPNB, and LPPNB/PPNC communities, we offer a provisional interpretation of figurine use and meaning during these periods. We realize that this scenario is purely conjectural and is affected by sample size and publication gaps. At the same time, it is important to note that size and frequency of figurines in itself is an interesting question. We believe that the higher proportion of ambiguity in human figurines in the MPPNB and the marking of secondary sexual characteristics in the PPNA and LPPNB/PPNC may be related to the socioeconomic structures of lifeways in these communities. During the MPPNB people lived in larger, growing communities, building up the scale of established subsistence, residential, and ritual practices. During this period we witness an emphasis on ambiguity and masking of individuality in figurines as well as in mortuary practices and the built environment. Both the PPNA and the LPPNB/PPNC encompass periods in which subsistence, settlement, and scales of social complexity shifted radically. In the PPNA period many people were moving from a hunting/gathering/foraging to a fully sedentary food-producing lifeway. For the first time, they lived in large, sedentary communities, experimenting with and establishing their food production system. With the advent of storage and sedentism, these communities also began to negotiate and develop mechanisms for limiting social differentiation. Similarly, the LPPNB/PPNC people were dealing with stresses on their subsistence and social structures at the other end of the spectrum. Very large and densely populated communities struggled with overcrowding, sufficient food production, and resource depletion. Essentially, both of these periods could be viewed as times in which society struggled greatly with changing residential patterns, stress from living together in sedentary settlements, and subsistence changes. It is during these shifting and stressful times that people represented male and female sexed bodies (or portions of bodies), although to a limited extent. Perhaps during periods when social, economic, and ritual practices were under contention, aspects of individuality and social differentiation entered into the negotiation of everyday life. Importantly, the built environment and the mortuary practices in LPPNB/PPNC and PPNA show more diversity, underscoring the ways that people worked to live together in sedentary settlements despite the pressures socially, economically, and politically.

Final Thoughts

With so little contextual information published, it is important to highlight the unresolved nature of figurine research: specifically, how little we understand about the interrelationship between the size of communities, ritual and political action, and the social context of figurine manufacture, use, and discard. Any attempt to formulate a synthesis of "What Neolithic Figurines Mean" is very conjectural and potentially premature. Nevertheless, we hope that this work highlights the challenges that Neolithic researchers face in interpreting figurine use in the world's earliest agricultural communities, and offers a limited critique of existing interpretive approaches. We conclude by returning to two points that need further exploration.

First, why did Neolithic people represent ambiguity in the majority of their human figurines, and alternatively mark or not mark sex or gender attributes on a small percentage of human representations? There are several possible interpretations, including the masking or emphasis of individual or structural differences to help negotiate social and economic changes experienced by these early agricultural communities in which we witness the initial development of storage technologies, surplus economy, and social differentiation. Similarly, these people may not have conceptualized male and female bodily differences as important aspects in their worldviews in understanding what it meant to be a person in a body. Conversely, these differences may have been crucially important in everyday interactions, and therefore they found it important to mask them in creating idealized social memories of the way life should be.

A second question that future researchers should address is one posed by Ucko (1996): why make figurines at all? We can draw on ethnographic analogies of bodily representation in ritual and non-ritual contexts to help us address this question, as the topic obviously holds important implications for functionalist interpretations. In a related way, we can also ask, "Why make different types of figurines (human, zoomorphic, or geometric)?" We argue that there is a definite shift in the manufacture of these figurine classes through the Pre-Pottery Neolithic, and that future exploration of this issue may enhance our understanding of the Neolithic.

Posing this last question leads us to our second point for consideration: the continued need for contextual analysis of figurines. We hope that it is clear that our own ability to make interpretations of these figurines is limited by the paucity of published contextual information. It is unfortunate that in many cases, the development of grand models and interpretations of Neolithic figurines is founded on a remarkably poor consideration of context and archaeological data. There is, for example, only limited understanding of the manufacture, use, and discard of figurines. While many interpretive models of the Neolithic use figurine data from secondary sources and there is very little contextual data published from the southern Levantine contexts, we do not feel any need to be pessimistic. Among others, Voigt (2000) has demonstrated the utility of contextual studies of Neolithic figurines from Turkey and Iran, and has established a strong analytical approach that focuses on context. In conclusion, we believe that studies sensitive to context will provide new insights into the social, economic, and ritual world in which figurines were used in the past.

Acknowledgments

We thank R. Bernbeck and S. Pollock for asking us to participate in this volume. M. Cochrane and A. Lowe provided assistance with the illustrations and data gathering. Discussions with M. Voigt, R. Joyce, S. Blum, G. Rollefson, O. Bar-Yosef, and several anonymous reviewers have been crucial to the development of this essay. While not agreeing with some of the concepts and interpretations presented in this essay, the constructive criticism and advice of all of these folks have immeasurably improved the clarity and organization of this essay.

NOTE

1 The context information for the human figurines from 'Ain Ghazal is currently available on Schmandt-Besserat's webpage (http://link.lanic.utexas.edu/menic/ghazal/). While the context information is very helpful, most of the objects are identified as PPNB (as opposed to MPPNB, LPPNB, or PPNC) and therefore we could not incorporate specific data from these tables into this analysis.

REFERENCES

Arensburg, Baruch, and Israel Hershkovitz, 1989 Artificial Skull "Treatment" in the PPNB Period: Nahal Hemar. *In* People and Culture in Change: Proceedings of the Second Symposium on Upper Paleolithic, Mesolithic, and Neolithic Populations of Europe and the Mediterranean Basin. Israel Hershkovitz, ed. pp. 115–133. Oxford: British Archaeological Reports International 508.

Bailey, Douglas, 1996 The Interpretation of Figurines: The Emergence of Illusion and New Ways of Seeing. Cambridge Archaeological Journal 6:281–307.

Bar-Yosef, Ofer 1997 Symbolic Expressions in Later Prehistory of the Levant: Why Are They So Few? *In* Beyond Art: Pleistocene Image and Symbol. Margaret Conkey, Olga Soffer, Deborah Stratmann, and Nina Jablonski, eds. pp. 161–187. San Francisco: California Academy of Sciences.

Bar-Yosef, Ofer, and David Alon, 1988 Nahal Hemar. 'Atiqot 18:1–81.

Bar-Yosef, Ofer, and Avi Gopher, eds. 1997 An Early Neolithic Village in the Jordan Valley. Part I: The Archaeology of Netiv Hagdud. Cambridge, MA: American School of Prehistoric Research, Peabody Museum.

Bar-Yosef, Ofer, and Richard Meadow, 1995 The Origins of Agriculture in the Near East. *In* Last Hunters–First Farmers: New Perspectives on the Prehistoric Transition to Agriculture. T. Douglas Price and Anne Gebauer, eds. pp. 39–94. Santa Fe: School of American Research.

Bonogofsky, Michelle, 2001 Cranial Modeling and Neolithic Bone Modification at 'Ain Ghazal: New Interpretations, Paléorient 27(2):141–146.

Butler, Judith, 1990 Gender Trouble: Feminism and the Subversion of Identity. New York: Routledge.

Butler, Judith, 1993 Bodies That Matter: On the Discursive Limits of "Sex." New York: Routledge.

Cauvin, Jacques, 1994 Naissance des divinités. Naissance de l'agriculture. La révolution des symboles au néolithique. Paris: CNRS.

Cauvin, Jacques, 2000a The Birth of the Gods and the Origins of Agriculture. Cambridge: Cambridge University Press.

Cauvin, Jacques, 2000b The Symbolic Foundation of the Neolithic Revolution in the Near East. In Life in Neolithic Farming Communities: Social Organization, Identity, and Differentiation. Ian Kuijt, ed. pp. 235–251. New York: Kluwer Academic/Plenum.

Conkey, Margaret, and Joan Gero, 1997 Programme to Practice: Gender and Feminism in Archaeology. Annual Review of Anthropology 26:411–437.

De Contenson, Henri, 1967 Troisième campagne à Tell Ramad 1966. Rapport préliminaire. Annales Archéologiques de Syria XVII (1–2):17–24.

Douglas, Mary, 1982 Natural Symbols: Explorations in Cosmology. 3rd edition. New York: Pantheon Books.

Echegaray, Joaquin González, 1966 Excavaciones en la Terrza de El-Khiam (Jordania). Madrid: Consejo Superior el Investigaciones Cientificas.

Ferembach, Denise, and Monique Lechevallier, 1973 Découverte de deux crânes surmodelés dans une habitation du VIIème millénaire à Beisamoun, Israel. Paléorient 1:223–230.

Forest, Jean-Daniel, 1994 Towards an Interpretation of the Çatal Höyük Reliefs and Wall Paintings. In 1993 Yılı Anadolu Mediniyetleri Müzesi Konferansları. pp. 118–136. Ankara: Museum of Anatolian Civilizations.

Foster, Brian, 1993 Before the Muses. Bethesda, MD: CDL Press.

Garstang, John, and J. B. E. Garstang, 1940 The Story of Jericho. London: Hodder and Stoughton.

Gilchrist, Roberta, 1999 Gender and Archaeology: Contesting the Past. London: Routledge.

Gopher, Avi, and Estelle Orelle, 1996 An Alternative Interpretation for the Material Imagery of the Yarmukian, A Neolithic Culture of the Sixth Millennium B.C. in the Southern Levant. Cambridge Archaeological Journal 6:255–279.

Goren, Yuval, Nigel Goring-Morris, and Irena Segal, 2001 The Technology of Skull Modeling in the Pre-Pottery Neolithic B (PPNB): Regional Variability, the Relation of Technology and Iconography and Their Archaeological Implications. Journal of Archaeological Science 28:671–690.

Goren, Yuval, Irena Segal, and Ofer Bar-Yosef, 1993 Plaster Artifacts and the Interpretation of the Nahal Hemar Cave. Journal of the Israel Prehistoric Society 25:120–131.

Goring-Morris, Nigel, 2000 The Quick and The Dead: The Social Context of Aceramic Neolithic Mortuary Practices as Seen from Kfar Hahoresh. In Life in Neolithic Farming Communities: Social Organization, Identity, and Differentiation. Ian Kuijt, ed. pp. 103–136. New York: Kluwer Academic/Plenum Press.

Goring-Morris, Nigel, and Anna Belfer-Cohen, 1998 The Articulation of Cultural Processes and Late Quaternary Environmental Changes in Cisjordan. Paléorient 23:71–93.

Griffin, Patricia, Carol Grissom, and Gary Rollefson, 1998 Three Late Eighth Millennium Plastered Faces from 'Ain Ghazal, Jordan. Paléorient 24:59–70.

Haaland, Gunnar, and Randi Haaland, 1996 Levels of Meaning in Symbolic Objects. Cambridge Archaeological Journal 6:281–307.

Hamilton, Naomi, 1996 The Personal is Political. Cambridge Archaeological Journal 6:281–307.

Hermanson, Bo Dahl, 1997 Art and Ritual Behaviour in Neolithic Basta. In The Prehistory of Jordan II. Perspectives from 1997. Hans-Georg Gebel, Zeidan Kafafi, and Gary Rollefson, eds. pp. 333–343. Studies in Early Near Eastern Production, Subsistence, and Environment 4. Berlin: Ex oriente.

Hertz, Robert, 1960 Death and the Right Hand. Rodney Needham and Claydia Needham, trans. Glencoe, IL: Free Press.

Hodder, Ian, 2001 Symbolism and the Origins of Agriculture in the Near East. Cambridge Archaeological Journal 11:107–112.

Joyce, Rosemary, 1993 Women's Work: Images of Production and Reproduction in Pre-Hispanic Southern Central America. Current Anthropology 34:255–274.

Joyce, Rosemary, 2000 Gender and Power in Prehispanic Mesoamerica. Philadelphia: University of Pennsylvania Press.

Kafafi, Zaidan, and Gary Rollefson, 1995 Excavations at 'Ayn Ghazal: Preliminary Report. Annual of the Department of Antiquities of Jordan 39:13–29.

Kan, Sergei, 1989 Symbolic Immortality. Washington: Smithsonian Institution Press.

Kenyon, Kathleen, 1981 Excavations at Jericho, vol. III. The Architecture and Stratigraphy of the Tell. London: British School of Archaeology in Jerusalem.

Kirkbride, Diana, 1968 Beidha 1967 – an Interim Report. Palestine Exploration Quarterly 100:90–96.

Knapp, A. Bernard, and Lynn Meskell, 1997 Bodies of Evidence on Prehistoric Cyprus. Cambridge Archaeological Journal 7:183–204.

Kuijt, Ian, 1997 Interpretation, Data, and the Khiamian of the South-Central Levant. Neo-Lithics 3:3–6.

Kuijt, Ian, 1998 Trying to Fit Round Houses into Square Holes: Re-examining the Timing of the South-central Levantine Pre-Pottery Neolithic A and Pre-Pottery Neolithic B Cultural Transition. In The Prehistory of Jordan II: Studies in Early Near Eastern Production, Subsistence, and Environment. Hans-Georg Gebel, Zaidan Kafafi, and Gary Rollefson, eds. Berlin: Ex oriente.

Kuijt, Ian, 2000a Keeping the Peace: Ritual, Skull Caching and Community Integration in the Levantine Neolithic. In Life in Neolithic Farming Communities: Social Organization, Identity, and Differentiation. Ian Kuijt, ed. pp. 137–163. New York: Kluwer Academic/Plenum Press.

Kuijt, Ian, 2000b People and Space in Early Neolithic Villages: Exploring Daily Lives, Community Size and Architecture in the Late Pre-Pottery Neolithic. Journal of Anthropological Archaeology 19:75–102.

Kuijt, Ian, 2001 Meaningful Masks: Place, Death, and the Transmission of Social Memory in Early Agricultural Communities of the Near Eastern Pre-Pottery Neolithic. In Social Memory, Identity, and Death: Intradisciplinary Perspectives on Mortuary Rituals. Meredith Chesson, ed. pp. 80–99. Washington: American Anthropological Association.

Kuijt, Ian, and Bill Finlayson, 2002 The 2001 Excavation Season at the Pre-Pottery Neolithic A Period Settlement of Dhra', Jordan: Preliminary Results. Neo-Lithics 2(1):12–15.

Lacqueur, Thomas, 1990 Making Sex: Body and Gender from the Greeks to Freud. Cambridge, MA: Harvard University Press.

Lesure, Richard, 2002 The Goddess Defracted: Thinking about the Figurines of Early Villages. Current Anthropology 43:587–610.

Lock, Margaret, 1993 Cultivating the Body: Anthropology and Epistemologies of Bodily Practice and Knowledge. Annual Review of Anthropology 22:133–155.

Mahasneh, Hamzeh, and Hans Dieter Bienert, 1999 Anthropomorphic Figurines from the Early Neolithic Site of es-Sifiya (Jordan). Zeitschrift des Deutschen Palästina-Vereins 115:109–126.

Mahasneh, Hamzeh, and Hans-Georg Gebel, 1999 Geometric Objects from LPPNB es-Sifiya, Wadi Mujib, Jordan. Paléorient 24:105–110.

Marcus, Joyce, 1996 The Importance of Context in Interpreting Figurines. Cambridge Archaeological Journal 6:281–307.

Martin, Emily, 1987 The Woman in the Body. Boston: Beacon Press.

Mellaart, James, 1967 A Neolithic Town in Anatolia. New York: McGraw-Hill.

Meskell, Lynn, 1999 Archaeologies of Social Life: Age, Sex, Class, etc. in Ancient Egypt. Oxford: Basil Blackwell.

Nissen, Hans, Mujahid Muheisen, and Hans-Georg Gebel, 1991 Report on the Excavations at Basta 1988. Annual of the Department of Antiquities of Jordan 35:13–40.

Noy, Tamar, 1991 Art and Decoration of the Natufian at Nahal Oren. In The Natufian Culture in the Levant. Ofer Bar-Yosef and François Valla, eds. pp. 557–568. Ann Arbor: International Monographs in Prehistory.

Perrot, Jean, 1966 Le gisement Natoufien de Mallaha (Eynan) Israel. Paris: Association Paléorient.

Postgate, J. Nicholas, 1994 Text and Figurine in Ancient Mesopotamia: Match and Mismatch. In The Ancient Mind, Elements of Cognitive Archaeology. Colin Renfrew and Ezra Zubrow, eds. pp. 176–184. Cambridge: Cambridge University Press.

Rollefson, Gary, 1986 Neolithic 'Ain Ghazal (Jordan): Ritual and Ceremony II. Paléorient 12(1):45–52.

Rollefson, Gary, 2000 Ritual and Social Structure at Neolithic 'Ain Ghazal. In Life in Neolithic Farming Communities: Social Organization, Identity, and Differentiation. Ian Kuijt, ed. pp. 165–190. New York: Kluwer Academic/Plenum Press.

Rollefson, Gary, 2001a The Neolithic Period. In The Archaeology of Jordan. Burton MacDonald, Russell Adams, and Piotr Bienkowski, eds. pp. 67–105. Sheffield: Sheffield Academic Press.

Rollefson, Gary, 2001b 2001: An Archaeological Odyssey. Cambridge Archaeological Journal 11:112–114.

Rollefson, Gary, and Zeidan Kafafi, 1996 The 1995 Excavations at 'Ayn Ghazal: Preliminary Report. Annual of the Department of Antiquities of Jordan 40:11–28.

Rollefson, Gary, Denise Schmandt-Besserat, and Jerome Rose, 1999 A Decorated Skull from MPPNB 'Ain Ghazal. Paléorient 24:99–104.

Rollefson, Gary, Alan Simmons, Marcia Donaldson, William Gillespie, Zeidan Kafafi, Ilse Köhler-Rollefson, Ellen McAdam, Scott Rolston, and Kathryn Tubb, 1985 Excavations at the Pre-Pottery Neolithic B Village of 'Ain Ghazal (Jordan), 1983. Mitteilungen der Deutschen Orient-Gesellschaft zu Berlin 117:69–116.

Schiller, Anne, 1997 Small Sacrifices, Religious Change and Cultural Identity among the Ngaju of Indonesia. Oxford: Oxford University Press.

Schmandt-Besserat, Denise, 1997 Animal Symbols at 'Ain Ghazal. Expedition 39(1):48–58.

Schmandt-Besserat, Denise, 1998a 'Ain Ghazal "Monumental" Figures. Bulletin of the American Schools of Oriental Research 4:1–17.

Schmandt-Besserat, Denise, 1998b A Stone Metaphor of Creation. Near Eastern Archaeology 61(2):109–117.

Soffer, Olga, James Adovasio, and David Hyland, 2000 The "Venus" Figurines: Textiles, Basketry, Gender, and Status in the Upper Paleolithic. Current Anthropology 41:511–537.

Stekelis, Moshe, and Tamar Yizraeli, 1963 Excavations at Nahal Oren, Preliminary Report. Israel Exploration Journal 131:1–12.

Strouhal, Eugen, 1973 Five Plastered Skulls from Pre-Pottery Neolithic B Jericho: Anthropological Study. Paléorient 1:231–247.

Ucko, Peter, 1968 Anthropomorphic Figurines of Predynastic Egypt and Neolithic Crete with Comparative Material from the Prehistoric Near East and Mainland Greece. Royal Anthropological Institute Occasional Paper No. 24. London: Andrew Szmidla.

Ucko, Peter, 1996 Mother, Are You There? Cambridge Archaeological Journal 6:281–307.

van Dijk, Jan, Albrecht Goetze, and Mary India Hussey, 1985 Early Mesopotamian Incantations and Rituals. New Haven: Yale University Press.

Voigt, Mary, 1983 Hajji Firuz Tepe, Iran: The Neolithic Settlement. Hasanlu Excavation Reports I. Philadelphia: University of Pennsylvania Museum of Archaeology and Anthropology.

Voigt, Mary, 1985 Village on the Euphrates: Excavations at Neolithic Gritille, Turkey. Expedition 27:10–24.

Voigt, Mary, 2000 Çatal Höyük in Context: Ritual at Early Neolithic Sites in Central and Eastern Turkey. In Life in Neolithic Farming Communities: Social Organization, Identity, and Differentiation. Ian Kuijt, ed. pp. 253–294. New York: Kluwer Academic/Plenum Press.

Weinstein-Evron, Mina, and Anna Belfer-Cohen, 1993 Natufian Figurines from the New Excavations of the el-Wad Cave, Mt. Carmel, Israel. Rock Art Research 10(2):102–106.

Yakar, Regita, and Israel Hershkovitz, 1990 Nahal Hemar Cave: the Modeled Skulls. Atiqot 18:59–63.

9

The State: The Process of State Formation as Seen from Mesopotamia

Jean-Daniel Forest

Foreword

In common thought, the archaic state is related in some way to ours. When conceiving of humankind as continuously progressing, evolving by developing more and more complexity, the archaic state may appear as some far-off ancestor, and the interest paid to it is the more natural as it left behind concrete evidence of its high level of civilization. Hence that endless fascination for Egypt and Mesopotamia, the Indus Valley, China, Mexico, and Peru. For scholars the primitive state is a baffling topic: quite rare, it is the outcome of a far-reaching process that has to be explained. The question is not so much one of analyzing a particular kind of polity, but rather of revealing the mechanisms which eventually led to its appearance. The process is a long-term one, which took place over millennia, and the whole trajectory must be considered rather than only its final stage. To put it another way, the nature of the state question is dynamic as well as systemic. Here I will consider mainly the dynamic aspect.

That quest, already initiated in antiquity by Plato and Aristotle among others, was renewed during the 17th and 18th centuries by some philosophers, including Hobbes, Locke, and Hume in England, and Diderot, Montesquieu, and Rousseau in France, who contributed substantially to the elaboration of concepts we still use. During the 19th century, the West became more interested in remote cultures. It became concerned with its past through the study of ancient texts and remains, and it discovered "exotic" cultures through colonial ventures. It is at that time that sciences were constituted as separate fields, among which archaeology found its place. But archaeology at first had to excavate and classify a large series of data, and for that reason those who got involved in the question of the state were not archaeologists but rather historians, jurists, economists, and sociologists including de Tocqueville (1805–59), Fustel de Coulanges (1830–89), Morgan (1818–81), Maine (1822–88), Marx (1818–83), Engels (1820–95), Spencer (1820–1903), and

Durkheim (1858–1917). Since that time, the available data have expanded, but sociocultural anthropologists maintained their leadership over the subject, for their sources are more easily accessible and more directly exploitable than those of archaeology. Yet, every case within their reach has come under the influence of external and more evolutionarily developed entities, and they are therefore only by-products of a piece of history played out elsewhere.

Fried (1967) is one of the first scholars to have considered the whole scale of the problem, for he was careful to distinguish between primary (pristine) and secondary states. At the same time, he was well aware of the fact that primary states were quite rare and too ill-defined to ground his thought on, but he believed that the difficulty could be circumvented by replacing the missing data by cultural anthropological evidence, which he supposed to be equivalent. Unfortunately, there are drawbacks to such an approach. First, the evolutionary trajectory lasted for millennia, even if the state proper (depending on how it is defined) appears quite abruptly. The historical perspective which would enable cultural anthropologists to perceive such long-term change is never available, so their reconstructions of the dynamics of evolution cannot but be inferential. Second, the "traditional" societies that we know at present are quite diverse, and not all can be representative to the same extent of the past societies which eventually led to the state. When using them to build his four-part scheme, Fried probably mingled different trajectories, and for reconstructing change used societies which had nothing to do with the particular line of evolution that led to the state. Third, the reconstruction of the whole trajectory supposed that every preliminary stage still has some equivalence in the world today. That is not the case (the city-state, for example, has completely disappeared), and Fried himself acknowledges the point when writing of stratified societies. So it becomes apparent that the origins of the pristine state escape the scope of cultural anthropology. In order to understand the process, its form, character, and rhythm, we must undertake the difficult study of those few cases which, whether they were used as models by other societies or not, nonetheless deeply influenced the history of surrounding societies. Knowledge about such ancient states depends entirely on archaeology. Ideally, archaeologists and cultural anthropologists should collaborate in the task, but both parties have become trapped in the particularisms of their respective fields and hardly understand each other.

Archaeology is still handicapped by the very nature of its data and the time-consuming procedures that give access to them. It is at once clear that what we know about the different primary centers of evolution varies greatly from case to case. For example, the most ancient phases of development are ill-documented in Egypt, the Indus Valley, and China, so that it is very difficult to make comparisons, and at present, those centers can only be examined on their own. Mesopotamia is probably one of the most suitable cases for analysis. Second, the very complexity of the cases under study raises particular problems of representativeness. The data are quite diverse, and it is more difficult to acquire a significant part of them and to find the rarest kinds which often are at the same time the most spectacular. Within hierarchized societies, the elites represent but a very small part of society, so that chances are few for us to perceive them, through their tombs or their residences, for example. Third, our data are quite particular in that they are always material: architectural remains, objects, bones and botanical remains, and cultural deposits. Texts only appear within the most complex societies and at best inform us about a very late stage of the evolutionary trajectory.

Archaeology has to give sense to its ambiguous data, and at present different attitudes prevail concerning how this is to be done – either arguing at one extreme that the data are forever mute or, at the other, that anything may be said about them. Both result in denying any interest to archaeology. Solutions do exist, but first it must be recalled that the process of reasoning which leads from raw data to interpretation always depends on analogy (Verhoeven, this volume). This means that reasoning is grounded in experience, and knowledge accumulated through time, which may be used as a model. The critical point is to appeal to the best analogical basis, the one most suitable for the question to be addressed. In everyday life, our common sense plays such a part, but it depends upon socialization, and this culturally defined baggage prevents us from understanding something truly different. For understanding past societies through the material remains they left, common sense is inappropriate, and it must be replaced by something better, to be found, in my opinion, in what our cultural anthropological colleagues have been able to learn from the "primitive" societies they have analyzed. The arbitrary features – superficial, in some ways – which make a culture particular have to be put aside and only structural features and underlying mechanisms retained. Only that way may comparisons be drawn through space and time. Ethnographic analogies are most useful for the "simpler" societies of the past, but this utility declines as the societies we study become more complex. In any case, cultural anthropological studies as a basis for analogy are much more suitable than common sense.

It is as a specialist of archaic Mesopotamia that I will grapple here with the question of the origins of the state. My contribution is divided into four parts. After a brief overview of current theories, I present the main lines of Mesopotamian history, as we may reconstruct it at present. Then I consider what may be inferred from the analysis of specific data for understanding the evolutionary process in general and the formation of the state in particular. Finally, I come back to current theories in order to compare them to my conclusions.

An Overview of Current Theories

The particular phenomenon of the advent of the state has given rise to many interpretations that can only be considered here in a schematic way (cf. Haas 1982 for further details). First we must recall the two major options that divided 17th- and 18th-century philosophers. The one side argued that the state was grounded in a social contract, the other that it was imposed by force. Later theories which sought to explain the advent of the state in Mesopotamia and elsewhere generally waver between the same poles – contract and constraint, or integration and conflict – even when combining elements of both. Most often, some particular element is put forward as a "prime mover," that is, as either an initial or a main factor, depending on whether the determinant is conceived as being historical or structural. Such prime mover models have been criticized and have tended to be replaced by the idea of complex causality drawn from cybernetics, and exemplified by the work of Johnson, Wright, and Flannery (Flannery 1972; Wright and Johnson 1975; Wright 1977). In my opinion, traditional theories still deserve some attention, but they have to be evaluated according to the quality of the available data and the analogical field employed in their formulation.

The factors that have been drawn upon to explain the origins of the state are not numerous. They deal mainly with production and circulation of essential resources, demography, war, ideology and especially religion, social differentiation, and the quest for power. These features have been used to build networks of causal relationships, and differences between theories lie in the main elements chosen to construct the argument. With few exceptions (such as Spencer [1967], who brings war to the foreground), a prime place is granted to the economic roots of society. Agricultural practice, especially when irrigation is involved, has sometimes been taken as the prime determinant (Wittfogel [1957] is the best example), in the sense that the very conditions of production drive society to make needed organizational adjustments. But generally, agricultural constraints are linked to other features, such as trade and demography. Trade enables people to exchange local goods for products that are not otherwise available. It creates relations of dependency among the social groups involved and necessitates organizational agencies in order that those relations be regular and ensured. Trade may take place at a regional scale, either because of the geographic juxtaposition of contrasting ecological zones (Sanders 1976a, 1976b; Sanders et al. 1979) or because populations that live together exploit the environment in complementary ways, for example agriculturalists and pastoralists (Johnson 1973; Wright and Johnson 1975). Trade may also function at a larger scale and give rise to the long-distance trade thesis, as developed by Childe for Mesopotamia and Rathje (1971, 1972) for central America. Demography is probably the most popular element drawn upon in scholars' explanations (Smith 1972). The general idea is that demographic growth brings with it difficulties in meeting subsistence needs, resulting in an unbalanced situation between people and their environment, and hence the famous notion of "carrying capacity." "Demographic pressure" is thought to have given rise to reactions which either drove people to intensify their production (Boserup 1965; Smith and Young 1972), promoted competition (Fried 1967:196–204), or induced war (Carneiro 1970, 1978).

Whatever the scenario for explaining change – aspects of production, the desire to procure goods that were unavailable locally, or demographic pressure – centralization, hierarchy, and inequality are presumed to develop, either because the situation transformed those responsible into exploiters or because certain people found themselves with an opportunity to use their position for their own benefit (Adams 1984:88). Depending on the point of view, the state may then be conceived in contrasting ways. It may be seen as a solution for going beyond a dead-end economic situation, either through better organization (Service) or through conquest (Carneiro). Conversely, it may be viewed as a solution to class conflicts induced by an increasingly uneven distribution of wealth, a solution that benefits the elite (Childe 1936, 1942; Engels 1954; Fried 1967:235). But even granting that the state emerged spontaneously for practical reasons, it always remains somewhat ambiguous, being valued as both positive (from the point of view of organization) as well as negative (in terms of inequality).

The Mesopotamian Case

Mesopotamia – the lower Tigris and Euphrates alluvial plain of southern Iraq – was a great center of pristine evolution. In the span of about five millennia, simple groups of villagers developed more and more complexity until the advent of a state-level polity. The Mesopotamian development is among the most ancient ones (along with Egypt), among the best documented after more than a century of excavations, and in my opinion the one to which our Western civilization is the most indebted.[1]

As previously explained, our data are mute and only make sense through analogy. In the present state of archaeological research, the choice of analogy is left to the judgment of each particular scholar, leading to contrasting conclusions. The particular data base on which my own reconstruction of past social organization[2] rests seeks to replace common sense by anthropological knowledge that is structural in character. Nevertheless, that reconstruction remains quite personal, and it is not the only possible interpretation, as may be acknowledged by consulting other syntheses reflecting different approaches.[3] In any case, the explanations are not to be evaluated in terms of right or wrong, but rather according to their ability to make sense of or bring some order to a muddle of data, and so to help us grasp the past.

Several "cultures" are implicated in the trajectory of change. They follow one another without a break and most probably do not involve any major change in the make-up of the population. The first, called Ubaid after a site near Ur, lasted for more than 2,500 years. Because of its duration, it has been subdivided into phases according to the evolution of pottery shapes and decoration. The most ancient levels (called Ubaid 0, because Ubaid 1–4 were already in use when these levels were discovered) have been brought to light at Tell el Oueili, north of the present day town of Nasiriyeh. These earliest levels may be dated to about 6500 cal. B.C.E., but the levels that have been more extensively excavated (Ubaid 0 and 1) are somewhat later, around 6000 cal. B.C.E. They contained the foundations of granaries and private dwellings (figure 9.1). The dwellings are large, tripartite buildings, comprising one main common room in the center and private apartments on both sides that may have been occupied respectively by an elder couple and a younger one with its children. Three generations might therefore have lived together, constituting a stem-family. That particular kind of family group indicates that we are already dealing with developed village societies, for in societies in which decision-making lies in the hands of family heads, the enlargement of the family group is intended to maintain some stability in the numbers of people who assume responsibilities.

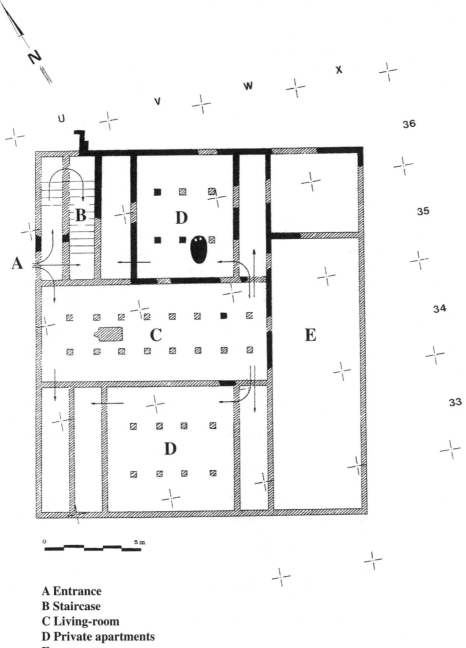

A Entrance
B Staircase
C Living-room
D Private apartments
E annexes

Figure 9.1 Plan of an Ubaid-period house from Tell el Oueili (Ubaid 0, ca. 6000 cal B.C.E.) (author's original)

Over time, Ubaidian social groups grew, so that they had to find political, social, and ideological solutions for dealing with larger populations. They developed a more pronounced hierarchy, so that the most recent phases of the Ubaid culture (Ubaid 4–5) may be conceived as "chiefdoms," in which decision-making was taken over by a few lineage heads. By Ubaid 3 (ca. 5500–4500 cal B.C.E.), large tripartite buildings built on a terrace are found, with a central hall and a row of utilitarian rooms on both sides. They are probably assembly chambers, where eminent persons may have gathered in order to manage public affairs. The buildings became progressively larger, their façades more elaborate, and their terraces higher, until they towered above the surroundings. We know hardly anything more, but our lack of data may be balanced in part by sources from northern Mesopotamia. There, around the end of the sixth millennium cal B.C.E., a local culture known as Halaf adopted Ubaidian features, and by so doing turned into what we call Northern Ubaid to distinguish it from the Ubaid proper. While the Halaf changed little, the Northern Ubaid (as well as the so-called Gawra culture which later takes over from it) evolved under the impulse of new values borrowed from its southern neighbor, and it continues along the trajectory that had already been experimented with by the Ubaid a millennium earlier. It follows that some knowledge about the fifth millennium Ubaid may be gained from the northern culture of the fourth millennium. In this particular case, such a derivation is not problematic, for the secondary evolution in the north is directly induced by the primary center in the south in such a way that both cultures are intimately related, as would be the case between a copy and its original.

At the site of Tepe Gawra, near Mosul, it may be ascertained that after a phase in which the family unit is of the stem-type (as in Ubaid 0–1, but with clearly different house plans [cf. figure 9.2]), there comes another phase in which the nuclear family, living in small tripartite buildings, dominates. In order to minimize the numbers of people entitled to take decisions, decision-makers had to represent a larger group than ever before, and one that was too large to be sheltered in a single house. The stem-family, which had the same purpose at a lower level of integration, ceased to be of interest, and the nuclear family (the minimal social unit) recovered the part it had played much earlier. Archaeology proves to be able to bear testimony to those people who concentrated the power of decision-making in their hands and who may be described as leading citizens. Some dwellings at Gawra stand out by their large size, the thickness of their walls, and the decoration of their facades, while some peculiarities in their plan show that they are much more open to the outside than is usually the case (figure 9.3). These are the residences of eminent persons, and it appears that, due to the functions they exercised, these people opened their houses to ordinary people who depended on them. At first, such fine residences were distributed throughout the settlement, but later they tended to occur in one spot at the top of the site. This means that leaders eventually became aware of having more in common with each other than they had with ordinary people – they now constituted an elite. At their head, a prominent individual lived in a larger and more elaborate house, where he probably received his subordinates as well as his peers. But after some generations, one of these para-

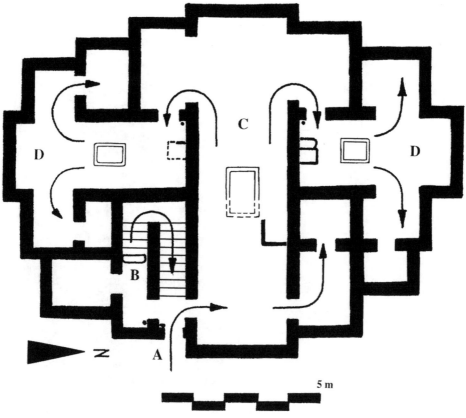

A Entrance
B Staircase
C Living-room
D Private apartments

Figure 9.2 Plan of an Ubaid-period house from Kheit Qasim (beginning of the fifth millennium cal B.C.E.) (author's original)

mount leaders built an audience hall which, with its courtyards and granary, constituted the heart of a compound that was the prototype of a palace. The gradual hierarchization of society is also reflected by changes in burial practices, with status differences more and more accentuated and very wealthy tombs appearing at the end. Such pieces of evidence bear testimony to successive levels of a chiefdom, and no doubt the Ubaid in the south experimented with an evolution of the same kind.

At about 4100/4000 cal B.C.E. the Ubaid culture was replaced by the Uruk (the change in terminology being based solely on the disappearance of painted pottery) which lasted until the end of the fourth millennium. Cities are now to be found, and the alluvial plain was soon divided into a series of small principalities, the populations of which were mainly urban. These principalities have been called city-states.

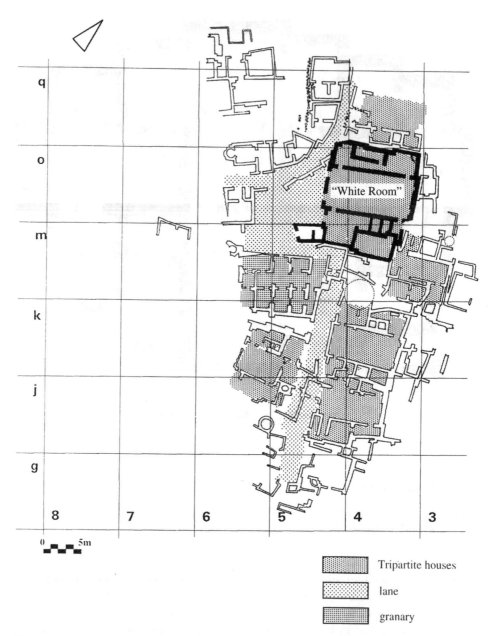

"White Room"

8   7   6   5   4   3

q   o   m   k   j   g

0 ▬▬▬ 5m

▨ Tripartite houses

▨ lane

▨ granary

Figure 9.3 Plan of a notable's residence and small tripartite houses from Gawra XII (Northern Ubaid, end of the fifth millennium cal B.C.E.) (after Tobler 1950: Pl. VIII)

No doubt these are state-like formations, but, as will be explained below, they must be distinguished from the state proper. Hierarchy became more pronounced, even while the economic basis remained on the whole the same. A hereditary elite settled into place, with one individual of higher rank named as leader, or king. In order to mark its distinction, the elite had luxury goods manufactured for itself. Skilled craftsmen were therefore necessary, and demand was sufficient to promote inventiveness and the elaboration of new techniques. But most of all, rare materials were needed, which were to be found only abroad. By the middle of the fourth millennium, expeditions to distant areas were organized, and colonies were implanted in northern Syria in order to acquire precious ores, among other things, obtained from local populations in Anatolia. Some colonial towns, built where none previously existed and sometimes quite rapidly, bear witness to the most ancient urbanism. In order to accommodate waves of settlers, much organization was required: regular streets were laid out, occasionally with systems for draining sewage, and plots of land were distributed according to a process of allotment. The housing was quite uniform, comprised of several buildings distributed around a courtyard, with the house proper on one side and a large reception room on the other. The doubling of entryways as well as fireplaces indicates that the genders are now more markedly opposed within the family group.

For control of the town, a council chamber, or town hall, was built on a high terrace or acropolis. The huge capitals in the south have been relatively little explored, but the late fourth millennium acropolis of Uruk has been excavated, revealing a series of buildings that show a degree of inventiveness that is never again found in later periods (figure 9.4). Those buildings are exceptional by their size (up to 4,600 sq. m), their plan, their technique (the use of gypsum, either let between planks or moulded), and their decoration (clay or stone cones, the colored heads of which were arranged to create geometric patterns). Together these buildings constitute a kind of palace, but one in which the different functional components were not yet integrated into a whole. Not far from this building, in the so-called "Anu-ziggurat" area, the "White Temple" was, like the "Painted Temple" at Uqair, actually a council room built on a high terrace, where eminent people (most probably lineage leaders) gathered in order to manage public affairs. Henceforth the elite were relieved of agricultural labor for which they were dependent on commoners, because they were placed in charge of the community and assumed the function of ensuring the group's prosperity. Fields were placed at their disposal as well as workmen to cultivate them. Because those fields were large, new techniques were perfected, and the swing-plow, for example, was invented. The elite also had to dispense some goods in order to remunerate those to whom they were obliged as well as in exchange for imported materials. It is possibly for such purposes that large flocks of sheep were raised – for their wool rather than their meat – and spinning factories (which are explicitly mentioned in the texts of the subsequent Early Dynastic period) were built.

In the elite sphere, the flow of goods had to be supervised and controlled, and, because human memory was unable to grasp the sheer volume of this information, new techniques of management were invented: cylinder seals for certifying sealings, tokens for accounting, and writing (the medium for communicating a language called Sumerian [see Zimansky, this volume]) for keeping more detailed records. In order to ensure the cohesion of a larger society, new ideological tools were required as well. A whole set of figurative images appeared that exalted kingship, and temples were built to demonstrate the presence of the gods among mortals and therefore guarantee social order. New trends can be detected among commoners

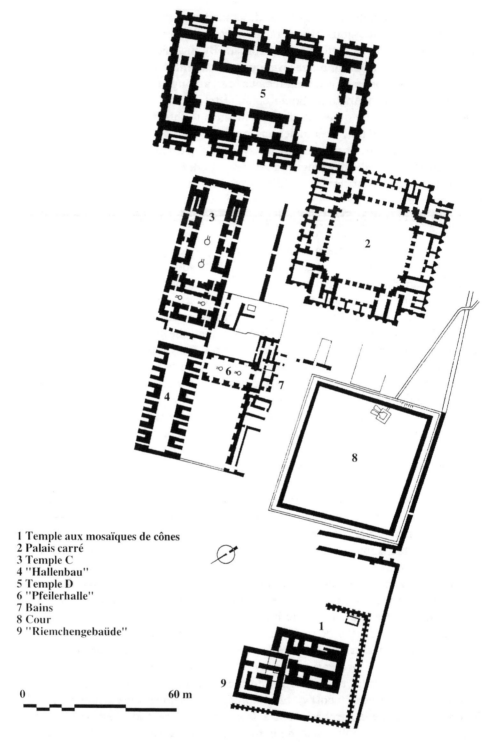

1 Temple aux mosaïques de cônes
2 Palais carré
3 Temple C
4 "Hallenbau"
5 Temple D
6 "Pfeilerhalle"
7 Bains
8 Cour
9 "Riemchengebaüde"

0   60 m

Figure 9.4 Plan of Eanna area of Uruk at the end of the fourth millennium B.C.E. (after Lenzen, as published in Amiet 1977:526)

as well. The city had become so large that all of its inhabitants could not know one another. Anonymity was the rule as kinship ties weakened. The multiplication of needs, the diversity and elaboration of techniques made it difficult for people to make everything for themselves. For some aspects of everyday life, people tended to rely on others and, because kinship could not remain the sole reference, exchange increased, probably leading to the appearance of standards and of places where equivalents could be defined and normalized.

The city-states of the alluvium were quite prosperous and active, but their very dynamism soon brought their interests into opposition and led them to rise up against one another. A climate of endemic war ensued, which became a characteristic of the following Early Dynastic period (third millennium B.C.E.). City walls were constructed, and weapons of copper or bronze became more frequent. Images were still closely bound to royal power (recalling that the king led, fed, and protected his people), but war commanded more attention (as seen in the "Standard of Ur" and the "Stele of the Vultures" [figure 16.3]). The elite's needs for ostentation were not reduced; to the contrary, long-distance trade with Iran, Afghanistan, Northern Syria, and Anatolia recovered after an earlier decline and spread in new directions, to the Gulf and the Indus Valley. Art and craftsmanship developed, as shown by the princely tombs of the Ur "Royal Cemetery," which contained hoards of luxury items made of gold, silver, and lapis, but which also give evidence of the gruesome practice of burying eminent people with all of their attendants. Palaces have been exposed, with compounds comprising the whole set of required functions, and temples of prime importance are known (at Khafajah, Al Hiba, Tell el Ubaid).[4] Built on top of high terraces in the middle of large enclosures, they towered above the towns around, demonstrating that the gods were looking after society. Some smaller buildings, at Khafajah and Tell Asmar, also considered to be temples, are more probably courtrooms where eminent people received their dependents and dealt with the common problems of the population. Written texts become more numerous and more easily understandable, but their interpretation is still tricky: for years scholars believed that temples were omnipresent in the economy of the Early Dynastic city-state, but recent analysis indicates that the texts are related rather to the administration of large estates held by lineages. Just as palaces of the time, the ordinary house integrates its different components better than houses of earlier periods, while still retaining the principle of a central courtyard. Abu Salabikh, a site more extensively explored than most, shows that a regular road system organized the urban texture and delimited belts of construction in which private houses were built side-by-side in four rows, with dead-end lanes serving the inner enclaves (Vallet 1999).

War was a conventional practice not intended to destroy the opponent and take control of territory but rather to initiate a tributary relation. Before long the defeated city-state would recover its strength, and war resumed with renewed vigor. Centuries were necessary before the rise of the concept of hegemony and the idea of subduing the whole country. Such an exploit was achieved at about 2300 cal B.C.E. by Sargon, an individual from the northern part of the plain who spoke a Semitic language called Akkadian. Sargon and his successors transformed the army into a powerful instrument of domination and conquest, and war, or the threat of it, was at the basis of their regime. In such a framework, new elites formed, based on criteria of bravery and fighting efficiency, and quite different from the former statutory aristocracy. At the same time, the new kingdom was reorganized, agents were installed alongside local princes, the circulation of goods and information (through the imposition of the Akkadian language) was improved, new imagery was created, often representing files of prisoners of war, and an attempt was made to deify some kings. But we are now in the field of history proper rather than one of structure.[5] In any case, the Sargonic venture in some way puts an end to the evolutionary process as it had functioned up until then. What follows in Mesopotamian history is nothing but a lengthy variation around the same theme, until the advent of larger empires that went far beyond the Mesopotamian region and which proved to be much too ambitious to last very long. Indeed, it proves to be the case that any center of evolution tends to foster secondary dynamics around it, which are often related to the development of trade. In their desire for ostentatious status exhibition, Mesopotamian elites invested in obtaining precious materials from abroad. By so doing, they gave the culturally less complex societies they met the contingent opportunity to make use of the situation as well as the desire and ability to imitate the model they thereby discovered. Put in another way, the pristine center tends to initiate secondary polities around it, which come to be potential opponents that may ultimately imperil it.

What is to be Gained from Such a Reconstruction?

As simplified and tentative as it is, this overview gives us some idea of Mesopotamian evolution as we understand it at present and leads us toward the reasons for change, the evolutionary dynamics in general as well as the advent of the state proper.

The opportunity to evolve in the direction of greater complexity first requires, at least in pristine situations, sedentism, agriculture, and animal husbandry. However, such neolithization, even when achieving full success, is not enough to generate an evolutionary dynamic, as shown by the extreme scarcity of centers of further development. It is significant in this regard that the Mesopotamian center did not develop in the areas (the Levant, Taurus, and Zagros foothills) where the neolithization process had taken place. As a second prerequisite, population growth is needed. It cannot be properly demonstrated, but no doubt such growth did occur, for it is a normal consequence of the new mode of production. With high infant mortality, people endeavor to have as many children as they can, in order to have helpers during their active years and to be sustained later in their lives. It is a kind of exchange of services between generations, somewhat like our own old-age pension schemes. But here again, population growth is not the whole explanation, for many groups of villagers have continued until the present day without having changed in any structural way (although their cultural features, arbitrary and superficial as they are, may very well have changed). The roots of evolutionary dynamics are ultimately to be found in the fact that members of some groups stay together despite their increasing numbers, whereas most village societies are segmentary, that is, they separate and found new settlements. Such a behavioral difference is induced by the mode of production and ultimately by peculiarities in the environment. In the most common case of dry farming, there are few environmental constraints, and relatively small human groups are quite easily able to survive. As a result people prefer to split up, rather than to face the problems that community growth might engender. Such societies exhaust their vitality by expanding spatially and therefore have no reason to change. On the other hand, when societies settle in some areas where agriculture requires more investment and greater collaboration (as may be the case with irrigated agriculture), they do not fission and instead have to solve the practical problems induced by their growth.

Here therefore is the scenario I propose: when, at the outset of the pre-pottery Neolithic (eighth millennium B.C.E.), the new mode of production was fully assimilated (implying the reorganization of kinship, alliance, and beliefs), the experience thereby acquired was soon adopted by hunter-gatherers living in inhospitable areas of Mesopotamia. The societies which then developed here and there in the Near East shared many features (and might be compared to many present-day societies): sedentarism, agriculture (wheat and barley), and animal husbandry (sheep, goat, cattle, pig), but also the tendency to promote childbirth. Nevertheless, natural conditions had enough influence on their mode of production for them to react in different ways. The few whose members had to collaborate more closely for common survival renounced segmentariness and therefore were obliged to find new political, social, and ideological solutions to deal with growing population. Evolutionary dynamics are basically adaptive in character, in the sense that they are related to the necessity to react to changes induced by peculiarities in the natural setting and hence the mode of production. As time goes by, it becomes more difficult to revert to former situations. When an irrigation network has been built and improved for centuries or millennia, nobody is likely to cast off such a heritage and start over again without endangering his or her way of life and without being condemned to radical adjustments implying renouncement of numerous cultural attainments. This difficulty does not depend only on agricultural practice: society is structured by kinship networks which constitute a social net, including the possibility of finding a spouse, a political system which ensures order and common security, and monuments which are the manifestation of society's prosperity. In a word there is a series of advantages, either actual or perceived, which tend to dissuade people from leaving the group. Conversely, the largest settlements – more prosperous, better organized, and provided with more impressive buildings – may be conceived as poles of attraction, able to draw people to them from surrounding areas. The growth of human groups therefore accelerated, and this prompted them to become more organized in order to manage problems that arose.

The topic of the state proper is another matter. Taken here as a particular kind of society, the state is not something one recognizes at the outset, but a concept that depends upon the perspective adopted. It needs a definition that is necessarily relative to other kinds of societies, other state formations (for example, present-day), or a particular field. A definition implies a process of classification, that is, the distribution of a limited series of data into separate categories according to some specific aim. In the present case, the field to be explored is Mesopotamia, which does not prevent using the conclusions to examine other pristine cases.

Everyone would agree on granting the state a high degree of complexity. That term does not necessarily mean that a situation is complicated or difficult to tackle (although that may well be the case), but rather that it is composite and multiform, referring, for example, to a wider range of social positions and behaviors, a greater diversity among (political, religious, administrative) agencies, and therefore larger sets of building and object categories. Indeed, it is through material that complexity may be perceived, among other things through:

- site distribution, for larger settlements tend to repel smaller ones, not so much because they need a sizeable territory, but rather because they tend to attract inhabitants of surrounding villages;
- architecture, with achievements requiring a large collective investment, specialized buildings (temples, administrative units), highly differentiated dwellings (from palaces to simple houses), features indicating particular relations within society (the family retires within its house) and the family (genders are more strongly contrasted);
- burial practices, with a larger range of possibilities, in particular more elaborate and wealthier tombs, occasionally human "sacrifices";
- craftsmanship, with a trend toward specialization and innovation, the multiplication of prestige goods (for keeping the elite content), often the use of precious materials from abroad, but also more standardized and occasionally mass production;
- new techniques of management (cylinder seals, tokens, writing).

These features, and many others, reflect particular social relations that imply distance, either vertical (hierarchy) or horizontal (anonymity). It is only at a very late stage of the evolutionary process that those features are supplemented by written texts which may throw some light on social organization, politics, ideology and much else, but they are often anecdotal and ambiguous. In any case, complexity was growing in Mesopotamia as early as the Ubaid period, increasing in Uruk and Early Dynastic times, and culminating with the Akkadian kingdom. There were different stages of local evolution, each requiring its own label. Many scholars consider the state to have appeared in Uruk times. Such a position may be maintained, but with the disadvantage of obscuring the specific characters of subsequent polities. That is why I prefer to distinguish the city-state and the state proper, reserving the latter term for Sargon's unification of the country at about 2300 cal B.C.E. It is not only because there is a drastic change of scale, but mainly because the sources of change are completely different than before. Until that time, access to higher levels of integration had been based upon internal mechanisms, slow and invisible to anyone; change was collectively assumed through initiatives grounded in the opacity of habitus (Bourdieu 1990), a kind of general agreement stemming from long tradition. Conversely, it is through brute force that Sargon imposed a new order, and his undertaking, violent and painful, was based on an initiative of its own, which lay at the extreme fringes of habitus. He took on his hegemony quite self-consciously, whatever might have been the actual circumstances which led him to conceive such extremes and rendered them possible. The city-state thus appears as the final outcome of a normal evolutionary process: every principality had become too structured to give rise peacefully to any further development. The state became an ultimate means of finding a solution – in a transgressive way – to evolutionary mechanisms that could not play out further. Change was provided by an historical event, but it still belongs to structure in the sense that the stalemated situation required an answer. No matter that the solution was brought about by an individual called Sargon rather than someone else. Indeed, others before him (such as Lugalzaggesi) had already tried their luck, with less success. It is also to be noted that the state associated with Sargon and his successors is quite invisible archaeologically and would remain in darkness, had we no texts.

Perspectives

Finally, we may compare this reconstruction of a particular case to current theories. The traditional opposition between contract and constraint is not, in my opinion, completely satisfactory, for any society is built upon habitus. A process of socialization is at work beginning at birth, leading to some degree of assimilation to current standards, however non-egalitarian they might be. At the same time, individual initiatives that lead to change depend primarily on what Bourdieu refers to as strategies without a strategist. Being the outcome of habitus, they are perceived as normal and do not draw attention; they are so numerous that none is able to measure the scope of their rationality; most of all, people neither know how much they are dependent upon their ancestors' choices, nor that their own choices bind their descendants. In this way, the notions of contract and constraint fade behind the enormous opacity of time and numbers. But if I had to choose between those perspectives, the consensual version would clearly get my approbation for the spontaneous evolution preceding the brutal advent of the state. Any society implies some rules (of kinship, alliance, and so on) that rest on the power of some individuals to make decisions (men as opposed to women and children, lineage heads, the elite). Those people who for some time enjoy power constitute what might be called the structure of control of society, which is intended to manage the interests of the group as a whole. That structure, either informal and diffuse or organized (the state apparatus, for example), ensures social reproduction on all planes (production, biological reproduction, standards) through particular practices (exchange of women, sharing or redistribution of goods) intended to keep everything as it should be. For the individual, society is therefore providential, in the sense that we may speak of the welfare state. Nevertheless, order is not inconsistent with inequality and exploitation (of women by men, youth by elders, society by elites), for individual interest is always subordinate to the common one. The structure of control is less to ensure individual well-being than to preserve social stability.

After Sargon, a new general agreement appeared, and the UrIII Dynasty hastened to lay claim to the heritage of the Akkadian kingdom and to improve on its main achievements by constructing a managerial, rather than a warlike, state. The Sargonic venture was in some ways a parenthesis, a breach in the consensual network of history, even if it came from a distortion of the habitus under the weight of circumstances. Nevertheless, the new concept of hegemony on the one hand and the development of secondary polities on the periphery of the alluvium on the other promoted war as the prime motor of change. The evolutionary process faded behind an eventful history until an ultimate level of integration appeared – the empire. From this point of view, the Sargonic venture may be conceived as a definitive rupture. In any case, it was revolutionary, because the passage to a higher level of integration rested upon unprecedented mechanisms.

The appraisal of current theories depends on the definition of the state. It depends as well on the perspective taken, whether one has in mind the long evolutionary process leading to the state or the advent, in a relatively short time, of the state proper. On the whole these two approaches are rarely distinguished, for most scholars imagine rapid change, implying historical rather than structural factors. I am, in any case quite sceptical about theories which adopt the conflictual perspective and argue that some people strove to control the basic resources of their own group. Traditional societies are very reluctant to control people through material (land, water, or tools). Indeed, it is much easier and much more efficient to use networks of relations and ideology. Within village societies the ability to control anything is a matter of status. The authority of an elder comes not from the fact that he controls supplies, tools, or women, but from the fact that he is an elder. It is his status in the group according to genealogical criteria which leads him to exert certain managerial and organizational responsibilities. The same holds true for complex societies, such as the third millennium city-states. The elite, as defined by standards of that time, was maintained for the services it performed, just as are the state and public offices at present. There need be no justification given to the population (at most some proofs of efficiency), and nothing to be sought after that the elite did not already have. From this point of view, there is no need to suppose that people are searching for power; rather, it is spontaneously given to them. Power may be the target of an individual, but only within the small group which already possesses it. When a king has canals dug, he is playing his part as guarantor of common prosperity, and the ability to gather public labor for the occasion proves that power is in his hands. On this point, I agree with Service (1975:8): "Political power organized the economy, not vice versa. The system was redistributive, allocative, not acquisitive. Personal wealth was not required to gain personal political power. And these first governments seem clearly to have reinforced their structure by doing their economic and religious jobs well – by providing benefits – rather than by using physical force." On the other hand, Sargon's conquest by force is contrary to traditional principles. His action, made possible only by a degraded situation and habitus gone adrift, shows clearly that the growing influence of personal motivations is the consequence rather than the cause of change.

Many scholars argue that the state solves – to the benefit of the elite – class conflicts induced by the uneven distribution of wealth (Childe 1936:115–116, 1942:106–107, 124–125; Engels 1954; Fried 1967:230). But by considering the Mesopotamian case, it is clear that the state (as I have defined it) is detrimental to elite interests. It puts power into the hands of people who, until then, were kept far from it and in that way deprives the local elite of part of its revenue. The new social order is in no way more egalitarian than before, and it does not change anything but gives power to people who have not been chosen according to the usual rules. It does not let commoners speak, but makes right of might. The state does not solve class conflict, and it may be thought that, in a world where the individual hardly counted, forces of integration were usually strong enough to prevent popular uprisings. If the state solved any conflict, it was the endemic one among city-states.

The models elaborated in the consensual perspective are more interesting, but some nuancing is necessary. Society is supposed to organize itself to solve material problems: difficulties in the mode of production (in particular in the case of irrigation), environmental deficiencies, and problems related to population growth. The mode of production is of prime importance, but mainly when agriculture and animal husbandry were adopted by people living in the alluvial plain and adapted to local conditions. The social order which then emerged conformed to the logic of the new mode of production and irrigation played a major part, for it contributed to the emergence of a habitus which promoted integration and, by so doing, evolution. Irrigation is only related very indirectly to the advent of the state, nearly 5,000 years later. Adams (1965:40–41, 1966:66–68, 1982) explains that in Mesopotamia large waterworks are developed long after the state, while Gibson (1974) argues that irrigation leads to nothing but economic disaster. Without going that far, it is obvious that a society uses irrigation according to its means as well as its needs (Fernea 1970; Downing and Gibson 1974). As early as the seventh millennium, Ubaidian villagers mastered (irrigated) agriculture, and the basis of the economy was firm, so that the reasons for change are to be found elsewhere, related to population growth.

I am quite prepared to acknowledge the prime importance of population growth, but not for the reasons currently put forward. Population growth, as a logical consequence of the mode of production, is much too common to explain anything. Boserup (1965) rightly observes that traditional societies are reluctant to modify their agricultural practices, because increasing production through intensification would involve more time and labor. For new practices to appear, people need strong motivations, and Boserup thinks that those are to be found in demographic pressure. In my opinion, growth has never been sufficient to induce such pressure, and the concept of carrying capacity may be applied only to exceptional situations. Although in favor of Boserup's thesis, Sanders admits, "Calculations of the carrying capacity of regions and measures of population sizes of prehistoric populations living in these regions usually show population levels well below carrying capacity"

(1984:23). In Mesopotamia, in any case, there is no trace of change in agricultural practice until the fourth millennium, with the introduction of the swing-plow, which is related to the size of lands allotted for elite maintenance.

In the same vein, Carneiro's thesis is in some way an extreme, for the conquest of one society by another means that the latter has been unable to solve its local problems of production. When the Mesopotamian city-states engaged in war, it was not so much because their economic basis was in danger, but because they became competitors in particular fields that interested the elite. In the same way, Sargon's conquest of Mesopotamia was not related to an imbalance between people and environment, for the Mesopotamian population remained the same whether unified or not. While the advent of the state was based upon force, the reasons, already alluded to, bear no relation to problems of subsistence. The important point is not population growth itself, but the neglected fact that people stay together for practical reasons: social structure changes in order to accommodate groups, according to the ways defined by habitus.

While the demographic argument may be revamped, the trade one lacks any foundation. It is quite clear that any traditional society, whatever its mode of production, relies primarily on its environment for its survival. Any other solution is inconceivable, be it only for practical reasons. It is very difficult for traditional agriculture to produce enough surplus to participate significantly in the maintenance of neighboring groups. Even assuming that irrigation, with its greater yields, might make it possible – although sowing and harvesting impose unavoidable constraints – the movement of goods would have to face the weakness of the means of transportation. As Trigger rightly emphasizes (1972:580), "Pre-industrial technologies by their very nature impose narrow limitations on the degree to which agricultural production may be intensified and goods may be transported." No society may survive through trade, and we must abandon Childe's view, which relates the advent of the state to the need for locally absent basic resources (wood, ores, stone, flint), procured in exchange for grain produced in excess for that purpose. For centuries, Ubaidian people imported nothing but bitumen, obsidian, and possibly a few types of stones they needed for adornment. They had enough wood for their everyday needs, and they even had stone (Boehmer 1984), but it was much easier to use mud brick as a building material. They probably obtained flint from the western desert. The goods they imported were in no way essential, but they might be viewed as advantageous in some way. At the same time, the circulation of these goods by "down-the-line" exchange enabled people neither to modulate demand nor to obtain any large quantity of them. The trade network developed only with the advent of complex societies during the fourth millennium. The conditions of that trade were quite different, and its function was to satisfy the needs of the elite. Imported goods were primarily raw materials for producing luxury goods, the circulation of which was carefully restricted, rather than goods for everyday consumption. It was hierarchy that gave rise to substantial long-distance trade and not vice versa. As articulated by Trigger (1972:585), "Because of the high cost of transportation in non-industrial societies, long distance trade is restricted mainly to goods and materials that are of great value or can be produced only in limited areas."

Conclusion

The Mesopotamian state emerged about 5,000 years later than the first villages in the area. We may trace the slow evolution leading to the state and isolate six levels of organization prior to the state proper. Each may be characterized by its most salient feature:

- in simple village societies decisions concerning the group were taken in common by heads of nuclear families under the care of an elder;
- in complex village societies stem families appeared in order to limit the numbers of people responsible, and the right to take decisions was temporarily delegated to certain individuals until the elders were replaced by new generations;
- in simple chiefdoms authority was further concentrated, and responsibilities were delegated to a few individuals (probably lineage heads) selected according to genealogy, so that the basic social unit reverts to the nuclear family;
- in complex chiefdoms the same responsible people became isolated from commoners and formed a class of their own;
- city-states were characterized by the appearance of hereditary, royal power;
- city-states ran into difficulties and ultimately declined as rivalry and warfare arose among them, problems that were solved only through Sargon's conquest.

The criteria that differentiate these levels of organization depend on what I have called the structure of control of society. Such a perspective resulted from the sense that the most salient features of the data (whether architecture, burials, or movable items) allude to particular individuals whose status led to prestige and authority. This allows the unambiguous detection of the ranking of society, status differentiation, and corresponding responsibilities. The evolution of the structure of control towards greater hierarchy was not intentional and therefore cannot be attributed to a search for personal achievement. It is the society which, through its members and especially the most eminent ones, adopts the most appropriate solutions for mastering problems encountered, in particular the necessity of integrating increasing numbers of people. Indeed, the mode of production encourages population growth, while particular environmental conditions incite people to stay together. If the relations between people and their environment thus appear so strong as to seem deterministic, it is because they are based upon numerous personal reactions which, leading in the same direction, tend to exclude any random drift. As Bourdieu put it (1990:55–6), "being the product of a particular class of objective regularities, the *habitus* tends to generate all the 'reasonable', 'common-sense' behaviors (and only these) which are possible within the limits of these regularities, and which are likely to be positively sanctioned because they are objectively adjusted to the logic characteristic of a particular field, whose objective future they anticipate. At the same time, 'without violence, art or argument', it tends to exclude all 'extravagances' . . . , that is, all the behaviors that would be negatively sanctioned because they are incompatible with the objective conditions."

As society increases in size, its structure of control must be reorganized. Insofar as responsible people are nominated according to general agreement (e.g., genealogical order), the trend towards inequality is due only to the need to face demographic changes. One of the most noteworthy implications of such a process is urbanization. In my opinion, the pristine state cannot come into being without some preliminary phase of urbanization, because it is the failing of integration at the urban stage that leads to state formation. The city-states of the alluvial plain became too similar to one another and too structured for a higher level of integration to appear spontaneously, and their vitality was consumed in enduring conflicts – until an exceptional leader took advantage of the situation to set up a new order for his own benefit.

NOTES

1 In the near future, I will be publishing a volume specifically devoted to particular aspects of that debt (Forest in press).
2 A much more detailed account of that reconstruction, with many bibliographic references, may be found in Forest (1996).
3 For example, Adams (1966), Redman (1978), Nissen (1988), Maisels (1990, 1999), Frangipane (1996), Pollock (1999), Charvát (2002).
4 Forest (1999).
5 For further details, cf. Liverani, ed. (1993).

REFERENCES

Adams, Robert McC., 1965 Land Behind Baghdad. A History of Settlement on the Diyala Plains. Chicago: University of Chicago Press.
Adams, Robert McC., 1966 The Evolution of Urban Society: Early Mesopotamia and Prehispanic Mexico. Chicago: Aldine.
Adams, Robert McC., 1982 Die Rolle des Bewässerungsbodenbaus bei der Entwicklung von Institutionen in der altmesopotamischen Gesellschaft. In Produktivkräfte und Gesellschaftsformationen in vorkapitalistischer Zeit. J. Hermann and I. Sellnow, eds. pp. 119–140. Berlin: Akademie Verlag.
Adams, Robert McC., 1984 Mesopotamian Social Evolution: Old Outlooks, New Goals. In On the Evolution of Complex Societies – Essays in Honor of Harry Hoijer 1982. Timothy Earle, ed. pp. 79–129. Malibu: Undena Publications.
Boehmer, Rainer M., 1984 Kalkstein für das urukzeitliche Uruk. Baghdader Mitteilungen 15:141–147.
Boserup, Esther, 1965 The Conditions of Agricultural Growth. Chicago: Aldine.
Bourdieu, Pierre, 1990 The Logic of Practice. R. Nice, trans. Stanford: Stanford University Press.
Carneiro, Robert L., 1970 A Theory of the Origin of the State. Science 169:733–738.
Carneiro, Robert L., 1978 Political Expansion as an Expression of the Principle of Competitive Exclusion. In Origins of the State: The Anthropology of Political Evolution.

Ronald Cohen and Elman R. Service, eds. pp. 205–224. Philadelphia: Institute for the Study of Human Issues.

Charvát, Petr, 2002 Mesopotamia Before History. London & New York: Routledge.

Childe, V. Gordon, 1936 Man Makes Himself. London: Watts and Co.

Childe, V. Gordon, 1942 What Happened in History. London & New York: Penguin Books.

Downing, Theodore E., and McGuire Gibson, eds., 1974 Irrigation's Impact on Society. Anthropological Papers of the University of Arizona, 25. Tucson: University of Arizona Press.

Engels, Friedrich, 1954[1884] L'origine de la famille, de la propriété privée et de l'État. Paris: Éd. sociales.

Fernea, Robert A., 1970 Shaykh and Effendi: Changing Patterns of Authority among the El Shabana of Southern Iraq. Cambridge, MA: Harvard University Press & London: Oxford University Press.

Flannery, Kent, 1972 The Cultural Evolution of Civilizations. Annual Review of Ecology and Systematics 3:399–426.

Forest, Jean-Daniel, 1996 Mésopotamie. L'apparition de l'État, VIIe–IIIe millénaires. Paris: Éd. Paris-Méditerranée.

Forest, Jean-Daniel, 1999 Les premiers temples de Mésopotamie (4e et 3e millénaires). BAR International Series, 765. Oxford: Archaeopress.

Forest, Jean-Daniel, In press L'Épopée de Gilgamesh et sa postérité. Paris: Éd. Paris-Méditerranée.

Frangipane, Marcella, 1996 La nascita dello stato nel vicino oriente, dai lignaggi alla burocrazia nella Grande Mesopotamia. Padua & Bari: Laterza.

Fried, Morton, 1967 The Evolution of Political Society. An Essay in Political Anthropology. New York: Random House.

Gibson, McGuire, 1974 Violation of Fallow and Engineered Disaster in Mesopotamian Civilization. In Irrigation's Impact on Society. Anthropological Papers of the University of Arizona, 25. Theodore E. Downing and McGuire Gibson, eds. pp. 7–19. Tucson: University of Arizona Press.

Haas, Jonathan, 1982 The Evolution of the Prehistoric State. New York: Columbia University Press.

Johnson, Gregory, 1973 Local Exchange and Early State Development in Southwestern Iran. Anthropological Papers, 51. Ann Arbor: University of Michigan, Museum of Anthropology.

Liverani, Mario, ed., 1993 Akkad, the First World Empire. Structure, Ideology, Traditions. Padua: Sargon srl.

Maisels, Charles, 1990 The Emergence of Civilization, from Hunting and Gathering to Agriculture, Cities, and the State in the Near East. London: Routledge.

Maisels, Charles, 1999 Early Civilizations of the Old World. London: Routledge.

Nissen, Hans J., 1988 The Early History of the Ancient Near East, 9000–2000 BC. Chicago: University of Chicago Press.

Pollock, Susan, 1999 Ancient Mesopotamia: The Eden that Never Was. Cambridge: Cambridge University Press.

Rathje, William L., 1971 The Origin and Development of Lowland Maya Classic Civilization. American Antiquity 36:275–285.

Rathje, William L., 1972 Praise the Gods and Pass the Metates: A Hypothesis of the Development of Lowland Rainforest Civilizations in Mesoamerica. In Contemporary Archaeology. Mark P. Leone, ed. pp. 365–392. Carbondale: Southern Illinois University Press.

Redman, Charles, 1978 The Rise of Civilization: From Early Farmers to Urban Society in the Ancient Near East. San Francisco: Freeman & Co.

Sanders, William T., 1976a The Natural Environment of the Basin of Mexico. *In* The Valley of Mexico. Eric R. Wolf, ed. pp. 59–68. Albuquerque: University of New Mexico Press.

Sanders, William T., 1976b The Agricultural History of the Basin of Mexico. *In* The Valley of Mexico. Eric R. Wolf, ed. pp. 101–160. Albuquerque: University of New Mexico Press.

Sanders, William T., 1984 Pre-Industrial Demography and Social Evolution. *In* On the Evolution of Complex Societies, Essays in Honor of Harry Hoijer 1982. Timothy Earle, ed. pp. 7–39. Malibu: Undena Publications.

Sanders, William T., Jeffrey R. Parsons, and Robert S. Santley, 1979 The Basin of Mexico: Ecological Processes in the Evolution of a Civilization. New York: Academic Press.

Service, Elman R., 1975 Origins of the State and Civilization: The Process of Cultural Evolution. New York: Norton.

Smith, Philip E. L., 1972 Changes in Population Pressure in Archaeological Explanation. World Archaeology 4/1:5–18.

Smith, Philip E. L., and T. Cuyler Young, 1972 The Evolution of Early Agriculture and Culture in Greater Mesopotamia: A Trial Model. *In* Population Growth: Anthropological Implications. Brian J. Spooner, ed. pp. 1–59. Cambridge, MA: MIT Press.

Spencer, Herbert, 1967 The Evolution of Society (Selected Papers from Principles of Sociology 1876, 1882, 1896). Chicago: University of Chicago Press.

Trigger, Bruce, 1972 Determinants of Urban Growth in Pre-Industrial Societies. *In* Man, Settlement and Urbanism. Peter J. Ucko, Ruth Tringham, George W. Dimbleby, eds. pp. 575–599. Gloucester: Duckworth.

Vallet, R., 1999 La formation de l'habitat urbain en Mésopotamie: Abu Salabikh, une ville neuve sumérienne. *In* Habitat et société, XIXe Rencontres Internationales d'Archéologie et d'Histoire d'Antibes. Frank Braemer, Serge Cleuziou, Anick Coudart, eds. pp. 151–165. Antibes: Éditions APDCA.

Wittfogel, Karl A., 1957 Oriental Despotism. A Comparative Study of Total Power. New Haven: Yale University Press.

Wright, Henry T., 1977 Toward an Explanation of the Origin of the State. *In* Explanation of Prehistoric Change. James N. Hill, ed. pp. 215–230. Albuquerque: University of New Mexico Press.

Wright, Henry T., and Gregory Johnson, 1975 Population, Exchange and Early State Formation in Southwestern Iran. American Anthropologist 77:267–289.

10

Archaeology, Bible, and the History of the Levant in the Iron Age

Israel Finkelstein

The questions of the historicity of the biblical narrative on ancient Israel and the ability of archaeology to contribute toward a better understanding of the text have hovered like black clouds over both academic research and public discussion for decades (see Yahya, this volume). The debates have been influenced not only by academic research in the fields of archaeology and biblical studies, but also by larger cultural and historical processes (see also Bernbeck, this volume). In recent years we have seen a new "high tide" in the discussion, this time focusing on the problem of the United Monarchy and in a way on the question of the validity of the entire historical narrative in the Bible (Davies 1992; Lemche 1994:165–190; Thompson 1999).[1]

Since so much is at stake here, the scholarly discussion has drifted into a bad-tempered debate, characterized, unfortunately, by harsh language and name calling. Together with the offensive language have come the generalizations: one is expected to be a "nihilist" or a "fundamentalist"; nothing in between. For a while it seemed that the center had disappeared. But the fact of the matter is, that one should distinguish between at least three – not two – camps.

Scholars in the conservative camp follow the biblical text on the history of Israel in the way the ancient writers wanted us to read it, that is, as a reliable record of Israel's history, narrated in sequential chronological order from earlier to later periods.[2] Conservative scholars agree that the biblical materials – be they the Pentateuch ("The Five Books of Moses") or the Deuteronomistic History (the books of Joshua, Judges, Samuel, and Kings) – got their final shape relatively late in the history of Israel, in late-monarchic and post-Exilic times (seventh to fifth centuries B.C.E.). Yet, many would still claim a tenth–ninth century date for the crystallization of much of the material in the Pentateuch and would also argue that in both literary works the later redactors incorporated early traditions and even older written sources. True, only a few in the conservative camp would still try to identify a "Period of the Patriarchs" in the second millennium B.C.E. or to explain a destruction of a major Late Bronze city as an outcome of the Israelite conquest of Canaan.[3] Yet, many would still read the description of the Exodus on a New Kingdom background (Frerichs and Lesko 1997; Sarnah 1999:33–54; Malamat 2001:57–67), and all scholars in this camp would stand behind the biblical portrayal of a glorious "United Monarchy" of David and Solomon (Mazar 1990:368–402; Dever 2001).

Scholars belonging to the radical camp date the texts to the Persian or Hellenistic Period and see the description of ancient Israel as strongly influenced by the ideology, needs, and realities of these later times (Davies 1992; Lemche 1993:163–193; Lemche 1994; Thompson 1999). Hence they minimize – if not discount altogether – the historical value of the biblical description of Ancient Israel, preferring to see it as an entirely ideological – and almost entirely fictional – work of the Jerusalem Temple establishment in these later periods.

The third camp – where I belong – though positioned in the center, is far from both poles. Scholars in this camp accept a late-monarchic or Exilic date (seventh or sixth centuries B.C.E.) for a large portion of the Pentateuch and much of the Deuteronomistic History. Hence they acknowledge the value of these texts as preserving real evidence on the history of Israel in monarchic times. However, they see the stories – in the way they are presented in the text – as highly ideological and adapted to the needs of the community during the time of the compilation. Hence, the most meaningful difference from the conservative camp is that the adherents to the center camp tend to read the texts in an *opposite* "direction" – seeing evidence of later periods in the descriptions of Israel's early history. In other words, they try to understand them in their historical context as creative compositions, rather than objective facts (Van Seters 1983; Niemann 1993; Finkelstein and Silberman 2001). This does not mean that the texts have no historical value, but it does mean that in many cases they tell us more about the society and politics of the writers than about the times described in them.

Before I continue, I wish to pause and briefly clarify my views on the question of dating the texts. Since the 19th century, it has become clear that the Old Testament (OT) texts were not written at the time of the events they relate and that various sources can be identified for both the Pentateuch and the Deuteronomistic History. Regarding the Pentateuch, I accept the main outline of the Documentary Hypothesis, in contrast to scholars – mainly German – who have recently started drifting away from it.[4] For reasons which stem from the realm of archaeology, and which will be partially disclosed later, I would date J (the Pentateuch source which uses the tetragrammaton YHWH for the God of Israel) to the seventh century B.C.E. – later than the ninth–eighth centuries B.C.E. date recently given in Friedman (1999), and a bit earlier than the Exilic date advocated by Van Seters (1992). J deals first and foremost with the centrality and superiority of Judah over its neighbors – Israelites and non-Israelites alike. It provides a common early history for all Israel and delineates the ethnic lines between the "we" (Judah) and the "them" (all the others). As such it is soaked with the ideology of late-monarchic Judah. And I would support those scholars who argue that P (the Priestly source in the Pentateuch) has a late-monarchic layer (from the late seventh or early sixth century B.C.E.), though in the main it is a post-Exilic work (of the fifth century B.C.E.) (Haran 1981:321–333; Hurvitz 2000:180–191).

Regarding the Deuteronomistic History,[5] I adhere to the "Harvard school" of Frank Cross and his students, that is, to a Josianic (after the name of Josiah king of Judah, who ruled from 639 to 609 B.C.E.) date for the first "edition" of the History labeled "Dtr1" and an Exilic date for the second, final edition, labeled "Dtr2" (Cross 1973:274–288; Nelson 1981b; Halpern and Vanderhooft 1991:179–244; Mckenzie 1991). As I will try to demonstrate later, archaeology can strongly support this view and seriously undermine many of the arguments of the Göttingen school, which would break the Deuteronomistic History into several sources, all dating after the fall of Jerusalem (Smend 1971; Dietrich 1972; Veijola 1977).

This means that I would support biblical scholars who argue for a thematic and chronological relationship between the two great literary works, the Pentateuch and the Deuteronomistic History.[6] I would see big portions of both of them as supplying the ideological platform for the political program of Judah in later monarchic times. I refer to the Pan-Israelite idea, which, to the best of my understanding, first surfaced in a full-blown shape at that time. It argued that the Davidic kings, with their seat of power in the city of Jerusalem in the Southern Kingdom of Judah, are the only legitimate heirs to the territories of the Northern Kingdom of Israel, which was vanquished by the Assyrians in the late eighth century B.C.E., and to the leadership over the Israelites still living in these territories, and that the cult of all Israelites should be centralized in the Temple in Jerusalem. As such, the texts are highly ideological, on both the theological and political levels. They represent the point of view of one faction of the Judahite society (we have no idea if it ever formed the majority in late-monarchic times); they certainly do not represent the Northern Kingdom of Israel or, what Morton Smith called years ago, the "syncretistic" ideas in Judah (Smith 1971). We can only imagine how different a history of Israel would be if written by scribes from the Northern Kingdom or by other factions of the Judahite society, had they survived.

As highly ideological texts, even the treatment of periods close in date to the time of the compilation cannot be read uncritically. A good example can be found in the treatment of the "Assyrian century" in the history of Judah (Naaman 1991:55–160; Naaman 1994:235–254). In most of this period Judah was ruled by three kings: father, son, and grandson. The first, Ahaz, is depicted as a sinner and as one who cooperated with the Assyrians and compromised Judah's independence. His son Hezekiah is described as the second-most righteous king from the lineage of David and as a hero who stood firmly and courageously against Assyria. The Deuteronomistic Historian makes a special effort to hide the fact that Judah remained under Assyrian domination many years after the "miraculous" rescue of Jerusalem from the Assyrians. The grandson, Manasseh, who ruled in Jerusalem over half a century, is described as the most evil of all apostates and head of all villains. Dtr2 (see above) flatly puts the responsibility for the fall of Jerusalem on his head.

Archaeology has given us a completely different story – or at least a completely different perspective on Judahite affairs. Ahaz saved Judah from the bitter fate of the Northern Kingdom and incorporated it into the Assyrian economy. His policy led Judah to an unprecedented prosperity, in which Jerusalem and Judah experienced dramatic demographic growth. This was the time when Jerusalem expanded to the western hill (Broshi 1974:21–26). Judah apparently participated in the Assyrian-led Arabian trade and, as a result, the Beer-sheba valley flourished (Singer-Avitz 1999:3–74). In contrast, Hezekiah took a reckless decision to rebel against Assyria and was therefore responsible for the events that led to the utter devastation of Judah (Halpern 1991:11–107). Archaeology demonstrates the extent of the catastrophe. Almost every site excavated in the Shephelah and the Beer-sheba valley revealed evidence for destruction (Naaman 1979:61–86; Ussishkin 1982). The Shephelah – the bread basket of Judah – never recovered from the shock; surveys reveal the dramatic decrease in the number of settlements there in the seventh century.

Again in contrast, archaeology shows us that Manasseh saved Judah from annihilation. Under his *realpolitik* of cooperation with Assyria, the Southern Kingdom emerged from the ashes, was reincorporated into the Assyrian economy, and reached an unprecedented prosperity. Judah increased its role in the Assyrian-led southern trade and the Beer-sheba valley experienced a record settlement density (Finkelstein 1994:169–187). And Judah must have been the main supplier of olives for the extensive Assyrian oil industry at Tel Miqne-Ekron (Gitin 1987:81–97); as a result, the Shephelah at least partially recovered. Ostraca, seals and seal impressions, weights, and other finds indicate that in Manasseh's days Judah reached full statehood and an impressive literacy rate (Jamieson-Drake 1991; Finkelstein 1999b:35–52).

The lesson here is clear and simple. If a period so close to the compilation of the text shows such a great gap between the heavy ideological intent of the text and the more nuanced economic and social content of the finds, one should be even more cautious when dealing with the description of earlier periods, in which the Deuteronomistic Historian could have been even freer to advance his ideology, as the memory of the real events was much vaguer. Let us take the Northern Kingdom as an example. The Deuteronomistic Historian treats Israel in a highly negative way, making every effort to diminish its importance and delegitimize its very existence. At the same time, he contends that the Israelite population in the territories of the Northern Kingdom *does* belong to the "nation." One could almost argue that in order to learn about the real Northern Kingdom, we need to turn the Deuteronomistic description upside down. The period of the Omrides (the Israelite dynasty of Omri, Ahab, and the sons of the latter) is especially distorted. The text paints the Omrides as apostates and villains. It does not mention their military power and only vaguely refers to their great building activities. Without archaeology – in the broader sense – we would never know about Ahab's great chariot forces (from Shalmaneser III king of Assyria), about the Omrides' conquests in Moab (from the stele of Mesha, king of Moab in Transjordan), about their expansion to the north (from the Tel Dan stele, erected by Hazael, King of Aram Damascus), and about their Herodian-like building achievements at Samaria, Jezreel, Hazor, and Megiddo (Finkelstein 2000:127–128). Without archaeology we would never know that the Omrides established the first real territorial state in the Levant, a state which covered both highlands and lowlands, with their varied populations, a state which engaged in intensive trade with Phoenicia, Cyprus, and the south (Finkelstein 1999b).

Once we become aware of the fact that the texts are relatively late in date, and that they tell the stories from the subjective point of view of the needs of the writers, then we can acknowledge the tremendous power of archaeology as the real-time witness to the events. Archaeology, which in past years was almost completely subjected to the text and used mainly to "decorate" the stories, is now taking the lead in writing the history of ancient Israel.

First, there is the formative period, where archaeology is the only witness. The conquest and judges stories, even if containing a few vague memories of heroic events – mythological or real – are almost completely expressions of the political and theological ideology of Josianic times (Nelson 1981a:531–540; Van Seters 1990:1–12; Younger 1990; Finkelstein and Silberman 2001). The Bible, then, provides only those impressions of the rise of Early Israel that the late-monarchic writer wanted to – or could – give us. Only archaeology can tell us about the material culture of the Iron I sites in the highlands, about the dispersal of their settlements, about their economy and about their relationship with their neighbors. And it gives us the long-term perspective on the demographic history of the highlands, which reveals the origin of the settlers in the Iron I sites (Finkelstein 1988; Finkelstein 1995:349–365). In the same way archaeology is the sole witness for the tenth century B.C.E. – the time of the United Monarchy (see below).

Archaeology actually goes far beyond this. It can also tell us a lot about the texts themselves, by providing information about their possible date of compilation. As I have already noted before, many biblical scholars date two of the three main sources of the Pentateuch – J and E – to early monarchic times, in the tenth century or a bit later. And many more argue that the Deuteronomistic History, even if compiled in the seventh or sixth centuries B.C.E., incorporated written material from earlier centuries. Archaeology, I would argue, shows that both theories are highly unlikely.

It is quite clear that these great literary works were meant to convey theological, cultural, and political messages. As such, they were probably directed at a wider public, far beyond the circles of the writers. They were meant to be read by (or to) people in the capital and in the countryside of Judah alike. I would argue therefore that the "standardized" literary works narrating the history of (all) Israel (in contrast to scattered, contradictory, and partial oral traditions) must have been written in an urban society, with high level of knowledge, sophistication, and literacy in the elite and the circles around it; they must have been written when the community was already quite advanced from the socio-political point of view; and they must have been written in a period when literacy spread not only in the capital, but also in the countryside of the kingdom. Having these conditions in mind, we should now look at the demographic and cultural developments in Jerusalem in particular and Judah in general.

Archaeology demonstrates that in the tenth and early ninth centuries Jerusalem was no more than a poor, small highland village. This period of time is represented only by meager pottery finds (Steiner 1998:26–32, 62; Finkelstein 2001:105–115; Ussishkin forthcoming). Jerusalem grew to become a major urban center in the late eighth century B.C.E. (Broshi 1974). The destruction of the Northern Kingdom by the Assyrians in 720 B.C.E., and the devastation of the Judahite lowlands by Sennacherib in 701 B.C.E., sent torrents of refugees to Jerusalem and Judah. And the incorporation of Judah into the Assyrian system gave it a major economic boost. The city quickly developed and expanded far beyond the limited area of the City of David, was surrounded by massive fortifications (Avigad 1984:46–60),[7] and was provided with a sophisticated water system.

Archaeology also indicates that until the eighth century B.C.E. the countryside of Judah was very sparsely settled, by no more than a few small villages. The population of the Judahite countryside grew dramatically in the late eighth century B.C.E., as a result of the same processes that brought about the expansion of Jerusalem (Ofer 1994:102–106).

And archaeology shows that the population of Judah reached the level of significant literacy only in the seventh century B.C.E. There is almost no sign of writing in Judah in general and Jerusalem in particular before the eighth century. Inscriptions – ostraca and seal impressions – first appear in the eighth century, and their number grew significantly in the course of the seventh century B.C.E. (Naveh 1982; Sass 1993; Renz 1995:38–39; Avigad and Sass 1997).[8]

To sum up this point, in the tenth and early ninth centuries the southern hill country was still characterized by demographic and political conditions similar to those which prevailed in the Late Bronze Age and are reflected in the Amarna letters. A "king" ruled over a large, relatively empty, dimorphic countryside, with a few villages and a large number of pastoral people. The capital was no more than a small highland stronghold, probably comprised of a modest palace, a shrine and a few more buildings for the elite (Naaman 1996:17–27). There is no way, to my mind, to imagine major literary activity under these conditions. The great historical works, which aimed to serve the propaganda of the Davidic dynasty and the Deuteronomistic movement, could not have been written much before 700 B.C.E.

Archaeology can help date a text even more precisely. The most obvious case may be that of the J source in the Pentateuch. Scholars have noticed long ago that a few themes in Genesis cannot predate the first millennium B.C.E. I refer mainly to the mention of Philistines and Arameans, who did not come to prominence in the region before the eleventh and ninth century B.C.E., respectively (Mazar 1986:49–62; McCarter 1999:1–31). But they tended to treat the mention of these people as anachronisms. The first who took a different approach was Thomas Thompson, who argued 25 years ago that the "anachronisms" in the text are, in fact, those aspects which specifically distinguish the narratives from the rest of the ancient Near Eastern folk-tales. Their removal would make the stories insignificant for Israelite history (Thompson 1974:324).

Indeed, there is much beyond Arameans and Philistines in J. I will limit myself to a few examples. Genesis 36:31–39 lists the early kings of Edom. Both extra-biblical sources and archaeology indicate that there were neither real kings nor a real state in Edom before the late eighth century B.C.E. Edom rises after the con-quest of the region by Assyria and the beginning of prosperity in the arid zones of the south as a result of the lucrative Arabian trade under Assyrian domination. The evidence for sedentary occupation in Edom prior to the Assyrian take-over is scanty. The first large-scale wave of settlement there, and the establishment of large settlements and fortresses, may have started in the eighth century B.C.E., but reached a peak only in the seventh and early sixth centuries B.C.E.[9] And no less important, the area was again very sparsely inhabited after the Babylonian take-over, until the Nabatean prosperity in the Hellenistic period.

Also significant is the appearance of certain toponyms in Genesis. Chapter 14 – the story of the great war between the kings of the east and the kings of the cities of the plain – mentions "En-mishpat that is, Kadesh", Tamar, and Ashteroth-karnaim. The first is no doubt Kadesh-barnea, the great oasis in the south, which is safely identified with Ein el Qudeirat in eastern Sinai. The main period of set-tlement activity in this site is in the seventh and early sixth century B.C.E. Tamar should most probably be identified with Ein Haseva in the northern Araba. Exca-vations there uncovered a great fort which functioned mainly in the late Iron II (late eighth and seventh centuries B.C.E.) (Ussishkin 1995:118–127; Naaman 1997:60). The combination Ashteroth-karnaim refers to the city of Ashteroth in southwest-ern Syria, and makes a reference to the fact that it is located in the Neo-Assyrian district of Karnaim. Chapter 14 forms a singular source, very different from the rest of the material in Genesis, which may be dated to Exilic or post-Exilic times. But it seems that at least part of the geographic information in it best fits late-monarchic times.

Finally, I wish to refer to the mention of Gerar as a Philistine city in the narra-tives of Abraham and Isaac (Genesis 20, 26 – E and J stories, respectively). Gerar is safely identified with Tel Haror northwest of Beer-sheba. Excavations there showed that in the Iron I – the early phase of Philistine history – it was no more than a small, quite insignificant village. But in the late Iron II it was built as a strong, heavily fortified, Assyrian administrative stronghold. The site was not occupied in the sixth century B.C.E. (Oren 1993:582–584). Hence the combination of Philistines and Gerar best fits the reality of the period of Assyrian domination in the region. Indeed, Naveh has recently proposed to identify Abimelech, king of Gerar in Genesis, with Ahimilki, king of Ashdod, who is mentioned in seventh-century Assyrian sources (Naveh 1998:36).

Ideology is no less important than topography for a reading of Genesis. The notion of the centrality and superiority of Judah – a centerpiece in the J narratives – cannot be understood before the destruction of the Northern Kingdom in 720 B.C.E. Until that date Israel was the dominant power while Judah was a marginal, dependent entity. From the late eighth century and in the seventh century Judah developed this sense of importance, power, and message. It saw itself as the heir to the Israelite territories and the Israelite population which remained in the north after the fall of the Northern Kingdom and the deportation of large segments of its population by the Assyrians.

That the stories in Genesis are Judah-centric is best reflected in the negative attitude toward its neighbors. The best example is the mocking of Ammon and Moab by mentioning (Genesis 19:30–38 – a J text) that the eponymous fathers of these nations were born of an incestuous union of a father with his daughters. And the Edomites and the Arab tribes in the south were portrayed as savages, compared to sedentary Judah. These perceptions, too, fit late-monarchic times more than any other period, including post-Exilic times, when some of these neighbors were quite insignificant.

Still, though the Pentateuch and the Deuteronomistic History were put in writing relatively late in Israelite history, most biblical scholars would accept that they include materials earlier than the time of the compilation. The problem is that in most cases the old memories are so vague, or so manipulated by the later writers, that the early realities in them are beyond recovery. Only archaeology can help, in certain cases, in identifying such earlier traditions. I wish to briefly demonstrate this with two examples, both from the Deuteronomistic History.

The excavations at Shiloh in the 1980s have shown beyond doubt that the site reached its peak of activity in the late Iron I, in the eleventh and early tenth centuries B.C.E. In the Iron II there was only meager activity at the site and in most of this long period it seems to have been deserted (Finkelstein et al. 1993). It is clear therefore that the stories in I Samuel about the importance of Shiloh in pre-monarchic times cannot reflect late-monarchic realities. Rather, they must represent some sort of memory of the prominence of the site in earlier times. The same holds true for the cycle of stories about the wandering of David and his men along the southern fringe of Judah. These narratives clearly fit a description of a band of Apiru (a term describing outlaws, uprooted bandits in Bronze Ages texts) moving in a sparsely settled region, far from the reach of central authority. This kind of background does not fit the period when the Deuteronomistic History was put in writing. At that time the area was densely settled, with no trace of Apiru reality left. Therefore, I see no alternative but to argue that the stories reflect what I have labeled before "the Amarna-like" situation in the Judahite hill country prior to the great demographic growth in the late eighth century B.C.E.

But recognizing the possible historical value of isolated elements is something very different from accepting the entire story of the rise of a united Israel from earliest times. Should we therefore consider the biblical materials on the *formative* periods in the history of Israel as ahistoric and therefore useless? The answer is both positive and negative. Positive, because the biblical material cannot help us reconstruct this formative history. Negative, because it tells us a lot about the society and realities of the time of the writing. And this is the point which I have tried to emphasize throughout this chapter, that the main contribution of the "view from the center" is to demonstrate that these texts should not be read as a sequential history, from ancient to later times, but the other way around – from the time of the writing back to more remote periods of history. I wish to conclude this paper with two examples.[10]

The first is the Conquest of Canaan in the book of Joshua. Central to the Deuteronomistic ideology was the idea that all Israelite territories and people should be ruled by a Davidic king and that all Israelite cult should be centralized in the temple in Jerusalem. This ideology probably emerged after the fall of the Northern Kingdom, but could not have been fulfilled as long as Assyria dominated the region. But when the Assyrians pulled out ca. 630 B.C.E., it seemed possible to accomplish. Thus at the time when possession of the Land was of great concern, the Book of Joshua offered an unforgettable epic with a clear lesson – creating a vivid, unified narrative out of vague memories of how, when the People of Israel *did* follow the covenant with their God to the letter, no victory could be denied to them. That point was made with some of the most vivid folk tales recast as a single epic against a highly familiar seventh-century background and played in places of the greatest concern to the Deuteronomistic ideology.

So, the towering figure of Joshua is used to paint a metaphorical portrait of Josiah, the would-be savior of all the People of Israel. Josiah is the new Joshua (Nelson 1981a), and the past, mythical conquest of Canaan is a battle plan for the present fights and for a conquest to be.[11] Indeed, the overall battle plan in the book of Joshua fits seventh-century realities. The first two battles – at Jericho and Ai (that is, the area of Bethel) – were fought in territories which were the first target of the Josianic expansionism after the withdrawal of Assyria from the province of Samaria. Jericho was the southeastern outpost of the Northern Kingdom and the later Assyrian province, which flourished after the Judahite takeover. Bethel was the main, much hated cult center of the Northern Kingdom.

Likewise, the story about the Gibeonites who have "come from a far country" and asked to make a covenant with the invading Israelites has a basis in the historical reality of the seventh century B.C.E. Expanding northward into the area of Bethel, Judah faced a problem of how to integrate the descendants of the deportees brought by the Assyrians from afar and settled there a few decades earlier.[12] The (old?) story of the Gibeonites could provide an "historical" context in which the Deuteronomists explained how it was possible to integrate these people though they were not Israelites by origin.

Next comes the conquest of the Shephelah, probably symbolizing the renewed Judahite expansion into this important, fertile region, expansion which is evident from the distribution of late-monarchic finds (Kletter 1999:19–54). This area – the traditional breadbasket of the Southern Kingdom – was taken from Judah by the Assyrians a few decades earlier and given to the cities of the coastal plain.

Then the story turns to the north. And this time the conquest of the past becomes a utopic conquest in the future (cf. Bernbeck, this volume). The reference to the famous city of Hazor calls to mind not only its reputation in the distant past as the most prominent of the Canaanite city-states, but certainly the realities of more recent times, when Hazor was the most important center of the Kingdom of Israel in the north. No less meaningful is the mention in the same chapter of Naphot Dor, probably alluding to the days when the city of Dor on the coast served as a capital of an Assyrian province. And most important, the territories described in relation to the war in the north perfectly match the Galilee territories of the vanquished Northern Kingdom of Israel. These were the territories which were conceived in seventh-century Judah as lawfully and divinely belonging to the Davidic kings in Jerusalem.

To sum up this point, in reading and reciting these stories of conquest of the entire Land of Israel, the Judahites of the late seventh century B.C.E. saw their own deepest wishes fulfilled.

The same approach to the biblical text should be utilized regarding the United Monarchy. Archaeology shows absolutely no sign of a great tenth-century territorial state ruled from Jerusalem. First, as I have already noted, tenth-century Jerusalem was no more than an Amarna-type highlands stronghold. Second, the Judahite countryside was very sparsely settled at that time. There were no human resources available for conquest and domination of large territories. Third, I see no reason why the marginal, underdeveloped southern highlands would become a center of the only territorial state in the Levant; state formation in this region came only in the ninth century and was closely related to Assyrian expansionism (Finkelstein 1999b). Fourth, as far as I can judge, and as far as recent radiocarbon dates indicate, the strata with monumental architecture in the north, which formed the basis for the reconstruction of a material culture of a great tenth-century state – mainly the Megiddo palaces – should be redated to the early ninth century B.C.E. (Finkelstein 1996:177–187; Finkelstein 1999a:55–70).[13]

And there is more. In the northern valleys, the tenth century is characterized by a revival of the Canaanite system of the second millennium B.C.E. The main cities in this landscape (Megiddo, Rehov, Dor, and Kinneret), which I have recently labeled "New Canaan" (Finkelstein 2003), probably served as centers of city-state territorial entities. Almost all their features – pottery, metallurgical and architectural traditions, layout of the main cities, cult, and settlement patterns of the countryside around them – show clear continuation of second-millennium traditions. The tenth-century monarchs in Jerusalem could not have ruled, therefore, in the northern valleys. The idea that poor Jerusalem, with its sparsely settled hinterland ruled over the far away, rich, and prosperous cities of the lowlands is an absurd one.

Biblical scholars have long acknowledged that the description of the United Monarchy, especially the glamour of the days of Solomon, draws a picture of an idyllic Golden Age wrapped in later theological and ideological goals (Van Seters 1983:307–312; Garbini 1988:32; Auld 1996:160–169; Miller 1997:1–24; Niemann 1997:252–299). Indeed, in this case, too, it is not difficult to identify the landscapes and costumes of seventh-century Judah as the stage setting behind the biblical tale (Knauft 1991:167–186). The lavish visit of Solomon's trading partner, the Queen of Sheba, to Jerusalem no doubt reflects the participation of seventh-century Judah in the lucrative Arabian trade. The same holds true for the description of the building of "Tamar in the wilderness" and the trade expeditions to lands afar setting off from Ezion-geber in the Gulf of Aqaba – two sites which were securely identified and which were not inhabited before late-monarchic times. And David's royal guard troops of Cheretites and Pelethites, long assumed by scholars to have been Aegean in origin, should probably be understood against the background of the service of Greek mercenaries in the armies of the seventh century – certainly in the Egyptian and possibly in the Judaean armies (Finkelstein forthcoming). Many other items in the story (such as the frequent mention of copper and horses and the mention of Achish as king of a Philistine city in the Shephelah) also fit late-monarchic realities.[14]

The tale of a glamorous United Monarchy had obvious power for the people of Judah. A new David had now come to the throne, intent on "restoring" the glory of his distant ancestors. This is Josiah, the most devout of all Judahite kings. He was able to roll history back from his own days to the time of the mythical United Monarchy. By cleansing Judah from the abominations of the nations and undoing the sins of the past he could stop the cycle of idolatry and calamity forever. He could reenact the United Monarchy of David before it went astray. So Josiah embarked on reestablishing a United Monarchy. He was about to "regain" the territories of the now destroyed Northern Kingdom, and rule from Jerusalem over the territories of Judah and Israel combined.

Now back to the tenth century. Neither archaeology nor the biblical text supply the slightest clue for the extent of the Jerusalem territory of that time. The only clue – if there is one – is the appeal of the Deuteronomistic Historian to the collective memory of his compatriots, that in the distant past the founders of the Davidic dynasty ruled over a territory larger than the traditional boundaries of the Southern Kingdom in late-monarchic times. We can say no more.

I have tried to demonstrate in this chapter the role of modern archaeology in the study of ancient Israel. Archaeology can be successfully utilized in this endeavor only after being liberated from the simplistic reading of the text, which made it a secondary character in the play and forbade it from raising its own, genuine voice. Indeed, in recent years archaeology has taken the lead in the quest for biblical history.

NOTES

1   For rejoinders see, for instance, Halpern 1995:26–47; Dever 2001.
2   For the founder of this school of thought see Albright 1957. More recently see Dever 2001; Malamat 2001.
3   But see Ben-Tor 1998:456–467.
4   For the Documentary Hypothesis see Friedman 1987. For overviews of the state of research see de Pury and Römer 1989:43–80; Van Seters 1999.
5   Unlike some current scholars, e.g., Knauft (2000:388–398), I belong to the majority, who continue to work in the framework of a Deuteronomistic History.
6   See summaries with bibliographies in Whybray 1987:221–235; de Pury and Römer 1989:58–67; Römer and de Pury 2000:82–8.
7   For recent excavations in the City of David see Shanks 1999:20–29.
8   But see Millard 1998:33–39.

9   See various articles in Bienkowski 1992; Hart 1986:51–58.
10 For detailed treatment see Finkelstein and Silberman 2001.
11 See also Lohfink 1991:125–141.
12 On these deportations see Naaman and Zadok 1988:36–46; Naaman and Zadok 2000:159–188.
13 For radiocarbon results see Gilboa and Sharon, forthcoming in *Radiocarbon*.
14 For Achish see Naveh 1998.

REFERENCES

Albright, William F., 1957 From Stone Age to Christianity. Garden City: Doubleday.

Auld, Graeme, 1996 Re-Reading Samuel (Historically): "Etwas mehr Nichtwissen". *In* The Origin of the Ancient Israelite States. Volkmar Fritz and Philip R. Davies, eds. pp. 160–169. Sheffield: Academic Press.

Avigad, Nahman, 1984 Discovering Jerusalem. Oxford: Blackwell.

Avigad, Nahman, and Benjamin Sass, 1997 Corpus of West Semitic Stamp Seals. Jerusalem: The Israel Academy of Sciences and Humanities.

Ben-Tor, Amnon, 1998 The Fall of Canaanite Hazor – the "Who" and "When" Questions. *In* Mediterranean Peoples in Transition, Thirteenth to Early Tenth Centuries B.C.E. Seymour Gitin, Amihai Mazar, and Ephraim Stern, eds. pp. 456–467. Jerusalem: Israel Exploration Society.

Bienkowski, Piotr, ed., 1992 Early Edom and Moab. Sheffield: J. R. Collins.

Broshi, Magen, 1974 The Expansion of Jerusalem in the Reigns of Hezekiah and Manasseh. Israel Exploration Journal 24:21–26.

Cross, Frank M., 1973 Canaanite Myth and Hebrew Epic. Cambridge: Harvard University Press.

Davies, Philip, 1992 In Search of "Ancient Israel". Sheffield: Academic Press.

Dever, William G., 2001 What Did the Biblical Writers Know and When Did They Know It: What Archaeology Can Tell Us about the Reality of Ancient Israel. Grand Rapids: Eerdmans.

Dietrich, Walter, 1972 Prophetie und Geschichte: Eine redaktionsgeschichtliche Untersuchung zum deuteronomistischen Geschichtswerk. Göttingen: Vandenhoeck & Ruprecht.

Finkelstein, Israel, 1988 The Archaeology of the Israelite Settlement. Jerusalem: Israel Exploration Society.

Finkelstein, Israel, 1994 The Archaeology of the Days of Manasseh. *In* Scripture and Other Artifacts: Essays on the Bible and Archaeology in Honor of Philip J. King. Michael D. Coogan, Cheryl J. Exum, and Lawrence E. Stager, eds. pp. 169–187. Louisville: Westminster John Knox Press.

Finkelstein, Israel, 1995 The Great Transformation: The "Conquest" of the Highlands Frontiers and the Rise of the Territorial States. *In* The Archaeology of Society in the Holy Land. Thomas E. Levy, ed. pp. 349–363. Leicester: Leicester University Press.

Finkelstein, Israel, 1996 The Archaeology of the United Monarchy: An Alternative View. Levant 28:177–187.

Finkelstein, Israel, 1999a Hazor and the North in the Iron Age: A Low Chronology Perspective. Bulletin of the American Schools of Oriental Research 314:55–70.

Finkelstein, Israel, 1999b State Formation in Israel and Judah, a Contrast in Context, a Contrast in Trajectory. Near Eastern Archaeology 62(1):35–52.

Finkelstein, Israel, 2000 Omride Architecture. Zeitschrift des Deutschen Palästina-Vereins 116:114–138.

Finkelstein, Israel, 2001 The Rise of Jerusalem and Judah: The Missing Link. Levant 33:105–115.

Finkelstein, Israel, 2003 City States and States: Polity Dynamics in the 10th–9th Centuries B.C.E. *In* Symbiosis, Symbolism and the Power of the Past: Ancient Israel and its Neighbors from the Late Bronze Age through Roman Palestine. Proceedings of the W. F. Albright Institute of Archaeological Research and the American Schools of Oriental Research Centennial Symposium. William Dever and Seymour Gitin, eds.

Finkelstein, Israel, forthcoming The Philistines in the Bible: A Late-Monarchic Perspective. Journal for the Study of the Old Testament.

Finkelstein, Israel, and Neil A. Silberman, 2001 The Bible Unearthed: Archaeology's New Vision of Ancient Israel and the Origins of its Ancient Texts. New York: Simon and Schuster.

Finkelstein, Israel, Shlomo Bunimovitz, and Zvi Lederman, 1993 Shiloh, The Archaeology of a Biblical Site. Tel Aviv: Institute of Archaeology.

Frerichs, Ernest S., and Leonard H. Lesko, eds., 1997 Exodus: The Egyptian Evidence. Winona Lake: Eisenbrauns.

Friedman, Richard E., 1987 Who Wrote the Bible? San Francisco: Harper.

Friedman, Richard E., 1999 The Hidden Book in the Bible. San Francisco: Harper.

Garbini, Giovanni, 1988 History and Ideology in Ancient Israel. New York: Crossroad.

Gilboa, Ayelet, and Ilan Sharon, forthcoming Early Iron Age Radiometric Dates from Tel Dor: Preliminary Implications for Phoenicia and Beyond. Radiocarbon.

Gitin, Seymour, 1987 Tel Miqne-Ekron in the 7th C. BC: City Plan, Development and the Oil Industry. *In* Olive Oil in Antiquity. Michael Heltzer and David Eitam, eds. pp. 81–97. Haifa: Haifa University Press.

Halpern, Baruch, 1991 Jerusalem and the Lineages in the Seventh Century BCE: Kinship and the Rise of Individual Moral Liability. *In* Law and Ideology in Monarchic Israel, Baruch Halpern and Deborah W. Hobson, eds. pp. 11–107. Sheffield: JSOT Press.

Halpern, Baruch, 1995 Erasing History, The Minimalist Assault on Ancient Israel. Bible Review (December 1995):26–47.

Halpern, Baruch, and David Vanderhooft, 1991 The Editions of Kings in the 7th–6th Centuries BCE. Hebrew Union College Annual 62:179–244.

Haran, Menahem, 1981 Behind the Scenes of History: Determining the Date of the Priestly Source. Journal of Biblical Literature 100:321–333.

Hurvitz, Avi, 2000 Once Again: The Linguistic Profile of the Priestly Material in the Pentateuch and its Historical Age. Zeitschrift für die alttestamentliche Wissenschaft 112:180–191.

Hart, Stephen, 1986 Some Preliminary Thoughts on Settlement in Southern Edom. Levant 19:51–58.

Jamieson-Drake, David W., 1991 Scribes and Schools in Monarchic Judah: A Socio-Archaeological Approach. Sheffield: Almond.

Kletter, Raz, 1999 Pots and Polities: Material Remains of Late Iron Age Judah in Relation to its Political Borders. Bulletin of the American Schools of Oriental Research 314:19–54.

Knauft, Axel E., 1991 King Solomon's Copper Supply. *In* Phoenicia and the Bible. E. Lipinski, ed. pp. 167–186. Leuven: Peeters.

Knauft, Axel E., 2000 Does "Deuteronomistic Historiography" (DH) Exist? *In* Israel Constructs its History. Deuteronomistic Historiography in Recent Research. Albert de Pury, Thomas Römer, and Jean-Daniel Macchi, eds. pp. 388–398. Sheffield: Academic Press.

Lemche, Niels Peter, 1993 The Old Testament – A Hellenistic Book? Scandinavian Journal of the Old Testament 7:163–193.

Lemche, Niels Peter, 1994 Is it Still Possible to Write a History of Ancient Israel? Scandinavian Journal of the Old Testament 8:165–190.

Lohfink, Norbert, 1991 Studien zum Deuteronomium und zur deuteronomistischen Literatur, II. Stuttgart: Katholisches Bibelwerk.

Malamat, Abraham, 2001 History of Biblical Israel. Leiden: Brill.

Mazar, Amihai, 1990 Archaeology of the Land of the Bible 10,000–586 B.C.E. New York: Doubleday.

Mazar, Benjamin, 1986 The Early Biblical Period: Historical Studies. Jerusalem: Israel Exploration Society.

McCarter, Kyle P., 1999 The Patriarchal Age: Abraham, Isaac and Jacob. *In* Ancient Israel: From Abraham to the Roman Destruction of the Temple. Hershel Shanks, ed. pp. 1–31. Washington: Biblical Archaeology Society.

Mckenzie, Steven L., 1991 The Trouble with Kings: The Composition of the Book of Kings in the Deuteronomistic History. Leiden: Brill.

Millard, Alan R., 1998 The Knowledge of Writing in Iron Age Palestine. *In* "Lasset uns Brücken bauen . . ." Klaus-Dietrich Schunck and Matthias Augustin, eds. pp. 33–39. Frankfurt: Peter Lang.

Miller, Maxwell J., 1997 Separating the Solomon of History from the Solomon of Legend. *In* The Age of Solomon, Scholarship at the Turn of the Millennium. Lowell K. Handy, ed. pp. 1–24. Leiden: Brill.

Naaman, Nadav, 1979 Sennacherib's campaign to Judah and the Date of the *LMLK* Stamps. Vetus Testamentum 29:61–86.

Naaman, Nadav, 1991 The Kingdom of Judah under Josiah. Tel Aviv 18:3–71.

Naaman, Nadav, 1994 Hezekiah and the Kings of Assyria. Tel Aviv 21:235–254.

Naaman, Nadav, 1996 The Contribution of the Amarna Letters to the Debate on Jerusalem's Political Position in the Tenth Century BCE. Bulletin of the American Schools of Oriental Research 304:17–27.

Naaman, Nadav, 1997 Notes on the Excavations at 'Ein Hazeva. Qadmoniot 113 (Hebrew):60.

Naaman, Nadav, and Ran Zadok, 1988 Sargon II's Deportations to Israel and Philistia (716–708 B.C.). Journal of Cuneiform Studies 40:36–46.

Naaman, Nadav, and Ran Zadok, 2000 Assyrian Deportations to the Province of Samaria in the Light of Two Cuneiform Tablets from Tel Hadid. Tel Aviv 27:159–188.

Naveh, Joseph, 1982 The Early History of the Alphabet. Jerusalem: Magnes.

Naveh, Joseph, 1998 Achish-Ikausu in the Light of the Ekron Dedication. Bulletin of the American Schools of Oriental Research 310:35–37.

Nelson, Richard D., 1981a Josiah in the Book of Joshua. Journal of Biblical Literature 100:531–540.

Nelson, Richard D., 1981b The Double Redaction of the Deuteronomistic History. Sheffield: JSOT Press.

Niemann, Michael H., 1993 Herrschaft, Königtum und Staat. Skizzen zur soziokulturellen Entwicklung im monarchischen Israel. Tübingen: Mohr.

Niemann, Michael H., 1997 The Socio-Political Shadow Cast by the Biblical Solomon. *In*

The Age of Solomon, Scholarship at the Turn of the Millennium. Lowell K. Handy, ed. pp. 252–299. Leiden: Brill.

Ofer, Avi, 1994 "All the Hill Country of Judah": From Settlement Fringe to a Prosperous Monarchy. *In* From Nomadism to Monarchy, Archaeological and Historical Aspects of Early Israel. Israel Finkelstein and Nadav Naaman, eds. pp. 92–121. Jerusalem: Yad Ben Zvi.

Oren, Eliezer D., 1993 Haror, Tel. *In* The New Encyclopedia of Archaeological Excavations in the Holy Land 2. pp. 580–584. Jerusalem: Israel Exploration Society.

Pury, Albert de, and Thomas Römer, 1989 Le Pentateuque en question: position du problème et brève histoire de la recherche. *In* Le Pentateuque en question. Albert de Pury, ed. pp. 9–80. Geneva: Labor et Fides.

Renz, Johannes, 1995 Die Althebräischen Inschriften, Teil 1: Text und Kommentar. Darmstadt: Wissenschaftliche Buchgesellschaft.

Römer, Thomas, and Albert de Pury, 2000 Deuteronomistic Historiography (DH): History of Research and Debated Issues. *In* Israel Constructs its History. Deuteronomistic Historiography in Recent Research. Albert de Pury, Thomas Römer, and Jean-Daniel Macchi, eds. pp. 24–141. Sheffield: Academic Press.

Sarnah, Nahum A., 1999 Israel in Egypt: The Egyptian Sojourn and the Exodus. *In* Ancient Israel: From Abraham to the Roman Destruction of the Temple. Hershel Shanks, ed. pp. 33–54. Washington: Biblical Archaeology Society.

Sass, Benjamin, 1993 The Pre-Exilic Hebrew Seals: Iconism vs. Aniconism. *In* Studies in the Iconography of Northwest Semitic Inscribed Seals. Benjamin Sass and Christoph Uehlinger, eds. pp. 194–256. Fribourg: University Press Fribourg.

Shanks, Hershel, 1999 Everything You Ever Knew About Jerusalem is Wrong (Well, Almost). Biblical Archaeology Review 25(6):20–29.

Singer-Avitz, Lily, 1999 Beersheba – A Gateway Community in Southern Arabian Long-Distance Trade in the Eighth Century BCE. Tel Aviv 26:3–74.

Smend, Rudolf, 1971 Das Gesetz und die Volker: Ein Beitrag zur deuteronomistichen Redaktionsgeschichte. *In* Probleme biblischer Theologie. Hans W. Wolff, ed. pp. 494–509. München: Chr. Kaiser.

Smith, Morton, 1971 Palestinian Parties and Politics That Shaped the Old Testament. New York: Columbia University Press.

Steiner, Margret, 1998 David's Jerusalem, Fiction or Reality? It's Not There – Archaeology Proves a Negative. Biblical Archaeology Review 24(4):26–33, 62.

Thompson, Thomas L., 1974 The Historicity of the Patriarchal Narratives: The Quest for the Historical Abraham. Berlin: de Gruyter.

Thompson, Thomas L., 1999 The Bible in History: How Writers Create a Past. London: Jonathan Cape.

Ussishkin, David, 1982 The Conquest of Lachish by Sennacherib. Tel Aviv: Institute of Archaeology.

Ussishkin, David, 1995 The Rectangular Fortress at Kadesh-Barnea. Israel Exploration Journal 45:118–127.

Ussishkin, David, forthcoming Solomon's Jerusalem: The Text and the Facts on the Ground.

Van Seters, John, 1983 In Search of History: Historiography in the Ancient World and the Origins of Biblical History. New Haven: Yale University Press.

Van Seters, John, 1990 Joshua's Campaign of Canaan and Near Eastern Historiography. Scandinavian Journal of the Old Testament 4(2):1–12.

Van Seters, John, 1992 Prologue to History, The Yahwist as Historian in Genesis. Louisville: Westminster/John Knox.

Van Seters, John, 1999 The Pentateuch: A Social-Science Commentary. Sheffield: Academic Press.

Veijola, Timo, 1977 Das Königtum in der Beurteilung der deuteronomistischen Historiographie: Eine redaktionsgeschichtliche Untersuchung. Helsinki: Suomalainen Tiedeakatemia.

Whybray, R. N., 1987 The Making of the Pentateuch. A Methodological Study. Sheffield: Academic Press.

Younger, Lawson K., 1990 Ancient Conquest Accounts: A Study of Ancient Near Eastern and Biblical History Writing. Sheffield: JSOT Press.

11

Imperialism

Mario Liverani

Colonialism, Cultural Appropriation, and Empires

As a child does with his or her toys, Western culture quite often investigates what it is destroying, from alien peoples and cultural heritages to landscapes and material resources.

The archaeological and epigraphic rediscovery of ancient Near Eastern civilizations (Larsen 1996) started in the period of colonial appropriation of the Ottoman Empire and was a constituent part of that process. This holds true both in general terms and in detail: it should suffice to remember that the short period (1842–54) of excavations carried out by Emile Botta, Austen Layard, and their followers (E. Place, H. Rassam, W. K. Loftus) in the capital cities of Assyria took place in the interval between the end (1841) of the war of the Ottoman empire, supported by the major European countries, against Muhammad Ali and the beginning (1855) of the Crimean War and Indian Mutiny. From this perspective, archaeological excavations took place side by side with (or even slightly preceded) the European intrusion (under the label of assistance) in the financial system and communication infrastructures of the declining empire.

Besides political and economic aspects, cultural aspects played an important role in the process of appropriation (Silberman 1982; Larsen 1994): the shipment of stone reliefs to be exhibited in London and Paris museums is just a more apparent feature of the cultural appropriation of historical and cultural heritage. Specific research tools were invented by European colonizers in order to accomplish the task of assimilating alien cultures.

In the case of illiterate cultures of "primitive" peoples, the cultural tool invented by colonialism was ethnology. But in the case of Near Eastern (and other Asiatic) peoples and civilizations, a different tool had to be invented, namely Orientalism (Said 1979, 1993). Those cultures were literate and politically sophisticated, they had produced important insights in the fields of religion, philosophy, literature, and art, they were assumed by the Classical tradition to be the original homeland of wisdom and civilization, and they provided the historical background of the Holy Bible. For all these reasons their cultures could not be simply destroyed; they had to be appropriated by the European conquerors.

The cultures of the ancient Near East, moreover, were (and still are) considered especially important as providing the "roots" for our own civilization and religion. The early 20th-century *ex-libris* of James Henry Breasted, reproduced as a stone relief on the entrance of the Chicago Oriental Institute, shows modern Western archaeologists (backed by Roman legionaries and medieval crusaders) meeting ancient Egyptian and Babylonian kings and scribes (Larsen 1994).

The appropriation found ready-made help in the Biblical and Classical tradition of *translatio imperii* (Goetz 1958; Kratz 1991): imperial power shifted from Assyria and Babylonia to Media and Persia, then to the Greeks, finally to the Romans. In this way, a line of continuity linked the ancient empires to the European ones, the heirs of the Roman empire. Larsen has compared the Chicago relief to a painting representing Napoleon's meeting with the mummy of an ancient Pharaoh. The Napoleonic iconography, in its turn, can be traced to narratives about Alexander the Great meeting the statue of Nectanebo and inheriting Pharaonic power. This is important, since the transfer of empire inside the Near East (from Assyria to Babylonia, from Media to Persia) took place in the same geographic space and cultural tradition, while the application of the same paradigm to justify the Macedonian conquest was ideologically biased in that the transfer was in fact the result of a foreign conquest. The justification of Alexander's conquest is the first model for the modern appropriation of Middle Eastern cultural and political heritage by Western colonialism.

The idea of the *translatio imperii*, moreover, became part and parcel of a comprehensive model for world history. A Euro-centered world view assumed that high culture originated in the Middle East (Egypt and Mesopotamia), then passed to Greece and Rome, the Christian Middle Ages, and up to the Western European world of the Industrial Revolution. Such a basic line of development in world history is still accepted as "normal" by the Western public, who assimilate it through secondary school textbooks.

This is a selective pattern, however, one dictated by the Western point of view. The Islamic or Middle Eastern perspective would generate a different line of continuity, for instance a line connecting directly (with no shift in space) the Achaemenid empire with the Pahlavi dynasty, as materialized on the occasion of the 2,500th anniversary of Cyrus, celebrated in Teheran, 1971 (Anon. 1974). The case is not unique: the modern Lebanese, especially the Christian Maronites, engaged in Levantine trade pretend to be direct heirs of the Phoenicians, while the desperate Kurds claim to be descendants of the "mighty Medes" and celebrate Nowruz as an anniversary of the Medes' destruction of Nineveh in 612 B.C.E. Modern Egypt takes care – basically for purposes of tourism – of its Pharaonic antiquities. Similar processes of identification of modern and ancient peoples and re-appropriation of local heritage for various political, nationalist, or economic reasons have been under way in Iraq, Yemen, Turkey, and wherever conspicuous remains of ancient cultures are visible.

The local point of view, however, was not operative at the time of colonialist intervention, because traditional Islamic culture did not express any interest in pre-Islamic cultures, discarded as belonging to the period of *jāhilīya* (the state of ignorance in pre-Islamic paganism). As the territorial appropriation has been recurrently justified by "empty" spaces or their poor exploitation by local peoples, so also cultural appropriation has been justified by local disinterest in heritage abandoned in ruins and at risk of complete destruction if left to the care of its direct heirs. The 19th-century pictorial representations of Oriental ruins by David Roberts and other "Orientalist" painters vividly expressed such a state of affairs by populating the magnificent monuments of the past with picturesque yet miserable squatters. Since the late 18th century, the most attentive travelers in the Middle East (Volney 1792) established an explicit connection between the despotic rule of the Ottoman empire and the state of abandonment of a landscape populated with the remains of ancient cities and palaces. They pointed to a period when those regions hosted important civilizations and denounced the political (especially fiscal) and cultural causes of their collapse.

This was particularly true for the Biblical heritage (Silberman 1991), since the change in local religion, brought about by the Islamicization of the Middle East and the westwards displacement of Christianity, left "our" sacred places in the hands of the believers of another religion. We can quote the cry of Robert Mignan in Chaldea (1829:120) to express the common feeling of travelers visiting the Holy Places in Palestine or looking for the Tower of Babel in the Mesopotamian plains: "Can we ever sufficiently lament the circumstance of the country being in the hands of barbarians?" In this perspective, colonial appropriation was perfectly justified as the rescue of a heritage despised by its physical descendants but highly appreciated by its Western moral heirs.

Political and Moral Values: East vs. West

The European empires that destroyed and divided the spoil of the Ottoman empire were "bourgeois" empires, appreciating the values of freedom, democracy, individual enterprise, progress, and rational science. They conceived of, or at least pretended to justify, colonization as a valuable process of civilization and progress, applied to countries and peoples still in the hands of despots responsible for a state of generalized servitude and economic stagnation. Even Karl Marx (1960), certainly not an admirer of capitalism, evaluated the English colonization of India as progress, the only way to overcome political despotism and socio-economic stagnation.

The Western historians found in the ancient Near Eastern empires the models and forerunners of the Ottoman empire rather than of their own. They emphasized the negative values of despotism, generalized slavery, centralized economy, magic, stagnation, lust, and sadistic cruelty. Instead of building an unbiased story of progressive changes in political institutions, Western scholars were trapped in a preconceived opposition of East vs. West, where the negative values of the Oriental model were an obvious justification for the appropriation of their lands and culture, and even their history and cultural heritage. The concept of "opposition," though contradictory to that of "appropriation" in logical terms, nevertheless made the process even more effective.

The opposition of values had its origins in ancient Greece. The praise of the city-state vs. empire had first been expressed by Phocylides, ca. 540 B.C.E. ("A city which is small but on a lofty promontory and well ordered is stronger than foolish Nineveh"), but became a true clash of civilizations during the Persian Wars, as narrated by Herodotus. Freedom and democracy had the moral values to resist and even defeat the huge despotic empires of the Orient. In practical terms the small but determined (and better armed!) troops of the city-states were able to defeat the numberless armies of the emperor's slaves. The debate between Xerxes and Demaratos (Herodotus VII 103–104) applies the opposing virtues of despotism and freedom to warlike behavior. According to Xerxes, the Persians, "Were they under the rule of one, according to our custom, they might from fear of him show a valour greater than natural, and under compulsion of the lash might encounter odds in the field; but neither of these would they do while they were suffered to be free."

The answer by Demaratos turns the evaluation upside down: "[The Greeks], fighting singly, they are as brave as any man living, and together they are the best warriors on earth. Free they are, yet not wholly free; for Law is their master, whom they fear much more than your men fear you. This is my proof – what their law bids them, that they do; and its bidding is ever the same, that they must never flee from the battle before whatsoever odds, but abide at their post and there conquer or die" (trans. Godley 1982:407–409).

The final issue of the Persian wars was considered the practical demonstration that quality is superior to quantity, civic values are more effective than forced obedience, freedom works better than despotism. Following such a tradition more than two millennia later, the modern Greek Independence War (1823–28) was appreciated (and participated in) by members of the European intelligentsia as a repeat performance of the Persian wars, to be fought with a gun in one hand and Herodotus in the other.

But the archaeological discoveries in the mid-19th century provided a much better model for the "Empire of Evil": the Achaemenid empire replaced the Assyrian empire, which was also the first in line according to the "succession of empires" paradigm. The replacement had something to do with racist prejudices: the Persians were an Indo-European people, while the Assyrians were Semites. But the main reason for a criminalization of the Assyrian (and Neo-Babylonian) empire is to be found in the Biblical perspective. Assyria and Babylonia had been responsible for the conquest of Israel and Judah, the destruction of Jerusalem and the First Temple, and the deportations of the Jews – while Cyrus (the first Achaemenid emperor) was the author of the Edict (538) allowing the exiles to return to their homeland, an expression of a more enlightened political attitude. The Assyrian empire became the original model for the subsequent despotic empires down to the Ottomans. And the Ottoman empire acted as a model to more easily understand and reconstruct the Assyrian empire. The Ottoman model was effective in introducing terms like *harem, eunuchs,* and *vizier* into the description of Assyria, and in advancing fanciful reconstructions of Assyrian palaces embellished with domes and minarets (Fergusson 1851).

The Orient was not despotic in its entirety, however, and the Eastern Mediterranean belt had characters of its own. In modern times it hosted the "Levantine" communities of traders and dealers, largely Christian and building an intermediate zone between the Western and the Oriental worlds. In antiquity, the same belt was the seat of city-states and small kingdoms, assumed to have been more democratic and engaged in a desperate resistance against the advance of the aggressive and totalitarian empires of the Orient. The rescue and protection of Levantine dealers and Christian minorities, besides that of the Holy Places of Christianity, acted as an additional motivation and justification for colonial intervention.

Negative as they may have been from ethical and political points of view, the despotic empires were nevertheless a paradise for archaeology, especially the kind that dominated the colonial period. It was an archaeology of appropriation, and the aims of the first diggers are best defined by Layard: "to obtain the largest possible number of well preserved objects of art at the least possible outlay of time and money" (cf. Daniel 1975:152). The "objects of art," namely the sculptured slabs of the Assyrian palaces, were shipped to Paris and London, to be exhibited in the newly created museums for the admiration of a bourgeois audience. It is not by chance that the establishment of public (state-run) archaeological (and especially Oriental) museums went hand-in-hand with that of ethnographic collections, botanical gardens, and zoological parks: these are all cases of the Western imperial and colonial world exhibiting to its own public the spoils (both cultural and natural) of its conquests.

Classical scholars and art historians, however, were less enthusiastic about the artistic value of the Assyrian reliefs as compared to Greek ones, and the exhibit in the British Museum of the Assyrian reliefs and the "Elgin Marbles" materialized the uneven struggle (Bohrer 1989). Jacob Burckhardt (1905:65) mentions "the rude royal fortress of Nineveh" and "their miserable architectural structure and servile sculpture." Once again, our civilization owes a debt to the Orient in the "material" aspects of culture, but owes to Greece the most important values, those connected with a free development of individual personality, including aesthetic values. The Oriental empires, based as they were on compulsory dependence on the absolute will of the despot, did not produce good soldiers or good artists. Therefore the masterpieces of Greek art were exhibited for and perceived in their aesthetic values as a part of our own culture, while the Assyrian reliefs were exhibited as spoils from an inferior and alien civilization.

The physical appropriation of archaeological remains is just one aspect of colonial archaeology in its first phase. Another aspect was its exclusive interest in the "hard" structures of state and empire, as represented by palaces, temples, and fortifications, i.e., public architecture in general. The palaces excavated (if we can use

this term) by Botta and Layard were impressive enough in their graphic reconstructions; but when the German school of architects (R. Koldewey in Babylon and
W. Andrae in Assur) enabled excavators to make mudbrick structures visible, the
effect was impressive indeed and materialized the idea of a centralized totalitarian
empire.

For the early periods the concept of "Temple-City" as applied especially to
Sumerian culture demonstrated that the Orient was centralistic and totalitarian (in
this case, theocratic), not democratic, well before the existence of large empires.

The story of "Oriental Despotism" is a long one. After the end of the Ottoman
empire it found its best application to Soviet Russia (cf. Wittfogel 1957), considered as part of the "Eastern" side of slavery and stagnation, and fought against as
a terrible danger for the freedom of the Western democratic world. The story is still
alive in our times at the level of popular culture: in the movie "Star Wars" we are
the "Federation," a democratic and pluralistic organization fighting for freedom,
while the enemy is the "Empire" – "the Empire of Evil" – whose members speak
with a marked Russian accent.

While the despotic Oriental empires were criminalized, Western scholars could
not ignore Western empires, which were also studied in a critical way but characterized as networks rather than territories, aiming at economic rather than military
control. Lenin's definition of imperialism as the culminating phase of capitalism is
just a more popular (and more politicized) outcome of an important debate among
economists and modern historians (Brown 1974), but it had a very limited impact
on ancient Near Eastern studies. The basic point (faced differently by the various
schools) is that the prime mover of imperialism is economic, so that the "economy
of imperialism" is the pivotal subject for study. The military and political means to
accomplish expansion are left to the variable conditions of historical periods.

The Model of Empire and its Variations

During the colonial dominance (ca. 1920–50), the model of "empire" was applied
– both by specialized scholars and general audiences – to various polities of the
ancient Near East well before the time-honored line of the "classical" empires
(Assyria, Babylonia, Media, Persia). We still speak of an empire of Akkad (Westenholz 1979; Liverani 1993; but see Forest, this volume), of Ebla (Matthiae 1977;
Pettinato 1979), an Ur III empire (e.g., Goetze 1963), an empire of Hammurabi
of Babylon (e.g., Schmökel 1958), a Hittite empire (e.g., Gurney 1979), a Middle
Assyrian empire, and an Egyptian empire (especially in the New Kingdom: Kemp
1978; Frandsen 1979). Such a widespread use of the term seems to imply that every
Oriental state of some compactness and extent was an empire, without regard for
its inner structure or ideology. We might even suspect that some scholars feel more
rewarded by studying an empire than just a state – or cunningly hope their books
on the subject will sell better.

But over time, especially after the end of the colonial period around 1950 – when
real empires ceased to exist, or there was a pretense that they no longer existed as

such – a more "scientific" study of the characteristics of ancient empires began. Formerly, scholars were happy with a classification by way of analogy: an empire is a state similar to a model empire, be it the Assyrian (for antiquity) or the Ottoman one (for modern times). This mythical approach (based on a "first model" to be actualized in the course of time) was replaced by an historical one based on the analysis of specific features. Classifications and definitions of empires have been advanced many times, from the massive works of Wittfogel (1957) and Eisenstadt (1963) to the elegant "geometry" of Arrighi (1978). Various collective volumes on ancient (Garnsey and Whittaker 1978) or specifically ancient Near Eastern (Larsen 1979a; cf. also Garelli 1980) empires were produced, especially in the late 1970s.

Of course there is the risk of a vicious circle in this procedure: the specific features are those recurrent in a list of case studies selected in advance on the basis of a pre-conceived idea. A restricted list of cases closer to the "classical" model will produce a more specific definition, while a more varied list will produce a looser typology. The main problems arise from the solutions advanced for two important features. The first is the opposition of territorial, compact empires vs. loose (commercial or nomadic) empires. This problem is related to a value judgment, since territorial empires are mostly connected with (Oriental) despotism, loose empires mostly with (Western) commercial expansion.

The second problem is the minimum size necessary for an empire: is it reasonable to label as empire, or even as "universal" empire, a state controlling just a few hundred square miles of territory? Size is not an independent variable; it depends on the size of the *oikumene* known and frequented by a given society in a given historical time. Thus, the problem of size underscores the point that empires are better selected on the basis of their ideology – their pretension to exert a universal domination – than on actual extent. In a limited *oikumene*, it is possible that a small state may pretend to be the actualization of the universal domain, the unique kingdom entitled by God to exert legal power over the world.

In the case of ancient Near Eastern civilizations, however, these two problems were rather easily solved in practical terms (see Larsen 1979b for a general survey). Trade networks have seldom been labeled "empires." The system of Late Uruk period colonies (ca. 3200–3000), the Old Assyrian system of *kārum* (ca. 1900–1800), or the Phoenician network of colonies (ca. 750–500) can hardly be defined as "empires," as we shall see in a moment, although some scholars would like to identify the roots of imperialism in the Uruk period (Algaze 2001). Nomadic pastoralists in the Syro-Arabian steppe had neither the size nor the technical tools to establish any kind of enduring domain ("pastoral empire") over the country. As to size, any (assumed) ancient Near Eastern empire must be framed in its quite restricted *oikumene*, stretching from the Mediterranean to the Indian Ocean, in which it is easy to claim "universal" domain from coast to coast.

It would be wise to limit the use of the term "empire" to the Neo-Assyrian, Neo-Babylonian, and Achaemenid empires, reverting in fact to the "classical" list as already defined by the ancient (Biblical and Classical) authors. They developed a clear imperialistic ideology, were compact and despotic, and large enough to include a great part of the Near Eastern *oikumene* of their times. Previous polities in the third and second millennia were either too small or too loose to pretend to such a label. The Ur III state controlled directly only a restricted area in lower Mesopotamia; the Akkad empire had a more marked imperial ideology but a rather loose administrative structure; the Hittite empire had no imperial ideology and was regional in extent; and so on. An interesting case is Media, which was indeed a member of the classical list. More recent analyses (Sancisi-Weerdenburg 1988; Liverani in press), however, tend to describe the period ca. 650–610 as a secondary state generated by its proximity to the Assyrian empire and the interval ca. 610–550 as a loose confederacy of mountain chiefdoms under the hegemony of a Median ruler who acquired special prestige for having destroyed the Assyrian empire.

Dismounting Empires

In the post-colonial period, Near Eastern archaeology along with philology devoted an increased interest to clarifying the inner functioning of empires and unveiling their ideology. On the one hand, a growing interest in rural communities, rural landscape, domestic life and material culture, previously advanced primarily by Marxist scholars, became a common trend and resulted in a more variegated and less ideological approach to the real configuration of empires. On the other hand, the turning point of the late 1960s resulted in a more explicitly critical approach to received ideas and a true and proper "dismounting" of imperial ideologies and socio-economic structures. I single out here the most significant trends in addressing some key problems concerning ancient Near Eastern empires.

Imperial infrastructures: canals and roads

The epoch-making surveys carried out by Robert McC. Adams during the 1950s and 1960s in lower Mesopotamia (1965, 1981; Adams and Nissen 1972) explicitly contradicted the time-honored idea that hydraulic structures (the network of irrigation canals) were connected with empires – an idea that found its extreme supporter in Wittfogel (1957). According to Adams, the early development of irrigation canals was a local affair, carried out at a limited scale by local communities. Eventually the local networks were connected to wider systems, so that the growth of hydraulic structures went hand-in-hand with the growth of political systems and was not the result of centralized polities but rather a factor in their development.

A similar critique could be carried out regarding road systems. The Achaemenid empire is credited with the installation and running of a system of "kings' roads," the most important being the one from Susa to Sardis described by Herodotus (Seibert 1985:15–27; Koch 1986). Smaller sections of "kings' roads" are well attested in the Assyrian empire (Kessler 1980:27–78; 1997; Levine 1989), and a system of state-run post stations is known from the Ur III dynasty (Shulgi hymn:

Pritchard 1969:585–586). In this case as well it is a matter of the progressive establishment of a network connecting local roads to a more comprehensive system.

In current studies, the "imperial landscape" seems to be simply an enlargement
and systematization of previous local landscapes. Yet it is possible that recent trends
understate the role of empires in producing not only an enlargement in scale but
also a substantial improvement in agricultural and communication infrastructures.

Imperial capital cities

In earlier studies the large Assyrian and Babylonian capital cities were interpreted
as something different and even opposite to Western cities, by scholars of various
ideological backgrounds (Liverani 1997:86–87). According to Karl Marx they were
"princely encampments, superfetations of the real economic structure" (1983:39).
Jacob Burckhardt defines the "enormous military encampments of the Assyrian
dynasties," the Babylonian "common castle for all goods and gods," "the three temporary residences of the Achaemenids," and "the huge market-places of the Oriental trade" as a negative counter-model for the Greek *polis* (1898:61). It is only in
the mid-20th century that these capitals were accepted as real cities, so that the
problem of their provisioning – and consequently the relationships of city and countryside – became a subject for serious study (Oates 1968). More recently the parallel growth of the Assyrian capitals and decrease of minor settlements has received
attention as a significant historical process (Wilkinson 1995).

We can also outline a changing approach to the visualization of the palace, the
core of any imperial capital city. In the 19th century, when European "formal"
empires still existed, the royal palace was viewed as a residence of the emperor (like
Versailles or Schönbrunn) and the location of ceremony and display. The pictorial
representations of Assyrian palaces were populated by courtiers solemnly engaged
in doing nothing – as if the empire could rest on prestige rather than production.
In the first half of the 20th century, palaces became a kind of political machine, the
core and physical location of the administration of the imperial economy. They were
studied mainly through administrative documents and inner correspondence
exchanged between king and officials, complemented by the functional analysis of
architecture (Margueron 1982; on Assyrian palaces cf. Albenda 1986; Russell 1991;
Caubet 1995). The old search for the location of the harem and throne room was
enlarged to a definition of sectors devoted to residence, ceremony, administration
and archives, store-rooms and workshops, in this way providing a more precise idea
of the use of the palace as the center of the empire.

Imperial ideologies and their archaeological visibility

The study of imperial ideology and its archaeological visibility, developed during
the late 1960s and 1970s, started from the unveiling of royal inscriptions as biased
messages, in line with procedures of "counter-information" and literary analyses

applied to modern political addresses (Eco 1971; Klaus 1971; Faye 1972; Robin 1973) . The transfer of such studies to imperial ideologies (and their "propaganda") of the ancient Near East has been the main engagement of various scholars (cf. Liverani 1979; Oppenheim 1979; studies collected in Fales 1981; Tadmor and Weinfeld 1983; Tadmor 1997). The application of similar perspectives to iconic representations and monumental architecture has been especially relevant as applied to Assyrian (cf. most recently Lamprichs 1995; Winter 1997) and Persian (Root 1979) palaces and sculpted reliefs. The study of imperial ideology is especially important because it makes clear that the very same definition of an empire is not so much related to the size of the imperial state (which, as we have seen, can be quite small, if projected to a world scale), but to the ideological pretension of universal domain, and therefore to a mental rather than practical accomplishment.

In terms of extent, the basic concept is that of the "universal empire." Since the king is put in charge by the gods, with the ultimate task of ensuring a correct relationship between divine and human levels, it is clear that only one kingdom can really be entrusted with such a charge. Its task is to extend the correct relationships – already existent in the home country – to the "barbarian" periphery. The most typical royal title of imperial flavor is "king of the four quarters" (i.e., of the entire world) and the most typical task is to enlarge the empire to the very outer border of the *oikumene*. The Assyrian coronation ritual states this task most clearly: "By your right sceptre enlarge your land! May Assur give you authority and obedience, justice and peace!" (Müller 1937:12–13). The visible materialization of the universal domain is provided by the stelae set up at the farthest points reached by the king, generally in locations that are ideologically meaningful and allude to a far end: the sea coast or a high mountain, beyond which no land can be seen or imagined to exist.

Although imperial conquest is intended as a benefit for the subdued peoples, who will be finally inserted in the cosmos and subtracted to chaos, nevertheless foreign peoples resist such a transformation. This is because they still are part of the chaos and are characterized by wickedness and insanity (Haas 1980). They do not submit; they resist, they have to be vanquished or even eliminated. They trust in their numbers or in the protection of the landscape, and do not understand that the imperial army, secure in its divine support, will unavoidably win.

The imperial conquest is therefore a story of military campaigns, motivated according to the pattern of "holy war," which is also "just war" (cf. Oded 1992). The enemies (and not the imperial expansionist policy) are responsible for the war and for their final defeat: since they resisted or even threatened the safety of the central kingdom, it is their fault (not ours) if they are finally killed. Once again an Assyrian text, in this case a prayer of Tukulti-Ninurta I from the Middle Assyrian period, is the best example. The repeated plunder and destruction carried out by the Assyrian armies against the mountain tribes in the Zagros is justified as a defensive reaction against the wicked, foolish, aggressive enemies (Foster 1993:230–235).

The sculptured reliefs in the Assyrian palaces have also been read as an apparatus of imperial propaganda, which is certainly true. But the main question is about the "audience" (or addressees) of such a textual and iconic apparatus. A rather naive explanation is that the narrative and representation of imperial power were intended to impress foreign visitors, and more particularly the description and representation of violence and sadistic cruelty was intended to terrify enemies. A much more reasonable explanation is that such scenes were intended to mobilize and ensure the loyalty of the Assyrians themselves. In fact the basic intent of the "holy war" paradigm is to convince the internal public that "our" war is supported by the gods, that our army is superior to that of the enemy, that we will suffer no casualties, and that the enemy will be punished for its "original sin" of being an enemy (i.e., for resistance to imperial and divine power).

The study of the literary *topoi* and iconic motifs of the imperial apparatus of propaganda has become in recent years one of the most productive lines of research for an in-depth understanding of what an ancient empire really was in the minds of its promoters and its participants.

Center and periphery

The empires in the ancient Near East can hardly be visualized as compact territories, all uniformly governed by an emperor. Imperial structure is rather complex (cf. Frei and Koch 1984 on the Achaemenid empire) and includes in all cases a distinction between the "inner country" and the provinces. The inner country, the core of the empire, is inhabited by a people ethnically and functionally different from the conquered lands. The Assyrians, Babylonians, or Persians remain the leading people, in direct contact with the gods, even after they have been able to enlarge the cosmos to include peoples who were originally excluded from such a beneficial contact. Of course, processes of intermixture between governing and governed peoples take place, but they are not similar in both directions. The core receives an influx of subordinated foreigners, in the form of deportees and prisoners, who are used as a work-force to replace the voids produced by an ever problematic demographic balance and war losses. In contrast, the conquered kingdoms, transformed into provinces or satrapies, receive an influx of representatives of the ruling class: governors and administrative units, located in provincial palaces, garrisons of guards and soldiers to keep law and order, and in some cases merchants who profit from unbalanced economic relationships. Provincial palaces reproduce on a smaller scale the function and operative procedures of the central palace in the capital city.

Not all territory can be administered according to a provincial system. At the empire's periphery some form of autonomy can exist, for different reasons. One is transient: the submission of foreign kingdoms most often takes place in a two-stage procedure. First, the kingdom is vanquished and becomes a "vassal"; later, following a "rebellion," it is punished by loss of autonomy and transformation into a province. A second reason is structural: the mountain and steppe tribes do not have the internal political and economic requisites to become provinces. They do not have cities and palaces, their produce cannot be subject to formal taxation.

Therefore they remain in the status of dependent but autonomous peoples, governed by their own chiefs, linked to the emperor by loyalty oaths, and paying not taxes but tribute that is mostly disguised as gifts and receiving royal gifts in their turn. The imperial arrangement is basically a three-level structure: core, provinces, periphery (Steinkeller 1987; Marcus 1990).

In the periphery and also outside the empire, a process of adaptation takes place, according to which local tribes and chiefdoms, devoid of the markers of state formation (royal palace, formal administration, and taxation system), are led to imitate the state structures of the empire. This happens because of the political and economic relationships that the empire establishes with surrounding polities. Local elites build state-like structures in order to better express their prestige inside their country and to better interact with the empire. Such processes of "secondary state formation" (Brown 1986; Liverani in press) at the periphery of empires are archaeologically and textually attested, especially in the mountain ranges bordering Mesopotamia, but also in other areas.

The decision-making process

The inner structure is much more complex than old-fashioned presentations of ancient Near Eastern empires pretended it to be. It is true that the emperor is an absolute sovereign, whose power (assigned to him by the gods) has no limit. But "despotism" is a concept belonging to the field of ideology and needs to be qualified in reality. Nobody can even think to run an empire in isolation. The emperor is obviously assisted by a large number of officials and courtiers, competent in (and entrusted with) various special functions: scribes and administrators, astrologers and magicians, servants and body-guards. Of course such a political elite can influence the emperor in his decisions. We can single out three problems confronting the sovereign as especially meaningful.

The first problem is that the decision-making procedure is complicated by necessary recourse to two parallel channels. On the one hand the king has to collect and validate information, and eventually take decisions, on the human level. On the other hand he has to collect and validate information and warnings coming from the super-human level, which is considered to be the most significant (Pongratz-Leisten 1997, 1999). The Mesopotamian model of kingship has recourse to the two legendary sovereigns of Akkad, contrasting the correct behavior of Sargon, who follows divine advice even if human information is negative, with the impious behavior of Naram-Sin, who trusts in human intelligence against the negative advice of the omens. In fact the Late Assyrian kings, about whom we have the richest documentary evidence, followed both channels by collecting both human information and counsel and astral omens and prophecies, validating the information through extispicy, and confronting negative omens with prophylactic rituals (*namburbi*).

The second problem is that the king's advisors follow their own strategies of self-promotion and self-protection, not necessarily coincident with the interest of the empire. On the one hand, human advisors tend to be cautious, even too cautious, in order to avoid the risk of being held responsible for possible disasters. On the other hand, astrologers tend to be optimistic (and even to conceal negative signs) in order to avoid the risk of being considered boycotters of the king's projects and activities. In general, court officials follow a strategy of family consolidation, acquiring real estate and ensuring their sons' succession to the office, a strategy contrary to the king's interest in removing inefficient officials and keeping total control on people and resources. Recourse to eunuchs is the most obvious move in this direction, since eunuchs cannot hope to transmit their position to sons (Grayson 1995; Deller 1999).

The third problem is that the royal palace is not a safe place, and the emperor is subject to continuous stress in taking care of his personal safety. The atmosphere of the palace is one of competition and slander not only among officials but also inside the harem and royal family – not seldom ending in conspiracies against the king or designated heir to the throne. In the Hittite and Assyrian empires, regicide is one of the most common procedures of turnover, and most time and attention must be paid by the sovereign to avoid risks of assassination.

Outside the palace, the two basic structures of any empire are the bureaucracy (e.g., Gibson and Biggs 1987) and the army (e.g., Malbran-Labat 1982). In both, the basic technical tools at the disposal of empires are the same as for smaller states, only scale and spatial dissemination are greater and more complex. In the ancient Near East, personal relationships prevailed over functional structures. The distinction between members of the royal family, administrative elite, army officers, and provincial governors tends to be rather fluid. The king is personally responsible for political and administrative decisions (even of quite minor cases), but his personal relations with bureaucrats and officers becomes a less and less effective tool with the growing scale of the problems. In various cases from the Hittite to Late Assyrian empire, the king seems more concerned with ensuring the loyalty of his assistants than with fully exploiting their services.

The effects of ancient imperialism

The existence and tendency of an empire to grow have important effects on surrounding peoples and countries. In modern times, economic development of an empire parallels underdevelopment in the periphery, since it is based on the exploitation of the periphery's resources and labor power. In ancient times, the effect of imperial growth on the periphery seems to have been dissimilar in conquered countries and the outer periphery.

Doubtless, imperial growth has a devastating effect on conquered countries: destruction of towns and villages, devastation of agriculture, deportation of ruling elites and commoners brought about a vertical collapse of the local economy and culture. The imposition of imperial religion to the detriment of the local one, even if not coercive (Cogan 1974), affected both the elite (because of the ideological relationship between the gods' favour and political fortunes) and the common population (in a general loss of traditional reference points). Tribute (before annexation) and taxation (inside the empire) were burdensome for local economies (cf. Bär 1996 on tribute; Postgate 1974 on taxation).

Deportations (Oded 1979; Gallagher 1994) were a typical imperial procedure, meant to achieve two different results. The goals of breaking down political resistance and eliminating local centers of independent culture and trade were reached quite easily. Repopulating the core country, however, was achieved only to a minor degree. The effects of imperial devastations are quite evident in the archaeological record. Entire countries, previously the seat of brilliant cultures, were totally destroyed, and depopulation assumed unprecedented levels. It suffices to compare the demographic, economic, and cultural levels reached by Neo-Hittite, Aramean, and Levantine kingdoms before and after the Assyrian conquest to understand what the effect of ancient imperialism was to subjected peoples.

A major problem is that cross-deportations also produced an ethnic intermingling that persisted even after the empire collapsed and increased the effects of religious and ethnic competition not only between different countries, but also inside one country. The problems of minorities, refugees' diaspora, and resurgent nationalism are an effect of imperialism in the ancient Near East (the case of Israel is paramount) as in modern times (e.g., after the disruption of the Ottoman and Austro-Hungarian empires).

The effect of ancient imperialism on the outer peripheries seems to have been rather positive, in the sense of increasing their socio-economic complexity. We have already seen the "secondary" growth of formal polities (including urbanization, administration and writing, etc.). Furthermore, the economic relationships did not result in underdevelopment of the periphery, since trade items were rather specialized (metals, semi-precious stones, etc.) and did not affect the basic productive structure, but only stimulated the activity of specialized craftspeople.

Growth and collapse

The collapse of ancient empires has been the first and most conspicuous feature to attract the attention of modern historians. Ruins and desert, left behind by the despotic states of the ancient Near Eastern civilizations and still visible, were explained as the unavoidable issue of misgovernment and over-taxation. In Biblical studies, the ruins of Assyria and Babylonia were pointed to as proof of the effectiveness of the divine curse against cruel kings and peoples who conquered and destroyed Israel.

A "scientific" approach to the problem of collapse has been used especially during the 1980s in the framework of system theory, as a result of interaction between various factors and feedbacks (Tainter 1988; Yoffee and Cowgill 1988). Collapse is viewed mostly as a result of over-exploitation of limited human and material resources by overly ambitious programs of growth and dominance – a secular and properly political version of the moral or religious explanation. An external shock by invading barbarians is commonly considered an occasional factor, the final strike against an already declining system (Liverani 2001).

The problem of genesis and growth is less conspicuously visible in archaeological remains and has been more recently analyzed (e.g., Brinkman 1984). In earlier studies, the empire was visualized rather statically in its functioning, with no concern for the formative process. In contrast, this is now considered an important problem, not simply solved by recourse to the expansionist ideology of empires. Such an ideology can explain the motivations of the ruling class, but imperial expansion must be analyzed according to the procedures through which political and administrative control is established over ever larger areas. Recourse to models of "network of communications" and "territorial control" for the Assyrian empire in the formative period is just one example (Liverani 1988; cf. Postgate 1992). Even the most practical matters of costs and logistics for military campaigns should receive attention.

The Crisis of Imperialism

In this analysis, I have often underscored how historians' attitudes toward empires have changed through time. On the one hand, the more sophisticated procedures of analysis that are available today, both in archaeology and history, make possible a better articulated and critical view of empires, as compared to a rather simplistic and "totalitarian" view supported by scholars (and popular appreciation) in past generations. A recent collective volume (Alcock et al. 2001) includes so varied a typology of empires (territorial "classic" empires, trade networks, nomadic empires, city-less empires, enlarged chiefdoms, etc.) that the very effectiveness of the concept runs the risk of becoming lost.

On the other hand, the research trends that are visible – with the over-evaluation of empires before the Second World War and their under-evaluation in the following period – clearly depend on the modern political environment. After the end of Western colonialism, the scholarly approach had to change, even if rather reluctantly, to give space to a multi-centered perspective on world history – even if the Euro-centered line of development still finds its place in secondary school textbooks.

Once a source of pride, the word "empire" – alluding to colonial domination – became a reason for shame: nobody now claims to be an empire or to carry on an imperialistic policy, or if someone does it implies an overwhelming arrogance. Despotic empires are openly criminalized, but economic empires are also subject to opportunistic censure – or at least to an (unconscious?) understatement of their political relevance. The use of the term in ancient history has also become more critical and qualified. In order to conceal the opposition of West vs. Orient, an opposition that became unpopular both in Western democracies and Asiatic markets, the specific connotations of oppressive despotism, burdensome bureaucracy, and military expansion gave way to a multifarious and largely meaningless use of the term as applied to any form of multi-ethnic political domain. In economics, the crisis of imperialism generated recent trends – also visible in ancient Near Eastern studies – to complement the model of redistribution (best fitting an imperial apparatus) with one of market and private enterprise (Stolper 1985).

Of course, the end of the Western colonial hold on the Middle East did not mean that the Western world renounced its political, economic, and historical pretensions. It simply means that another strategy has been assumed, namely the neo-capitalist one of controlling resources rather than territories, exploiting the low costs of local work-forces and stimulating local markets. Even archaeological activities in the Middle East have now – quite often – a neo-capitalist flavor, with salvage projects and regional planning programs in the service of local states. The old model of "imperial" political relationships, which reserved an active role for the ruling partner only, has been complemented by others such as Frank's "underdevelopment," Wallerstein's "world system," or Renfrew's "peer polity interaction," or others that provide every component in a system with its own space and role.

The model of "underdevelopment" (Frank 1967; Emmanuel 1969; Amin 1973; also the historical approach by Wolf 1982), based on an analysis of the modern world, states that development in the core of (economic) empires brings about a parallel process of underdevelopment in the exploited periphery. This model has received scant attention in the field of ancient Near Eastern studies, yet its relevance has already been hinted at above. Ancient empires, like early modern ones, are based on the exchange of different kinds of resources; but, in the former cases, such imbalance did not bring about a different rate of development in the center vs. the periphery. Nevertheless, these problems deserve a specific analysis that is still missing.

In contrast, the "world system" model (Wallerstein 1974, 1980, 1989) has been influential in ancient Near Eastern studies, mostly applied to late prehistoric and proto-historic periods (Kohl 1987) with particular insistence on the Uruk period (Algaze 1993), rather than to fully historical empires. The use of this label has been criticized in various ways. The "world" covered by the Uruk network is too small, and a label such as "regional system" would be more appropriate. Moreover, long-distance trade probably affected a minor part of the societies involved, which remained basically concerned with the exploitation of local resources in agriculture and animal husbandry.

The model of "peer polity interaction" (Renfrew and Cherry 1986) is in fact most useful in describing the Late Bronze state of affairs, for example, when half a dozen states of regional extent (Egypt, Hittite, Mitanni, Assyria, Babylonia, Elam) interacted through trade and diplomacy more often than through war, with the impossibility for any of them to assume wider control or even some form of hegemony. Yet each of the interacting states could have been convinced that it was the "central empire" in the system (Liverani 1990).

In any case it seems clear that the last two generations of scholars have also been, consciously or not, influenced by their socio-political setting, both in discarding old ideas and in advancing new models. But the task of unveiling (and confessing) our own bias is much more difficult than underscoring that which influenced scholars of past generations.

REFERENCES

Adams, Robert McCormick, 1965 Land Behind Baghdad. Chicago: University of Chicago Press.

Adams, Robert McCormick, 1981 Heartland of Cities. Chicago: University of Chicago Press.

Adams, Robert McCormick, and Hans Nissen, 1972 The Uruk Countryside. Chicago: University of Chicago Press.

Albenda, Pauline, 1986 The Palace of Sargon, King of Assyria. Paris: Éditions Recherche sur les Civilisations.

Alcock, Susan, Terence D'Altroy, Kathleen Morrison, and Carla Sinopoli, eds., 2001 Empires. Perspectives from Archaeology and History. Cambridge: Cambridge University Press.

Algaze, Guillermo, 1993 The Uruk World System. Chicago: University of Chicago Press.

Algaze, Guillermo, 2001 The Prehistory of Imperialism: The Case of Uruk Period Mesopotamia. In Uruk Mesopotamia & Its Neighbors. Mitchell Rothman, ed. pp. 27–83. Santa Fe: School of American Research Press.

Amin, Samir, 1973 Le développement inégal. Essai sur les formations sociales du capitalisme périphérique. Paris: Les Éditions de Minuit.

Anon. 1974. Hommage universel. Commémoration Cyrus. Actes du congrès de Shiraz 1971 et autres études rédigées à l'occasion du 2500e anniversaire de la fondation de l'empire perse, I–III (= Acta Iranica, première série 1–3), Téhéran-Liège: Bibliothèque Pahlavi; Leiden: E. J. Brill.

Arrighi, Giovanni, 1978 La geometria dell'imperialismo. Milano: Feltrinelli. [Geometry of Imperialism. London: New Left Books.]

Bär, Jürgen, 1996 Der assyrische Tribut und seine Darstellung. Neukirchen-Vluyn: Neukirchener Verlag des Erziehungsvereins.

Bohrer, Frederick N., 1989 Assyria as Art: A Perspective on the Early Reception of Ancient Near Eastern Artifacts. Culture & History 4:7–33.

Brinkman, John A., 1984 Prelude to Empire. Philadelphia: Babylonian Fund.

Brown, Michael B., 1974 The Economics of Imperialism. Harmondsworth: Penguin Books.

Brown, Stuart C., 1986 Media and Secondary State Formation in the Neo-Assyrian Zagros. Journal of Cuneiform Studies 38:107–117.

Burckhardt, Jacob, 1898 Griechische Kulturgeschichte, I. Berlin–Stuttgart: Spemann.

Burckhardt, Jacob, 1905 Weltgeschichtliche Betrachtungen. Stuttgart: Alfred Kroner.

Caubet, Annie, ed., 1995 Khorsabad, le palais de Sargon II, roi d'Assyrie. Paris: Réunion des Musées Nationaux.

Cogan, Mordechai, 1974 Imperialism and Religion. Assyria, Judah and Israel in the Eighth and Seventh Centuries B.C. Missoula: Society of Biblical Literature and Scholars Press.

Daniel, Glyn E., 1975 A Hundred and Fifty Years of Archaeology. London: Duckworth.

Deller, Karlheinz, 1999 The Assyrian Eunuchs and their Predecessors. In Priests and Officials in the Ancient Near East. Kazuko Watanabe, ed. pp. 303–311. Heidelberg: Heidelberger Orientverlag.

Eco, Umberto, 1971 Le forme del contenuto. Milano: Bompiani.

Eisenstadt, Shmuel N., 1963 The Political System of Empires. London and New York: The Free Press of Glencoe.

Emmanuel, Arghiri, 1969 L'échange inégal. Essai sur les antagonismes dans les rapports économiques internationaux. Paris: François Maspero.

Fales, F. Mario, ed., 1981 Assyrian Royal Inscriptions: New Horizons (Orientis Antiqui Collectio 17). Roma: Istituto per l'Oriente.

Faye, Jean P., 1972 Les langages totalitaires. Paris: Hermann.

Fergusson, James, 1851 The Palaces of Nineveh and Persepolis Restored. London: John Murray.

Foster, Benjamin, 1993 Before the Muses, 2 vols. Bethesda, MD: CDL Press.

Frandsen, Paul J., 1979 Egyptian Imperialism. *In* Power and Propaganda. A Symposium on Ancient Empires (Mesopotamia 7). Mogens T. Larsen, ed. pp.167–190. Copenhagen: Akademisk Forlag.

Frank, Andre Gunder, 1967 Capitalism and Underdevelopment in Latin America. New York and London: Monthly Review Press.

Frei, Peter, and Klaus Koch, 1984 Reichsidee und Reichsorganisation im Perserreich (Orbis Biblicus et Orientalis 55). Freiburg: Universitätsverlag; Göttingen: Vandenhoeck & Ruprecht.

Gallagher, William R., 1994 Assyrian Deportation Propaganda. State Archives of Assyria Bulletin 8/2:57–65.

Garelli, Paul, 1980 Les empires mésopotamiens. *In* Le concept d'empire. Maurice Duverger, ed. pp. 25–47. Paris: Presses Universitaires de France.

Garnsey, Peter, and Charles R. Whittaker, eds., 1978 Imperialism in the Ancient World. Cambridge: Cambridge University Press.

Gibson, McGuire, and Robert Biggs, eds., 1987 The Organization of Power. Aspects of Bureaucracy in the Ancient Near East. Chicago: The Oriental Institute.

Godley, Alfred D., 1982 Herodotus, with an English Translation, vol. 3. Cambridge, MA: Harvard University Press; London: William Heinemann.

Goetz, Werner, 1958 Translatio Imperii. Tübingen: Mohr.

Goetze, Albrecht, 1963 Šakkanakkus of the Ur III Empire. Journal of Cuneiform Studies 17:1–31.

Grayson, A. Kirk, 1995 Eunuchs in Power. Their Role in Assyrian Bureaucracy. *In* Vom Alten Orient zum Alten Testament. Festschrift W. von Soden. Manfred Dietrich and Oswald Loretz, eds. pp. 85–98. Neukirchen-Vluyn: Neukirchener Verlag des Erziehungsvereins.

Gurney, Oliver R., 1979 The Hittite Empire. *In* Power and Propaganda. A Symposium on Ancient Empires (Mesopotamia 7). Mogens T. Larsen, ed. pp. 151–165. Copenhagen: Akademisk Forlag.

Haas, Volkert, 1980 Die Dämonisierung des Fremden und des Feindes im Alten Orient. Rocznik Orientalistyczny 41/2:37–44.

Kemp, Barry, 1978 Imperialism and Empire in the New Kingdom Egypt. *In* Imperialism in the Ancient World. Peter Garnsey and Charles R. Whittaker, eds. 1978, pp. 7–57. Cambridge: Cambridge University Press.

Kessler, Karlheinz, 1980 Untersuchungen zur historischen Topographie Nordmesopotamiens. Wiesbaden: Ludwig Reichert.

Kessler, Karlheinz, 1997 "Royal Roads" and Other Questions of the Neo-Assyrian Communication System. *In* Assyria 1995. Simo Parpola and Robert M. Whiting, eds. pp. 129–136. Helsinki: University of Helsinki.

Klaus, Georg, 1971 Sprache der Politik. Berlin: Deutscher Verlag der Wissenschaften.

Koch, Heidemarie, 1986 Die achämenidische Poststrasse von Persepolis nach Susa. Archäologische Mitteilungen aus Iran 19:133–147.

Kohl, Philip, 1987 The Use and Abuse of World Systems Theory. The Case of the Pristine West Asian State. *In* Advances in Archaeological Method and Theory 11. Michael Schiffer, ed. pp. 1–36. San Diego: Academic Press.

Kratz, Reinhard G., 1991 Translatio Imperii. Neukirchen: Neukirchener Verlag.

Lamprichs, Roland, 1995 Die Westexpansion des neuassyrischen Reiches. Neukirchen-Vluyn: Neukirchener Verlag des Erziehungsvereins.

Larsen, Mogens T., ed., 1979a Power and Propaganda. A Symposium on Ancient Empires (Mesopotamia 7). Copenhagen: Akademisk Forlag.

Larsen, Mogens T., 1979b The Tradition of Empire. *In* Power and Propaganda. A Symposium on Ancient Empires (Mesopotamia 7). Mogens T. Larsen, ed. pp. 75–103. Copenhagen: Akademisk Forlag.

Larsen, Mogens T., 1994 The Appropriation of the Near Eastern Past: Contrasts and Contradictions. *In* The East and the Meaning of History (Studi Orientali 13), 29–51. Rome: Dipartimento di Studi Orientali; Bardi Editore.

Larsen, Mogens T., 1996 The Conquest of Assyria. Excavations in an Antique Land 1840–1860. London and New York: Routledge.

Levine, Louis, 1989 The Zamua Itinerary. State Archives of Assyria Bulletin 3:75–92.

Liverani, Mario, 1979 The Ideology of the Assyrian Empire. *In* Power and Propaganda. A Symposium on Ancient Empires (Mesopotamia 7). Mogens T. Larsen, ed. pp. 297–317. Copenhagen: Akademisk Forlag.

Liverani, Mario, 1988 The Growth of the Assyrian Empire in the Khabur / Middle Euphrates Area: A New Paradigm. State Archives of Assyria Bulletin 2:81–98.

Liverani, Mario, 1990 Prestige and Interest. International Relations in the Near East ca. 1600–1100 B.C. (History of the Ancient Near East, Studies 1). Padova: Sargon. Republished (2001) as International Relations in the Ancient Near East, 1600–1100. Basingstoke and New York: Palgrave.

Liverani, Mario, ed., 1993 Akkad. The First World Empire. Padova: Sargon.

Liverani, Mario, 1997, The Ancient Near Eastern City and Modern Ideologies. *In* Die orientalische Stadt: Kontinuität, Wandel, Bruch. Gernot Wilhelm, ed. pp. 85–107. Saarbrücken: Saarbrücker Druckerei und Verlag.

Liverani, Mario, 2001 The Fall of the Assyrian Empire: Ancient and Modern Interpretations. *In* Empires. Perspectives from Archaeology and History. Susan Alcock, Terence D'Altroy, Kathleen Morrison, and Carla Sinopoli, eds. pp. 374–391. Cambridge: Cambridge University Press.

Liverani, Mario, In press The Rise and Fall of Media. *In* Continuity of Empire: Assyria, Media, Persia. Giovanni B. Lanfranchi, ed. Padova: Sargon.

Malbran-Labat, Florence, 1982 L'armée et l'organisation militaire de l'Assyrie. Genève and Paris: Librairie Droz.

Marcus, Michelle, 1990 Centre, Province and Periphery: A New Paradigm from Iron-Age Iran. Art History 13:129–149.

Margueron, Jean, 1982 Recherches sur les palais mésopotamiens de l'âge du bronze. Paris: Librairie Orientaliste Paul Geuthner.

Marx, Karl, 1960[1853] New York Daily Tribune 25.06.1853. *In* Werke, Band 9:131–132. Berlin: Dietz Verlag.

Marx, Karl, 1983[1857–58] Formen, die der kapitalistischen Produktion vorhergehen. *In* Werke, Band 42. Berlin: Dietz Verlag.

Matthiae, Paolo, 1977 Ebla. Un impero ritrovato. Torino: Einaudi.

Mignan, Robert, 1829 Travels in Chaldaea. London: Colburn & Bentley.

Müller, Karl F., 1937 Das assyrische Ritual, vol. 1. Leipzig: Hinrichs.

Oates, David, 1968 Studies in the Ancient History of Northern Iraq. London: The British Academy.

Oded, Bustenay, 1979 Mass Deportations and Deportees in the Neo-Assyrian Empire. Wiesbaden: Ludwig Reichert Verlag.

Oded, Bustenay, 1992 War, Peace and Empire. Justifications for War in Assyrian Royal Inscriptions. Wiesbaden: Ludwig Reichert Verlag.

Oppenheim, A. Leo, 1979 Neo-Assyrian and Neo-Babylonian Empires. *In* Propaganda and Communication in World History, vol. 1. The Symbolic Instrument in Early Times. Harold D. Lasswell, Daniel Lerner, and Hans Speier, eds. pp. 111–144. Honolulu: University Press of Hawaii.

Pettinato, Giovanni, 1979 Ebla. Un impero inciso nell'argilla. Milano: Mondadori.

Pongratz-Leisten, Beate, 1997 The Interplay of Military Strategy and Cultic Practice in Assyrian Politics. *In* Assyria 1995. Simo Parpola and Robert Whiting, eds. pp. 245–252. Helsinki: University of Helsinki.

Pongratz-Leisten, Beate, 1999 Herrschaftswissen in Mesopotamien (State Archives of Assyria Studies 10). Helsinki: University of Helsinki.

Postgate, J. Nicholas, 1974 Taxation and Conscription in the Assyrian Empire. Rome: Biblical Institute Press.

Postgate, J. Nicholas, 1992 The Land of Assur and the Yoke of Assur. World Archaeology 23:247–263.

Pritchard, James B., ed., 1969 Ancient Near Eastern Texts Relating to the Old Testament. 3rd edition. Princeton: Princeton University Press.

Renfrew, Colin, and John Cherry, eds., 1986 Peer Polity Interaction and Socio-Political Change. Cambridge: Cambridge University Press.

Robin, Régine, 1973 Histoire et linguistique. Paris: Armand Colin.

Root, Margaret C., 1979 The King and Kingship in Achaemenid Art. Essays on the Creation of an Iconography of Empire (Acta Iranica, troisième série 9). Leiden: E. J. Brill.

Russell, John M., 1991 Sennacherib's Palace without Rival at Nineveh. Chicago: University of Chicago Press.

Said, Edward, 1979 Orientalism. New York: Vintage Books.

Said, Edward, 1993 Culture and Imperialism. New York: Alfred Knopf.

Sancisi-Weerdenburg, Heleen, 1988 Was there ever a Median Empire? Achaemenid History 3:197–212.

Schmökel, Hartmut, 1958 Hammurabi von Babylon. Die Errichtung eines Reiches. München: Janus Bücher.

Seibert, Jakob, 1985 Die Eroberung des Perserreiches durch Alexander den Grossen auf kartographischen Grundlage. Wiesbaden: Ludwig Reichert Verlag.

Silberman, Neil A., 1982 Digging for God and Country. New York: Alfred Knopf; London and New York: Anchor Books, Doubleday.

Silberman, Neil A., 1991 Desolation and Restoration: The Impact of a Biblical Concept on Near Eastern Archaeology. Biblical Archaeologist 54:76–87.

Steinkeller, Piotr, 1987 The Administrative and Economic Organization of the Ur III State: The Core and the Periphery. *In* The Organization of Power. Aspects of Bureaucracy in the Ancient Near East. McGuire Gibson and Robert Biggs, eds. pp. 15–34. Chicago: The Oriental Institute.

Stolper, Matthew, 1985 Entrepreneurs and Empire. Leiden: Nederlands historisch-archaeologisch Instituut te Istanbul.

Tadmor, Hayim, 1997 Propaganda, Literature, Historiography: Cracking the Code of the Assyrian Royal Inscriptions. *In* Assyria 1995. Simo Parpola and Robert M. Whiting, eds. pp. 325–338. Helsinki: University of Helsinki.

Tadmor, Hayim, and Moshe Weinfeld, eds., 1983 History, Historiography and Interpretation. Jerusalem: The Magnes Press.

Tainter, Joseph, 1988 The Collapse of Complex Societies. Cambridge: Cambridge University Press.

Volney, Constantin-François, 1792 Les ruines, ou méditation sur les révolutions des empires. Paris.

Wallerstein, Immanuel, 1974, 1980, 1989 The Modern World-System. 3 vols. New York: Academic Press.

Westenholz, Aage, 1979 The Old Akkadian Empire in Contemporary Opinion. *In* Power and Propaganda. A Symposium on Ancient Empires (Mesopotamia 7). Mogens T. Larsen, ed. pp. 107–123. Copenhagen: Akademisk Forlag.

Wilkinson, Tony, 1995 Late-Assyrian Settlement Geography in Upper Mesopotamia. *In* Neo-Assyrian Geography. Mario Liverani, ed. pp. 139–159. Roma: Università "La Sapienza."

Winter, Irene, 1997 Art in Empire: The Royal Image and the Visual Dimensions of Assyrian Ideology. *In* Assyria 1995. Simo Parpola and Robert Whiting, eds., pp. 359–383. Helsinki: University of Helsinki.

Wittfogel, Karl A., 1957 Oriental Despotism. A Comparative Study of Total Power. New Haven: Yale University Press.

Wolf, Eric, 1982 Europe and the People without History. Berkeley: University of California Press.

Yoffee, Norman, and George Cowgill, eds., 1988 The Collapse of Ancient States and Civilizations. Tucson: University of Arizona Press.

Part III

Constructing Arguments, Understanding Perceptions

Reinhard Bernbeck
and Susan Pollock

The papers in this section are concerned with various avenues for approaching the Near Eastern past. Two of the most basic concerns are the dimensions of time and space. Despite their universal importance, both are culturally specific, and the recognition of their changing perception has led to the development of landscape archaeologies and a return to a more historically oriented archaeology. Representations from the past, whether texts or images, provide another set of ways to gain insights into past perceptions. Their intricate details may often reveal otherwise unrecoverable knowledge, but at the same time, such representations can conceal reality. Finally, since all knowledge of the past is fragmentary, a chapter on ethno-archaeology and analogies discusses some of the means archaeologists use to close evidential gaps.

A theme that recurs in this section under different guises is what is called *babylonische Eigenbegrifflichkeit* or "Babylonian conceptual autonomy" (Landsberger 1926). According to this concept, the Mesopotamian past needs to be understood and accounted for in its own terminology, implying a hermeneutic approach. Thus, if there is no word for either art or time in the ancient Mesopotamian languages (Ross, Charvát), one needs to think twice about applying those notions to the ancient Near East in the ways we commonly use them. Even for prehistoric periods or societies without writing, we need to make an effort to gain insights into the world of concepts, as Steadman argues in her plea for an analysis of landscape features. Thus, the original, purely linguistic idea of *Eigenbegrifflichkeit* needs to be broadened to the material record. In the absence of written documents, this search cannot result in the identification of words, but only in a matrix of concepts described in our present languages. Attempts to approach past worlds by including their own views are not necessarily new – indeed, they are the mainstay of much philological effort – but it is significant to note that they form a major part of the arguments of most chapters in this section, indicating their shift to center stage in Middle Eastern archaeology.

Opposed to the notion of *Eigenbegrifflichkeit* is the external perspective, often associated with rational argumentation. Rationality (to be precise: instrumental rationality) dominates Western thinking and praxis. If *Eigenbegrifflichkeit* is to be an integral part of accounts of the past, can there be any place for rationality, which is so typical for our ways of thinking? Steadman explicitly argues that rational considerations also played an important role in past decisions. Indeed, the fashionable dismissal in its entirety of instrumental rationality as Western and therefore inappropriate seems mistaken. Some of the postprocessual strands of contemporary archaeology have become so idealistic that they can no longer conceive of conditions in the past as existentially threatening. Instrumental rationality was likely an important aspect of both past worldview and praxis.

However, inner perspectives and *Eigenbegrifflichkeit* pose additional problems. On the level of intellectual concepts, the ancient Near East is often treated as one single historical unit, and some of the papers assembled here allude to this idea. Charvát contends that concepts of time, established in the Uruk period, remained unchanged down to the Hellenistic period. Steadman speaks of "stasis" when interpreting the habit of living on mounds, and Ross argues that basic iconography changed little over time. If time, praxis in space, or pictorial representations are approached with the goal of revealing an inner (past) perspective, one may reasonably ask, "whose perspective, and when?" In order to be useful, the idea of an *Eigenbegrifflichkeit* needs to be historically and socially contextualized. Some notions may change only in the *longue durée*, but that needs to be researched rather than assumed at the outset.

As Zimansky points out, literacy is not one of those constant phenomena. Rather, uses and degrees of literacy changed substantially in the history of the ancient Near East. Writing was not just a prosaic means to an end, but occupied a dynamic cultural position. Similarly, the idea that there was only one way of seeing, typical for millennia of ancient Near Eastern "art," is challenged by Ross. Such challenges are predicated on a long-term view, and are therefore only possible from an external, academic perspective, the one with which, by necessity, one starts. It is only a dialectical movement between past *Eigenbegrifflichkeit* and present academic ideas (Bourdieu 1997) that ensures an escape from both present-day preconceptions and a normative, ahistorical view of the past.

How do we explore such concepts as time and space, those highly abstract dimensions of Western modernity? Charvát points out that time was thought of as concrete by the ancient Sumerians. Time is not only partly analogous to space, but has "fullness," is related to natural events such as harvests, and is marked by eternal return and cyclicality. However, there is also an underlying directionality, and in that respect, ancient Near Eastern perceptions of time were eschatological. While we have no problems imagining a combination of cyclicality and linearity of time (since they are part of our own life in the cycle of weeks and months and the open-endedness of history), the development of watches has produced a modern life-world where *chronos* is an independent, abstract entity that threatens us with schedules and deadlines. Charvát reminds us that a precondition for understanding ancient worldviews is that we throw out this baggage of our own ideas and try to imagine a world without the notion of "time." We may conceptualize practical life as a series of passages, movements that eschew the abstract, and a cosmology where there is no past other than ancestor-time (Steadman). However, it is insufficient to try to leave behind our present self-understanding in order to capture the foreign past in an intellectual effort of phenomenological reductionism. In his contribution, Verhoeven argues that all archaeological argumentation is based to a considerable extent on analogies between past and present. The fragments of archaeological knowledge only become meaningful wholes through a medium that joins them (see also Bernbeck, this volume). The means to do so are derived principally from observations of and experiences with living people. One question that would merit further attention is the reach of analogies. Verhoeven's "structural analogy" seems to be based on the assumption that certain practices and their meanings have a universal relation, an idea that is against the current of particularism which dominates contemporary anthropology.

For space, another abstract anchor of modern life, Steadman proposes a multi-layered analytical approach that tackles spatial meanings. While landscape archaeology has promoted such an idea for quite some time, it has rarely been employed in studies of the ancient Near East (but see Smith 2003). Steadman shows that "cognitive landscapes" should not be read with one single set of meanings in mind, such as religion, but rather that space is a matrix on which multiple kinds of meanings can be grafted simultaneously, thus complicating the task of unraveling past spatial concepts. In her discussions, she employs both analogical reasoning and hermeneutics.

The chapters by Zimansky and Ross are concerned with matters of representation, textual and pictorial. Apart from their production, images and texts are in three major ways interesting to archaeologists. They can reveal elements of past reality that are otherwise not preserved, they contain components of ancient ideologies, and they can give hints about their audiences. Images often include details about clothing styles, gestures, and people involved in activities; cuneiform and other texts provide a wealth of insights about the names of individuals and groups and the nature of their relations. Any such knowledge is unattainable from standard archaeological data. However, both Zimansky and Ross point out that representations are deeply ideological in that reality is always rendered through a "filter" (Ross; see also Pollock, this volume), or what Zimansky calls a "smokescreen." Filters of representation are themselves historically specific, and provide additional glimpses into changing constructions of power relations. Texts and images are the main gateways to a history of ancient Near Eastern ideologies, a major research desideratum that is a necessary precondition for writing history itself, but as yet has been barely tackled (but see Liverani 1993). One of the reasons for this state of affairs is the assumption of an ancient Near Eastern "unchanging mind," an orientalist preconception that is still at the base of many syntheses of "Mesopotamian civilization" (e.g., Bottéro 2000).

Contexts in which representations were seen or read are an essential component of texts and imagery (see also Kujit and Chesson, this volume). Who was granted access to royal or divine statues and reliefs, who was allowed, and who could read ancient texts? As both Zimansky and Ross emphasize, this kind of information provides essential insights into past reception of representations. Accounts of the past that aim to integrate such inner perspectives must be concerned with these issues. Unfortunately, philologists who deal with texts are rarely concerned with the contexts from which their sources derive, thinking that texts "speak for themselves." In this way, as Zimansky notes, they spur – together with irresponsible art collectors – one sharply increasing mode of artifact retrieval, namely looting.[1]

Ancient texts and public images depict the world of the exceptional. Writing and reading were mostly elite activities, and even if images were exhibited in public, they were a distinctly urban phenomenon inaccessible to the majority of peasants. It is therefore highly unlikely that the details derived from such objects are representative of the routines and beliefs of ancient Near Eastern (non-elite) people. Only archaeological excavations of small villages and ephemeral camps of nomads can remedy this skewed picture. Unfortunately, data from such sites, destroyed by the hundreds every year in a vastly changing contemporary Middle East, are still so sparse that a "people's history of Mesopotamia" cannot be written. If we know anything about past habitual practices, it is the routines of the urban elites. Charvát's example of cylinder seals as material items that are so well tailored to the habitus of the ancient Mesopotamian *urbanites* is a case in point. We do not know whether the concepts Charvát sees exemplified in these tiny objects extended to the countryside.

Near Eastern archaeology is therefore in need of a fundamental change in emphasis. However, as Verhoeven reminds us, we are prisoners of our own habitus, of unquestioned ways of seeking financial support for projects, conceptualizing them, and carrying them out. Our own professional routines and the structures that frame and reconfirm those routines need to change to draw us towards the habitual rather than to value principally the exceptional.

NOTE

1 However, looting in countries strained by armed conflict, such as Afghanistan, Iraq, or the Palestinian territories has to be understood also as a desperate attempt to maintain a living. "Subsistence looting" should be differentiated from looting for financial profit.

REFERENCES

Bottéro, Jean, 2000 Religion and Reasoning in Mesopotamia. *In* Ancestors of the West, Jean Bottéro, Clarisse Herrenschmidt, and Jean-Pierre Vernant, pp. 3–66. Teresa Lavender Fagan, trans. Chicago: University of Chicago Press.

Bourdieu, Pierre, 1997 Pascalian Meditations. Richard Nice, trans. Stanford: Stanford University Press.

Landsberger, Benno, 1926 Die Eigenbegrifflichkeit der babylonischen Welt. Islamica 2:355–371.

Liverani, Mario, ed., 1993 Akkad: The First World Empire. Padua: Sargon.

Smith, Adam T., 2003 The Political Landscape. Constellations of Authority in Early Complex Polities. Berkeley: University of California Press.

12

Ethnoarchaeology, Analogy, and Ancient Society

Marc Verhoeven

Introduction

Ethnoarchaeology and analogy have long been, and still are, two significant topics of the archaeology of the Middle East and of archaeological theory in general. In this chapter I hope to make a contribution to the ongoing discussion about the use and usefulness of these closely related topics. There are already many general introductions about ethnoarchaeology and analogy; after a short overview I specifically wish to focus on the problems with and possible solutions to the use of ethnoarchaeology and analogy in the archaeology of the Middle East.

This chapter consists of three main parts. First, ethnoarchaeology in the Middle East is discussed: what is it, and what are the main studies? Second, analogy in archaeology is considered: how can it be defined, what kinds of analogies can be identified, what are the problems with the use of analogy in archaeology and what solutions are there? Third, as an example, I examine the interpretation of early Neolithic human skulls, found without the skeleton and sometimes plastered, from the Levant and Anatolia, and so-called structural analogies are introduced as a method for opening up a social past. In the conclusion the role of ethnoarchaeology in the modern Middle East for constructing the (distant) past is considered.

Ethnoarchaeology: Among the Living

Ethnoarchaeology in its widest sense is the study of contemporary cultures in order to obtain data that can be used to aid archaeological interpretation (see, most recently, David and Kramer 2001). It is an important means for making sense of the production, use, and discard of past material culture, or put more generally, for investigating the relationships between human practice and material culture. The ethnographic data that can be used are observations in living communities (formerly also referred to as "living archaeology," "action archaeology," or "archaeological ethnography"), artifact studies, and experiments.[1]

Middle Eastern scholars have practiced all three forms of ethnoarchaeology. In the following sections I shall discuss each of these categories briefly, starting with observations in living communities.

Village studies

Village studies refer to extended observations by archaeologists of human practice in "traditional" villages.[2] Studies of architecture, village lay-out, use of space, social structure, kinship regulations, functions of artifacts, formation processes, agriculture, etc., can all be part of this approach.[3] Pioneering village studies are those of Watson (1979) and Kramer (1982). In her studies in three Iranian villages in western Iran (Hasanabad, Shirdasht, and Ain Ali), Watson set out to present as many data as possible about technology and subsistence in these villages, in order to provide sources of hypotheses for archaeologists working with comparable materials. Her basic assumption was uniformitarian: she maintained that the past cannot be understood without reference to the present. She was particularly interested in relationships between village lay-out, nature of the domestic architecture and artifacts on the one hand, and population size and socio-economic structure on the other. The first part of Watson's study dealt with economic organization, agricultural methods, animals, domestic technology, kinship, and the supernatural in the three villages. In the second part, so-called behavioral correlates and uniformitarian principles (see below) are discussed, especially the relationship between archaeology and ethnography.

A more recent example of village studies is Horne (1994). Like the above-mentioned studies, Horne investigated relationships between the material and socio-cultural dimensions of human settlement, this time in a group of small agricultural villages in Khar o Tauran, a village district on the edge of the great central desert of the Iranian Plateau. Particularly interesting is the final chapter, in which Horne tests at three different levels the "fit" between selected spatial (rooms, houses, and fields) and social aspects (activities, households, and communities) of settlement.[4]

Artifact studies

Good examples of artifact studies are provided by the work of Ochsenschlager. During the excavations at the Sumerian site of al-Hiba in southern Iraq, Ochsenschlager collected ethnographic information in order to interpret archaeological data from the excavations. Modern use of sheep, pottery, mud objects, and weaving were studied (Ochsenschlager 1974, 1993). For example, combining the ethnographic information with the archaeological data, the spinning of thread and yarn, construction of fishing nets, and cloth weaving could be postulated and described for the site of al-Hiba (Ochsenschlager1993). Furthermore, on the basis of analogy to pottery in nearby villages, Ochsenschlager was able to designate six types of containers at this site. A similar approach was taken by McQuitty (1984) in an article about clay ovens in Jordan.

By explicitly investigating the use of archaeological and ethnographic objects and by contextualizing both sets of data, these studies go beyond traditional archaeological inferences, which on the basis of form-function resemblances assume, rather than investigate, functions of ancient artifacts from present examples.[5]

Experimental studies

There is an active type of research that focuses on obtaining experimental data regarding the production and use of artifacts in order to employ these data to interpret similar archaeological artifacts (e.g., Ingersoll et al. 1977). Especially well-known in this respect are experiments with flint (and obsidian) tools. Most often, traces of production and use are studied by means of microwear analysis (through reproduction of bodily movement with tools). Sickle blades are particularly popular in this respect. For example, in a study of glossed Neolithic "Çayönü" tools from sites in Anatolia and Iraq, Anderson found that, contrary to expectation, these artifacts were not related in any way to cereal harvesting. Instead, they seem to have been used for decorating stone objects. "Çayönü" tools, then, may indicate the finishing of "prestige" objects such as bowls and bracelets (Anderson 1994). Another example of experimental studies is the work of Campana, who made bone tools (such as awls and spatulas) and used them on a variety of materials in order to provide clues for interpreting Natufian and Neolithic bone tools from sites in the Zagros and the Levant (Campana 1989).

Analogy: the Only Way

Following Wylie (1985:28), I define analogy as the "selective transportation of information from source to subject on the basis of a comparison that, fully developed, specifies how the 'terms' compared are similar, different, or of unknown likeness." There is a source (most often the present)[6] and a subject (the past) side in the analogy. As indicated by many researchers, analogical reasoning is at the core of all archaeological interpretation; we can only understand the past through the present, which is our ultimate frame of reference. Ethnoarchaeology, then, is a particular form of analogical reasoning; it is a specific way of "enriching" our frame of reference (or habitus: see below) so as to interpret the past in an informed way.

Before discussing the basic problems with the use of analogy in archaeology, it is appropriate to introduce the different forms of analogy, as distinguished by Wylie (1985; see also Bernbeck 1997:85–108).

Genetic analogy

Genetic analogy refers to the nowadays rejected culture-historical practice of tracing a direct line of descent of cultures on the basis of formal similarities. A famous example of this is Sollas's (1911) parallel between ethnographically documented hunting groups and prehistoric cultures. Genetic analogy was based on two main principles: (1) evolutionism (or anti-evolutionism): modern and ancient societies were treated as equal; (2) diffusionism: migrations were postulated on the basis of the analogies. Of course, the main problem with genetic analogies is the premise of direct historical continuity between two cultures which are not only widely separated in time, but also in space.

Direct historical analogy

The direct historical analogy holds that when continuity between the past and the present can be assumed, many formal similarities between the information being compared may be acknowledged (e.g., Watson 1980:56).[7] There are two main problems related to this approach. First, problems related to the comparison of proper contexts may arise (e.g., Noll 1996:246, 248). For instance, two groups in the same area may have produced very different artifacts. Cultural change, furthermore, may have led to drastic changes in many other respects. With regard to the Middle East, for example, direct historical analogy involves a very long timespan: at least 2,500 years, if one considers the Ancient Near East to end with the Achaemenids. Therefore, no useful similarities may have survived, making direct historical analogies with modern Middle Eastern cultures very problematic. Second, direct analogies situated in the same region or period of interest are frequently unavailable.

New analogy

In 1961 Ascher introduced the concept of new analogy, formulating a new goal for analogies: reconstruction of human practice, something not immediately observable in the archaeological record. Continuity between source and subject side in the analogy is not necessary in this kind of comparison. For Ascher, source and subject sides in the comparison should be comparable in at least (but not only) two respects: (1) ecology, and (2) technology. Focusing on these two basic aspects, the new analogy was problematic, since it is questionable whether similar environments are always manipulated in a similar fashion, as was supposed (as technology is obviously related to the environment).

Formal analogy

Formal analogies, as opposed to the former direct historical and new analogies, are based on more than one source. Specific and similar features of different modern communities are used to interpret comparable features of past communities. Formal analogies, then, work from the assumption that if two artifacts or contexts have some common properties, they probably also have other similarities. There are three main problems with formal analogies. First, the source communities are only comparable with regard to certain elements, resulting in negligence of potentially important differences. Second, it must be proven that the various sources are historically independent. For instance, it must be established that different social groups on the source side are not in fact part of one (ancient) tradition. Third, correlation of specific and similar features does not necessarily indicate cause-effect relationships, and it may lead to rather mechanistic and generalizing reconstructions.

Relational analogy

Relational analogies are comparable to formal analogies, but there must be clear relationships between specific features on the source side of the analogy: a natural or cultural link between the different aspects in the analogy is sought after. According to Wylie (1985:95), they are based upon "knowledge about underlying 'principles of connection' that structure source and subject and that assure, on this basis, the existence of specific further similarities between them." In relational analogies it is not only the attributes of artifacts, but also their cultural context that are taken into account. The relevance of the association of two variables needs to be examined.

Complex analogy

In complex analogies, finally, *various* relational analogies are used. Through the combination of different, and therefore multiple sources for each aspect on the subject side, a new societal whole can emerge that has no one "precedent" in *one* source. In this way, the past can definitely be different from the (source-side) present.

The Problems with Analogy

As will be clear by now, "reasoning by analogy" is at the core of ethnoarchaeology, and in fact of all archaeological research; without comparisons, juxtapositions, and analogies, interpretive frameworks cannot be established. In this process of comparison, however, one runs the risk of transposing one's own cultural categories to the object of study (e.g., Shanks and Tilley 1987:7–28). It has been argued that if we interpret the past by analogy to the present, we can never find out about forms of society and culture which do not exist today. Furthermore, deterministic uniformitarianism must be avoided; it cannot be assumed that societies and cultures that are similar in some aspects are entirely similar. Another often heard criticism against the use of analogy is that analogies can never be checked or proven, because alternative analogies, which fit the data from the past equally well, can always be found.

In my view, the following four problems need to be addressed when using analogies in archaeological research: (1) formation processes, (2) the form-function problem, (3) hypothesis testing, (4) "normalization." In this section these problems will be introduced; in the next section some possible solutions will be discussed.

Formation processes

Put very generally, formation processes create the evidence of past societies and environments that remains for the archaeologist to study. There are natural and cultural formation processes. Cultural formation processes include the deliberate or accidental activities of humans; natural formation processes refer to natural or environmental events which result in, and have an effect upon, the archaeological record. Formation processes can be divided into discard processes, disposal modes, reclamation processes, and disturbance processes (Schiffer 1987). All these processes indicate that there is no one-to-one correspondence between the *systemic context* (a past cultural system) and the *archaeological context* (materials which have passed through a past cultural system, and are now the objects of archaeological research) (Schiffer 1972).

Formation processes, then, intervene between past practice and present discoveries. The past can only be described and interpreted via observations made in the present, and these observations are based on (or rather, filtered through) the formation processes of the archaeological record. With regard to the use of analogy in archaeology, formation processes show that the archaeological record is a very specific entity; it is, as it were, a distorted reflection of past practice, leaving the archaeologist with material culture only. Murray and Walker (1988:250–251) write in this respect about the "ontological singularity of the archaeological record." It has to be acknowledged that the source and subject sides, representing respectively a living social system and a dead one (or the remains of a living system) in an archaeological analogy are of a wholly different nature. The main problem here, in other words, is one of potential incompatibility of systemic and archaeological contexts.

Form-function correlations

The so-called form-function problem refers to the disputable practice of inferring a similarity in function on the basis of a similarity in form between source and subject sides, or etic and emic perspectives, in an archaeological analogy.[8] The problem, of course, is that formally similar objects may have entirely different functions and meanings (e.g., Noll 1996:247).

Hypothesis testing

Third, something should be said about the practice of *testing* analogies. In the traditional processual way of using ethnoarchaeology and analogy, information from the source side of the comparison was most often used to test hypotheses. A famous example of this is Narroll's average of 10 sq. m of living space per person, which was established on the basis of a cross-cultural analysis and which has been often used for archaeological population estimates (Narroll 1962). However, the basic problem with the "hypothetico-deductive method" is that: "The emphasis on hypothesis testing, and the necessity to formulate this hypothesis prior to the testing, leads to the definition of certain categories, into which the data are slotted if they do not deviate too much from the expected pattern," as van Gijn and Raemaekers (1999:50) have rightly argued (and see Hodder 1982:20–23; Wylie 1985:86–88). Moreover, part of the answer is already provided by the hypothesis. To return to the above example: Narroll's 10 sq. m living space per person excludes a different population density in the past: it is an assumption, not an outcome of the analysis. On the other hand, the formulation of hypotheses may have a healthy effect: when one does not find what was expected data may be re-evaluated, potentially leading to new information.

Normalization

The form-function problem is directly related to the concept of *normalization*, coined by Murray, who states that: "alongside the process of construction [or better: re-construction: M.V.] in archaeology there operates a parallel process of 'normalization' where the conventional concepts and categories which underwrite the interpretation of human action defuse potentially disturbing archaeological data" (Murray 1992:731). To put it dramatically, normalization denies a past that is different from the present, and therefore represents a denial of history (Murray 1992:734, and see also Binford 1968:13). Murray and Walker (1988:251) note in this respect that: "the bulk of practitioners sacrifice this significant property so that they may apply conventional interpretations and explanations of archaeological data thereby gaining meaning and plausibility which 'trickle down' from the contemporary social sciences."

At this point, it is the archaeologist who becomes the subject of (archaeological) research. Archaeologists, like any other social or natural scientists, have what the French sociologist Bourdieu (1977) called a (professional) habitus. This is a term that designates the cognitive framework which, largely unconsciously, is mobilized for the interpretation and attribution of meaning to material objects. Moreover, it refers, as the word implies, to habits, customs, and dispositions, which are at the basis of and which shape the above-mentioned framework. According to Bourdieu, the habitus is informed by structuring principles (e.g., social and ritual rules, taboos, etc.), together representing structure, which in their turn inform *practice*, or social action. Thus, archaeology is a specific form of *practice*, informed by *structure* and *habitus*. Inevitably, an archaeologist's reconstruction of the past is structured by his/her habitus. Normalization denotes the danger of wholly ethnocentric reconstructions, but as indicated earlier, the past can only be understood through the present, therefore, some form of normalization seems inescapable. Whether we like it or not, normalization, while presenting a problem, seems to be part of the "logic" of archaeological reasoning.

A Proper Use of Analogy in Archaeology?

Reasoning by analogy is indispensable and it will be clear that ethnoarchaeology and archaeology cannot do without it. Dispensing with analogical inferences, therefore, is no solution to the problems indicated above. How, then, should archaeologists go about using analogies? Obviously, there is no clear-cut solution, and I will not try to present a final answer. My purpose here is to provide some possible directions for a proper use of analogy in archaeology. To begin with, however, I want to make three general statements.

First, I would like to point out that while presenting a major problem for reconstructing past practice, analogy also opens up the past for us: the use of it is *at the same time both a prerequisite and an impediment* for analyzing and understanding past behavior. Secondly, ethnographic analogies should be regarded as "media for thought" (or examples) rather than as models to be either fitted to or tested against archaeological data (Tilley 1996:2). Thirdly, I think we have to agree with Parker Pearson (1999:21) who notes, with regard to the use of analogy in the archaeological study of death, that, "By looking at the diversity of the human responses to death, archaeologists trying to interpret the past can attempt to slough off ethnocentric presuppositions." This is of course true for all spheres of life. Thus, by studying many different examples, possible new and unexpected ways of interpreting the past may be discovered.

With regard to the basic problems with analogy in archaeology, it is my contention that before using an analogy formation processes of the archaeological record should be addressed. It is absolutely crucial to have a clear idea about the nature of the archaeological evidence used in the analogy, i.e., the subject side. Furthermore, the contexts (spatial, chronological, etc.) of the finds included in the analogy need to be taken into account. In other words, we need to know as much as possible about the fragmented archaeological database before using analogies. In an earlier study, dealing with the use of space and social relations in a Neolithic settlement in northern Syria, I have presented various methods for assessing the impact of formation processes and for reconstructing the use of space (Verhoeven 1999). Only on the basis of an understanding of these issues can a reconstruction of the past systemic context be attempted. Such a reconstruction is necessary in order to "enrich" the archaeological record, i.e., to be able to compare a (fragmented) past systemic context with a contemporary systemic context and to make the two sides of the comparison as compatible as possible.

Regarding the problem of hypothesis testing (and normalization), Murray and Walker (1988:251–252) have proposed that "working hypotheses drawn from analogical inferences be preferentially accepted inasmuch as they (a) may be refutable within the universe of data they are invoked to interpret, and (b) anticipate the likelihood of changes in one (or more) parameters vis-à-vis the analogical case(s), the detection of which (i.e., the changes) is susceptible to the strategy in (a)." Murray and Walker advocate a refutation strategy, rather than the common confirmation strategy, which often results in circularity and self-fulfilling prophecies, because an inability to refute a hypothesis helps to provide further justification for their acceptance (see also Tringham 1978:179). In a refutation strategy hypotheses that withstand refutation become those of choice for incorporation into provisional models for future inquiry. So-called biconditional analogical hypotheses (e.g., "if x, and only if x, then y") are proposed in this respect, since such biconditional propositions may offer working hypotheses that are potentially refutable within the universe of data.

With regard to refutation, however, I think we have to agree with Hodder (1982:22–23) when he argues that one cannot disprove in an absolute sense in archaeology any more than one can prove: any disproof is itself a hypothesis. So whether we "prove" or "disprove" an analogy, the problem remains the same.

Bernbeck (1997:101–104, 2000) advocates the use of different analogies ("a juxtaposition of different scenarios"), i.e., a use of complex analogies, instead of one single analogy. By using complex analogies, archaeological features are interpreted with the help of various contemporary features and/or communities. The following steps should be taken when using complex analogies: (1) comparison of each source with the subject in a systematic way (analysis of differences, similarities and incommensurables); (2) incomparable sources must be withdrawn from the study; (3) study of relationships between elements in sources which are used for interpreting a specific archaeological feature; (4) selection of elements that show a cause-effect relationship; (5) comparison of these source elements to subject elements; (6) synthesis of analyses of different elements. Bernbeck (1994, 2000) has applied complex analogies with some success in an analysis of Neolithic economy in Mesopotamia, e.g., for describing and interpreting the construction of clay buildings, the use of pottery kilns, and the herding of animals, using different sources for each of these spheres.

Structural Analogies: Opening up a Social Past

In this section, I would like to present an example of analogical reasoning in archaeology taken from my own work. As part of a research program dealing with the development and meaning of ritual practices of early Neolithic farming communities of the Pre-Pottery Neolithic B (PPNB: ca. 8600–7000 cal B.C.E.) in the Levant and Anatolia, I have analyzed human skulls, severed from the skeleton, found at sites such as Jericho, 'Ain Ghazal, Ramad, and Nahal Hemar in the Levant and Çayönü and Nevalı Çori in southeast Anatolia (Verhoeven 2002a, and see Verhoeven 2002b). These skulls (isolated or in groups) were found on house floors or in pits beneath house floors or courtyards (see e.g., Bienert 1991). Apart from undecorated skulls, plastered skulls have been found (Kuijt and Chesson, this volume). Generally speaking, these skulls have a "mask" of plaster covering the frontal parts of the skull, with modeled facial features (figure 12.1). The eye-sockets may be left open or are filled with plaster, and occasionally eyes are represented by shells. Most often the mask shows traces of paint. Clearly, the skulls (unplastered as well as plastered) were meant to be seen and circulated in PPNB communities.[9]

The traditional and most accepted interpretation with regard to the skulls (especially the plastered ones) is that they are part of an ancestor cult (Bienert 1991; Bienert and Müller-Neuhof 2000). However, there seems to have been more to human skulls than ancestor worship alone. First, quite a number of unplastered skulls of (young) children seem to have been removed and cached, and it is questionable that they were regarded as real ancestors, since they had of course no offspring. Secondly, it has been noted that plastered Neolithic skulls in the Near East were selected on the basis of their morphological characteristics; only abnormally wide skulls were plastered. Probably, these skulls were deformed *in vivo* at a young age (Arensburg and Hershkovitz 1988; Meiklejohn et al. 1992). Thus, there probably was a relationship between deformation and the selection of skulls for ritual treatment *post mortem*.

In order to better understand the meanings of plastered and unplastered human skulls, I have analyzed the ritual use of human skulls in ethnographic contexts, especially among the Naga of Assam and the Iatmul of the Sepik area in Papua New Guinea. After the presentation of the case study (which is a summary of Verhoeven 2002a) I will explain on which basis the selection of skulls was made, and in general how I have used analogy.

The Naga

The Naga believe in the existence of a powerful life-force which is principally located in the head. This life-force of a person can be transmitted in various ways, both during life and after death, and it can benefit individuals as well as the village as a whole. The life-force ensures well-being and fecundity. Fecundity is central to Naga life (Simoons 1968). In many and various rituals, life-force and fecundity are explicitly linked to human heads. For instance, taking an enemy head and bringing it back to the village is done in order to increase the "store of fertility." In the so-called Feasts of Merit, the source of the fertilizing power stems from the heads of human beings, which in various rituals is transferred to the symbols used in the feasts. Interestingly, like the Feasts of Merit, death rituals are related to harvest or sowing, thus again showing a connection between death and fecundity.

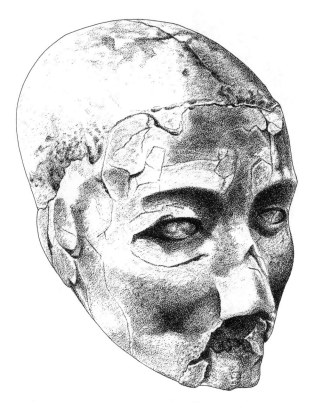

Figure 12.1 Plastered human skull from Jericho (*sources*: Kenyon 1981: Pl. 52; Verhoeven 2002a: Figure 8, reproduced by permission)

The Iatmul

Iatmul culture and ceremonial life are centered around the men's house. Very important ritual objects which are stored in the men's houses of the Iatmul are decorated (plastered and painted) human skulls, both of ancestors and of slain enemies. The skulls strongly resemble the PPNB plastered skulls (compare figures 12.1 and 12.2). The painting resembles the facial painting of both men and women on ritual occasions; it was a means of identifying oneself with mythical beings or ancestors. The skulls played a role in various rituals, especially fertility and death rituals (Smidt 1996). As in the Naga case, therefore, human skulls were not only related to death, but also to fecundity.

Meanings of PPNB skulls

Let us now look at how I have dealt with the ethnographic "examples," and how they fit in the process of interpretation. First of all, in the study referred to above

Figure 12.2 Decorated human skull from Papua New Guinea (Iatmul people, Sepik province) (*source*: Fur and Martin 1999:156; Verhoeven 2002a: Figure 9, reproduced by permission)

(Verhoeven 2002a) I have critically evaluated the current views concerning the meaning of PPNB (plastered) skulls. As it appeared that the notion of ancestor worship is not sufficient (see above), it became clear that other possibilities had to be looked for. I felt that it was first necessary to contextualize the PPNB skulls by relating them to other PPNB ritual practices. This has been attempted in an analysis of indications for rituals at five PPNB sites, located in the Levant ('Ain Ghazal and Kfar HaHoresh) and southeast Anatolia (Nevalı Çori, Çayönü, and Göbekli Tepe). The main indications of rituals at these places (and many other PPNB sites) seem to be "special" buildings, burials, skull caches, plastered skulls, large statuary, and human and animal figurines. Based upon an integrated analysis of these features, in which I searched for structural similarities in meaning, it appeared that there seem to be four basic so-called structuring principles characteristic of PPNB rituals in general: *communality* (many PPNB rituals are marked by public display), *dominant symbolism* (the use of highly visual, powerful, and evocative symbols), *people-animal linkage* (the physical and symbolical attachment of humans with animals), and *vitality*. Vitality is a complex issue, referring to three related notions: *domestication*, *fecundity*, and *life-force*. Domestication not only refers to the taming of wild animals and plants, but also to the social and ideological process of controlling society (through rituals). Fecundity in general refers to fertility (i.e., soil fertility and birth-giving), and the related notion of sexuality. With life-force is meant the vital power which principally remains in the head; this notion will be discussed in more detail below. Of course, all these terms are etic, but the analysis indicated that they denote important emic categories.

With regard to the skulls, as a next step, information about the ritual use and meaning of human skulls, plastered as well as unplastered, was gathered from ethnographic data (see also Bienert and Müller-Neuhof 2000:27). It is important to realize that this search for analogies was steered by my reconstruction of the four basic characteristics of PPNB ritual life. Initially, I chose the Iatmul example because of the remarkable similarities between decorated Iatmul skulls and decorated PPNB skulls. In other words: I explicitly used form-function correlations. Analysis of this example made me aware of the possible relationship between death and fecundity and of the concept of life-force. In fact, it appears that in many cultures all over the world human skulls, plastered as well as unplastered, are regarded as powerful symbolic and ritual objects which refer to life-force, fecundity, and related concepts (e.g., Fur and Martin 1999). The use of additional different cases (i.e., of complex analogy) would be interesting and necessary to validate the present argument.

To return to our PPNB skulls, I have argued that while ancestors as mythical persons were probably worshiped, human skulls (plastered as well as unplastered) taken from skeletons were specially honored because they were the seat of life-force, which could be used to ensure fecundity – of the fields, domesticated animals, and people – and well-being. Perhaps in the Levant there was a two-level ritual and ideological hierarchy with regard to human skulls and vitality, consisting of (1) plastered human skulls, which are all of adults and probably representing especially important persons (ritual leaders?), and of (2) unplastered skulls, which perhaps represented less important ancestors. In southeast Anatolia, however, the absence of plastered PPNB skulls may suggest an absence of such a hierarchy. While the skulls of adults were probably related to both an ancestor cult and vitality, it is suggested that children's skulls were mainly related to vitality. In the PPNB, then, the living and the dead were integrated into a system that seems to have been basically concerned with ancestor worship, fecundity, and life-force.

Structural analogy

I will now evaluate how I have used analogies on a more theoretical and methodological level. The basic questions here are: (1) geographically and chronologically the source and subject sides in the analogy are very far apart; how are they to be linked? and (2) have I normalized the past by imposing the analogies upon it?

First and foremost *relevance* ("principles of connection that structure source and object, supposing further similarities between them," see above) must be considered (Stahl 1993). I felt that notwithstanding the distance, the analogies used are relevant since they are formally quite similar, and, importantly, also on a deeper, structural level there seem to be concordances. In fact, I have attempted to isolate general structuring principles of meaning and symbolism, rather than culturally specific practices (which are analyzed later). In other words, I have used what I like to introduce as *structural analogies* in a search for an understanding of the *structure* of ancient features and practices by analyzing the structure of comparable features or practices in the ethnographic record.[10] In our example, structure was represented by the principles of fecundity and life-force; *practice* has been reconstructed by describing (interpreting) the way human skulls were used in PPNB communities.

Using structural analogies, then, it is argued that formal similarities between source and subject sides in the analogy (thus using form-function correlations, which seem inescapable) may indicate general principles of meaning and symbolism. When comparing formal similarities in structural analogies, information about structure on the source side is used to reconstruct structure on the subject side. However, as indicated above, archaeological objects and their context can be very important means for investigating and isolating structure on the source side of the analogy. Structure should not be transposed from source to subject; it should be used for acquiring a general idea about the structuring principles related to the archaeological objects in the comparison. Even if the number of formal similarities is limited, structural analogies can be used, since as Wylie (1985:106) has indicated: "A source that shares as little as a single attribute with the subject in question may be used as the basis for a (partial) reconstructive argument insofar as it exhibits clearly the specific consequences or correlates associated with this attribute that may be expected to occur in the subject context." To get access to more specific, local meanings (i.e., to contextualize the principles), ancient *practice* should be reconstructed, before and after the use of the structural analogy. This may be accomplished by generating archaeological context, for example through a spatial analysis, including the study of formation processes (Verhoeven 1999). Structural analogies thus move from general structures to specific practices, and the relations between structure and practice should be critically evaluated.

It should be emphasized here that structural analogies, like Ascher's "new analogy," refer to notions such as ritual, ideology, and symbolism, and not to detailed comparisons of artifacts. In other words, in structural analogies material culture is used to obtain access to non-material culture (e.g., Noll 1996:246, 249).

Now, dealing with the second question, it could be objected that I have normalized the past by imposing "modern" concepts upon it. Undeniably, I have used the present to interpret the past, but as has been indicated above, there does not seem to be any other way. By using various relevant (structural) analogies, and by explicitly paying attention to archaeological and ethnographic context, I believe I have opened up, and not closed down, the past, by suggesting an alternative interpretation of PPNB skulls. Of course, the PPNB "skull cult" was different from the veneration of skulls in Papua New Guinea or Assam, but at a deep, structural level the existence of similarities does seem to be defendable. The data on the source side should not be regarded as parallels, but as *examples*, once again indispensable for opening up, and not closing down, the past![11]

To summarize, in using structural analogies the following steps should be taken:

1   Critical evaluation of hypotheses concerning function and meaning of archaeological feature(s) or practice(s) to be interpreted.
2   Analysis of archaeological context (formation processes, spatial analysis, etc.) in order to reconstruct past systemic context.
3   Preliminary reconstruction of structuring principles of archaeological objects.
4   Preliminary reconstruction of ancient practice.
5   (Cross-cultural) search for comparable ethnographic examples.
6   Analysis of structure (or general structuring principles) underlying these examples.
7   Comparison of archaeological and ethnographic records (identification of similarities and differences).
8   Critical evaluation of the eloquence of the comparison: (a) relevance, (b) generality, and (c) "goodness-of-fit" must be assessed (Hodder 1982:22).
9   Reconstruction of structuring principles of archaeological objects.
10 Reconstruction of ancient practice.
11 Synthesis (structure, practice, function, meaning).

Conclusion: the Past, the Present, and the Future

The use of analogy and ethnoarchaeology – a particular form of analogy – in the archaeology of the Middle East and in archaeology in general is an indispensable method for making sense of the past. Without their use, archaeologists would be describers, and not interpreters, of the past, i.e., archaeology would not be what it should be: a social science, dealing with past social practice. The use of so-called structural analogies has been proposed as a way of opening up such a social and meaningful past.

Especially due to the pace of modernization in the Middle East, "traditional" ways of life (but see below) are rapidly vanishing (e.g., Watson 1980:59). Important and exemplary ethnoarchaeological studies in "traditional" villages like those of Watson, Kramer, and Horne will become more and more difficult to carry out. For the people living in these villages, modernization has obvious advantages, especially with regard to the often laborious agricultural and domestic activities. For archaeologists, however, "traditional" villages are an important source of information for a wide array of topics: function and meaning of artifacts, organization of labor, relations between wealth and material culture, kinship systems, agricultural systems, building techniques, production of artifacts and food, etc. Of course, one can find all these things in "modern" villages as well, but it can be assumed that "traditional" villages are more comparable to archaeological ones, at least in material respects. Many a Middle Eastern archaeologist will recall the experience of excavating artifacts and structures quite similar to those of the "traditional" village where his/her base camp is.[12]

This brings us to the important question of the extent to which present-day Middle Eastern societies, situated in a modernized setting and having witnessed dramatic political, economic, and social changes, are representative of the past (both of the Middle East and in general). Ethnoarchaeological research in "traditional" villages does not deal with "living fossils"; one would deny history by arguing so (cf. Wolf 1982). However, as already indicated, it is undeniable that while "traditional" villages are different in many aspects from (pre-)historic ones, there are also many formal similarities, suggesting at least some continuity in social and economic practices. Moreover, as has been argued, while there may be many differences between source and subject sides in analogies, it is especially *relevance* (formally and structurally) and *context* that are important in an assessment of the usefulness of analogies. Thus, even in "semi-traditional" or "modern" Middle Eastern villages relevant analogies may be found.

Therefore, ethnoarchaeological research will remain an important tool for providing data with regard to interpretation of the archaeological record. Such research should on the one hand be based on the kinds of questions archaeologists have, but on the other hand, practices or artifacts which are disappearing fast should be recorded as soon as possible, even if as yet no archaeologists are working on such practices or materials. Of course, in the case of village studies, settlements and their occupants are not museums or laboratories, where people turn into objects. Instead, we deal with subjects, with whom we should not only communicate about the past, but also about the present. The present, i.e., ethnoarchaeology and analogy, will remain an indispensable means for understanding the past, also in the future.

Acknowledgments

This research was supported by the Council for the Humanities, which is part of the Netherlands Organization for Scientific Research (NWO). I am indebted to Reinhard Bernbeck and Susan Pollock for their stimulating criticism and many useful suggestions which considerably improved the original version of this paper. Erick van Driel made the drawings. Ans Bulles corrected the English text.

NOTES

1   In a recent publication Owen and Porr use the term ethno-analogy as a synonym for ethnoarchaeology (Owen and Porr, eds. 1999).
2   In the conclusion I will return to the problematic concept of "traditional villages."
3   Bernbeck (1997:105) would call this "contextual ethnoarchaeology." His "Middle Range ethnoarchaeology" deals with archaeological formation processes.
4   For other village, and related, studies see e.g., Antoun 1972; Holmes 1975; Lutfiyya 1966; Mortensen 1993; Nicolaisen 1963; Sweet 1960.
5   *The Traditional Crafts of Persia* (Wulff 1966) remains useful for the interpretation of Near Eastern artifacts.

6   Apart from present sources, historical sources can also be used in an analogy.
7   A related term is *ethnohistory*, in which the history of a region is applied to archaeological problems in that region (Orme 1973:483).
8   The same holds for form-meaning relationships. In fact I should write form-function/meaning. For reasons of convenience, however, I here use the formulation form-function.
9   Garfinkel (1994:170) reconstructs the following stages in the "life-cycle" of PPNB skulls: (1) burial of corpse, usually under the floor of a house; (2) opening of the grave (after a year or so) and removal of the skull; (3) possible selection for decoration (for special persons?); (4) storage or display; (5) burial of skull.
10 For a critique of the (anthropological) search for structure see Guenther 1999:226–247.
11 Some researchers (e.g., Bernbeck 2000; Shanks and Tilley 1992) have argued that there is no past; that there is only a present discussion about a past time.
12 Fragmented and limited observations of traditional activities near their excavation sites by archaeologists are described as "fortuitous ethnoarchaeology" by Longacre (1991:6).

REFERENCES

Anderson, Patricia C., 1994 Reflections on the Significance of Two PPN Typological Classes in Light of Experimentation and Microwear Analysis: Flint "Sickles" and Obsidian "Çayönü" Tools. *In* Neolithic Chipped Stone Industries of the Fertile Crescent: Studies in Early Near Eastern Production, Subsistence, and Environment 1. Hans G. Gebel and Stefan K. Kozlowski, eds. pp. 61–82. Berlin: ex oriente.

Antoun, Richard, 1972 Arab Village: A Social Structural Study of a Transjordanian Peasant Community. Bloomington: Indiana University Press.

Arensburg, Baruch, and Israel Hershkovitz, 1988 Nahal Hemar Cave: Neolithic Human Remains. Atiqot 18:50–58.

Ascher, Robert, 1961 Analogy in Archaeological Interpretation. Southwestern Journal of Anthropology 17:317–325.

Bernbeck, Reinhard, 1994 Die Auflösung der häuslichen Produktionsweise: Das Beispiel Mesopotamiens. Berlin: Dietrich Reimer.

Bernbeck, Reinhard, 1997 Theorien in der Archäologie. Tübingen and Basel: A. Francke Verlag.

Bernbeck, Reinhard, 2000 Towards a Gendered Past: The Heuristic Value of Analogies. *In* Vergleichen als archäologische Methode: Analogien in den Archäologien. Alexander Gramsch, ed. pp. 143–150. Oxford: BAR International Series 825.

Bienert, Hans-Dieter, 1991 Skull Cult in the Prehistoric Near East. Journal of Prehistoric Religion, 5:9–23.

Bienert, Hans-Dieter, and Bernd Müller-Neuhof, 2000 Im Schutz der Ahnen? Bestattungssitten im präkeramischen Neolithikum Jordaniens. Damaszener Mitteilungen 12:17–29.

Binford, Louis, 1968 Archaeological Perspectives. *In* New Perspectives in Archaeology. Louis Binford and Sally Binford, eds. pp. 5–32. Chicago: Aldine.

Bourdieu, Pierre, 1977. Outline of a Theory of Practice. Cambridge: Cambridge University Press.

Campana, Douglas V., 1989 Natufian and Protoneolithic Bone Tools: The Manufacture and Use of Bone Implements in the Zagros and the Levant. Oxford: BAR International Series 494.

David, Nicholas, and Carol Kramer, 2001 Ethnoarchaeology in Action. Cambridge: Cambridge University Press.

Fur, Yves le, and Jean-Hubert Martin, eds., 1999 "La mort n'en saura rien": reliques d'Europe et d'Océanie. Paris: Éditions de la réunion des musées nationaux.

Garfinkel, Yosef, 1994 Ritual Burial of Cultic Objects: The Earliest Evidence. Cambridge Archaeological Journal 4/2:159–188.

Guenther, Mathias, 1999 Tricksters & Trancers: Bushman Religion and Society. Bloomington and Indianapolis: Indiana University Press.

Hodder, Ian, 1982 The Present Past: An Introduction to Anthropology for Archaeologists. London: Batsford.

Holmes, Judith E., 1975 A Study of Social Organisation in Certain Villages in West Khurasan, Iran, with Special Reference to Kinship and Agricultural Activities. Ph.D. thesis, University of Durham.

Horne, Lee, 1994 Village Spaces: Settlement and Society in Northeastern Iran. Washington and London: Smithsonian Institution Press.

Ingersoll, Daniel, John Yellen, and William Macdonald, eds., 1977 Experimental Archaeology. New York: Columbia University Press.

Kenyon, Kathleen, 1981 Village Ethnoarchaeology: Rural Iran in Archaeological Perspective. New York & London: Academic Press.

Kramer, Carol, 1982 Village Ethnoarchaeology: Rural Iran in Archaeological Perspective. New York and London: Academic Press.

Longacre, William, 1991 Ceramic Ethnoarchaeology: An Introduction. In Ceramic Ethnoarchaeology. William Longacre, ed. pp. 1–10. Tucson: University of Arizona Press.

Lutfiyya, Abdulla M., 1966 Baytin: A Jordanian Village. A Study of Social Institutions and Social Change in a Folk Community. The Hague: Mouton.

McQuitty, Alison, 1984 An Ethnographic and Archaeological Study of Clay Ovens in Jordan. Annual of the Department of Antiquities 28:259–267.

Meiklejohn, Christopher, Anagnostis Agelarakis, Peter A. Akkermans, Philip E. L. Smith, and Ralph Solecki, 1992 Artificial Cranial Deformation in the Proto-Neolithic and Neolithic Near East and its Possible Origin: Evidence from Four Sites. Paléorient 18/2:83–97.

Mortensen, Inge D., 1993 Nomads of Luristan: History, Material Culture, and Pastoralism in Western Iran. London: Thames and Hudson.

Murray, Tim, 1992 Tasmania and the Constitution of the Dawn of Humanity. Antiquity 66:730–743.

Murray, Tim, and Michael J. Walker, 1988 Like WHAT? A Practical Question of Analogical Inference and Archaeological Meaningfulness. Journal of Anthropological Archaeology 7:248–287.

Narroll, R., 1962 Floor Area and Settlement Population. American Antiquity 27:587–588.

Nicolaisen, Johannes, 1963 Ecology and Culture of the Pastoral Tuareg. With Particular Reference to the Tuareg of Ahaggar and Ayr. Copenhagen: The National Museum of Copenhagen.

Noll, Elisabeth, 1996 Ethnographische Analogien: Forschungsstand, Theoriediskussion, Anwendungsmöglichkeiten. Ethnografische und Archäologische Zeitschrift 37:245–252.

Ochsenschlager, Edward L., 1974 Modern Potters at al-Hiba, with Some Reflections on the

Excavated Early Dynastic pottery. *In* Ethnoarchaeology. Christopher Donnan and C. William Clewlow, eds. pp. 24–98. Institute of Archaeology, Los Angeles: University of California.

Ochsenschlager, Edward L., 1993 Village Weavers: Ethnoarchaeology at al-Hiba. Bulletin on Sumerian Agriculture 7:43–62.

Orme, Bryony, 1973 Archaeology and Ethnography. *In* The Explanation of Culture Change: Models in Prehistory. Colin Renfrew, ed. pp. 481–492. London: Duckworth.

Owen, Linda R., and Martin Porr, eds., 1999 Ethno-Analogy and the Reconstruction of Prehistoric Artifact Use and Production. Tübingen: Mo Vince Verlag.

Parker Pearson, Michael, 1999 The Archaeology of Death and Burial. Phoenix Mill, England: Sutton Publishing.

Schiffer, Michael, 1972 Archaeological Context and Systemic Context. American Antiquity 37/2:156–165.

Schiffer, Michael, 1987 Formation Processes of the Archaeological Record. Albuquerque: University of New Mexico Press.

Shanks, Michael, and Christopher Tilley, 1987 Social Theory and Archaeology. Oxford: Polity Press.

Shanks, Michael, and Christopher Tilley, 1992 Re-Constructing Archaeology: Theory and Practice. London: Routledge.

Simoons, Frederick J., 1968 A Ceremonial Ox of India: The Mithan in Nature, Culture, and History. Madison, WI: University of Wisconsin Press.

Smidt, Dirk, 1996 Sepik Art: Supernatural Support in Earthly Situations. *In* The Object as Mediator: On the Transcendental Meaning of Art in Traditional Cultures. Mireille Holsbeke, ed. pp. 60–67. Antwerp: Etnografisch Museum Antwerp.

Sollas, William J., 1911 Ancient Hunters and their Modern Representatives. London: Macmillan.

Stahl, Ann, 1993 Concepts of Time and Approaches to Analogical Reasoning in Historical Perspective. American Antiquity 58:235–260.

Sweet, Louise, 1960 Tell Toqa'an: A Syrian Village. Anthropological Papers, 14. Ann Arbor: University of Michigan Museum of Anthropology.

Tilley, Christopher, 1996 An Ethnography of the Neolithic: Early Prehistoric Societies in Scandinavia. Cambridge: Cambridge University Press.

Tringham, Ruth, 1978 Experimentation, Ethnoarchaeology and the Leapfrogs in Archaeological Methodology. *In* Explorations in Ethnoarchaeology. Richard Gould, ed. pp. 169–199. Albuquerque: University of New Mexico Press.

Van Gijn, Annelou, and Daan C. M. Raemaekers, 1999 Tool Use and Society in the Dutch Neolithic: The Inevitability of Ethnographic Analogies. *In* Ethno-Analogy and the Reconstruction of Prehistoric Artifact Use and Production. Linda R. Owen and Martin Porr, eds. pp. 43–52. Tübingen: Mo Vince Verlag.

Verhoeven, Marc, 1999 An Archaeological Ethnography of a Neolithic Community: Space, Place and Social Relations in the Burnt Village at Tell Sabi Abyad, Syria. Istanbul: Nederlands Historisch-Archaeologisch Instituut.

Verhoeven, Marc, 2002a Ritual and Ideology in the Pre-Pottery Neolithic B of the Levant and South-East Anatolia. Cambridge Archaeological Journal 12:233–58.

Verhoeven, Marc, 2002b Ritual and its Investigation in Prehistory. *In* Magic Practices and Ritual in the Near Eastern Neolithic. Hans Georg Gebel, Bo Dahl Hermansen, and Charlott Hoffmann-Jensen, eds. Berlin: ex oriente.

Watson, Patty Jo, 1979 Archaeological Ethnography in Western Iran. Tucson: University of Arizona Press.

Watson, Patty Jo, 1980 The Theory and Practice of Ethnoarchaeology with Special Reference to the Near East. Paléorient 6:55–64.

Wolf, Eric, 1982 Europe and the People without History. Berkeley: University of California Press.

Wulff, Hans E., 1966 The Traditional Crafts of Persia: Their Development, Technology, and Influence on Eastern and Western Civilizations. London and Cambridge, MA: MIT Press.

Wylie, Alison, 1985 The Reaction Against Analogy. Advances in Archaeological Method and Theory. Michael Schiffer, ed. pp. 63–111. New York: Academic.

13

The Ancient Sumerians in the Tides of Time

Petr Charvát

Introduction

The perception of time is one of the most important and most crucial characteristics of any civilization that existed in historical times or that exists even now. It could be demonstrated repeatedly that sensitivity to the flow of time and recognition of the temporal coordinate of reality constitute one of the basic traits of humanity, and, indeed, that the concern with the very notion of time may represent a component of the bundle of spiritual properties that distinguished the first humans from their animal environment. In fact, such a feature of human behavior as burial of the dead, which first occurred at least 100,000 ago, bears out the perception of the flow of time; here, of course, it assumes a rather prosaic form of protective measures taken against the decomposition of a human corpse that falls prey to the elements which take their share in the appropriation of material constituents of the dead body as time passes. Let us, however, notice that at least as early as the ninth–eighth millennium B.C.E., the plastered skulls of the aceramic Neolithic sites of the Near East first bear out a belief in an immaterial, and hence eternal, component of human nature, outlasting the bonds of physical existence of particular humans. Indications consistent with such a situation may even reach as far back as the Natufian culture (Bar-Yosef 1997:209, 211–212 with ref.). Nevertheless, while each civilization takes account of the essentials represented by the regular sequence of days, nights, and seasons of the year, the manner in which it includes time in the contexts of spiritual reflection on its world can constitute a telltale testimony of its scales and ladders of values. These values structure both the internal life of bearers of the respective civilizations and the unfolding of major events of public character, deemed to encode the "proper," "civilized" way of life and therefore constituting an "outer shell" of social life of every civilization of the world (on time in various cultures of the world cf. especially Gell 1992).

While the ideas sketched above are likely to arouse no contradictions or objections, we do encounter some difficulty in the decoding of the perception of time and temporality in early civilizations, especially those which thrived in the very distant past. Difficulties also arise in translating the testimony of historical evidence into terms and notions characterizing our own vision of any particular historical period. We all somehow realize, or tacitly assume, that we can understand ancient people because we are human beings just like them. This idea, first proposed at the beginning of the 18th century by the Italian scholar Giambattista Vico, has since gained ground. In fact, Jean Piaget, a French developmental psychologist investigating the development of abstract values in children, has demonstrated that there seems to exist a universal, pan-human mode of perception of time, similar to that of colors (on this Gell 1992:97–117, 132–145). What, however, might not be so evident is the idea that the employment of singular mental tools, by which human beings grasp the world surrounding them, is determined by the overall context of a given period's mode of thinking. "Cultural time" is at least as important as "biological time." Without a doubt we may assume that in the Middle Ages, those condemned as heretics and sent to the execution pyre were as scared to die as we are today. Nevertheless, the idea of the possible perdition of their immortal souls, which they wholeheartedly embraced, was stronger than the individual and absolutely natural fear of death, and it inspired in them an attitude of ultimate intransigence. They simply could go no further in giving up their "erroneous" views and returning to orthodoxy without putting their souls into peril of eternal damnation, as all readers of Umberto Eco's *The Name of the Rose* certainly realize.

It is exactly this kind of intellectual adventure that I wish to undertake here. Mine is an attempt at decoding a structured mode of thought in one of the world's earliest civilizations, that of the Sumerians living in the fourth and third millennia B.C.E. in Mesopotamia, a drainage area of the twin rivers Euphrates and Tigris, and at comparing it with the modern perception of time and temporality. What I am going to present is at best a nebulous and blurred vision of time as viewed by the ancients, of the relation between the temporal flow and the structure of the world as they perceived it.

Measuring Time in Ancient Mesopotamia

At least since the beginnings of their literacy in the late fourth millennium B.C.E., the Sumerians – whichever ethnic group or groups may be masked by this later ethnonym – were well aware of the individual segments of time (on the emergence of the Sumerian civilization cf. now Charvát 2002). The very first texts which they wrote in an early form of what is presently called the cuneiform script, best designated as proto-cuneiform, contain the notions of day, month, and year (most recently Friberg 1999; cf. also Glassner 2000a:179 [fig. 14], 283–284 [fig. 1]). The authors of these earliest texts were thus aware of the basic dimensions of time, as well as of the essentials of the motions of the principal celestial bodies which determine the seasons and thus also the year. We must nonetheless regrettably confess that we do not know whether these lexemes refer to actually measured segments of time or to abstract, "artificial" units created as a yardstick to approximate future sequences of vitally important events such as agricultural work or shepherding seasons. We may work with the assumption that the authors of the most ancient texts were familiar with the notions of days, months, and years. We would, however, be hard put to estimate how far they took pains to measure the time-unit lengths exactly or whether they worked with any abstract notions such as "man/woman-days," equal to pre-determined amounts of work.

The Sumerians were apparently not very much interested in the higher measures of time (such as, for instance, the *aeons* of Greek mythology or the *yugas* of Indian time reckoning), or at least they did not refer to them in their written records. The three basic manners of dating historical events, used subsequently throughout the whole history of Mesopotamian civilization, emerged as early as the third millennium B.C.E. These were:

1   The system of assigning an independent name to each past year and of referring to the dates of historical events as happening in those named years, lists of which were presumably kept. This is, in fact, a very traditional manner of dating, examples of which may be found throughout the world and in diverse human societies. The bison skins with symbols for year names kept by the shamans of some native American tribes point this out clearly.
2   Dating by measuring the temporal distance which has passed from a fixed point in time, usually from the enthronement of the ruling monarch, until the present. This system, which frequently gives the data in their barest possible form as numerals denoting the year, month, and day in which the recorded event took place, represents the form of dating later borrowed by the major religions of the world. It is most common even today, as is demonstrated by the various *Anno Domini*, *Hijrah*, or World-Creation datings.
3   Dates that made reference to the service periods of public appointees who took their turns of office at regular intervals. Reference to their names could thus help to indicate the moment at which the event in question took place. Such office turns, designated in Sumerian by the term BALA and written by a sign depicting (in all probability) a spindle with the whorl that kept it rotating, were also appropriated by successor civilizations. This is illustrated in the Roman system of annual dating by reference to the names of consuls who held office in the relevant year.

It goes without saying that all this would induce us to believe that the ancient Sumerians conceived time in much the same manner as we do. Such an assumption, however, would not be quite correct. In many aspects the Sumerian perception of time differed from ours, and that seems to have been the case from the beginning of their civilization onwards.

What Kind of Time?

The first, and rather considerable, difference pertained to the very notion of time itself. This term simply did not exist as such in the Sumerian language, though expressions denoting its various components and segments existed from the beginning of cuneiform (Wilcke 1982:33; Selz 1999:511).

The Sumerians also saw time as a component of a wider system, embedded in structures of spatiotemporal extension. Robert Englund has noticed that in the proto-cuneiform script of the late fourth millennium B.C.E., identical graphemes are used for the periods of day and directions of the wind, the latter most probably indicating the cardinal points (Englund 1988:165–166, from the Uruk Plant List). This probably wove time into a wider and more universal system in which it did not function independently but constituted one of the properties of a complex universe. In classic Chinese thought, for instance, time represented but a function of space and of the never-ending vegetational cycle with its proliferation and hibernation phases. Winter was equivalent to the north, the color black, the element water, and the supremacy of the major female principle (*yin*); spring was homonymous with the east, the color blue-green, the element wood, and the supremacy of the minor female principle, and so on.

Later on, the idea of the world as a fourfold spatiotemporal structure, from which the sun was supposed to depart and to which it returned through heavenly gates guarded by mythical doorkeepers stationed there (bison men and scorpion men), is clearly perceptible in Mesopotamian cuneiform texts (Huxley 2000). This enmeshing of time within a wider network of structural relationships might have resulted in profound social consequences: one of the commonly acknowledged functions of the early elites, of considerable importance for the proper functioning of the natural and societal bonds, might have been seen in "starting-off" the motion of the world. This happened in early China where the king had to determine the beginning of the calendar, the first day of the first month, by personally proceeding from one section of his Calendar house (Ming-T'ang) to another (Ching 1997:37), but it also occurred in a number of non-state societies (e.g., Gell 1992:306–313).

Such a wider notion of time, seen as a substance which, though integrated into the terrestrial universe as an organized whole, can crop up in many particularities of human interaction with the world, opened the way towards characterizations of temporal entities which may seem surprising to us. The perception of time as a function of space, coupled with the personally experienced sequence of natural fertility cycles built into the agropastoral enterprise, gave birth to such ideas as the "plenty" or "fullness" of time, expressed most clearly in the measurement of temporal segments by means of hollow measures (Selz 1999:471). But the ancients expressed themselves sometimes even more clearly: in the "Lamentation over the Destruction of Ur," Enlil, the divine father of Ur's own god Nanna, gives his son a hardly encouraging answer when Nanna comes to him to plead for the fate-stricken people of Ur: "Who has ever seen a kingdom which outlasted the time measured out to it? As to its [Ur's] kingdom, its regnal period is filled up" (Wilcke

1982:41). This general idea has been carried up to the present time especially by the text of the Bible. In its temporal determinations, in particular in the expectations of the moment of the end of the world, this notion of time figures prominently, most clearly in eschatological parts such as the Revelation (Rev. XV: 15: "Thrust in thy sickle, and reap: for the time is come for thee to reap; for the harvest of the earth is ripe."). The connection, of course, is neither a word-for-word nor a literal one, but the linking of the idea of time with the notion of fullness or ripeness, alluding clearly to vegetational symbolism, is there just the same.

As with most ancient civilizations, one would be tempted to assume almost automatically that the Sumerians lived with a cyclical notion of time. The reality is somewhat more complex. On the one hand, Claus Wilcke has convincingly demonstrated that the Sumerian word for "back of the body" is the same as that used for "the future" (EGER; Wilcke 1982:31). This shows that the cyclical or rather circular notion of time, enclosing the human bondage into one gigantic trajectory which is closed and along which things material and immaterial move in an eternally fixed circular course, was not alien to the ancient Sumerians. The slogan "back to the future" would clearly be comprehensible to them. On the other hand, inhabitants of ancient Mesopotamia did recognize an initial point in time at which civilization began. This is clearly indicated by the famous dictum of Uruinimgina's inscription, referring to the earliest possible time marker as to a time of NUMUN.È.A.TA, that is, "from the time when the seed sprouted forth" (Wilcke 1982:32). Though this could well be understood as a recurring event, it nonetheless implies an idea of a starting point fixed somewhere in the mythical past. Variants, of which the last one named here is most interesting for archaeology, do refer to the beginning of all things as the day "on which fates were decreed (UD.NAM.TAR.RA)" and even "on which the population was settled (UD.UL UN KI.GAR.RA)" (Wilcke 1982:32). A just measure of prudence is obviously in place here, as it transpires that both the notion of cyclical time and that of linear time might have been, at least *in nuce*, present in ancient Sumerian thought (also Selz 1999:467).

"Our" Time and "Their" Time

We need not unduly stress the considerable difference between this indigenous perception of Sumerian temporality and the present-day idea of time as a pure, crystalline, abstract current which swishes around our ears, being essentially independent of what we do, say, or think and defying all attempts at persuading it not to leave its traces on our material substance. We try to cheat time by jogging to keep our figures slim, by facelifting to conceal the dark spots and wrinkles, by makeup to pretend eternal youthfulness or by smoothly shaved faces to make septuagenarians look younger. We tend to imagine that somewhere in hoary antiquity, people were hardly more than crude barbarians who dressed in animal skins, ate raw meat, and drank blood still warm from the veins of the animals killed. We deem them low because they did not even know literacy, or, alternatively, the Immaterial Principle, Incarnate God, Prophet, or whatever it might have been right down to Adam

Smith's Treatise on the Wealth of Nations. We love to envisage our predecessors advancing only slowly, at great pains, and with considerable expense (and, of course, listening to the proper advice administered by the only political and spiritual leaders worth listening to) up to the present happy time of civilization where time ends because no regime could be better than ours. All this represents, of course, hardly more than a thinly disguised notion of time prevalent in the major monotheistic religions of the world, well illustrated by Christianity. The Christian history of the path of salvation, beginning with God's creation of the world and passing through the stages of the creation of first human beings and the first fall, followed by the apparition of Jesus Christ, Crucifixion, and Resurrection and ending with the Last Judgment and establishment of the Kingdom of God on earth, was taken over by the Enlightenment philosophers. They merely substituted the stages of "darkness," in which humankind lived before the introduction of 18th-century ideals, for the preceding idea of the times of "ignorance" of the major religions, and the illustrious and informed present for the time of victory of any of the major religions – some even for God's kingdom on earth. This is well discernible in archaeological thought with Gordon Childe's proposal of the Neolithic revolution, representing a sort of revelation of what was subsequently to become a bundle of the major civilization trends. Ever since the days of this great Australian-born archaeologist, his colleagues have perceived the time of Mesopotamian civilization as a linear "long-distance run" for more and more perfection, beginning somewhere in the dark times of "savagery" (cf. the following citation) and ending in the blessed sunlit days of the food-producing economy, or state and literate civilization, or the world's first empire, or the world's first multinational and multicultural state (for a beautiful example of this mode of thinking cf. the introduction to Braidwood and Howe 1960:1–9, as well as their discussion on pp. 175–176).

At present, it is, of course, easy to criticize views that held an enormous importance in their days. Without any doubt, our scholarly predecessors, to whom we owe much, paved the way towards the accessibility of the enormous amount of evidence at our disposal, with the aid of which we are now realizing that things are not so simple. Nevertheless, we only begin to comprehend today how difficult it is to reconcile this vision of ours with the views and opinions taken by the ancients.

Sumerians, Scholars, and Stochastic Events

It goes without saying that modern studies focusing on the long-term factors of Mesopotamian history have not failed to appear. One of the most inspiring ones appeared fairly early but is not cited too frequently up to the present time. This is Gibson's (1974) study on the impact of various irrigation strategies on the economy of ancient Mesopotamia. The author calls to our attention the fact that in the long run of Mesopotamian civilizations, there are certain limits which should not be transgressed, lest all Mesopotamian communities pay a heavy fine. Specifically, in order to make Mesopotamian agriculture productive, local populations had to let at least one half of the available soil lie fallow, an historically constant feature of which people of the time were undoubtedly aware. This, of course, must have been one of the components of their environment which was likely to have contributed to their conviction that there are certain things which not even time will overcome, constant features of the landscapes and life-style of the riverine plains of Mesopotamia belonging to the fate of the land decreed forever by the gods. The lure of bigger agricultural yields, which might have pushed the major empires of Mesopotamian history towards violation of this golden rule and which ended up in a disastrous salinization of large tracts of once fertile soil, might then very well have been seen by the rural communities as an outrage committed by the emperors defying the commands of the gods, demons, and spirits, eternal proprietors of the arable soil, an outrage that had immediate and drastic consequences not only for the leaders, but for their whole communities.

An interesting step has been taken by Jean-Daniel Forest in his last major treatise on the origins of the Mesopotamian state (Forest 1996, and this volume). Much as Gibson in the context of natural qualities of the Mesopotamian environment, Forest has based his analysis of the rural communities of prehistoric Mesopotamia on an explicit ethnographic model, formulated by the eminent French ethnologist and connoisseur of matters African, Claude Meillasoux – that of the Household-based Agricultural Community (Communauté Domestique Agricole, or CDA: Forest 1996:esp. 21–22, 27, 51–52, 90–91, and 113–114). Defined as a production-consumption unit based on blood kinship, sharecropping, domestic redistribution, and neighborly aid, the CDA is assumed to have existed in two modes. The segmentary one, represented by the Halaf culture, resulted in an unlimited fissioning and propagation of its member communities all over the accessible landscapes which displayed certain geographic properties favorable for human settlement of the past age. The integrated one, incarnated by the sedentary Neolithic cultures of southern Mesopotamia as exemplified by Tell el Oueili, offered, as an alternative source-procurement strategy, intense exploitation of resources available in abundance in certain geographic niches, allowing human settlements to be "permanently" fixed in time and space. The northern variant of Ubaid culture is perceived here as a successful "export" of the integrated CDA northwards, where it is suggested to have given birth to a secondary form of integrated CDA with chiefdoms, exemplified by the site of Tepe Gawra.

This is again a procedure which must be welcomed as it points out that there are certain societies which oscillate around a well-balanced state of relationships aimed both outside, towards their natural environment, and inside, in the direction of sets of rules governing people's social behavior. In Africa, where the natural abundance offered by nature to human populations dispenses with the necessity of building too complex and too permanent social networks, such communities may make students of these societies believe that they have not changed from time immemorial. Now this is exactly the heart of the problem when we apply an ethnological model to our primarily archaeological data. Regardless of the difference in natural environment, I believe it would be somewhat difficult to demonstrate that the CDA really does possess characteristics which are constant over long periods of time and is not, for example, the result of a set of simplification processes which have been going on for a considerable but measurable period of time. Take, for instance, early medieval Western Europe but also Byzantium, which carried on the sophisticated cultural tradition of Classical Antiquity. A student pursuing the medieval development of this culture would be tempted to assume that nothing changed as the centuries and millennia passed. The culture, however, persisted in an economic and social context utterly different from the environment in which Greek and Roman cultures had reached their greatest floruits. Furthermore, is the CDA model sufficiently broad to accommodate the range of possible social organizations to be expected in the past, and especially in the more distant past? How deep must be the source critique which would assess the fruitfulness of its application in various historical contexts – would it be permissible, for instance, to use the CDA model for sedentary communities of food-gatherers, such as, for instance, the tribes of the American Northwest Coast?

But the matter does not, in fact, rest there. Ethnographic models, however useful they may be in visualizing various trajectories which the lives of the people in the past might have taken, offer only very rarely unequivocal clues implying positive, tangible, and verifiable evidence on the history of the respective human communities. This is not a problem for Jean-Daniel Forest only – all of us who try to lean on ethnographic evidence in hopes of at least visualizing, if not recreating the past, must necessarily take the customary path of source critique which frequently leaves very little in place to go by (Verhoeven, this volume). Resorting to a model in an historical interpretation of any given society should entail, whenever possible, a close scrutiny of the model with the purpose of determining which parts represent long-term constituents (perhaps on the scale of Fernand Braudel's *longue durée*) and which parts tend to be changeable or transient over shorter time segments. The two paths divide in front of us, with one leading invariably to the assembly of constructions which, though frequently appealing and elegant, may nonetheless collapse on the first contact with reality. The other leads into the maze of Boasian factography which may be difficult, if not impossible to disentangle and master. It is, however, all the more important that we keep addressing questions of a wider order to those civilizations which do possess a very long record of written information, such as the Mesopotamian one. These questions may have a significant bearing on our understanding of other ancient cultures.

Some of the most intriguing conclusions concerning the relationship of ancient Mesopotamians to time have been put forward recently by two scholars, Jean-Jacques Glassner (1993; 2000b) and Gebhard Selz (1999). Having investigated questions concerning the Sumerian King List (SKL), Glassner has convincingly demonstrated that this is one of the documents in which the Mesopotamian comprehension of time comes out most clearly. His is a firm conviction, very relevant in our context, that not only the SKL but Mesopotamian civilization in general shows evidence for both circular and linear time (Glassner 1993:24–26). Glassner outlines the basic Sumerian unit of calculable time, a "round" or "shift," as he explains the Sumerian word BALA, which I have already mentioned. He demonstrates that it was conceived as a minor cycle of work done, or task fulfilled: a certain amount of time needed to finish a given piece of labor, issuing out of a balanced state and leading again towards another balanced but different state of things (Glassner 1993:80–81; Glassner 2000b:192–195). Glassner points out that the notion fits perfectly the grapheme by which it is referred to in the script, an image of a spindle with its whorl. He points to the fact that within a given time segment a spindle would rotate, doing a certain amount of work and bringing about a small but perceptible change in the previous state of things (Glassner 2000b:193). This, as he argues, is precisely the idea which is behind the perception of history in the SKL as a series of "revolutions" (in the Elizabethan-England sense, where the word meant a tour of the royal domain by the suzerain), bringing to the foremost position among the Sumerian cities only the four kingships – Kish, Uruk, Ur, and Akkad – in shifting order and with short-term irregularities.

An Interlude: Sumerian Kingship and Time

Uruk occupied a position of honor, though it had no king (LUGAL), it did possess a time-honored EN (pontifical-cum-temporal-direction) office, at least from the last centuries of the fourth millennium B.C.E. It can be argued that the Uruk pontifical couple, EN (male) and NIN (female), played a key social role in the performance of the NA$_2$ ceremony, probably an early variant of the "sacred marriage" act. This served as an instrument to release natural fertility, conferred upon the earth and living beings by the gods, sole masters of it (Charvát 1997:esp. 10–12).

In fact, the choice of the candidate cities for the topmost positions in Sumerian society appears also to have been substantially conditioned by time. While the position of Uruk was quite unique – as the Sumerian elites were clearly aware – the LUGAL title, borne by the Kish and Ur suzerains, shows that both cities were old enough to have begun their politically central roles at the beginning of the Early Dynastic period (soon after 3000 B.C.E.) when the social prestige of the LUGAL title first prevailed over that of EN (cf. Charvát 1997:esp. 41–81). How did this happen? In Ur (and Kish?), a problem might have arisen out of the fact that the local EN dignitaries were women. Having been married to divinities, they had no earthly husbands upon whom they could have conferred the right to the highest office of the state. Under such circumstances, the crucial social roles devolved upon the individual NINs who took as husbands LUGALs, made the latter rise to the status of highest dignitaries of their respective communities, and, as time went by, that of true "kings." I assume that much as in an overwhelming majority of preindustrial societies, Sumerian women usually did not assume high office, but could confer the right to hold it on their consorts.

The communities ruled by ENSIs betray their political birth in the advanced Early Dynastic age (27th–26th centuries B.C.E.) when this title was introduced by the administrators of the Shuruppak polity, which may perhaps have represented an agency of the Kish kingdom. These communities were perceived by the author(s) of the SKL as relative newcomers who had no right to appropriate any leading position vis-à-vis the "historical sequence" of Mesopotamian kingship.

Nevertheless, the whole sequence of shifts of government clearly assumed a uni-lineal temporal direction, as is indicated by the fact that in the eyes of the author of the SKL there was always and invariably only one supreme city-state within all Sumer. This is aptly expressed by Jean-Jacques Glassner in his denomination of the Sumerian kingship as "*monarchie une*" (= "Monarchy One," cf. also Glassner 1993:87). The analysis of the SKL thus led him to show with remarkable clarity the complex character of Sumerian comprehension of time, at once both cyclical and linear.

Sumerians, Scholars and Stochastic Events Again

To these comments Gebhard Selz has added still other, most pertinent observa-tions. Elaborating upon the observations of both Wilcke (cf. supra) and Glassner, he made two very important remarks. First and foremost, he has formulated what may be termed the "substantial core" and the "accidental periphery" of the Sumerian notion of time (Selz 1999:467). This seems to have been expressed by dating formulae of Akkadian-language legal texts from Old Babylonian Susa, which Glassner (2000b:201) translates from the original as "for continuity and change, for posterity." For Selz, the Sumerians were convinced that anything that is well-established and lasts for a considerable period of time has been sanctioned by usage and, in the eyes of the ancients, has acquired a quasi-permanent, "eternal" charac-ter, similar to the "substantia" of medieval Scholastic philosophy (Selz 1999:508). In fact, this idea sounds congenial to any archaeologist who, asking the question of how long the Sumerians preserved monuments of their ancestors, realizes that a number of Sumerian temples housed remains that might have stood in their sanc-tuaries for centuries, if not millennia (Wilcke 1982:37–41). What shows instability is apt to change and is transient, elusive, volatile, unreliable, and potentially danger-ous ("accidentiae"), though the visible reality surrounding us is invariably com-posed of both these entities. Selz has thus outlined for us the very important distinction between stabilized features of both the natural and human environment, tending to be perceived by the ancient Sumerians as permanent and "eternal," and changeable and impermanent things that constitute an outer "interface" at which the mythically and eternally conceived "pure" substance of time interferes with other entities of both the visible and the invisible world.

A perfect example of this is the effort of Nabonidus, the last Neo-Babylonian king, to find the earliest possible ancestors to the series of cultic buildings he rebuilt at various sacred places. The conscious and deliberate effort to establish cultic structures that would be as close as possible to the mythical prototypes, and therefore to the "eternal" models, led him to initiate truly "archaeological excava-tions," in the course of which he attempted to find the most ancient ground plan of any edifice occupying the site in question. Having identified such ancient build-ings, he directed his architects to build the new temple exactly on the ancient plan, with dimensions "neither a finger shorter, nor a finger longer" (Glassner 1993:241–242).

The second and no less important conclusion put forward by Selz is that of the possibly artificial character of the Sumerian temporal records, at least from the earliest, proto-cuneiform phase of Mesopotamian culture (Selz 1999:472–476, 487–506). He has rightly pointed to the fact that many of the earliest economic texts contain data that are "raw" in the sense that they are not calibrated with respect to any higher temporal entities. It thus cannot be excluded that these texts are related not to the past, where more exact determination of time might have been required, but rather to the future – in fact, that they represent "plans," assessments or evaluations of individual economic ventures for the days, months, and years to come. This accords very well with the hypothesis formulated by Glassner (2000a:esp. 161–215), according to which the introduction of writing represents a deliberate and well-prepared invention corresponding to the needs of a particular time period (cf. also numerous works by Nissen, e.g., 1995:95–100). I myself am also persuaded that the invention and introduction of writing is but the last piece of a creative effort of the Chalcolithic chiefly elites, who, having constructed a new mental image of the universe in which they presented themselves as masters of space and time, proceeded to build an entirely artificial world to their own taste and liking – a universe defined by the signs of writing. The possibility of a rather sophisticated handling of time in the ancient world is borne out by the fact that as late as Hellenistic times, the temporal data of the Ptolemaic astronomical canon were converted to Egyptian yearly count upon transfer from Babylon to Alexandria (Depuydt 1995:esp. 106–115, cf. also Glassner 1993:130–131).

Time Before Time Before Time Before Time . . .

All this indicates that the Sumerian notion of time is a rather complex affair. Being an eternal cycle of ever-returning marker entities, it was also conceived as linear, having an overall direction in which it proceeded. Short of being envisaged as an independent force, it was embedded in a series of other coordinates of the visible world, most notably in space and in the disposition of its material components. To a certain extent, time was also a function of processes involving the discharge of natural fertility and represented thus a "living" affair. Time had a mythical, "eternal" interior of components that were unchanging and stabilized, and an outer shell or rather "atmosphere" of unstable and transitory phenomena which, though superficial, did carry a certain amount of importance. This is borne out by the fact that at least from around the year 700 B.C.E., Babylonian astronomers took great pains to record with the utmost patience, night by night, details of the motions of the principal celestial bodies which must have represented just this kind of superficial and changeable evidence (Depuydt 1995).

It does seem that once the Sumerian notion of time had become well-established, there was hardly anything to replace it in the minds of the successor populations of Babylonians and Assyrians. We can, then, at least attempt to question when the essential ideational concepts behind the Mesopotamian perception of time began to emerge.

Alwo von Wickede (1986) has with great skill investigated the structural principles guiding the decoration of Mesopotamian prehistoric pottery, and we can use
the categories which he has outlined to attempt a glimpse of the notions and concepts used by the inhabitants of the plains and submontane areas of what was to
become Babylonia and Assyria. This procedure is based on the idea that in prelit-
erate societies, eating is considered a most important activity. By eating human
beings assimilate and appropriate substances of the outer world which have been
tamed, humanized, and hence rendered harmless by the processing of the food in
question. Patterns on eating vessels will then tend to represent basic positive values
of the society in question, entering those who ingest the food or producing in them
a desirable state of affairs. A case in point is the Melanesian *kava* ceremony in which
the *kava*-drinking chief identifies himself with ancestors, thereby guaranteeing the
desirable social order at the moment of partaking of the potion (on this in general
cf. especially Lévi-Strauss 1969).

Bearers of the Hassuna and Samarra cultures decorated their products with
patterns displaying rotation as the most characteristic principle (von Wickede
1986:32). This seems to follow out of the prehistoric principle that within a world
that is non-humanized and both potentially and actually hostile, only the point
where human settlement is established represents a safe abode, a lynch-pin from
which human civilization must be suspended and on which it can be anchored, and
which constitutes a reference point for all human activities within its radius.

Representatives of the Halaf culture advanced further in the sense that theirs was
a world of axial symmetry (von Wickede 1986:32). Here prevails the vision of sedentary human populations, acknowledging a hierarchically ordered world centered, as
before, on human settlements but, unlike in Neolithic times, perceiving them as
embedded in concentric tracts of humanized landscapes, beyond the frontiers of
which extended the wild, and therefore "in-human" and potentially dangerous landscapes. Thanks to studies by André Leroi-Gourhan, we know that while the perception of the world in nomadic societies knows only one certainty – the human
encampment – nomads tend to see the rest of the world as a loose series of environments in no logical relation to one another, existing in a more or less haphaz-
ard manner and not tied to any unifying structures. Such traits of human thought
as the notions of center and periphery emerge only within the systems proper to
sedentary societies. Such creations of Halaf-culture potters as bowls or plates
bearing concentric flower- or rosette-like ornaments surrounded by concentric
bands of chequered patterns (von Wickede 1986:20, Abb. 17) may well visualize a
notion of a "civilized" quadripartite world inclosed in a large circle of ever-flowing
time.

What, however, was a truly fundamental invention was undoubtedly the cylinder seal, invented and introduced perhaps some time during the Middle Uruk
period. In addition to its technological advantages, the cylinder seal represents a
nearly perfect materialization of the Sumerian perception of the spatiotemporal
structure of the world. The matching is so conspicuous that we may be tempted to
see in this construct of the immediately pre-state age a "major leap," when a whole
bundle of changes transformed, at a relatively rapid pace, essentials of the mental

apparatus used by humans over a very long period of time, reaching perhaps as far back as the beginnings of Neolithic (in terms of Fernand Braudel's *longue durée*). Having the faculty of being endlessly rolled along a wet and pliable surface, it represents symbolically, but also quite realistically, the circularity of time. Being capable of producing an infinite linear arrangement of images, it stands for the linearity of time. Being endowed with the capacity to impress images in the wet clay or any soft matter, and thus create a new form of materiality, it may not only function within a coordinate system of a different order than time, such as that of space, but it can actively create reality. At this stage of development of the human mind, practical operations involving the human environment tend to be performed both in actual fact and "magically," (also) by means of images; one approach is a prerequisite of the other. And, indeed, in view of the fact that cylinder seals were used to close deliveries of agricultural surplus to the elites, their impressions also "produced plenty," and the seals were, in a certain sense, correlates of the cycles of natural fertility.

In fact, there is hardly anything to add after this exposition of the Sumerian notion of time as incarnated in the cylinder seal. This symbolic-cum-functional artifact must have represented a powerful tool with the aid of which prehistoric elites convinced their followers that they were capable of creating a new world order. What came after was just a repetition of the original creative act, a solidification and clarification of a notion which had existed ever since the beginning of Sumerian civilization. No wonder that modern scholars are fascinated by the *Eigenbegrifflichkeit* of Mesopotamian culture (cf., for instance, Selz 1999:511–512). They invariably observe that nearly all creative acts were already performed by the anonymous members of late-fourth-millennium elites. Trapped in the results of the enormous spiritual effort of their ancestors, the Sumerians, Babylonians, and Assyrians contented themselves with the conservation of the cultural heritage which they took over from them. There was only one way to bring more perfection to a system of this kind: to abandon it altogether and to build something radically different. That, however, had to wait for the Hellenistic times.

Conclusion

In fact, this attempt to uncover the perception of time in one of humankind's earliest literate civilizations has raised more questions than it has answered. The Sumerians apparently had a peculiar manner of conceiving and handling time, a manner appropriate to them which has to be understood in its own right. This mental tool was sufficiently sophisticated to delineate both "eternal" (long-term) components of ancient Mesopotamian civilization and to accommodate the changes brought forth by the variety of common, everyday situations. It enabled Mesopotamian elites to create a basic spatiotemporal context for their society in which life was worth living, both for elite members and for the population strata whom they served and by whom they were served. Chance has offered us the possibility to witness the emergence of this basic concept of time in its material incarnation (the cylinder seal) in the Middle Uruk period, at a moment just preceding the creation of one of the world's first literate civilizations. The rotation of the cylinder seal stands for circular/cyclical time; the linear extension of the image impressed by the seal represents a linear orientation, the "vector" of time. The cylinder seal's faculty of making an impression in a malleable surface stood for the basic unity of time and space; and the fact that supplies marked by the cylinder seals brought plenty to elite households indicated the filling capacity, or "fruition" of time. How far this perception of time reflected notions developed in the preceding, prehistoric age, or how far it represented a deep-reaching transformation of the mental apparatus of bearers of Mesopotamian civilization, must be determined by future research.

REFERENCES

Bar-Yosef, Ofer, 1997 Prehistoric Palestine. In The Oxford Encyclopaedia of Archaeology in the Near East, vol. 4. Eric Myers, ed. pp. 207–212. New York and Oxford: Oxford University Press.

Braidwood, Robert, and Bruce Howe, 1960 Prehistoric Investigations in Iraqi Kurdistan. Studies in Ancient Oriental Civilization No. 31. Chicago: University of Chicago Press.

Charvát, Petr, 1997 On People, Signs and States – Spotlights on Sumerian Society, c. 3500–2500 B.C. Prague: The Oriental Institute, Academy of Sciences of the Czech Republic.

Charvát, Petr, 2002 Mesopotamia Before History. London & New York: Routledge.

Ching, Julia, 1997 Son of Heaven: Sacral Kingship in Ancient China. T'oung-pao 83/1–3:3–41.

Depuydt, Leo, 1995 "More Valuable than all Gold": Ptolemy's Royal Canon and Babylonian Chronology. Journal of Cuneiform Studies 47:97–117.

Englund, Robert, 1988 Administrative Timekeeping in Ancient Mesopotamia. Journal of the Economic and Social History of the Orient 31:121–185.

Forest, Jean-Daniel, 1996 Mésopotamie – L'apparition de l'état, VIIe–IIIe millénaires. Paris: Méditerranée.

Friberg, Jöran, 1999 Counting and Accounting in the Proto-Literate Middle East. Examples from Two New Volumes of Proto-Cuneiform Texts. Journal of Cuneiform Studies 51:107–138.

Gell, Alfred, 1992 The Anthropology of Time – Cultural Constructions of Temporal Maps and Images. Oxford & Providence: Berg.

Gibson, McGuire, 1974 Violation of Fallow and Engineered Disaster in Mesopotamian Civilization. In Irrigation's Impact on Society, Anthropological Papers of the University of Arizona, 25. Theodore E. Downing and McGuire Gibson, eds. pp. 7–20. Tucson: University of Arizona Press.

Glassner, Jean-Jacques, 1993 Chroniques mésopotamiennes, présentées et traduites par Jean-Jacques Glassner. Paris: Les Belles Lettres.

Glassner, Jean-Jacques, 2000a Écrire à Sumer – l'invention du cunéiforme. Paris: Éditions du Seuil.

Glassner, Jean-Jacques, 2000b Historical Times in Mesopotamia. In Israel Constructs its History – Deuteronomistic Historiography in Recent Research. Journal for the Study of

the Old Testament, Supplement Series 306. Albert de Pury, Thomas Römer, Jean-Daniel
    Macchi, eds. pp. 189–211.
Huxley, Margaret, 2000 The Gates and Guardians in Sennacherib's Addition to the Temple
    of Assur. Iraq 62:109–138.
Lévi-Strauss, Claude, 1969 Du cru au cuit. Paris: Plon.
Nissen, Hans-Jörg, 1995 Grundzüge einer Geschichte der Frühzeit des Vorderen Orients.
    Darmstadt: Wissenschaftliche Buchgesellschaft.
Selz, Gebhard, 1999 Von "Vergangenem Geschehen" zu "Zukunftsbewältigung", Über-
    legungen zur Rolle der Schrift in Ökonomie und Geschichte. *In* Munuscula Mesopotam-
    ica – Festschrift für Johannes Renger. Barbara Böck, Eva Cancik-Kirschbaum, Thomas
    Richter, eds. pp. 465–512. Münster: Ugarit-Verlag.
von Wickede, Alwo, 1986 Die Ornamentik der Tell Halaf-Keramik – Ein Beitrag zu ihrer
    Typologie. Acta Praehistorica et Archaeologica 18:7–32.
Wilcke, Claus, 1982 Zum Geschichtsbewusstsein in Alten Mesopotamien. *In* Archäologie
    und Geschichtsbewusstsein (Kolloquien zur Allgemeinen und Vergleichenden
    Archäologie Bd. 3). Hermann Müller-Karpe, ed. pp. 31–52. München: C. H. Beck.

14

Reliquaries on the Landscape: Mounds as Matrices of Human Cognition

Sharon R. Steadman

Introduction

Across most of the Middle East, as well as parts of central Asia and southeastern Europe, human-made mounds dot the landscape. These have resulted from count-less generations of individuals carrying out everyday activities in exactly the same place as their ancestors did hundreds or thousands of years before. What prompted the peoples of this Middle Eastern landscape to form such an attachment to place that they return again and again, finally to permanently occupy that *exact place*? This prehistoric and early historic behavior eventually produced a terrain inter-spersed with testaments to a human tenacity in residential choice.

At the outset this contribution focuses on explanations that can be labeled "functional" or "rational." Such explanations have formed the mainstay of settle-ment archaeology for decades, and should always serve as basic linchpins for under-standing human settlement patterns. However, there is more to the human behavioral construct than simple reaction to practical needs. Whether choosing a name for a newborn daughter, deciding on a location for residence, or following ritual practice in the treatment of deceased relatives, humans make choices based on an intricate web of beliefs, perspectives, and worldviews that guide them toward certain behaviors. It is these webs of meaning that form the basis of the majority of discussion in this study. In particular, attention will be paid to humans' perceptions of the landscape and how such cognitions led to the formation of Middle Eastern mounds. Beyond just human-made marks on a natural landscape, mounds serve as matrices of meaning in their role as reliquaries of prehistoric lifeways.

Figure 14.1 A Turkish village on the Anatolian Plateau (author's original)

The Middle Eastern Landscape

Across the vast Middle Eastern landscapes are kilometers of agricultural fields or grazing lands, broken only by the occasional village, town, or encampment (figure 14.1). Many of these rise above the landscape, the material result of human processes of production, consumption, and deposition. This is not to say, however, that all these settlements are inhabited today. Many stand as tenantless memorials to the countless individuals who lived, loved, and died on these places hundreds and thousands of years ago. These silent sentries of the past carry names such as "höyük," "tepe," "tell," and "chogha," but all can be translated to mean "human-made mounds."

It is these mounds of human-produced detritus which have, in large part, inspired archaeological exploration of the Middle East, from Layard (Lloyd 1980:87–92), to Kenyon (1985:14–15), to the far less famous, but no less enthusiastic, present author. My first thought upon seeing Çadır Höyük (the site where I've worked over the last decade) was that the *mound* was breathtakingly beautiful (figure 14.2). One must wonder whether it is the physicality of the actual *mound* that inspires an archaeologist's thoughts of beauty, or perhaps more likely, the knowledge that secrets about past lives lie within the layers. The desire to *excavate*, to *reveal*, and to finally understand those successive habitations recorded in the stratigraphy of the mound is nearly irresistible. Fortunately, many have *not* resisted, and thus the history and prehistory of the Middle East have been laid out before us.

Figure 14.2 Çadır Höyük, the author's excavation site, central Turkey (author's original)

But what is it about the Middle Eastern landscape that makes it worthy of consideration, indeed worthy of an entire chapter in this volume? The topography and climate are varied; depending on the region described, adjectives ranging from "lush" to "spare" to "desolate" can be applied. It is not, however, just the environmental characteristics that are of interest, but the nature of the settlements themselves. There is a fundamental difference between agricultural towns in the Western world, particularly those found in North America and parts of Western Europe, and those in the Middle East. Most simply put, one can distinguish between "dispersed" settlements such as those found across the mid-western United States, and "nucleated" settlements in the Middle East.

In general, the North American small-scale farmer lives *on his land*. His farmhouse rests alongside the barn, silos, stock holding-pens, chicken coops, and fields. The family pick-up is used to travel *into* town for supplies. The point is that those engaged in a farming or herding lifestyle in large areas of the Western world live in dispersed settlements, inhabiting the actual land they work, alongside the animals they husband. A brief look at most villages and towns in western Asia will find the opposite. Farmers travel *from* town *to* their fields via four-wheeled or four-legged transport. Settlements are nucleated; residents live side-by-side and fields surround the settlement but lie open, without built structure (see figure 14.1). The narrow alleyways separating houses, the twisting town streets, the deeply furrowed pathways leading to the village springs and gathering places, all testify to the antiquity of such nucleated settlements.

The existence of such settlements, nucleated, crowded, persistent as to place, and the subsequent emergence of human-produced habitus rising above the natural landscape, leads to numerous questions. First and foremost: what led to the choice of that spot for habitation? Also of curiosity is: why stay there? Finally, one is moved to ask: why live in crowded (sloping?) towns on ever higher localities, rather than down "on the ground" nearer fields and grazing lands? This, of course, is not the first time such questions have been asked of archaeological settings. There is a rich literature on the origins of sedentary settlement, settlement choice, and the growth of cities (Chang 1968; Kostof 1991; Fletcher 1995). There is no need to recount the excellent ideas of these scholars here. Rather, the aim is to lead the researcher to view the Middle Eastern landscape with an eye toward two alternative (although not necessarily mutually exclusive) conceptual frameworks: the functional and rational approach, and the cognitive and symbolic approach. The former is an essential component to any study of land use in the ancient or present-day world. The latter is, admittedly, a more unconventional direction of inquiry, but one which may, in the end, be even more productive. Indeed, some suggest that to seek a rational and functional explanation for something that, in their opinion, is born entirely of symbolic patterns reflective of myth, ritual, and cultural consciousness (Rykwert 1976; Cosgrove 1995) is near to folly. However, folly would also plague an approach to landscape studies devoid of rationality.

Functional Landscapes: Rational Choices for "Place"

There has been no lack of archaeological research on the subject of why people settle in certain places. However, many research agendas seeking to explain settlement location have been unintentionally biased by underlying assumptions based on notions of "practicality" and "rationality" from a modern Western perspective. In other words, much of early modern Western settlement and residential choice has employed a selection process anchored in criteria such as land quality and natural resources, access to goods, and safety. These are certainly rational and logical questions to consider when deciding where to make a permanent home. An added bonus is that such models are testable archaeologically, using a variety of standard and scientific techniques.

These are entirely valid avenues of investigation into settlement choice issues. In fact, the archaeologist who did not at least ponder the physical and social landscape in which her settlement was located would likely be ignoring components crucial to building a complete culture history. People want to survive, and the choices they make about any number of things, including where to build a house, are heavily influenced by rational choices that aid in that struggle to survive. Whether those settling humans are transitioning from mobile foraging, migrating farmers rejecting their over-populated village, or city-dwellers looking for a simpler lifestyle, those humans will have certain requirements for their new home; of primary importance would be access to fresh water, wild plants and animals, and arable/grazing land, of considerable importance might be access to trade routes and a protected location. There are innumerable variables that would affect the hierarchical importance of these requirements, including the type of environment in question, the needs of the settlers, levels of competition for resources, socio-economic complexity, and so on. For instance, those founding new settlements on the British Isles would be more at liberty to choose locations close to natural resources such as flint and chalk (e.g., Field 1997), since fresh water and fertile land are not at a premium. In contrast, during the transition to sedentarism in the Levantine Natufian, hamlets were located at those relatively uncommon junctures of hill, mountain, and valley (providing a range of exploitable plant sources), while also providing easy access to river or stream (Henry 1989:48). Perhaps one of the best examples of hunter-gatherer settlement choice comes from the Syrian site of Abu Hureyra. Epipaleolithic residents settled next to abundant fresh water (the Euphrates River), amongst oaks, wild grasses and grains, berries and legumes, and were treated to an annual springtime migration of Persian Gazelle for their meat lockers (Moore et al. 2000:327–439). Without question, any analysis of settlement across the landscape *must* take into consideration the availability of natural resources that necessarily governed settlement choice.

Social pressures must also enter into consideration of settlement location, depending on the politico-economic structures of the inhabitants in question. While access to natural resources will remain crucial, other factors such as defensibility, or easy proximity to long-distance trade routes may also affect settlement location choice. In illustration of the former one may simply look at the location of nearly any Maori *pa* settlement in pre-colonial New Zealand. The Maori people, known for their stellar abilities in warfare, were vitally concerned with protection of territorial lands and resources, and therefore prepared for attack and defense at any time (Davidson 1984). Their palisaded *pa* settlements were typically located on steep-sided hills, rocky promontories, or on any location that afforded them an adequate view of approaching intruders and limited outside access to their homes. Thus, warfare and defense figured heavily into settlement choice in the Maori settlement of the landscape. Similar constraints on settlement choice might be exerted by the desire for easy and immediate access to raw material resources important to trade routes (such as metal ores, obsidian, semi-precious stones, etc.). It would behoove any researcher to carefully consider the practical concerns such as political, economic, and social needs inherent in the decision-making process of choosing a settlement location. However, a functional and rational approach can, and often does, go hand in hand with symbolic considerations whenever humans engage in activities that serve to shape their daily lives. It is crucial to recognize that choices based on both expediency and ideation are powerful actors in the human settlement of the landscape. Thus, a researcher must venture into explanations that extend beyond a practical analysis of the landscape into the matrices of human cognition.

Cognitive Landscapes: Mounds as Matrices

The human-generated mounds decorating the Middle Eastern landscape demand an explanation from archaeologists. In the previous section the more functional, and admittedly more easily traceable, frameworks for interpretation were briefly addressed. However, such strategies can conceivably be considered "group strate-gies for survival," even "commonsensical approaches" to settlement location choice. The question arises as to whether there is something more to the doggedly persis-tent settlement of place than just access to resources and a constantly sought measure of safety. The picture feels incomplete. What in fact is missing are the emo-tional and psychological components of the living, breathing humans who occupied the space on these mounds. As residents began to connect with a "place," living, working, and raising their children on it, how did that place begin to figure into their routine, their beliefs, and their actions? More specifically, what did they think and feel about the entire space (the ground, their house, the surrounding land-scape)? What did it mean to them? Such questions are infinitely more difficult to answer, and consequently require more complicated, less "concrete," explanatory frameworks. However, such avenues of inquiry are filled with potential for under-standing the western Asian prehistoric and early historic landscape.

The "landscape" as "built environment"

There has been a significant amount of important investigation on how the build-ing of structures both shapes human behavior (e.g., Giddens 1984; Wilson 1988; Hodder 1990) and is a reflection of that behavior (e.g., Rapoport 1988; Kent 1990). What is sometimes left out of these equations is the landscape in which the built structure is situated. The archaeological inclination is to focus on the material remains of a domicile and the information about human behavior that can be derived from them. Symbolic meaning may be inferred from tool assemblages and their locations (Rapoport 1990), room layouts (Blanton 1994), or house structure (Waterson 1990). However, the location of that house or village in the overall land-scape is often absent from the explanation of the human behavioral and cognitive networks responsible for the construction of that "built environment." In all likeli-hood, the natural environment, i.e., the landscape, had a crucial influence on pre-historic inhabitants as they "built" their "environments." Indeed, the natural setting may be just as strongly "constructed" an environment as any stone or mudbrick home (Feld and Basso 1996; Zedeño 2000).

The object here, then, will be to present models for understanding mounds of the Middle East from a "nested" perspective: human-constructed environments (houses) in significative and ideational places (mounds), set within the symbolic-cognitive natural environment (landscapes). By recognizing that humans live not just in their houses, but on the landscape that surrounds those houses, we may come even closer to understanding prehistoric human behavioral and cognitive constructs.

Investigatory models

The following discussion offers two approaches to how one might intertwine ma-terial data and ideational approaches to landscape interpretation. The first draws on Middle Eastern historical sources demonstrating the concept of "ownership of place" and its associated property. Extrapolating back in time, a concept of "connection to place" by individuals or within a lineage or kinship group may have induced preceding generations of early farmers to build and rebuild on ancestral land (thereby producing a mound). The second explores the concept of sacred spaces and how such power-filled localities may have influenced settlement patterns and longevity of place in Middle Eastern settings. Although presented as two distinct models and methodologies, aspects of kinship, ancestor, and sacred places may very well have been, and probably were, inextricably tied in the minds of the ancients. The two approaches offered here suggest only two of the many intertwined pathways a researcher might follow to understand the symbolically rich landscape.

Kinship and ancestral lands

What does it mean to "own" something? Most anthropologists can demonstrate that the Western concept of "ownership" is not a universal one. Egalitarian cultures such as the Penan of Borneo or the MButi of Africa have no sense of personal (individual) ownership of goods or places (Turnbull 1962; Davis et al. 1995), while other cultures, usually those practicing a subsistence-based farming and/or herding economy such as the Tsembaga of New Guinea and the Turkana of Kenya, consider ownership of goods and land to be clan or lineage-based, or of a more "corporate" nature (Ingold 1980; Johnson and Earle 1987; Earle 1991; Sanderson 1999:88–94). Decisions regarding the disposition of kin-owned land are corporate in that everyone has a "vote" or at least a right to voice an opinion. Thus an underlying principle of "ownership," or territoriality, exists in such cultures, but the notion of complete and utter control over the administration of land or material goods by an individual is absent.

The Western perception of individual ownership of goods and land, at least as old as classical Greek civilization, became well-ensconced in Western thought through the medieval European land-tenure system (Landes 1999:29–38). However, the concept of private (individual) ownership of land and its association with the Western ideals of power and wealth are found in earlier and more Eastern contexts, calling into question the "Westernness" of this principle. Evidence of individual ownership of land (and goods) is found in textual remains from the towns and cities of the ancient Near East; such texts detail third and second millennium B.C.E. examples of the transmission of land through inheritance and sale from one private individual to another (Alster 1980; Morrison 1987:172–189; Stone 1987; Haring 1998). Though the particulars of ownership were certainly culturally variable (and probably more loosely defined in comparison to the rigid regulations of present-day Western/U.S. private land ownership laws), the premise of individual ownership stretches back in time as much as five millennia, which leads us to ask whether this might be an even more ancient concept in Middle Eastern contexts.

Is it possible that a deeply felt ancestral relationship to a certain place on the earth might be at the root of Middle Eastern mounds? A kin group, clan, or even individual who established a relationship with a particular place, thus grounding identity and integral kin consciousness in that place, would pass such ideology down through the generations (see Chapman 1997 for similar views). In essence, a sense of "ownership" of that place would emerge so that succeeding generations would occupy, protect, and revere that locality. The connection between place and kin group would become so intertwined that the "space," which might include the earth, and that which is in it and on it, would essentially be inherited as the ancestral home. Over the generations, which might stretch into centuries or millennia, that place would see the building and rebuilding of homes. These would grow and contract to accommodate the needs of those inhabiting them, and configurations would change as dictated by the "fashion" of the times. But the essential *place* would never alter. How does one document this in the archaeological record? The model requires a mixture of cross-cultural ethnographic review of mobile and settled peoples' attitudes toward "space," which then must be used to interpret extant Middle Eastern archaeological contexts. With such an approach, a "timeline" of kin-related ancestral connections to place, consequently producing mounds, can be advanced.

Though areas such as southern Mesopotamia were first peopled by subsistence-based farmers and herders, the earliest inhabitants on much of the Middle Eastern landscape were mobile hunters and gatherers. Such residents offer artifactual and ecofactual remains that are minimal and transitory. Although much can be determined from hunter/gatherer lithic scatters and paleofaunal/floral remains (e.g., Hillman et al. 1989; Bar-Yosef 1991), such materials are hardly conducive to providing a framework for interpreting ancestral relationships to place.

A researcher can turn to numerous examples of present-day hunter-gatherers who view the landscape with a sense of territoriality and kinship/ancestral interconnections. Such group interrelationships with a region are found in Australian Aboriginal societies (Tilley 1994:37–54). Numerous studies recount the Australian Aboriginal "Dreaming Myths" (also known as "Dreamtime") that recount the origins of humans, kin/clan groups, and their totemistic ancestors as they either created, or were created from, the landscape (Fullagar and Head 1999; Layton 1999). An excellent example of this is found in Jackson's study of the Walpiri in central Australia (1995). He cites numerous examples of a Walpiri pointing out a feature on the landscape that is intimately twined with his totem's deeds and thus his kin group's history (on this topic see also Smith 1999). In most cases the myths associated with the place are known, in their entirety, only to members of that totem's clan (Jackson 1995). Needless to say, such places are considered the embodiment of the kin group, and members do not stray terribly far from their ancestral locations. If previous centuries had left Australia uncolonized, and the aboriginals had embarked upon a process of semi- or permanent settlement, would not kin groups claim sacred kin-centered landscapes as their "birthrights" with regard to residence?

Similar attitudes of familial relationship to the landscape can be found among the Ju'Hoansi of the African Kalahari Desert (Lee 1984:87–89). The idea of "ownership" amongst the Ju'Hoansi has more of a force of "belonging to" or being "identified with" a place (Wilson 1988:29). In fact, many mobile societies maintain a sense of kin and place: the closer you are to the locality of the kin-based space, the closer your kinship ties with your relatives (Wilson 1988:32–41). Thus, if we extrapolate to the prehistoric past of the ancient Near East, the notion of mobility and yet connectivity to place is not so far-fetched, and is perhaps simply a given. Group mentality of kinship and territory, and even an ancestral (totemistic) relationship to a location can be conjectured. The next step is to trace this connectivity as groups began to visit, revisit, and eventually live upon "their" places.

Without a written record, how can archaeologists possibly trace corporate (kin-based) territorial ownership in the earliest sedentary communities? Fortunately many researchers have undertaken these types of inquiries and have offered solid methodologies for tracing family-based cultural constructs. Ideally, the researcher must first ask how the kinship group is structured and how it expresses itself spatially. This path of inquiry can then be followed up with the investigation of kin-based ownership of *place*; i.e., the intricately woven relationship between family and the locality on which it has chosen to situate itself (for successful applications of such methodologies see Tilley 1996; Bradley 1998; Parker Pearson 1999; Porter 2002). Offered here is only one possible explanatory framework for recognizing the presence of kin-based notions of ownership among mobile foragers turned village inhabitants. Attention is focused not on the *structures* that make up the built environment, but what residents placed *inside, outside,* and *under* them.

A brief examination of mortuary ritual in the earliest (semi-)sedentary habitations of the Near East offers a glimpse into one possible version of the emergent family/land relationship as mobile peoples embarked on semi- or permanent settled life. Of particular interest here is the practice of "ancestor veneration" as expressed in "skull altars" inside homes, and subfloor burials. Such "house-floor burials" are common at early Neolithic sites in Iran and Iraq (Al-Soof 1968; Smith 1972), Abu Hureyra in Syria (Moore et al. 2000), sites in the Levant such as Jericho, 'Ain Ghazal, and Beidha (Kirkbride 1966; Cornwall 1981; Rollefson et al. 1992), and at Anatolian sites such as Çatal Höyük and Mersin (Garstang 1953; Mellaart 1967; Hamilton 1996). Thus, burial under one's house floor, and to some extent, placement of skulls inside houses, can be viewed as fairly prevalent Near Eastern practices. Accordingly, we can ask how such practices might reveal an ancestral relationship to the land. A focused examination of subfloor burials offers the suggestion that ancestral ideation is located *in the land* both symbolically and physically.

The literature on the meaning of "house-floor burials" is extensive, especially with regard to burial goods that accompany the interments. Grave goods are ideal indicators for a plethora of social behavioral patterns including social ranking, territoriality, and even ethnic subgroupings within a population (Henry 1989:202–210; Byrd 1994; and see Kuijt 2000a for discussion and literature review). Burial patterns are fairly consistent with regard to the interment; skeletal remains (sometimes after defleshing) were buried in subfloor or subcourtyard contexts, usually in flexed positions. In addition to the burials themselves, scholarly interest has been piqued by specialized treatments of the skeletal remains or inclusions of anthropomorphic plaster figurines in the burials or caches (see Kuijt and Chesson, this volume). In Anatolia, at the site of Çatal Höyük, the skulls of some of the individuals in the subfloor group burials had been painted with red, green, or blue pigments (Mellaart 1967:206–208); examples of more spectacular treatments of skeletal remains, particularly skulls, come from sites across the Levant (see Cauvin 1972 and Kuijt 2000b for discussion and examples). In these cases skulls are removed from the rest of the remains and either interred separately, often painted, or in an eerie prescience of modern forensic anthropology, modeled plaster was placed on the skull, in essence "remaking" the face of the deceased, with facial characteristics then applied with paint or shells (Kenyon 1985:38–39; Rollefson and Simmons 1987). In some cases skulls were then exhibited *inside* the house, on what might be termed pedestals, or even "altars" (see Kuijt 2000b for numerous examples of skull treatments).

Explanation of these burial and skull treatments ranges from the placing of them as representative of a death cult or ancestor veneration (Kenyon 1985:34–38), or as ghost expulsion or evocation devices (Scurlock 1995), to their identification as representatives of gods and goddesses (Schmandt-Besserat 1998). While any of these might be equally plausible, most scholars interpret these ritual burials as indicative of ancestor veneration (but see Verhoeven, this volume). Burial of the corporeal ancestral remains, treatment of skull, and burial of plaster statues (after, it might be conjectured, some ritual has imbued the statue with the essence/soul/identity of the dead ancestor), were apparently chosen by these early settlers as proper methods of recognizing their descent from those who came before. The placement of these forbears under or in the abode cleaves their ancestral power and protectiveness to those continuing the line. But it also establishes the ancestral line *in that place*. Possession of that particular locality is established not only by the presence of the living, but the presence of the dead as well. It would be a very brave usurper, or more likely an ignorant non-resident, who would take such a place from the "rightful" owners and thus risk the wrath of the ancestral protectors of lineage and place.

One of the most spectacular discoveries at 'Ain Ghazal in Jordan were caches of plaster figurines. These anthropomorphic statues, with painted faces, were made to stand on a platform or base (Rollefson 1986:45–47; Rollefson and Simmons 1987:43). Few would dispute the excavator's suggestion that these statues were representative of ritual-based activities; more specifically he suggests that "these two types of statues [some standing 90 cm high, some half that height] indicate a two-tiered religious hierarchy, one in which the larger statues fulfilled more important and most likely public functions, while the busts represent more specific, perhaps kin-related functions" (Rollefson and Simmons 1987:43). What is of particular interest to the discussion here is that the excavator notes that these statues appear at a time of unanticipated agricultural abundance at 'Ain Ghazal. This early farming village was so successful in its agricultural production that the population began to expand tremendously, in part due to newly arrived settlers (Rollefson and Simmons 1987:43–44). Is it possible, then, that the well-established inhabitants felt it necessary to demonstrate possession of their portion of the landscape not just through the subfloor burial of ancestors, but with the above-ground physical representation of those ancestors? As the population rose, and more settlers needed to establish residences, the desire to firmly embed the notion of "ownership of place," well-rooted in the veil of protectiveness exerted by the ancestors, may have resulted in rituals imbuing ancestral powers not just in the dead who rested beneath the floors, but in the symbolic representation of those ancestors in statuary stationed above the floor. Such powerful imagery would certainly cause a newcomer to think twice before trying to rout out a long-time resident, living or dead.

The concept of ancestral protectors of family land is commonly found in societies that practice both sedentary and mobile lifestyles. Though more commonly associated with societies that feel pressure to protect lines of inheritance and maintain societal divisions between kin-groups and power-structures, there is reason to believe that there exists a "universality of ancestor worship" among all cultures, past and present (Steadman et al. 1996). The conceptual approach to ancestor recognition is as diverse as the cultural spectrum; cultures such as the Wape of New Guinea rely on ancestors to protect kin-based hunting territories (Mitchell 1987), villages in Madagascar must maintain ancestral tombs in the village center or suffer the consequences, including human death and village destruction (Graeber 1998). In Near Eastern contexts, therefore, the placement of one's ancestor under the floor, whether skeletal remains or plaster representative, and ancestral altar with skull within the home, accomplishes two elements of action and effect: the burial identifies the place as the property of the kin-group that occupies it, and the maintenance of the altar and burials ensures continued ancestral protection of place and descendants who rightfully inhabit that place (as long as the residents faithfully maintain their ritual obligations).

As time carried on and generations of that kin group inhabited their place, the claim to a sacrosanct ownership of property would have become linked in the minds of all inhabitants. In essence, the identity of person would have become inextricably bound with the locality of her place in the settlement or on the landscape. When such a strong tie is built between person and place, it is not surprising to see generations and centuries pass with a dogged persistence of stasis with regard to residential location – the lifeblood of mound formation. The concept of ownership, now deeply embedded in the minds of the residents of these places, was transformed from a symbolic relationship with the ancestors who lived *in* the place, to a more legalistic and market-based ownership of a commodity – one that could be sold, rented, or traded, as has been traced in texts such as those described above.

Certainly the preceding discussion is not the culminating explanation of the human behavioral practices that led to the long-inhabited villages, towns, and cities of western Asia. It is rather but one example of how a researcher might employ a noetic approach in combination with material culture analysis to yield an explanation of the intersection between territory, place, kinship, and ancestor as a cognitive framework for understanding mounds across the Middle Eastern landscape.

The sacred landscape

An alternative cognitive approach offers the opportunity to view the landscape as one filled not only with ancestors, but with the more overtly spiritual and sacred as well. Quite possibly the landscape, or more accurately places on the landscape, signified powerful meaning for those choosing residence there. That the landscape represented a matrix of cosmological meaning for prehistoric inhabitants is an attractive, and even likely, scenario. As mobile foragers settled into farming or herding societies, a cosmological landscape may have guided their decision for settlement location and longevity of place.

Such perceptions of landscape studies may have substantial coincidence with more functional considerations for settlement and permanency. The key is to identify the "markers" on that cosmological and thus sacred landscape as they factored in the human behavioral construct of settlement choice. In order to interpret tell settlement as a product of the residents' belief system, the investigator must first recognize the existence of a multi-dimensional sacred landscape in the prehistoric past. A researcher seeking the prehistoric sacred landscape would find Tim Ingold's views quite helpful: "[the landscape] is not 'land', it is not 'nature', and it is not 'space'," but rather, "through living in it, the landscape becomes a part of us, just as we are a part of it" (1993:153, 154). That people perceive their landscapes as living beings, and that they themselves are *part* of those entities, is a commonly understood notion among anthropologists studying present-day non-Western cultures. However, all too often researchers are reluctant to carry such conceptual frameworks into the past as they attempt to divine the answers to settlement practices and behavioral constructs. Because we have no living informants, or oral traditions, to recount the mythologies of the landscape, archaeologists do not automatically consider manifestations of a sacred landscape as a prime mover in occupation and interaction with the land (economic, ritual, or otherwise). Nonetheless, it is not at all unlikely that the mobile inhabitants of the prehistoric Near East believed the landscape to be alive beneath their feet: that the winds originated from the breaths of the spirits, rivers and streams flowed from their lifeblood, and the mountains and valleys were contours of their corporeal forms.

There is ample evidence to suggest that a culture's mythology is instrumental in the decision-making processes involved in settlement choice and continued permanency. Several recent volumes focus on the sacrality of the landscape (Carmichael et al. 1994; Feld and Basso 1996; Ashmore and Knapp 1999). Such a cognitive approach would include a phase-based research agenda for understanding the prehistoric sacred landscape: (1) recognition of the presence of landscape features that might have held spiritual significance for ancient inhabitants and acknowledgement that such places served as matrices of power; (2) evaluation of the use of the landscape, and the settlement itself, for clues to document the existence of a sacred landscape as a determinant in settlement choice and longevity of place; (3) interpretation of the significance of those landscape matrices of spirituality within the cosmography of the prehistoric inhabitants of that locality.

The first step, identifying significative landscape features, is certainly the most straightforward. Recent research has already offered a type of "categorization" of potentially sacred landscape features (Tilley 1994; Taçon 1999:37; Crumley 1999). Among these are mountains and valleys (Brady and Ashmore 1999), forests, trees, or places with specialized vegetation (Parker Pearson et al. 1999), places with natural water flows (Taçon 1999), and locations with unusual features such as a cave or a jutting high place, perhaps offering a far-reaching view (Theodoratus and LaPena 1994; Saunders 1994). Particularly powerful are locations at which any of these features intersect (Carmichael 1994:92; Taçon 1999:37).

Across the Middle Eastern landscape, whether the Anatolian plateau, the Levantine littoral, or the alluvium of Mesopotamia, topographical features such as natural rises, fresh water sources, vegetational oddities, and caves and rock shelters, should capture the researcher's interest. Such features have already been discussed as crucial to functional and rational considerations when choosing a settlement location. However, there is no reason why these topographic features were not also part of a "living," sacred landscape to which the inhabitants saw themselves as inextricably tied. Thus, a researcher's "first step" in recognizing a sacred landscape is to search the region for likely nodes of intersection between human cognition of the sacred and the human-built environment. Such localities may be as dramatic as a mountain peak or as understated as an unusual rock formation. The challenge is to recognize the significance of that place to those who occupied the landscape centuries or millennia before.

The identification of potentially critical features in the surrounding landscape allows the researcher to next consider the location of the settlement within that landscape and the material culture within that settlement. A close evaluation of clues to a prehistoric cosmology is indeed fraught with difficulties, but essential. At times such clues are so vivid they nearly strike the archaeologist in the face: the animal motifs, and even more specifically, the wall-painting of a village nestled against a volcano, at Çatal Höyük (Mellaart 1967:176), the Palaeolithic European cave paintings, or the female figurines found in Bronze Age Minoan contexts, are examples of what might be termed remains with "obvious" ritual meaning. However, the presence of such material remains does not necessarily make the job of interpreting religious meaning *pro forma*, they simply give researchers more overt data to work with, and indeed, argue over. In other cases, material remains are far more ambiguous and identifying them even as bearing ritual import is problematic. It is sometimes more profitable to focus not on the artifactual remains but on the settlement itself.

The built environment often harbors ritual meanings embodied in room, house, and even village layout and orientation. The Tukanoans of Amazonia, for instance, construct their malocas (longhouses) to reflect "the nested imagery of womb and child, compartment and family, longhouse and community"; the dwelling itself emulates the structure of the cosmos embodied in the Tukanoan belief system

(Hugh-Jones 1995:233–234). The Tewa of the American Southwest construct villages that reproduce their cosmos, including orientation to cardinal directionality and representation of landscape features (i.e., mountains, rivers, etc.), all carefully relating creation myths and sacred stories (Tilley 1994:63–66; Snead and Preucel 1999). Thus, the built environment itself, including its very construction materials, decoration, orientation, and layout, can instruct the researcher regarding the sacred landscape and its interconnections with those who inhabit it.

The previous examples show that an intimate knowledge of the occupying culture's cosmology is, of course, enormously helpful, but it is not necessarily imperative. An example of understanding the settlement in the context of its landscape comes from my own project in central Turkey. Çadır Höyük is a 33m tall mound, situated on a natural rise above a river valley surrounded by gentle hills. The settlement offers occupational remains spanning the Late Chalcolithic to Byzantine period, with few gaps in this long sequence of habitation. The remains that are of particular interest to the present study are those from the Late Chalcolithic where we have carried out our most extensive excavations (Gorny et al. 1999, 2000, 2002). The Late Chalcolithic inhabitants of Çadır Höyük, based on our paleobotanical and paleozoological reports, practiced a mixed farming and herding lifestyle; it appears that settlement, from the earliest known occupation (ca. 5200 B.C.E.), was year-round. Previous studies of these remains have offered methods for interpreting the architecture, inter- and intra-room spatial analysis, and long-distance trade connections (Steadman 1995, 2000). It is in the preparation of my contribution to this volume that my investigation turns in earnest to the consideration of the settlement's placement in its larger landscape.

A practical analysis of the location offers some easily recognizable selection choices: Çadır rests at the confluence of two rivers, the Egri Su and the Kanak Su; it is surrounded by arable lands that would also have supported grazing; the site lies near or on a trade route heavily used in the Bronze Age, and perhaps in earlier periods as well. Also of interest is the decision of Çadır's first inhabitants to settle on a natural rise; though initial explanations might suggest defense as a factor, there is, as yet, no evidence to support this interpretation. The decision to settle on the bedrock outcropping may simply reflect a desire to avoid wasting valuable arable land, as well as to offer residents a pleasant view of the countryside. However, taking a step beyond practical matters of settlement choice guides me to acknowledge the prominence of a conically-shaped peak rising from behind the lower hills southeast of the site. This peak, today known as Çaltepe, is the highest elevation visible to the residents of Çadır. I note it here because it may have played a role in the original and successive Late Chalcolithic settlements at the site. The original inhabitants, presumably faced with a choice with regard to orientation of the village, chose a southeast/northwest axis in direct line with the rise of Çaltepe peak. The rectangular homes, pathways, and at least some doorways, are oriented so that ingress and egress offer views of this natural monument. Two other architectural features at the site are also built on this orientation, possibly with this peak in mind: the impressive stone gateway into the settlement faces Çaltepe, and an enigmatic stepped platform leading to what may have been a "high place" or even a structure more overtly ritual in nature (unfortunately, the destination of the stepped platform was destroyed by erosion and a later Hittite house), appears built with Çaltepe in mind.

The very brief description of architectural features and orientation at Çadır is inadequate to give the reader a clear understanding of the Late Chalcolithic settlement; rather, the intention was to provide a glimpse into the avenues of investigation the present author might follow with regard to identifying the role a sacred landscape may have played in Çadıran settlement choice and stasis of place. Though fresh water must have been of crucial importance to the earliest settlers, it was the high place on the landscape that commanded their attention. Mountains, not caves, earth, or water, may be the focus of my future investigations. Thus, the identification of features that, in ancient times, may have been imbued with sacrality, paves the road to the third and final step in this phased research design.

This "third step" is, by far, the most daunting. Seemingly it requires a giant leap of faith, or perhaps to put it more prosaically, a rather active imagination. When presented with a mountain, a water source, or perhaps a cave, without an explanatory framework in place, the researcher would be free to develop any number of ideas about the meaning of these features in a prehistoric cosmology. However, there are, in fact, interpretive models that can help the researcher anchor her reconstruction of prehistoric belief systems in more data-driven hypotheses. These methods rely first and foremost on one's familiarity with the culture: an understanding of the basic economy, an awareness of the material culture, and knowledge about architectural layouts and functions of buildings are all essential. Secondly, theoretical frameworks that include ethnographic components and methodologies for interpreting belief systems can provide a supportable intersection between landscape and cosmology (e.g., Brady and Ashmore 1999; Snead and Preucel 1999; Fullagar and Head 1999).

At the outset the researcher must bring the willingness to apply more cognitive-symbolically based interpretations to artifactual remains that might otherwise spend their lives in a utilitarian framework of explanation. For instance, the warclubs of the North American Winnebago culture are, indeed, used for war, but they also represent symbolically the culture's two major moieties (earth and sky), through the stylized designs of constellatory systems carved on the warclubs (Hall 1989). In the same vein, obsidian in Neolithic Anatolia may be viewed as more than just a valuable material for tool construction. Hasan Dağ, probably the mountain painted on the wall of one of the Çatal Höyük structures (shrines?), is represented as part of the landscape in which the settlement is situated. Clearly the artist meant to symbolize the importance of this peak to the village, possibly because of its valuable resource, obsidian. Obsidian was a vital component to Çatal's economy, and it is not a terrific stretch of the imagination to suspect that more symbolic interpretations should be piggy-backed onto the more utilitarian interpretations of its use.

But what did Hasan Dağ mean to the Çatalians, or Çaltepe to the Çadırans, or the other landscape features so prominent visually yet so intransigent to interpretation? It is here that one must turn to the work of one's colleagues and to models that have generated guidelines that may point toward elusive solutions to one's questions. The selection of appropriate research ranges from studies so broadly based that their explanations offer pan-cultural approaches, while others are so specific to peculiar circumstances that they are useful to perhaps a single investigator.

Examples of more broadly conceived explanatory frameworks include the compendia of research accomplished on the subjects of gender-based religions using evidence such as human figurines, environmental settings, and economic pursuits. Such studies explore possible connections between agriculture and the female principle, and animal husbandry as a male pursuit (see Sanday 1981 and Bowie 2000 for summaries of research; also Kuijt and Chessson, this volume). Already touched upon is the extensive literature on the relationship between domicile, cosmology, and perception of landscape. It is with astonishing frequency that inhabitants build their environments to mirror, symbolically, their cosmographical perception of the larger landscape (e.g., Bourdieu 1977; Hugh-Jones 1979; Hodder 1990). Perhaps of even greater use to the individual researcher might be studies that focus on particular elements within cultural settings. Such specific studies have become plentiful within the last decade as volumes devoted to the archaeology of landscape (Parker Pearson and Richards 1994; Carmichael et al. 1994; Hirsch and O'Hanlon 1995; Ashmore and Knapp 1999; Ucko and Layton 1999) have appeared. Contained within this vast literature, advanced by scholars who have opened themselves to the cognitive past, are potential clues to the meaning of mounds rising across a sacred landscape.

The researcher, faced with a landscape that demands interpretation, must commence upon that endeavor. However, the starting point in completing the "third step" of the phase-based research outlined above is far from clear. Is it best to begin with the notable landscape features, employ the archaeo-history of the region, and attempt to intuit their meaning? In other words, the researcher chooses an inductive approach that focuses specifically on a particular region's landscape, features, and inhabitants. Who better to rebuild the symbolic landscape, in essence "from the ground up," than the archaeologist who is intimate with every extant scrap her culture left behind. From those scraps we build the actions, and the thoughts behind the actions, of those who lived before. This is precisely the method I used in the preliminary interpretation of the Çaltepe peak at Çadır Höyük.

Based on my years of work at Çadır Höyük, in combination with my research interests, I can certainly say I came by my interpretations honestly. My interests in landscape archaeology had led me to explore how other researchers attempted to explain their landscapes. Many of these works are referenced in this chapter; they are not limited to the Middle East but span the Americas, Asia, and Africa. Thus, the natural inclination of the *re*searcher, i.e., to re*search*, provides the background necessary to engage in the investigation of one's own particular setting. In other words, the cumulative data from cross-cultural investigation allowed for a general beginning, and then narrowed to a specific interpretation of a particular landscape feature located within the context of the culture with which I am most familiar. However, the question here is not what my own methodology was, but rather, what is the "*correct*" methodology to pursue? Or, even further, is there a correct methodology at all?

An answer to the proposed question(s) is, of course, impossible. Nor is it feasible to review all the theoretical models that would act as the perfect complement to a researcher's attempts to unravel the secrets embedded in the ancient inhabitants' landscape. The closest to suggesting a "methodology" that this particular study can come is to report that the process employed by the author seemed the most productive at Çadır. Thus, one reviews cross-cultural approaches, in conjunction with an inductively (hermeneutically) based investigation of features of the landscape that coincide with one's perceived sensibilities, nationalities, ideations, and beliefs of the past culture who inhabited that landscape.

Indeed, it is the quest for answers that drives us to uncover the past and reassemble it into a complete picture. It is quite possible, even likely, that a researcher may never satisfactorily (with regard to her own expectations) fully achieve the most difficult third step in modeling a sacred landscape. The appearance of a full-fledged cosmology reported in a site report, and written as if an informant sat for hours as the tape-recorder ran, would most likely be met with suspicion and even derision. The line between data-based inference and utter imagination must be carefully drawn and assiduously followed. However, it should never be doubted that spirituality and mysticism most probably played a significant role in the settlement practices and indeed in the remarkable stasis of place that created mounds as matrices of meaning across a sacred landscape.

Conclusions

Middle Eastern mounds contain secrets to the past that will never be unearthed. The fact that these secrets may be conceptual rather than material in nature makes our work even more daunting. Ancestors and spirits may have been far from the minds of prehistoric inhabitants as they chose to settle and remain on a portion of soil for decades, centuries, millennia. But we, as the illuminators of the past, have spent too long envisioning mindless and faceless figures making decisions based purely on survivability and practicality. The past that we study was created by actors who thought about, emoted over, and believed in the natural world around them in terms that must have reached far beyond the functional. As we stretch our own minds beyond the functional, into the cognitive, we will surely be led to places that allow us to view those actors as living, breathing, *thinking* beings whose homes high atop a human-made hill evoked deeply-felt faith and emotion as they carried out their daily lives. To connect with even a fraction of that perception of the living landscape moves us exponentially forward as we carry out our roles as elucidators of those who made the past, for those who inhabit the present.

REFERENCES

Al-Soof, Behnam Abu, 1968 Tell Es-Sawwan Excavations of the Fourth Season. Sumer 24:3–16.

Alster, Bendt, ed., 1980 Death in Mesopotamia: XXVIe Rencontre Assyriologique Internationale. Copenhagen: Akademisk Forlag.

Ashmore, Wendy, and A. Bernard Knapp, eds., 1999 Archaeologies of Landscape: Contemporary Perspectives. Oxford: Blackwell.

Bar-Yosef, Ofer, 1991 Stone Tools and Social Context in Levantine Prehistory. In Perspectives on the Past: Theoretical Biases in Mediterranean Hunter-Gatherer Research. Geoffrey A. Clark, ed. pp. 371–395. Philadelphia: University of Pennsylvania Press.

Blanton, Richard E., 1994 Houses and Households, a Comparative Study. New York: Plenum.

Bourdieu, Pierre, 1977 Outline of a Theory of Practice. Cambridge: Cambridge University Press.

Bowie, Fiona, 2000 The Anthropology of Religion. Oxford: Blackwell.

Bradley, Richard, 1998 The Significance of Monuments: On the Shaping of Human Experience in Neolithic and Bronze Age Europe. London: Routledge.

Brady, James E., and Wendy Ashmore, 1999 Mountains, Caves, Water: Ideational Landscapes of the Ancient Maya. In Archaeologies of Landscape. Wendy Ashmore and A. Bernard Knapp, eds. pp. 124–145. Oxford: Blackwell.

Byrd, Brian F., 1994 Public and Private, Domestic and Corporate: The Emergence of the Southwest Asian Village. American Antiquity 59:639–666.

Carmichael, David L., Jane Hubert, Brian Reeves, and Audhild Schanche, eds., 1994 Sacred Sites, Sacred Places. London: Routledge.

Carmichael, David L., 1994 Places of Power: Mescalero Apache Sacred Sites and Sensitive Areas. In Sacred Sites, Sacred Places. David L. Carmichael, Jane Hubert, Brian Reeves, and Audhild Schanche, eds. pp. 89–98. London: Routledge.

Cauvin, Jacques, 1972 Religions néolithiques de Syro-Palestine. Paris: Maison-neuve.

Chang, Kwang-Chih, ed., 1968 Settlement Archaeology. Palo Alto: National Press Books.

Chapman, John, 1997 The Origins of Tells in Eastern Hungary. In Neolithic Landscapes. Peter Topping, ed. pp. 139–164. Oxbow Monographs 86. Oxford: Oxbow.

Cornwall, Ian W., 1981 The Pre-Pottery Neolithic Burials. In Excavations at Jericho, vol. 3. Thomas A. Holland, ed. pp. 395–406. London: British School of Archaeology in Jerusalem.

Cosgrove, Dennis, 1995 Landscapes and Myths, Gods and Humans. In Landscape: Politics and Perspectives. Barbara Bender, ed. pp. 281–305. Oxford: Berg.

Crumley, Carol L., 1999 Sacred Landscapes: Constructed and Conceptualized. In Archaeologies of Landscape. Wendy Ashmore and A. Bernard Knapp, eds. pp. 269–276. Oxford: Blackwell.

Davidson, Janet, 1984 The Prehistory of New Zealand. Auckland: Longman Paul.

Davis, Wade, Ian Mackenzie, and Shane Kennedy, 1995 Nomads of the Dawn: The Penan of the Borneo Rain Forest. San Francisco: Pomegranate.

Earle, Timothy, 1991 Property Rights and the Evolution of Chiefdoms. In Chiefdoms: Power, Economy, and Ideology. Timothy Earle, ed. pp. 71–99. Cambridge: Cambridge University Press.

Feld, Steven, and Keith H. Basso, eds., 1996 Senses of Place. Santa Fe: School of American Research.

Field, David, 1997 The Landscape of Extraction: Aspects of the Procurement of Raw Material in the Neolithic. In Neolithic Landscapes. Peter Topping, ed. pp. 55–67. Oxford: Oxbow Books.

Fletcher, Roland, 1995 The Limits of Settlement Growth: A Theoretical Outline. Cambridge: Cambridge University Press.

Fullagar, Richard, and Lesley Head, 1999 Exploring the Prehistory of Hunter-Gatherer Attachments to Place: An Example from the Keep River Area, Northern Territory, Australia. *In* The Archaeology and Anthropology of Landscape: Shaping your Landscape. Peter J. Ucko and Robert Layton, eds. pp. 322–335. London: Routledge.

Garstang, John., 1953 Prehistoric Mersin: Yümük Tepe in Southern Turkey. Oxford: Clarendon.

Giddens, Anthony, 1984 The Constitution of Society: Outline of the Theory of Structuration. Berkeley: University of California Press.

Gorny, Ronald L., Gregory McMahon, Samuel Paley, and Sharon Steadman, 2000 The 1999 Season at Çadır Höyük. Anatolica 26:153–171.

Gorny, Ronald L., Gregory McMahon, Samuel Paley, Sharon Steadman, and Bruce Verhaaren, 1999 The 1998 Alisar Regional Project Season. Anatolica 25:149–183.

Gorny, Ronald L., Gregory McMahon, Samuel Paley, Sharon Steadman, and Bruce Verhaaren, 2002 The 2000 and 2001 Seasons at Çadır Höyük in Central Turkey: A Preliminary Report. Anatolica 28:109–136.

Graeber, David, 1998 Dancing with Corpses Reconsidered: An Interpretation of *Famidihana* (in Arivonimamo, Madagascar). *In* Religion in Culture and Society. John R. Bowen, ed. pp. 69–93. Boston: Allyn and Bacon.

Hall, Robert L., 1989 The Material Symbols of the Winnebago Sky and Earth Moieties. *In* The Meanings of Things: Material Culture and Symbolic Expression. Ian Hodder, ed. pp. 178–184. London: Unwin Hyman.

Hamilton, Naomi, 1996 Figurines, Clay Balls, Small Finds and Burials. *In* On the Surface: Çatalhöyük 1993–95. Ian Hodder, ed. pp. 215–263. Cambridge and London: McDonald Institute for Archaeological Research and British Institute of Archaeology at Ankara.

Haring, B., 1998 Access to Land by Institutions and Individuals in Ramesside Egypt (Nineteenth and Twentieth Dynasties; 1294–1070 BC). *In* Landless and Hungry? B. Haring and R. de Maaijer, eds. pp. 74–89. Leiden: CNWS.

Henry, Donald O., 1989 From Foraging to Agriculture: The Levant at the End of the Ice Age. Philadelphia: University of Pennsylvania Press.

Hillman, Gordon C., Susan Colledge, and David R. Harris, 1989 Plant-food Economy during the Epipalaeolithic Period at Tell Abu Hureyra, Syria: Dietary Diversity, Seasonality, and Modes of Exploitation. *In* Foraging and Farming: The Evolution of Plant Exploitation. David R. Harris and Gordon C. Hillman, eds. pp. 240–268. London: Unwin Hyman.

Hirsch, Eric, and O'Hanlon, Michael, eds., 1995 The Anthropology of Landscape. Oxford: Clarendon.

Hodder, Ian, 1990 The Domestication of Europe. Oxford: Basil Blackwell.

Hugh-Jones, Christine, 1979 From the Milk River: Spatial and Temporal Processes in Northwest Amazonia. London: Cambridge University Press.

Hugh-Jones, Stephen, 1995 Inside-out and Back-to-front: The Androgynous House in Northwest Amazonia. *In* About the House: Lévi-Strauss and Beyond. Janet Carsten and Stephen Hugh-Jones, eds. pp. 226–252. Cambridge: Cambridge University Press.

Ingold, Tim, 1980 Hunters, Pastoralists and Ranchers. Cambridge: Cambridge University Press.

Ingold, Tim, 1993 The Temporality of the Landscape. World Archaeology 25:152–174.

Jackson, Michael, 1995 At Home in the World. Durham, NC: Duke University Press.

Johnson, Allen, and Timothy Earle, 1987 The Evolution of Human Societies. Stanford: Stanford University Press.

Kent, Susan, 1990 A Cross-cultural Study of Segmentation, Architecture, and the Use of Space. *In* Domestic Architecture and the Use of Space. Susan Kent, ed. pp. 127–152. Cambridge: Cambridge University Press.

Kenyon, Kathleen M., 1985 Archaeology in the Holy Land. 5th edition. New York: Thomas Nelson Publishers.

Kirkbride, Diana, 1966 Five Seasons at the Pre-pottery Neolithic Village of Beidha in Jordan. Palestine Exploration Quarterly 98:8–72.

Kostof, Spiro, 1991 The City Shaped: Urban Patterns and Meanings Through History. Boston: Little, Brown, and Co.

Kuijt, Ian, 2000a Keeping the Peace: Ritual, Skull Caching, and Community Integration in the Levantine Neolithic. *In* Life in Neolithic Farming Communities: Social Organization, Identity, and Differentiation. Ian Kuijt, ed. pp. 137–164. New York: Plenum.

Kuijt, Ian, ed., 2000b Life in Neolithic Farming Communities: Social Organization, Identity, and Differentiation. New York: Plenum.

Landes, David S., 1999 The Wealth and Poverty of Nations. New York: Norton.

Layton, Robert, 1999 The Alawa Totemic Landscape; Ecology, Religion and Politics. *In* The Archaeology and Anthropology of Landscape: Shaping your Landscape. Peter J. Ucko and Robert Layton, eds. pp. 219–239. London: Routledge.

Lee, Richard, 1984 The Dobe !Kung. Fort Worth: Holt, Rinehart, and Winston.

Lloyd, Seton, 1980 Foundations in the Dust: The Story of Mesopotamian Exploration. Revised edition. London: Thames and Hudson.

Mellaart, James, 1967 Çatal Hüyük: A Neolithic Town in Anatolia. New York: McGraw-Hill.

Mitchell, William E., 1987 The Bamboo Fire: Fieldwork with the New Guinea Wape. 2nd edition. Prospect Heights, IL: Waveland Press.

Moore, Andrew M. T., Gordon C. Hillman, and Anthony J. Legge, 2000 Village on the Euphrates: From Foraging to Farming at Abu Hureyra. Oxford: Oxford University Press.

Morrison, Martha A., 1987 The Southwest Archives at Nuzi. *In* Studies on the Civilization and Culture of Nuzi and the Hurrians, vol. 2. David I. Owen and Martha A. Morrison, eds. pp. 167–201. Winona Lake: Eisenbrauns.

Parker Pearson, Michael, 1999 The Archaeology of Death and Burial. College Station: Texas A & M University Press.

Parker Pearson, Michael, and Colin Richards, eds., 1994 Architecture and Order: Approaches to Social Space. London: Routledge.

Parker Pearson, Michael, Ramilisonina, and Retsihisatse, 1999 Ancestors, Forests and Ancient Settlements: Tandroy Readings of the Archaeological Past. *In* The Archaeology and Anthropology of Landscape. Peter J. Ucko and Robert Layton, eds. pp. 397–410. New York: Routledge.

Porter, Ann, 2002 The Dynamics of Death, Ancestors, Pastoralism, and the Origins of a Third-millennium City in Syria. Bulletin of the American Schools of Oriental Research 325:1–36.

Rapoport, Amos, 1988 Levels of Meaning in the Built Environment. *In* Cross-Cultural Perspectives in Non-verbal Communication. Fernando Poyatos, ed. pp. 317–336. Toronto: Hogrefe.

Rapoport, Amos, 1990 Systems of Activities and Systems of Settings. *In* Domestic Architecture and the Use of Space. Susan Kent, ed. pp. 9–20. Cambridge: Cambridge University Press.

Rollefson, Gary O., 1986 Neolithic 'Ain Ghazal (Jordan): Ritual and Ceremony II. Paléorient 12/1:45–52.

Rollefson, Gary O., and Alan H. Simmons, 1987 The Life and Death of 'Ain Ghazal. Archaeology 40:38–45.

Rollefson, Gary O., Alan H. Simmons, and Zeidan Kafafi, 1992 Neolithic Cultures at 'Ain
Ghazal, Jordan. Journal of Field Archaeology 19:443–471.

Rykwert, Joseph, 1976 The Idea of a Town: The Anthropology of Urban Form in Rome, Italy
and the Ancient World. Cambridge, MA: MIT Press.

Sanday, Peggy R., 1981 Female Power and Male Dominance: On the Origins of Sexual
Inequality. Cambridge: Cambridge University Press.

Sanderson, Stephen K., 1999 Social Transformations: A General Theory of Historical Development. New York: Rowman and Littlefield.

Saunders, Nicholas J., 1994 At the Mouth of the Obsidian Cave: Deity and Place in Aztec
Religion. In Sacred Sites, Sacred Places. David L. Carmichael, Jane Hubert, Brian
Reeves, and Audhild Schanche, eds. pp. 172–183. London: Routledge.

Schmandt-Besserat, Denise, 1998 'Ain Ghazal 'Monumental Figures'. Bulletin of the
American Schools of Oriental Research 310:1–17.

Scurlock, Joanne A., 1995 Magical Uses of Ancient Mesopotamian Festivals of the Dead. In
Ancient Magic and Ritual Power. Marvin Meyer and Paul Mirecki, eds. pp. 93–107.
Religions in the Graeco-Roman World 8. Leiden: Brill.

Smith, Claire, 1999 Ancestors, Place and People: Social Landscapes in Aboriginal Australia.
In The Archaeology and Anthropology of Landscape. Peter J. Ucko and Robert Layton,
eds. pp. 189–218. New York: Routledge.

Smith, Philip E. L., 1972 Ganj Dareh Tepe. Iran 10:165–168.

Snead, James E., and Robert W. Preucel, 1999 The Ideology of Settlement: Ancestral Keres
Landscapes in the Northern Rio Grande. In Archaeologies of Landscape: Contempo-
rary Perspectives. Wendy Ashmore and A. Bernard Knapp, eds. pp. 169–197. Oxford:
Blackwell.

Steadman, Lyle B., Craig T. Palmer, and Christopher F. Tilley, 1996 The Universality of
Ancestor Worship. Ethnology 35:63–76.

Steadman, Sharon R., 1995 Prehistoric Interregional Interaction in Anatolia and the
Balkans: An Overview. Bulletin of the American Schools of Oriental Research 299/300:
13–32.

Steadman, Sharon R., 2000 Spatial Patterning and Social Complexity on Prehistoric Near
Eastern 'Tell' Sites: Models for Mounds. Journal of Anthropological Archaeology
19:164–199.

Stone, Elizabeth C., 1987 Nippur Neighborhoods. Studies in Ancient Oriental Civilization
44. Chicago: Oriental Institute, University of Chicago.

Taçon, Paul S. C., 1999 Identifying Ancient Sacred Landscapes in Australia: From Physical
to Social. In Archaeologies of Landscape. Wendy Ashmore and A. Bernard Knapp, eds.
pp. 33–57. Oxford: Blackwell.

Theodoratus, Dorothea J., and Frank LaPena, 1994 Wintu Sacred Geography of Northern
California. In Sacred Sites, Sacred Places. David L. Carmichael, Jane Hubert, Brian
Reeves, and Audhild Schanche, eds. pp. 20–31. London: Routledge.

Tilley, Chistopher, 1994 A Phenomenology of Landscape: Places, Paths and Monuments.
Oxford: Berg.

Tilley, Christopher, 1996 An Ethnography of the Neolithic. Cambridge: Cambridge
University Press.

Turnbull, Colin M., 1962 The Forest People. New York: Simon and Schuster.

Ucko, Peter J., and Robert Layton, eds., 1999 The Archaeology and Anthropology of
Landscape. London: Routledge.

Waterson, Roxanna, 1990 The Living House: The Anthropology of Architecture in South-East Asia. Oxford: Oxford University Press.

Wilson, Peter J., 1988 The Domestication of the Human Species. New Haven: Yale University Press.

Zedeño, Maria N., 2000 On What People Make of Places: A Behavioral Cartography. *In* Social Theory in Archaeology. Michael B. Schiffer, ed. pp. 97–111. Salt Lake City: University of Utah Press.

15

Archaeology and Texts in the Ancient Near East

Paul Zimansky

From its infancy as a discipline, archaeology in the Middle East has been intimately tied to the written record. Inscriptions were among the first artifacts from Mesopotamia and Iran brought to the attention of early modern Europe by travelers, whose interests were inspired in the first place by a text[1] *par excellence* – the Bible. When excavations were initiated in Mesopotamia in the 1840s and 1850s, they produced a flood of tablets and monumental inscriptions that facilitated the decipherment of Akkadian and led to the identification of additional hitherto unknown languages and cultures such as Elamite, Urartian, Hurrian, and Sumerian.[2] When George Smith announced the discovery of a Mesopotamian flood story in 1873 (Lloyd 1980:146) many saw cuneiform as a window on the most remote periods of the past, if not on the origins of humanity itself. Although this illusion was gradually undermined by advances in geology and evolutionary biology, finding tablets remained one of the primary objectives of archaeology in the ancient Orient.

The extent to which this was a priority is revealed in a controversy that took place in the late 1880s among the planners of America's first overseas field project in the Middle East, the University of Pennsylvania's Nippur expedition. Its epigrapher and later director, Hermann Hilprecht, contended that it would be more efficient to purchase tablets from local diggers than to deal with the logistics and supervision of excavation directly (Kucklick 1996:49). While this policy was not enacted, the fact that it was even considered shows the extent to which the archaeology of southern Mesopotamia was a tablet hunt, with sites like Telloh and Nippur mined for their lode of new epigraphic material. Emphasis on recovering artifacts that could speak for themselves in writing was not unreasonable in an era when the potential of archaeology for establishing chronological sequences, defining contexts, and attacking questions of historical interest through mute material remains had yet to be realized.

The methods that eventually gave archaeology legitimacy as a discipline in the late 19th and early 20th centuries were developed, for the most part, in other areas, but there are a few specifically associated with the Middle East. W. M. Flinders Petrie is remembered in introductory archaeology textbooks today as the creator of an ingenious system of sequence dating for pre-Dynastic Egypt. During a brief sojourn in Palestine, he also first recognized the potential of using pottery and exhibited an appreciation for the stratigraphy of tells for cross-dating and chronological coordination (Moorey 1991:28–29). The arrival of German excavators at Zincirli, Babylon, Assur, and Uruk, with their emphasis on broad horizontal exposures and recovery of architectural remains, did much to foster an appreciation for context that could give voice to artifactual information in its own right (Lloyd 1980:174).

Once effective methods for investigating prehistory were developed, the Middle East assumed a pivotal role in the study of the human past for reasons such as the origins of agriculture and the emergence of state-organized complex societies, that had little to do with the inscriptions its archaeologists continued to uncover. Nevertheless, the Middle East remains an arena of exceptional interchange and feedback between philological and archaeological research. Writing itself is an archaeological concern here. The first fully developed system of recording language graphically, cuneiform, can be traced back to its origins in less sophisticated recording devices through the findings of archaeologists in the tells of southern Mesopotamia (Gelb 1963:61–72). The alphabet was also an invention of the ancient Orient, and its evolution from a local experiment in the early second millennium to the inspiration for Phoenician, Greek, Etruscan, and Latin scripts of the first millennium B.C.E. is manifest in small inscribed artifacts of modest philological content.

It is not just the historical priority of writing or the unparalleled time depth of the record that makes it a concern to the archaeologist: a key point is that an extraordinary proportion of the written record for the Middle East has been extracted from the soil, and thus has an archaeological context. Most of the writing germane to Mesopotamia, Assyria, the Hittites, pre-Achaemenid Iran, etc. does not come from external observations or information transmitted from generation to generation as does, for example, the historical documentation for the emergence of Rome or the early dynastic history of China. It is instead reconstructed from materials largely composed in the time and culture to which they are relevant and recovered as physical objects.

Less direct means of historical transmission between the ancient Near East and the present are not inconsequential, but there have been significant disruptions. Discontinuity is bridged only imperfectly by accounts of such writers as Herodotus, Cteisias, Xenophon, Berossos, and Strabo. The Bible constitutes an exception, obviously, but it is a late and parochial collection of documents in comparison to the corpus of cuneiform materials in various languages (see Finkelstein, this volume).[3] On the other hand, an unrivaled volume of written material survives thanks to the durability of the primary media of literacy in the ancient Near East, clay tablets and stone monuments. A good part of what comes out of the ground is quite mundane: lists of commodities like sheep or beer rations, receipts, private correspondence, tablets on which a scribe in training jotted a few signs, etc. The information these documents transmit is of a different character than what is available to ancient historians who work only with documents that were intended for posterity, and opens windows onto aspects of daily life that would be hidden to us had they been written on perishable materials like parchment, wood, or papyrus. These make it possible to write "history from below," to use the phrase of one modern practitioner (Van de Mieroop 1999).

This is not to deny that a very real historical tradition existed within the ancient Near East or to claim that *all* written documents are contemporary with the periods on which they shed light. Some texts report on events long in the past and others fraudulently purport to be earlier compositions than they actually are. As early as the end of the third millennium B.C.E., scribes were actively incorporating local dynastic lists into a master framework for the history of southern Mesopotamia (Jacobsen 1939:128–164). The Assyrian King List presents a chain of succession that spans nearly 1,500 years (Pritchard 1969:564–566). Among the Hittites, to cite a particularly prominent case, older tablets were frequently recopied by scribes and classic texts originally composed several centuries earlier were found in several copies in the royal archives at Boğazköy (Bryce 1998:420). In royal chancelleries and temple communities throughout the Near East, professionals maintained a stream of religious and literary continuity as well as propagating texts for the audience of posterity. This included documents in Sumerian, which, like Latin, was maintained as a written language centuries after it ceased to be spoken.

The interplay of epigraphy, archaeology, and ancient concepts of tradition is clearly illustrated by Nabonidus of Babylon (555–539 B.C.E.), who excavated sequences of temple foundations, linked them with previous rulers on the basis of inscriptions, and performed restorations of buildings and monuments to legitimize his own imperial policies (Beaulieu 1989:138–148). One of the subjects of Nabonidus's antiquarian interests, Hammurabi, also presents an interesting case of a textually documented individual leaving a strong imprint in the archaeological record. He is best known for his law code, which survives as a diorite stele in the Louvre, and has been replicated in many modern casts, providing the first text that many contemporary students encounter in learning Akkadian. The original was recovered in 19th-century C.E. excavations at Susa, where it had been brought as an item of booty by the Elamites in the 12th century B.C.E. The tradition of these laws was sufficiently independent of the original monument that at least one copy of them is attested in a tablet inventory of the Neo-Assyrian Empire (Fales and Postgate 1992:69). Hammurabi's numerous surviving letters show him to be an administrator for whom almost no matter was too trivial (e.g., Kraus 1968:passim). His destruction of the palace of Mari, one of the richest sites in the Near East, speaks for the effectiveness of his armies and left behind a trove of tablets that enlighten us on many aspects of the politics and society of his age. Thus the career of one individual has left its imprint on the archaeological record in several different ways, from the mundane to the monumental, and in historical traditions fostered by ancient libraries and modern cultural institutions.

With these mutual dependencies, one would expect philology and archaeology to be thoroughly integrated, yet there is a tension between the fields that leads practitioners of both to lament that the potential integration has not been fully realized (Liverani 1999). One factor that has complicated the exchange of information between textual and archaeological sources is the division between archaeology and epigraphy as academic specialities (Van de Mieroop 1999:5). Training in ancient languages such as Akkadian, Hittite, and Sumerian, is demanding, but not greatly in demand. It is only offered at a few elite institutions and most Assyriologists – as cuneiform specialists are called in deference to the original source of cuneiform tablets, whether or not they have any interest in Assyria proper – generally devote their efforts to the interpretation of tablets themselves. Although there are rare individuals who have shown equal capacities in philology and archaeology, and certainly some cross-training between the disciplines, most analysis of texts is done by people who are not actually concerned with the contextual recovery of artifacts. There is also apt to be a somewhat different conception of audience for the products of the research in the two specialties. Philology is, by its very nature, culturally specific and particularistic, often focusing on unique creations and individual behavior. Archaeologists, on the other hand, usually attempt to understand human behavior in the aggregate (Childe 1956:13–15), and may move from culture to culture during their careers, or even in the course of a single stratigraphic excavation. Such factors often lead to breakdowns in communication and a failure of both disciplines to exploit the potential offered by actually finding written documents in the ground. I shall return to this point after a discussion of the character of the written record.

Writing Systems of the Ancient Near East

Mechanisms for recording linguistic information graphically have a longer history in the Middle East than anywhere else in the world, but it is important to recognize that writing is very unevenly represented in both time and space. Some systems are in fact quite defective in recording clear links to language, functioning more as mnemonic devices for limited types of information than fully developed mechanisms capable of transmitting any and all thought. While it may be technically correct to speak of literacy beginning five thousand years ago in Mesopotamia, this starting point is not as dramatic a boundary as is, for example, the divide between prehistoric and historical archaeology in North America. For long stretches of time after the invention of cuneiform the archaeologist must work without the benefit of documentary evidence, which is often silent on some of the most essential aspects of even relatively "literate" societies, including the large proportion of the population that made no use of writing whatever.[4]

The cuneiform system originated in southern Mesopotamia in the late fourth millennium B.C.E., where the earliest tablets, found in level IV of the Eanna district of Uruk, appear to be purely numeric (Nissen et al. 1993:13–14). It has been suggested that the system of notation may have been developed to replace a system of tokens or tallies that were sealed in tangerine- or orange-sized clay envelopes, or bullae, in the years preceding its introduction, but the thesis that the first signs were originally pictorial representations of "complex tokens" (Schmandt-Besserat 1992: vol. 1, 142–150) remains unsubstantiated. There can be little doubt, however, that the primary emphasis in early recording was keeping track of commodities. Nearly simultaneously with Uruk's development of the precursors of the sign forms that were to remain in use in the following millennia, another script, also making use of clay as the basic medium but having a slightly different inventory of signs, appeared in the neighboring Susiana Plain, undoubtedly stimulated by the same social needs that generated writing in Mesopotamia. Despite some continuity with later writing, this "Proto-Elamite" script remains undeciphered (Walker 1987:41; Damerow and Englund 1989).

The primary historical value of fourth-millennium writing is in the light it sheds on bureaucratic procedures in the earliest state-organized societies. Linguistically, it is not particularly informative. Only Uruk has produced a substantial corpus of documents, and in these there is almost no grammar or phonological information. Most of the texts are "economic" or "administrative" in that they are simple tags, records of quantities of commodities, or cryptic notes of transactions. A few "lexical" lists seem to have served as exercises devoted to scribal training (Nissen et al. 1993:19–24). There are a large number of signs and different counting systems in evidence. What language lay behind the writing is uncertain.[5]

Tablets and inscribed stone objects dating to the following centuries have been found at several sites in southern Iraq and Syria. General continuity with the script of the Uruk period is clear, but there are also significant changes. The signs, initially pictorial, develop more abstract forms and are now wedges made with a triangular stylus rather than drawings, although many numbers continue to be made by impressions of an instrument (presumably the opposite end of the stylus) with a circular rather than triangular cross section. A significant development is the standardization of signs and a great reduction in their number from over 1,000 to approximately 600 basic forms. The writing became increasingly phonetic, with many signs being used for their syllabic value rather than standing for whole words (Nissen et al. 1993:116–124).

Mesopotamia appears to have been multilingual well before it was literate, with place names and certain technical terms indicating the erstwhile presence of non-Semitic, non-Sumerian speaking groups. With the rise of Sargon and his dynasty to power in the twenty-fourth century, cuneiform came to be used for recording the Akkadian language, but even earlier Sumerian tablets found at Tell Abu Salabikh appear to have been written by scribes with names that are etymologically Akkadian (Biggs 1967). Before it disappeared in the first century C.E. (Walker 1987:17–18), the logo-syllabic cuneiform system spread throughout the Near East and was also used to write Eblaite, Elamite, Hittite, Hattic, Hurrian, Luwian, Palaic, and Urartian.[6] Two additional scripts, Ugaritic and Old Persian, invented independently in the second and first millennia B.C.E., respectively, are sometimes called "cuneiform," although they operate on quite different principles. Their characters are indeed wedge-shaped, but in each case they are restricted in number to around thirty and function essentially as defective syllabaries (consonant with vowel unspecified) or consonantal alphabets (Walker 1987:44–47).

The Semitic alphabet, ancestral to our own, also emerged in the Middle East. Its history is much more difficult to trace than the development of cuneiform because it was normally written on perishable materials and comparatively few documents survive. The first attempts at alphabetic writing are generally thought to have come about through the interaction of Semitic speaking peoples of the Levant with Egypt around the beginning of the second millennium B.C.E. (Healey 1990:16–19). The gradual evolution of the characters can be traced from the second millennium Levant to the Phoenician alphabet in the early Iron Age and thence via Greece, Etruria, and Rome, to their form on the present page. Vowels, it should be noted, were not added to this writing system until it reached Greece (Healey 1990:35–39).

In the Iron Age, variations of the alphabetic script were used to record a number of related languages such as Hebrew, Moabite, and Aramaic. Sealings, ostraka, papyri, and a few royal display inscriptions present evidence for these in some quantity. Ultimately, Aramaic was the linguistic survivor, and the Hebrew Bible the most substantial text in the ancient Near Eastern alphabetic tradition. By the end of the first millennium B.C.E., these scripts were in competition with Greek and Latin, but their prevalence is demonstrated by such documents as the Dead Sea Scrolls and their subsequent replacement by Arabic was never total.

One other quite distinctive script was developed in ancient western Asia, although its importance pales in comparison to cuneiform and the Semitic alphabets. In the Hittite Empire, various symbols first seen on sealings were elaborated to create a logo-syllabic hieroglyphic writing system. It is now recognized that the language conveyed by these "Hittite hieroglyphs," whenever there is sufficient indication of phonology to judge, is not Hittite at all, but rather Luwian, its cousin in the Anatolian branch of the Indo-European family. When Hittite and Luwian ceased to be written in cuneiform with the demise of the Hittite Empire around 1200 B.C.E., this hieroglyphic script came into widespread use in successor principalities of southern Anatolia and northern Syria. Artifactually, it survives largely in the form of royal display inscriptions, although the existence of a small number of private letters on lead strips suggests that it had wider uses (Hawkins 1986).

Texts as Artifacts

Although there is some justification for the belief that Mesopotamian civilization was at times unusually bureaucratic and literate, there can be no doubt that taphonomic factors are primarily responsible for the wealth of mundane documentation available for study. The cuneiform system was designed for clay, virtually the only thing available to write on in southern Mesopotamia. Although most tablets were merely sun dried, they still survive extraordinarily well in normal archaeological deposits such as trash dumps and on floors of abandoned houses. Archaeologists in other areas, for example the Aegean, despair of finding clay tablets in contexts where there has not been a conflagration to at least partially fire them (Chadwick 1976:18), but this is not a necessary condition for survival in the Middle East. They endure even in damp soils, and I have personally observed unbaked tablet fragments and seal impressions retain their legibility and decoration after having been inadvertently washed in a flotation machine. In southern Mesopotamia excavated tablets are sometimes shattered by crystals of salt that form in the clay as they dry out, and of course any tablet that lies unprotected on a site's surface for any length of time will weather away, but otherwise, once buried, they have a high survival rate.

Tablets could be baked, of course, and this was done primarily to documents for which some sort of permanence was expected. Some of the most spectacular examples of the latter are the clay prisms on which the annals of Assyrian kings were recorded, recovered in the early days of excavation. Formal sealed treaties, literary texts, and other archival documents were treated in this way, but archaeological recovery of these, particularly in modern excavations, is far less common than unbaked tablets. Perhaps the most common class of durable inscribed object is the baked brick, which is often stamped with a short text giving the name of a king and the structure for which the brick was created.

The contexts in which tablets are found are quite varied. In some celebrated cases, it is quite appropriate to speak of the recovery of archives or libraries. The first of these to be discovered, and still probably the most important, was Assurbanipal's Library at Nineveh, a collection made by the last great king of Assyria (Oppenheim 1977:15–18). There are inventories that suggest that an important part of the material assembled was not on tablets, but on writing boards, which unfortunately do not survive (Parpola 1983:4–8). There is also testimony pertinent to the original sources of the tablets in the form of letters indicating the king's interest in collecting tablets (Oppenheim 1977:244). The majority of texts from the Hittite capital also come from imperial archives, of which there was one in the royal palace on the citadel of Büyükkale and another in the principal temple of the city below. The discovery of a completely unexpected major archive was made in 1975 at Tell Mardikh, Syria, where tablets of the third-millennium kingdom of Ebla lay in rows as they had been shelved in an annex at the side of a palace courtyard.

Many sites produce massive numbers of tablets that were not in any way intended for posterity. There are indeed palace archives at Ugarit, but excavation there has produced thousands of additional tablets in various contexts, especially in the level that marks the destruction of the site at the end of the Bronze Age (Pedersén 1998:68–80). One group of letters, reportedly found in kilns, reflects exchanges between the king of Ugarit and other potentates reporting on the approach of the enemies who apparently destroyed the site. A similar situation is seen at the palace of Mari, where the soldiers of Hammurabi, who destroyed it, left documents in the ruins that inform us of the politics of the period immediately preceding the destruction, as well as all other aspects of palace life. These destructions, which were no doubt catastrophes for those who lived at the time, tend to produce masses of evidence of a single time and place, upon each of which generations of Assyriologists have been able to build their research careers.

One may contrast these epigraphic extravaganzas with the more prosaic forms of archaeological recovery in which tablets are found in smaller numbers in contexts less likely to reflect their use than their discard. The site of Nippur in southern Mesopotamia may be taken as an example of the latter. It has multiple periods of occupation, in most of which scattered documents are found, albeit unevenly. School tablets, upon which a student has clumsily jotted a few lines, occasionally corrected by a teacher, are a fairly common appearance in trash deposits throughout the site. One quite important group of tablets from the early first millennium – a period in which documents are generally quite rare – was found in soil that was thrown in around a coffin to fill an isolated grave (Cole 1996:1). But even in these instances they provide useful dating information. Tablets of this non-public type, regardless of their subject and completeness, are sensitive chronological indicators, which archaeologists use to anchor stratigraphic sequences. Sometimes they are quite precise. For example, legal and economic texts are often dated to the year, month, and day. All types of writing are sensitive to subtle changes in fashion which make them roughly datable on the basis of style. Datable tablets, or more usually tablet fragments, are used by archaeologists in much the same way that dated coins are used in later archaeological contexts – at a minimum they establish a *terminus post quem* for the archaeological level in which they are found. Since they are generally short-lived in their use and it is a relatively simple matter to discern whether they are in use or discard contexts, they also often suggest, granted less precisely, the end of a range as well.

Display inscriptions have contextual value on those occasions when they survive *in situ*. Foundation deposits, in which inscribed figurines, clay cones, and ceremonial tablets were sometimes placed under the walls of buildings, provide quite reliable information on their sponsors. The same information is provided by stamped bricks, which rulers created in massive numbers in some periods, but these were frequently re-used in other buildings. Inscriptions on stone were often set up as stelae or architectural components to commemorate building activities and historical events, such as military campaigns. These reach a pinnacle of decorative and narrative value in the royal palaces of the Neo-Assyrian kings of the earlier half of the first millennium B.C.E. at Nimrud, Khorsabad, and Nineveh. The findspots of isolated display inscriptions can also provide quite useful historical information. For example, the distribution of building and campaign inscriptions on cliff faces and semi-portable stone blocks, all datable to the reign of a given ruler, are the primary means by which the expansion and decline of the kingdom of Urartu can be traced (Zimansky 1985:48–76). They provide the dates for individual sites, which in turn yield dated pottery and other artifacts.

The issue of context is one in which archaeologists, who view tablets as artifacts, sometimes find themselves in ethical conflict with philologists, who see them as documents that can, to a considerable degree, speak for themselves. Cuneiform tablets and other inscribed objects have, unfortunately, a monetary value and are traded on the antiquities market, despite the fact that they reach that market through illegal excavation and export. Misinformation about their findspots is often provided as a smokescreen. Moreover, the trade favors whole tablets and ignores fragments, although the latter often contain quite valuable information. In the ground the archaeologists generally find roughly ten fragments per whole tablet, so an illegal excavation is apt to destroy much more textual information than it brings to light. When a document does appear under such circumstances, the ethical position of the archaeologist is absolutely clear. It has been stripped of its context and therefore of much of its value, to say nothing of the damage that is done to archaeological sites generally by unrestrained burrowing. One does not wish to reward the thieves and the operators of the fencing networks in the West or encourage them in greater destruction by publishing and validating their offerings. For those who specialize in reading documents, however, these objects are a great temptation. Cuneiform is sufficiently difficult to counterfeit that Assyriologists are generally confident they can distinguish forgeries from genuine documents, although there are controversies enough on specific cases to raise suspicion on this point. They are used to working with unprovenienced materials since many museum collections were put together almost entirely by purchase, and even catalogues of early excavated tablets contain little more than the name of the site and the date of acquisition. It is only recently that archaeologists have had the opportunity to provide detailed contextual information on tablet findspots and demonstrate the value this adds to the text, and to this day the convention of publishing tablets separately from other excavated artifacts persists. Under these circumstances, many feel that the information in the inscription simply cannot be sacrificed to the deficiencies of its pedigree, thus insuring continued grounds for divorce between archaeology and tablet.

With other, less portable or more perishable written media, this problem of illegal trade and context damage is less pervasive, but still present. The same sorts of information found in cuneiform were committed to these other forms of writing on occasion, but much less of it has survived. We have already noted, for example, the minimal private correspondence incised on lead strips in Luwian hieroglyphs. Hebrew, Aramaic, and Arabic alphabetic writing of the early Iron Age for private purposes has been discovered painted on sherds at such sites as Lachish (Torczyner et al. 1938) and Arad (Aharoni 1981) in Israel. Some of these were letters and others had to do with palace administration. Perhaps the most celebrated discovery is a storage jar sherd from Kuntillet Ajrud on which is written an imprecation to Yahweh and "his Ashera" – the latter a subject of much speculation but looking rather like a wife or female principle that the monotheism of the Biblical text did not prepare us to find in an eighth-century B.C.E. context (Dever 2001:183–187).

With regard to the documentation deliberately created with posterity or a broad propagation of information in mind, alphabetic and Luwian hieroglyphic monuments constitute a corpus similar in character to that in other parts of the world, such as in Rome or among the classic Maya. Most monumental display inscriptions were carved in stone and many were associated with images that bring them into the purview of the history of art. The inscriptions reinforce ideological positions of religion or politics and are themselves a demonstration of power in the mere fact that their creators had sufficient resources to control the written word.

The Scope of Literacy

The number of people who were literate or made use of literacy through scribal intermediaries varied according to time and place, but was undoubtedly more circumscribed than in modern societies. Scribes were trained professionals, and their instruction began at an early age, as a literary composition on the subject in Sumerian makes clear (Kramer 1961:35–45). It is sometimes claimed that the difficulty of the cuneiform writing system itself held back the development of literacy, and societies in which the impact of writing spread beyond the sphere of a small group of palace and temple-based elites could not develop until the alphabet was invented (e.g., Cross 1989:77). The percentage of people who can read, however, seems much more a consequence of societal demand than the technology of writing. The high literacy rates of modern societies like China and Japan undermine the proposition that logo-syllabic writing systems cannot be learned without years of specialized training, and there is, if anything, less evidence for writing in the parts of the Near East that had the alphabet in the second millennium than in Mesopotamia, where cuneiform prevailed.

The Law Code of Hammurabi contains some interesting testimony on literacy. In the epilogue, it states: "Let any wronged man who has a lawsuit come before the statute of me . . . and let him have my inscribed stela read aloud to him, thus may he hear my precious pronouncements" (Roth 1995:134). He is not expected to read it himself. In the Code there is also a law that stipulates a marriage without a formal contract is no marriage (Roth 1995:105). It should be noted, however, that actual marriage contract tablets are not nearly as common in the archaeological record as one would expect if the latter statute is construed as meaning a *written* contract.[7] Assurbanipal's claim to have actually learned Sumerian and Akkadian, albeit in a different context, suggests that it was unusual enough for a king to be literate to make it worth boasting about.

Within the cuneiform sphere, there is tremendous variation over time and space in the amount of writing and the purposes for which it was employed. In some instances, tablets are associated almost exclusively with large institutions. This is true, for example, in Early Dynastic Mesopotamia, when temple and palace both employed scribes to manage their economies as well as create dedicatory and propagandistic inscriptions. At other times, most dramatically in the Old Babylonian and Neo-Babylonian periods in southern Mesopotamia, the penetration of literacy into the private realm is much more extensive and deep. There are letters from merchant to merchant, wives to husbands, and servants to masters (Oppenheim 1967:73–110, 183–195). Contracts, inheritance documents, transactions in tiny plots of land, etc. demonstrate that practically everyone was making use of the written word, at least indirectly.

It must be emphasized that there is no linear trend in the spread of literacy. There are eras, such as the early Kassite period in southern Mesopotamia, when almost nothing is being written. This is because the sedentary population nearly vanishes, and along with it most of the need for writing, which had its original *raison d'être* in social complexity and the impersonal nature of large urban environments. In the face-to-face, tribally organized, world of the Kassites there was no more need for writing than there was in Dark Age Europe. At the end of the Bronze Age, writing disappeared from the Anatolian Plateau, which thereafter remained outside the sphere of "cuneiform culture," of which it had so conspicuously been a part during the Hittite Empire.[8] There are counter-examples of rejuvenation and spread of what might have been assumed to be moribund writing systems: examples of this may be seen in the reappearance of masses of tablets from southern Mesopotamia in the Neo-Babylonian period after centuries of relative scarcity, and the spread of Assyrian-inspired cuneiform in hitherto illiterate eastern Anatolia in the Iron Age.

Chance plays no small role in what archaeologists have recovered. Until the 1970s no writing was known from Early Bronze Age Syria. This situation was suddenly reversed with the discovery of the Ebla archive, as substantial a group of texts as any from Mesopotamia itself in that era. Similar surprises may await us in other areas. The dark age Kingdom of Mitanni, a one-time rival of the Hittites and Egyptians for supremacy in Syria, is known to have made use of writing, but its capital is not securely identified, to say nothing of any royal archives, which could conceivably be as rich as those found at Boğazköy. There are hundreds of display inscriptions from Urartu, but only about two dozen tablets – just enough evidence to demonstrate that writing was being used for mundane administrative purposes and to offer the potential for opening a completely new window on this mysterious kingdom (Zimansky 1985:80–83). This unevenness of coverage over space, time, and societies has a profound impact on the concerns of archaeologists who conduct their research in the broad framework of civilizations that are generally characterized as "historical."

Near Eastern Archaeology as "Historical Archaeology"

The way in which the documentary evidence whose character and availability have been discussed above is integrated with the archaeological record depends to a great extent on the scholarly objectives and philosophical outlook of the individual scholar. Both history and archaeology embrace a variety of perspectives on the methods and ultimate objectives of the study of the human past. In the broadest approach, there is no fundamental difference in the types of evidence. Late in his career, V. Gordon Childe summed up his position in the following terms: "Archaeology is a source of history, not just a humble auxiliary discipline. Archaeological data are historical documents in their own right, not mere illustrations to written texts. Just as much as any other historian an archaeologist studies and tries to reconstitute the process that created the human world in which we live – and us ourselves in so far as we are each creatures of our age and social environment" (Childe 1956:9).

Alternatively, those who construe "history" in a narrower sense as the study of documentary evidence alone, view the scope and specificity of information provided by the written word as potentially so much greater than anything the material record can supply that archaeology is seen playing a supplemental role, filling in lacunae where documents are lacking or correcting biases of epigraphic sources at best. To the extent that written records are deficient the importance of archaeology increases, but the problems are essentially defined by what has been committed to writing. To cite but one authority: "only *written* documents can give us an assured knowledge of our past that is precise, detailed, and analytical. Prehistorians and archeologists as such can only see a hazy and uncertain outline of the past. This is why *history begins at Sumer*, as is emphasized by the title of a popular book. In other words, history begins in Lower Mesopotamia in the first part of the third millennium" (Bottéro 1992:28 [emphasis original]).

Archaeologists who do not share Childe's view that history is the primary objective of their discipline have yet another orientation. In theoretical literature developed primarily by students of the prehistoric cultures, archaeology is often seen as being a mainstream social science dedicated to explaining human behavior in broadly valid and abstract terms. The very specificity of the written record, and the undeniable fact that it illuminates only selected and specialized components of any given society, relegate it to the margins in the eyes of those who share this orientation. Students of the texts have themselves long recognized that what gets written down is often the atypical rather than the typical; normative practices are not usually recorded (Civil 1980:228). In addition to this, the focus of texts is generally on very limited parts of society. For example, the question of how cities are formed and configured is one upon which written documents can indeed have a bearing, but tablets rarely penetrate to the countryside and do not embrace broad enough sweeps of time to give a sufficiently coherent picture of how the whole economy functions. Thus, the offerings of the tablets can be seen almost as a smokescreen.

This is directly relevant to the appreciation of ancient ideologies, for whose power there is so much concern in the social sciences today. The specific and deliberate communications committed to writing by individuals have material analogues in art, which has an equally vivid capacity for transmitting narrative detail, idiosyncrasy, bombast, and propaganda. The most elaborate of both forms of these "graphic" creations, however, tend to reflect the beliefs and postures of very select individuals. The masses of figurines that archaeologists uncover in greater Mesopotamia, on the other hand, rarely illustrate anything we know of from written myths, legends, and rituals, and certainly do not convey very specific information about popular ideologies, but they do mark out the parameters of shared belief systems.

In short, there are differences in both the methods and aims of using texts in archaeological research in the Middle East, as there are in the study of textually documented cultures elsewhere. These are dependent upon the questions being asked. Few scholars, however, would deny the utility of combining all forms of evidence at some level. Let us consider several examples of the mutual reinforcement of archaeological and documentary evidence, beginning with very general problems and concluding with reference to some that are much more focused. It should be emphasized that virtually all research in the Bronze and Iron Age Near East is conducted within an historical framework, and cases treated here only hint at the range of possibilities.

The investigation of ancient urbanism in southern Mesopotamia has long engaged the energies of scores of anthropologically trained archaeologists. In the 1960s and 1970s, pioneering survey work of Robert McC. Adams on shifting patterns of settlement in the Tigris-Euphrates alluvium documented the emergence of the first cities and plotted their changing fortunes in subsequent millennia. This has been supplemented by other scholars in southern Mesopotamia and surveys are now routine in all parts of the Middle East. The basic field strategy consists of visiting sites and analyzing pottery scattered on their surfaces, which is the primary material evidence available without recourse to excavation. Except for the rare instances where inscribed objects like stamped bricks are recovered, there is little direct recourse to written evidence, granting that pottery sequences excavated from contexts dated by cuneiform tablets elsewhere lend chronological precision to the historical part of the sequence.

The Mashkan-shapir project, conducted between 1986 and 1990 in southern Iraq, was designed to carry this investigation into Mesopotamian urbanism further by focusing on a question of the spatial organization at a single site (Stone and Zimansky 1995). Were institutions such as palace and temple centrally located with residences of elites in close proximity, as they were in some ancient societies, or was power more decentralized, with rich and poor intermingled throughout the urban environment? There were some obvious criteria for selecting a site at which to treat this problem efficiently – it had to be well preserved with visible surface remains, belong to a single period, and be of sufficient size to be regarded as a city. But the project directors also wanted a site dating to the Old Babylonian period, because that is when tablets were most widely used by different segments of society and offer the best prospect of identifying spatial variations in behavior. In the course of the initial surface survey, dedicatory inscriptions identifying the site as ancient Mashkan-shapir were discovered near a city gate. The existence but not the location of this city had been known from existing texts such as the Code of Hammurabi. Finding the ancient name of the site was neither expected nor required information for the original aims of the project, but did greatly enhance understanding of the context in which the site came into being and was destroyed, by linking it to the political history of the age. Inscribed evidence found in excavation helped to identify what activities were practiced in certain areas. For example, numerous door sealings from a building showed it to have been administered by two brothers. Although the project was cut short by the Gulf War in 1990 after two very short exploratory seasons and one campaign of four months, it did generate a relatively detailed picture of an entire urban setting in which textual evidence played a role in recognizing specialized areas, albeit one of less significance than the purely archaeological identification of such features as streets, temple platforms, harbors, residential structures, manufacturing areas, and graves.

A much better known site, Kültepe (ancient Kanesh), already noted above, provides an example in which textual and archaeological information are much more in balance, and together provide the most detailed information of an ancient trading network available to modern scholarship.[9] In this case, the tablets inspired the archaeology. They first appeared on the antiquities market in the late 19th century C.E. and hope of discovering more eventually brought archaeologists to the site, where they were not disappointed. A Turkish team under the direction of Tahsin Özgüç has worked at Kültepe annually since 1948, and tens of thousands of tablets have now been recovered. The site consists of a main mound – a high tell of almost circular plan upon which palatial buildings of the early second millennium B.C.E. have been excavated – and a residential area that arcs around it known as the *karum*, in which merchants from Assyria resided. Almost all of the tablets come from private houses in the *karum* and are concerned with a long-distance trade in metals and textiles. They are the earliest documents from Anatolian soil and have been exploited for evidence on such subjects as the early migrations of Indo-Europeans, the emergence of the Hittites, and the character of the Old Assyrian city-state. In relating texts to archaeology, however, they are most interesting on the subject of trade.

In theory, trade is relatively amenable to archaeological investigation, and objects thought to have moved from one place to another are frequently noted in excavation reports. The mechanisms by which goods are exchanged, are, of course, much less obvious, and there is much controversy in anthropological literature about such matters as whether modern concepts like the law of supply and demand, abstract value, etc. should be applied to ancient societies, or what archaeological traces these would leave if one accepts their existence. Thanks to the tablets, we are in an almost unique position of knowing what goods were being traded, who did the trading, and what institutions were associated with it at Kültepe. We also have the physical remains of the trading colony to look at for correlations. It is a sobering lesson for archaeologists. We see nothing of the tin and textiles that the texts tell us were being brought to Anatolia, nor any of the "money" (gold and silver) sent in return to Assyria. The Assyrian merchants themselves, who were hundreds of miles from home and living in a foreign culture, apparently adopted the living styles of Anatolia and left very little indication of their presence, except for the cuneiform tablets and the seals and sealings associated with them. Yet when the various sources of evidence, textual and archaeological, are taken together, they provide us with a remarkably full picture of how this trading network functioned.

I will limit myself to referring to two additional case studies of the coordination of textual and archaeological evidence, both from Nippur. In the 1950s and 1960s, a University of Chicago expedition there uncovered substantial numbers of tablets dating to the late third and early second millennia B.C.E. from residential areas (TA and TB) and from a temple dedicated to the goddess Inanna. In the case of the latter, Richard Zettler was able to piece together the temple archive, only 10% of which was found *in situ* and the rest in secondary contexts associated with later rebuildings of the temple. He was able to construct a genealogy of temple admin-istrators five generations deep and demonstrate that the temple operated more or less as a family operation, with junior members looking after administrative tasks like sealing doors on no other authority than kinship (Zettler 1987). Elizabeth

Stone, working with documents in more direct contexts from residential areas, was able to correlate real estate transactions with house plans, and trace the history of a family and its fortunes over seven generations (Stone 1987). These two studies present information in the realm of social history that is very far removed from the kind of "kings and battles" theme associated with more public documents. We operate here at the same level as historical archaeology of much more recent periods, with the benefit of documents that are actually found in direct association with artifactual remains.

Conclusions

The study of the ancient Near East offers unique opportunities for the coordination of documentary and archaeological evidence largely because so much of the former is transmitted to us in the form of the latter. There is a great wealth of textual information of different kinds, particularly in what has come to us through cuneiform, which was widely used by numerous civilizations, committed to relatively imperishable materials, and is quite well understood as a writing system by modern scholars. We can hear the voices of the royal propagandists and bureaucrats, and contemplate – if not understand – ancient ideologies through mythological and literary texts. Chronologies and social identities are more perceptible here than they are for most other ancient civilizations.

There are, of course, many caveats and pitfalls in the application of these sources to historical and cultural understanding. The full potential of integrating textual and archaeological data has seldom been realized or even recognized. The overwhelming majority of cuneiform inscriptions were unearthed with little attention to their archaeological context, either before controlled methods of digging were understood or in clandestine excavations directed solely to acquiring marketable portable artifacts. The scholars working with the enormous body of material thus put at their disposal had little incentive for insisting on precise contextual information, nor providing it to their colleagues operating in the field.

Differences in the training, capacities, and objectives between the fields of Assyriology and Near Eastern archaeology have also retarded communication. Interpreting the texts is not always as straightforward as non-specialists might assume. Scribes, presuming knowledge that we simply do not have, leave out much information that we would dearly love to have. This is particularly true in letters, which are rarely dated and emerge from contexts that were well understood by the correspondents, but utterly opaque to us. It is often the exceptional things that get written down, not the routine, and we always run the risk of generalizing from very particular cases with texts. On the other hand, archaeology's strength comes from its concern with the most basic and recurrent elements of human existence. Granted that its data sets are invariably incomplete and often unrepresentative, they still embrace larger segments of society and broader chronological ranges than texts. The primary challenge here is to make reliable and convincing inferences on the basis of large shadows rather than individual points of light.

Yet there is no inherent conflict between these disciplines. Both are mechanisms for recovering information about the past – tools, as it were, for answering questions that the modern world deems important. It is in the questions that the most profound transformations take place, as our cumulative knowledge increases and priorities are altered by shifting perspectives. In most cases, these shifts are toward issues that demand input from archaeology and testimony on peoples, social forces and developments that are not directly addressed by the written word alone. There are numerous approaches to the past, and both historians who work primarily with documents and archaeologists come in different stripes. They have, in the Middle East, more sources for their various quests than those concerned with any other part of the ancient world, and more to gain by recognizing the potential of integrating them.

NOTES

1   The term "text" has become so charged in contemporary academic discourse that its use without qualification is no longer possible. In this chapter, I employ the term to refer specifically to documents written in a formal script that transmits information on the basis of human speech – physical manifestations of the specific words of their creators. This restricted definition is adopted not to denigrate the approach of those who see the entire archaeological record as a text to be read and interpreted through culturally conditioned interchange between creators and interpreters. Rather, it is offered to frame and limit the discussion to the arena in which Near Eastern archaeology has one of its more important claims to distinction – the survival of documentary evidence over a longer time range than anywhere else.

2   For a succinct overview of the languages written in cuneiform, see Walker (1987, especially pp. 40–47).

3   Biblical archaeology constitutes a special case of correlation between material artifact, text, and ideology, which has generated an enormous literature that limitations of space prevent us from treating in detail. For a sampling of some of the recent methods, concerns and controversies of this field, see Bartlett (1997), Dever (2001), Finkelstein and Silberman (2001), King and Stager (2001), and Finkelstein (this volume).

4   A concise overview of the types of cuneiform documents available for each period in Mesopotamian history is presented by Van de Mieroop (1999:9–38).

5   The few traces of information that have been used to argue that the underlying language was Sumerian, e.g., the arrow, read TI, as a rebus for the word meaning "life" (Bottéro 1992:79–82), have been challenged in detail by Englund, who argues that Sumerian did not enter the country until after the archaic Uruk tablets had been written (Englund 1998:73–81).

6   For the non-specialist in cuneiform, an excellent overview on how cuneiform was used to write Elamite, Hurrian, Urartian, and Hattic, as well as the state of our understanding of these languages, is to be found in Gragg (1995).

7   Van de Mieroop (1997:10–12) accepts that these were verbal agreements and argues that the only reason "marriage contracts" were put in writing at all was that a transfer of property with monetary value was involved. He cautions that the purposes for which writing was undertaken have to be considered when evaluating cuneiform documents as histor-

ical sources and these were much more limited than for modern documentation. Using modern rubrics such as "wills" can be quite misleading.

8 Gernot Wilhelm has developed the concept of "*Keilschrift-Kultur*" to reinforce the point that a great deal of cultural baggage went along with the writing system that was developed in Mesopotamia when it was borrowed by other societies. This included literary works and religious concepts. The area of this commonality shrank dramatically at the end of the Bronze Age (Wilhelm 1986:95–7).

9 A succinct overview of Kanesh and the Old Assyrian trade may be found in Veenhof (1995), which also includes a brief bibliography of accessible sources on the subject.

REFERENCES

Aharoni, Yohanan, 1981 Arad Inscriptions. Jerusalem: Israel Exploration Society.

Bartlett, John, 1997 Archaeology and Biblical Interpretation. London and New York: Routledge.

Beaulieu, Paul-Alain, 1989 The Reign of Nabonidus, King of Babylon 556–539 B.C. New Haven and London: Yale University Press.

Biggs, Robert, 1967 Semitic Names in the Fara Period. Orientalia 36:55–66.

Bottéro, Jean, 1992 Mesopotamia: Writing, Reasoning, and the Gods. Zainab Bahrani and Marc Van de Mieroop, trans. Chicago and London: University of Chicago Press.

Bryce, Trevor, 1998 The Kingdom of the Hittites. Oxford: Oxford University Press.

Chadwick, John, 1976 The Mycenaean World. Cambridge: Cambridge University Press.

Childe, V. Gordon, 1956 A Short Introduction to Archaeology. London: Frederick Muller.

Civil, Miguel, 1980 Les limites de l'information textuelle. *In* L'Archéologie de l'Iraq du début de l'époque néolithique à 333 avant notre ère. Marie-Thérèse Barrelet, ed. pp. 225–232. Paris: CRNS.

Cole, Steven W., 1996 Nippur IV. The Early Neo-Babylonian Governor's Archive from Nippur. Oriental Institute Publications 114. Chicago: Oriental Institute Press.

Cross, Frank M., 1989 The Invention and Development of the Alphabet. *In* The Origins of Writing. Wayne M. Senner, ed. pp. 77–90. Lincoln: University of Nebraska.

Damerow, Peter, and Robert Englund, 1989 The Proto-Elamite Texts from Tepe Yahya. American School of Prehistoric Research Bulletin 39. Cambridge, MA: Harvard University Press.

Dever, William J., 2001 What Did the Biblical Writers Know and When Did They Know It? Grand Rapids, MI/Cambridge, UK: Eerdmans.

Englund, Robert, 1998 Texts from the Late Uruk Period. *In* Mesopotamien: Späturuk-Zeit und Frühdynastische Zeit. Josef Bauer, Robert K. Englund, and Manfred Krebernik, eds. Freiburg and Göttingen: Vandenhoeck & Ruprecht.

Fales, F. M., and J. N. Postgate, 1992 Imperial Administrative Records, Part I. State Archives of Assyria, vol. 7. Helsinki: Helsinki University Press.

Finkelstein, Israel, and Neil A. Silberman, 2001 The Bible Unearthed: Archaeology's New Vision of Ancient Israel and the Origin of Its Sacred Texts. New York: Free Press.

Gelb, I. J., 1963 A Study of Writing. 2nd edition. Chicago: University of Chicago.

Gragg, Gene B., 1995 The Less-Understood Languages of Ancient Western Asia. *In* Civilizations of the Ancient Near East, vol. 4. Jack M. Sasson, ed. pp. 2161–2179. New York: Scribners.

Hawkins, [John] David, 1986 Writing in Anatolia: Imported and Indigenous Systems. World Archaeology 17:363–375.

Healey, John F., 1990 The Early Alphabet. Reading the Past. London and Berkeley, CA: British Museum/University of California Press.

Jacobsen, Thorkild, 1939 The Sumerian King List. Oriental Institute of the University of Chicago Assyriological Studies No. 11. Chicago: University of Chicago Press.

King, Philip, and Lawrence Stager, 2001 Life in Biblical Israel. Louisville and London: Westminster John Knox Press.

Kramer, Samuel, 1961 History Begins at Sumer. 2nd edition. London: Thames & Hudson.

Kraus, F. R., 1968 Briefe aus dem Archive des Šamaš-Hāzir in Paris und Oxford. Altbabylonische Briefe in Umschrift und Übersetzung, Heft. 4. Leiden: E. J. Brill.

Kucklick, Bruce, 1996 Puritans in Babylon: The Ancient Near East and American Intellectual Life 1880–1930. Princeton: Princeton University Press.

Liverani, Mario, 1999 History and Archaeology in the Ancient Near East: 150 Years of a Difficult Relationship. *In* Fluchtpunkt Uruk: Archäologische Einheit aus methodischer Vielfalt. Schriften für Hans Jörg Nissen. Hartmut Kühne, Reinhard Bernbeck, and Karin Bartl, eds. pp. 1–11. Rahden/Westf.: Marie Leidorf.

Lloyd, Seton, 1980 Foundations in the Dust: The Story of Mesopotamian Exploration. Revised edition. New York: Thames & Hudson.

Moorey, P. R. S., 1991 A Century of Biblical Archaeology. Cambridge: Lutterworth Press.

Nissen, Hans, Peter Damerow, and Robert Englund, 1993 Archaic Bookkeeping. Paul Larsen, trans. Chicago and London: University of Chicago Press.

Oppenheim, A. Leo, 1967 Letters from Mesopotamia. Chicago: University of Chicago Press.

Oppenheim, A. Leo, 1977 Ancient Mesopotamia: Portrait of a Dead Civilization. Revised edition. Chicago: University of Chicago Press.

Parpola, Simo, 1983 Assyrian Library Records. Journal of Near Eastern Studies 42/1:1–29.

Pedersén, Olof, 1998 Archives and Libraries in the Ancient Near East 1500–300 B.C. Bethesda, MD: CDL Press.

Pritchard, James B., ed., 1969 Ancient Near Eastern Texts Relating to the Old Testament. 3rd edition. Princeton: Princeton University Press.

Roth, Martha T., 1995 Law Collections from Mesopotamia and Asia Minor. Atlanta: Scholars Press.

Schmandt-Besserat, Denise, 1992 Before Writing. 2 vols. Austin: University of Texas Press.

Stone, Elizabeth, 1987 Nippur Neighborhoods. Chicago: Oriental Institute Press.

Stone, Elizabeth, and Paul Zimansky, 1995 The Tapestry of Power in a Mesopotamian City. Scientific American 272/4:92–97.

Torczyner, Harry, et al., 1938 Lachish I (Tell ed Duweir): The Lachish Letters. London, New York and Toronto: Oxford University Press.

Van de Mieroop, Marc, 1997 Why Did They Write on Clay? Klio 79:7–18.

Van de Mieroop, Marc, 1999 Cuneiform Texts and the Writing of History. London and New York: Routledge.

Veenhof, Klaas R., 1995 Kanesh: An Assyrian Colony in Anatolia. *In* Civilizations of the Ancient Near East, vol. 2. Jack Sasson, ed. pp. 859–871. New York: Charles Scribner's Sons.

Walker, C. B. F., 1987 Cuneiform. Reading the Past. London and Berkeley, CA: British Museum/University of California Press.

Wilhelm, Gernot, 1986 Urartu als Region der Keilschrift-Kultur. *In* Das Reich Urartu: Ein altorientalischer Staat im 1. Jahrtausend v. Chr. Volkert Haas, ed. pp. 95–113. Konstanz: Universitätsverlag.

Zettler, Richard L., 1987 Administration of the Temple of Inanna at Nippur under the Third Dynasty of Ur: Archaeological and Documentary Evidence. *In* The Organization of Power: Aspects of Bureaucracy in the Ancient Near East. McGuire Gibson and Robert D. Biggs, eds. Chicago: Oriental Institute Press.

Zimansky, Paul, 1985 Ecology and Empire: The Structure of the Urartian State. Chicago: Oriental Institute Press.

16

Representations, Reality, and Ideology

Jennifer C. Ross

To residents of ancient Near Eastern cities and towns, the visual imagery they regularly encountered was not "art" in the aesthetic sense of the word. Philosophers of art maintain, in fact, that the aesthetic concept is a relatively recent one, and that most imagery produced in the ancient world belonged to the category denoted by Latin *ars* and Greek *techne*, or "skill" (Mortensen 1997). At the same time, the traditional art historical terminology of art, artist, and patron can provide a useful framework for discussion, if applied cautiously.[1] In the ancient Near East, representations on wall surfaces and freestanding stelae, on seals and vessels, functioned within a larger cultural system to convey ideas and information relating to the order and organization of society. Each patron, artist, and viewer, even each act of creation or observation, constituted part of a process by which meaning was constructed, interpreted, challenged, and incorporated into the prevailing social and political systems.

Images were produced in a variety of forms and media during the period covered by this chapter, the third through the first millennium B.C.E. Here, however, I will narrow the focus to exclude "decorative" designs, whether geometric, natural, or figural.[2] I will also concentrate on Mesopotamian imagery, that of the Tigris and Euphrates River valleys of modern Iraq, but my comments should be applicable to other areas of the ancient Near East as well. Most of my discussion in this chapter will refer to public art, primarily the monumental sculptural works of Mesopotamia, commissioned by the elite to signify their devotion to the gods, dedication to their land and people, and achievements. In focusing on these, I will be giving rather scant attention to works, such as votive statuary and representational art situated in houses, commissioned or created for private consumption and devotion. I will offer a methodology for assessing the public imagery in particular, with special attention to how representations were perceived and interpreted by a range of potential witnesses.

Art historians and archaeologists are equipped with a variety of methods and theoretical approaches with which to evaluate artistic works; these have been applied to the study of some of the best-known ancient Near Eastern images. A first step in the assessment of a work is descriptive, examining the iconographic content of the image, identifying the figures and recording such features as size, shape, and material. This stage encapsulates and translates the image into a different medium of representation; it may highlight particular features of the work felt by the analyst to be most significant, while passing over others. A second stage comprises stylistic appraisal. Stylistic analysis may be synchronic, locating an individual work within its time period and particular place of origin. While individual artists' hands have seldom been recognized in the art of the ancient Near East (nor were such works ascribed to particular artists in the textual records), the products of some regional workshops have been identified (Collon 1981, 1985; Winter 1981a). Another level of stylistic analysis is diachronic, examining the development of motifs, techniques, and artistic styles over longer spans of time.

The analytical methods offered here take for granted the need for descriptive and stylistic analyses, but are more interpretive, attempting to place individual works, and artistic production as a whole, into an active context as the products, expressions, and generators of ideologies. The term "ideology" is used here in the Marxist sense, as a collection of strategies and shared meanings deployed by an elite class to make present realities, including social and economic stratification and political inequalities, appear natural and beneficial to society as a whole (Liverani 1979:298; Pollock 1999:173). For artistic representations, this implies an adaptation, refocusing, selective representation, or even a misrepresentation of events and conditions. An ideological approach to art requires that there be a sponsor and creator of the work in question, a receptive and understanding audience toward whom the imagery was directed, and a distinct message being communicated and received, though not necessarily consciously (Wolff 1993:115). Ideology manifests itself in a number of ways, including but not limited to visual modes of expression (art and architecture), ritual performance, and verbal devices such as stories. Through strategic use of one or more of these methods, societal leaders declare and reaffirm their own roles and status (De Marrais et al. 1996:16). At the same time, ideological expression may leave room for reinterpretation, and its meanings can be contested, revised, or even negated by the population it tries to manipulate. Societies may maintain multiple, nested, or conflicting ideologies, though one will usually dominate others; such multivocality and diversity can challenge and transform social structures (Liverani 1979:300).

Because it requires an audience that has been socialized in the dominant forms of cultural representations, even if not actively aware of this, much ideological expression is set in a public forum; in the case of art, this often takes place on a monumental scale and in accessible locations. As described below, artistic representations in the Near East began to proliferate in the kin-based societies of the Neolithic. The growth of urbanism in Mesopotamia in the Late Uruk period (the late fourth millennium) coincided with the appearance of the earliest artistic representations of the roles and responsibilities of leaders. It is not a coincidence, from

the standpoint of the ideological analysis offered here, that production of monumental art and architecture expanded rapidly during this period.

This first appearance of artistic expressions of ideology of leadership, and its
further development during the third millennium, also corresponded with the earliest examples of narrative art in Mesopotamia. Pictorial narrative, imagery that tells
or alludes to a particular story, has been an object of art historical research for
several decades. Scholars have offered examples of and explanations for the narrative art produced in ancient Egypt (Kantor 1957; Davis 1992, 1993), Greece (most
recently Stansbury-O'Donnell 1999), and Italy (von Blanckenhagen 1957). The
richness of the pictorial repertoire that has survived from these cultures has encouraged the development of narrative approaches to art. The pictorial narratives created
in the ancient Near East, on the other hand, have been examined in less detail, with
attention paid most often to particular pieces or periods (Güterbock 1957; Perkins
1957; Reade 1979b; Winter 1981b, 1985; Russell 1993). Here, I will offer the viewpoint that the ideological and narrative approaches to artistic representation can be
more widely applied to all periods of production. Narrative art requires an intuitive
contemporary "reader" to reconstruct the story it tells; that same reader, according to an ideological perspective on art, may regard and (unconsciously) interpret
the imagery as culminating in the social and political circumstances of his or her
own time, explaining and naturalizing the status quo and thus the dominant ideology of the time. The techniques and goals of narrative expression and ideological
communication thus appeared nearly contemporaneously in the ancient Near East,
and often worked together to reinforce the sense that societal norms were logical
and natural.

Origins of Near Eastern Art

The earliest surviving art from the ancient Near East comes from the Epipaleolithic
and Neolithic periods, over 10,000 years ago. Incised stones and carved bones from
Epipaleolithic levels at 'Ain Mallaha ('Eynan) and the Carmel cave complex in
northern Israel were perhaps important first steps toward visual expression (Noy
1991; Belfer-Cohen 1991). In the permanent agricultural villages of the Neolithic,
however, there is evidence for more intensive and widespread image production.
Both the scattered Epipaleolithic evidence and the more extensive data from permanent Neolithic settlements around the Fertile Crescent suggest that the beginnings of artistic production intersected with other critical social and economic
changes related to the development of permanent settlements and an agricultural
economy.

The figurines, relief sculpture, and wall paintings produced at such Neolithic
sites as Jericho (Kenyon 1960:54), Nevalı Çori and Göbekli Tepe (Hauptmann
1999), and, particularly, Çatal Höyük (Mellaart 1967; Hodder ed. 1996), portrayed
the interdependence and interconnectedness of the natural and cultural worlds
(Yakar 1991:310; Voigt 2000). At a time when humans sought to extend and intensify their manipulation of nature, through intensification of hunting and gathering

practices or by means of incipient agriculture, such images may have served to model behaviors, express and affect desired outcomes, or record important events of the natural and human life cycles. At Çatal Höyük, the amount and variety of artistic work indicates that community members were continually interacting with, manipulating, and being influenced by imagery. The artistic content differed from building to building, but each resident of the town may have had daily opportunities to see and interpret the representations. The regular renewal and transformation of images (through repainting of walls) suggests that, despite changes in content, artistic expression was of enduring value and potential benefit to the residents. The emerging evidence of the variety, scale, and complexity of Neolithic representational art indicates that image production and consumption played an important role in the transition to permanent settlement and eventually to food production, and in attendant social transformations throughout the Near East during the Neolithic (Cauvin 1994).

More salient to the ideological analysis of ancient Near Eastern art offered here, however, are the phases of image production that coincided with the establishment and consolidation of more complex sociopolitical forms, those characterized by urban and state organizations. These societal changes began in the fourth millennium, and the artistic transformations that accompanied and supported them principally expressed the roles and responsibilities of leaders. Art functioned to support societal hierarchies, focusing on an active ruler who served the gods and his community,[3] and maintained the ordered workings of both society and nature. Some fundamental iconographic scenes, particularly images depicting rulers, developed during the Uruk and Early Dynastic periods (late fourth to mid-third millennium), and remained important in subsequent phases of Mesopotamian art. Such scenes included the royal hunt, the construction of buildings, and the presentation of offerings to gods. It is vital to note, however, that despite the continuity of such iconography, the precise execution of images, and more importantly, their meaning and evaluation changed over time. Art, and particularly art that served ideological purposes, is embedded in specific historical settings, and must be assessed in localized terms (Wolff 1993:61–65). Artistic change may offer evidence of change in political, social, economic, and religious circumstances; on the other hand, artistic representations that use traditional iconography of legitimacy may not shift concurrently with changes in the wielders of power.

While the first uses of visual narrative and the production of ideological messages coalesced in the late fourth millennium, artistic expression was just one of a number of mechanisms developed in the Uruk period to support and enhance the emergent bureaucracy. Writing, seal use, monumental architecture, and other visible expressions of control and leadership also justified and affirmed the organization of society. The roles and responsibilities of a leader expanded as the population he answered to also increased in number. Under these circumstances, the physical presence and availability of the ruler had to be supplemented by images, to serve as visible substitutes, and to stand in as symbols of his authority. Ruler and image became one and the same. Other forms of expression, such as speech acts and rituals, which are less detectable archaeologically, would also have served similar ideological goals.

Ideology and the Locus of Artistic Production

The analysis of the art of the ancient Near East in terms of its sociopolitical context and content that I suggest is also appropriate given the absence of written evidence for the appreciation of art on an aesthetic level. Sumerian and Akkadian lacked words for "art" and "artist." Instead, according to historical and dedicatory inscriptions of all phases of ancient Near Eastern written documentation, the ruler served as designer and executor of most artistic and architectural programs. Texts of the Neo-Assyrian period (the time that furnishes the most comprehensive royal artistic corpus) specifically state that the king (usually in the first person) "created" images of the gods, and of himself performing a variety of activities. These he also "erected," usually in public spaces, for others to witness.

The textual record also indicates how little of the art of Mesopotamia has been preserved. The Akkadian term ṣalmu (Sumerian ALAN or AN.DÙL)[4] is a general word for image, referring to statues in the round and to reliefs.[5] The images thus described included statues of gods and kings, in a variety of materials. Year-names from the second millennium commemorated the production and erection of such representations as major events in processes of temple construction and furnishing (Ungnad 1938; Horsnell 1999; Sigrist and Damerow 2001). The expense, materials, and public nature of image production and presentation made these appropriate events to mark the year. Inscriptions record the production of other types of images as well. Among them, we find narû (Sumerian NA.RU or NA.RÚ.A)[6] referring to a freestanding stone monument, or stele; in some cases, a narû had an inscription only, but at other times it included an image. The term uṣurtu (GIŠ.HUR)[7] designated incised drawings, occasionally figural, but usually building plans. Finally, tamšilu,[8] deriving from mašālu ("to be similar, equal"), meant "copy" or "portrayal." This word pertained specifically to images produced in direct "likeness" to physical objects, animals, and individuals, both human and divine; it was used sparingly, and for a limited time, as a synonym for ṣalmu.

The ability to commission and create images was not a royal prerogative alone. Ritual texts of the first millennium such as maqlû attest to the extensive production and use by ordinary citizens of figurines (also called ṣalmu, NU, or ALAN) for magical purposes. These could represent gods, demons, or humans (particularly adversaries). While occasionally made of stone or metal, these figurines were usually of less durable materials – wax, unbaked clay, or wood – and were deposited in out-of-the-way places or in rivers, where they could no longer do harm to the sufferer. These texts suggest, therefore, that large numbers of images were produced in Mesopotamia that have left little or no impact on the archaeological record.

The reality of production

Despite royal assertions claiming credit for artistic production ("I made a representation of . . ."), most images were probably produced by specialized craftspeople working, usually, for the public institutions of palace and temple. These individuals appear in economic and administrative texts as recipients of rations and of materials needed to complete their work. The craftsmen were often organized into workshops incorporating a variety of productive tasks, from textile production to metalwork. This type of organization, under an official overseer, fostered some degree of integration and coordination among crafts. Production for the temple and palace was probably not, in most periods, a full-time or year-round occupation.[9] Nevertheless, the importance of craft production to the public institutions is indicated by the antiquity of certain professional designations. Logograms for craftworkers, such as SIMUG (smith) and NAGAR (carpenter), are found in lexical literature at least as early as the Early Dynastic period (Civil 1969:10–11). A few references, in addition, attest to foreign craftsmen brought to Mesopotamia for particular projects. These individuals were particularly adept at manipulating raw materials from their own lands, as suggested, for example, by the ruler Gudea's comment that "Magan and Meluhha, (coming down) from their mountain, loaded wood on their shoulders for him, and in order to build Ningirsu's House they all joined Gudea (on their way) to his city Girsu" (Gudea Cylinder A XV 8–10; Edzard 1997:78). Similarly, the foundation inscription from Darius' palace at Susa laid claim to multinational support and resources for construction; this functioned in part as a propagandistic statement of territorial control (Darius Sf 30–55; Kent 1950:142–144).

Overall, however, the cuneiform texts offer very little information about the distinctiveness of individual crafts or art forms, and the archaeological evidence for workshops or craft quarters is meager. Even the verb for creation, *epēšu* (DÙ), is unspecific; its typical definition is "to make," and it could connote any form of production, including building, weaving, and sculpting. For the most part, scribes and administrators of the ancient Near East were unconcerned with the artistry and even the specific content of artistic production, except as it consumed precious raw materials or conveyed the proper attitude of support and reverence toward the ruler. The ruler thus stood as the ultimate authority in matters of iconography, material, and design, perhaps communicating his expectations and desires directly to the artists.

Ancient Near Eastern rulers, thus, claimed responsibility and credit for artistic production and manipulated images to support the legitimacy of their rule. Like other ideological forms of expression, these official statements of creative prowess served as misrepresentations of the actual locus of production, placing artistry in the hands of the king, and denying the artisans a creative role in image production.

Ideology, Iconography and Medium

Iconography and medium

The examination of the extant images from the ancient Near East offers a means beyond the textual evidence to formulate nuanced perspectives on the potential audience for and message of the images, as well as a view of changes in audience and message over time. Artistic representations were created from a variety of materials, in all shapes and sizes, and on items with a wide range of functions. Given the variability of this evidence, it may be possible to identify patterns of material, form, content, and function that reflect the preferences and intentions of the makers and observers of artistic works.

Through art, its designers and producers attempt to convey a certain reality to viewers from their own and other societies. This reality, though, is a selective one; artists may choose from a range of possible strategies of representation, and from a series of moments in time. The reality they evoke is generally portrayed from the perspective of one individual or group: note how Assyrians never lose a battle, or even suffer a casualty, in first millennium art. Through specific strategies of representation, actions and circumstances are "re-presented." They are removed from their original time and space by being carved from stone or modeled in metal, materials that preserve the events in a continual present tense, and they are re-placed in a new physical setting. Reality therefore is perceived through a filter, retold and reorganized for a diverse audience, both divine and human, ruler and ruled.

The principal filter through which reality becomes image is ideology, though image production is also conditioned by convention and ability. Ideology determines how the real conditions of lived experience should be presented, or re-presented, in art. Representations affect the experience of an audience, and guide its reactions and perceptions. The affective properties of visual representation, backed as they are by a dominant ideology, communicate to the viewer the proper workings of society, and his or her own place (or lack thereof) within it. If public and lasting, visual images may be subject to repeated viewings, constantly re-integrated into consciousness, the details of the events perhaps forgotten but the dominant themes becoming symbolic of societal order.

In the ancient Near East, accessible imagery, whether public and monumental, such as much of the relief sculpture from Mesopotamia, or small but widely disseminated, like seals, had the potential to educate and incorporate new groups of subject peoples into a political system (Eisenstadt 1979:21). It also integrated individuals and groups already within that system more fully into the values and ambitions of their rulers. In each historical period, artists and designers of visual images may have had access to the art of preceding periods; they then made both intentional and unconscious use of elements of past imagery, and transformed those elements for their own purposes (Root 1990). All of these factors were potentially significant in the design of artistic programs, and to their variation and continuity over time and space in the ancient Near East.

The use and reception of Near Eastern art were always conditioned by the political, social, and religious structures at work in specific historical settings, and by the ideological requirements within those settings. Particular aspects of the representations served as active mediators in the communication between producer/patron and audience; for this reason, it is important to examine in detail the visual cues through which meaning was constituted, communicated, and perceived. The use of images to communicate is made possible in part by the knowledge and experience held in common by both the makers/commissioners of the image and their audience. This common perception does not have to be "real" or practical; it may include experiences of divine presence or knowledge of past events not participated in directly, as well as culturally regulated ways of seeing.

The basic iconographic content of the art of ancient Mesopotamia was relatively narrow, and changed little over time. The precise details of setting and the identity of specific figures, however, as well as the context of display, did vary; here we may detect the particular historical settings of images and the shifting ideological messages they conveyed. The primary types of scenes portrayed either the realm of the supernatural or that of humanity, though the lines between these were frequently crossed. Specific identifiable myths are few and mainly limited to the Old Akkadian period; particular deities (identifiable by their attributes), on the other hand, are not uncommon. Scenes of ritual, in which humans appeared in direct contact with the gods, were also widespread in Near Eastern art; their purpose was to reveal a relationship continually reenacted and reaffirmed by human acts of worship.

More clearly on the human plane are scenes representing actions of a ruler; the gods are often present in these images as well. Most common among these, particularly on monumental representations, was the battle scene. Battles in Near Eastern art were depicted as large-scale incidents pitting army against army. In contrast, human combatants locked in isolated hand-to-hand contests or fighting animals are often interpreted as "heroes" or, more specifically, as Gilgamesh and Enkidu.[10] In both hunts and combats against animals, the ruler-hero displayed his superiority over the dangerously wild portions of his realm, and symbolized his protection of society against predation of all types (Weissert 1997).

Imagery with nonviolent content conveyed the roles and responsibilities of rule in more peaceful times. Central themes in such images included the reception of tribute and gifts, and occasionally scenes of formal alliance with a foreign power (as on Shalmaneser III's throne base; Mallowan 1966:445). In addition, rulers could be portrayed as architects and builders, actively promoting the growth of their settlements, and offering allegiance and honor to the gods through temple construction.

Beyond these few basic types, other representations are more difficult to interpret. These include, in particular, images of animals, singly, in heraldic pairs, or in procession, as are found in several periods of glyptic art. A number of scenes depict day-to-day activities, such as plowing or milking. These depictions may stem from a need or desire to represent aspects of daily life. In other cases, such imagery may have had an apotropaic or protective force, or functioned to communicate group identity.

Medium and ideology

While the philological discussion above requires that we regard all Mesopotamian art equally as "image," a general distinction existed between three-dimensional statuary, which was usually limited in iconographic range and function, and the much more multi-functional two-dimensional media. Three-dimensional art was restricted to statuary in divine, human, and animal form, in various materials (stone, clay, metal, and a variety of perishable materials) and sizes. Larger figures mainly stood in temple or other ritual settings, or were cached after outliving their dedicatory function. The context, physical and cultural, of this statuary may have set limits on variability and innovation; cross-culturally, religious modes of expression are more conservative than other types.[11] Smaller figurines and images were more mobile, and could have been transported to new settings, kept on the body as ornaments or talismans, or set in a variety of architectural and functional locales. Statues and statuettes also could have been manipulated in ritual settings to act and interact; their meanings may not have been so fixed as we often suppose.

Two-dimensional imagery, on the other hand, appears to have offered a broader canvas for expression, and carried the majority of the ideological messages found in art of the ancient Near East. The reasons for this distinction are manifold, and some are, perhaps, obvious. A two-dimensional medium usually offered greater flexibility in the portrayal of more than one individual, and thus gave the artist the ability to convey action and interaction, sequence and story. The artist could experiment with notions of scale and size, gesture and movement (see below), in ways not available with sculpture in the round. In contrast to statuary, two-dimensional images in the ancient Near East were established and experienced in a wider array of contexts (to be discussed below), and were therefore more liable to reinterpretation over time.

Two-dimensional artistic media varied in size, form, and materials; yet similar types of scenes were distributed across these media. The most common and widely-distributed medium was the seal. Despite their relatively small surface area, seals could accommodate a combination of two or even three scenes, as well as an inscription to identify the individual or institutional owner, or to express a prayer or incantation. Different scene types dominated glyptic imagery in different periods. Seals also offer an opportunity to study the diffusion and accessibility of imagery to an extended audience; because seal ownership was not always restricted to the highest-ranking administrators, and their potentially multiple impressions extended even further through the social ranks, visual knowledge and experience encoded in imagery was made available to non-elites. Porada (1980:10) emphasizes that even this extension was historically contingent; seals expanded in function over time, with a particularly dramatic shift in the Ur III period, during a time of tremendous growth in bureaucracy. Because of their variety, portability, distribution, and survival, seals and seal impressions have been the focus of extensive scholarly study; for the same reasons, they had the potential to be bearers of both narrative and ideological information (Bernbeck 1996:203).[12]

While seals and seal impressions were the most common two-dimensional media in the ancient Near East, a variety of other forms existed. In general, these artistic formats were significantly larger than seals and therefore afforded artists a monumental surface for visual expression. For this reason, these genres are sometimes, perhaps wrongly, regarded as more likely than seals to incorporate narrative scenes and ideological messages. Two-dimensional art forms included relief sculpture (in stone, clay, and metal), painting (wall paintings, but also on pottery), and inlay (in a variety of materials). Painted designs, in particular, have suffered damage over time and are poorly documented archaeologically; in addition, a number of perishable materials, especially textiles, may also have borne representations. As mentioned above, ritual texts point to the extensive use of such poorly preserved materials.

On the other hand, stone relief is well preserved archaeologically, and is one of the best sources of information on the settings and functions of monumental art in the ancient Near East. Various types of scenes were carved in stone, particularly designs relating to historical and ritual events. Stone may have been selected intentionally for monumental and ideologically themed imagery because of its durability; the later confiscation and appropriation of such monuments as Naram-Sin's victory stele indicate the lasting significance of stone reliefs (Winter 1996:19). Smaller ceramic and metal reliefs, and composite inlay scenes, portrayed a similar range of subject matter, including ritual scenes and battles, as well as extracts from myths and scenes from daily life. Additionally, abstract and apotropaic designs were sometimes set on these media.

Material also was a potent symbol of value, and varied according to genre. As indicated above, stone was particularly important in the production of art, both monumental and modest in scale. Available tools and technologies affected the choice of particular stones; as technologies improved, for example, stones of greater hardness were preferred for seal manufacture (Sax et al. 2001). At the same time, softer stones and alternative materials (clay, wood, or frit) also remained in use in all periods of glyptic production. Particular materials may have been chosen for their color or talismanic value (Collon 1987:100). Cultural value was also conferred on specific materials because of their relative rarity and expense. In Mesopotamia, all raw metals, and some stones (especially harder stones such as diorite and quartz) had to be imported. Because of their relative expense, certain materials were restricted in circulation; some, particularly metals, would also have undergone repeated recycling to keep them in use. Artists were also restricted by the particular size and shape of imported resources, and adapted designs to make maximum use of the available material (Azarpay 1990:101). A number of scholars have examined the interrelationship of long-distance trade and political development in Mesopotamia; certain periods of territorial or imperial expansion may have been driven, in part, by elite desire to control raw material resources and the routes over which they were transported (Alden 1982; Algaze 1993). Historical inscriptions specifying the sources of rare stones and metals implied the extension, whether real or hoped for, of royal power into distant lands (Ross 2001:420). In this way, rulers made explicit use of the ideological value of imported and expensive materials.

Context

Public contexts

A number of factors beyond iconographic content and medium contributed to the design and interpretation of individual works of ancient Near Eastern art. Cues to meaning were embedded within individual pieces, and also supplied by the circumstances of viewing. Among the most important of visual indicators, and most difficult to ascertain archaeologically, was the architectural context of the work. This setting, whether public or private, affected experience through the control of spatial perception and of the movement of the body as a viewer approached, observed, and withdrew from the image.[13] The particular setting also determined how many people could see a piece at one time, or at all.

The extant images from primary archaeological contexts in the Near East come largely from public spaces such as temples and palaces. Thus, it appears that much imagery, especially those pieces illustrating royal themes, was intended for sizable and diverse audiences.[14] This impression is corroborated by dedicatory inscriptions on statues and stelae, and by historical texts, which describe public settings in which monuments stood. During most phases of Mesopotamian artistic production, two- and three-dimensional representations were installed in temples. Temple courtyards formed the setting for ritual depictions and battle scenes (Reade 1979a:339), as well as dedicatory statues. Courtyards were also used for ritual performances, wherein some portion of the population participated (Winter 1992:38 n. 19). There, they would have encountered and interacted with the monuments, walking around the double-sided stelae, approaching the statues, and perhaps leaving offerings to past and present rulers as well as to the gods (Winter 1992:29). In smaller, more restricted spaces within the temple building, votive statues may have been intended for both divine and human witnesses. Monuments dedicated by rulers, found throughout temple precincts, communicated explicit ideological statements about the conditions of governance and sociopolitical hierarchy: they showed the ever-present, ever-renewed bond between god and ruler, an intimate relationship reinforcing the ruler's right to rule, and demonstrating his commitment to service on behalf of the gods.

Secular spaces also held imagery for public viewing. According to royal inscriptions of the first millennium, these locales included open areas within cities (including those in conquered territories), along roadways, at symbolically significant spots, such as the sources of the Tigris and Euphrates, and on mountainsides (the latter two practices of image placement are attested in the extant material remains as well).[15] Surviving first millennium images of royal power in these locations consisted of free-standing statues, stelae, and rock-cut reliefs. The content varied, ranging from representations of king and god to images of a victorious ruler. Given the distribution of such imagery, the audience would have included both native Mesopotamians, already experienced in the symbolism of power, and newly-conquered peoples, learning through the art about the roles and authority of their new rulers, and simultaneously of their own positions in society.

Presumably more restricted in access, royal palaces also contained meaningful visual portrayals of the social and political order, particularly artistic and ideological messages concerning the ruler. The earliest Mesopotamian palace from which extensive decoration has been preserved is at Mari, where Old Babylonian-period wall paintings depicted the relationship between the king and gods (Parrot 1974:115). Reuse of this palace through multiple generations suggests that its imagery expressed a long-lasting power structure. Much more is known of the decorative programs of Neo-Assyrian palaces (Reade 1979b, 1980; Winter 1981b, 1983); at this time, in contrast to the second millennium, the conventions of power required each king to construct and furnish a palace that encapsulated his particular accomplishments. Not all Neo-Assyrian kings attained this goal; those who did, however, left an unparalleled record of the ideological underpinnings of their power, and of the developments in artistic expression over a 200-year period. In Neo-Assyrian palaces, both public and private spaces held relief and painted decoration. It was in the public areas, and particularly the throne room, however, that the ideological content of the visual imagery was most vigorously displayed. Here, despite the variety of scene types portrayed, the viewer perceived consistent and emphatic statements concerning divine protection of the king, and about royal provision for the people and the ruler's prominent role in the military expansion of his empire. Irene Winter (1983:27) concludes that these scenes were intended for a diverse audience of gods, kings (current and future), Assyrian officials and palace workers, and local and foreign visitors. Each viewer regarded and read the scenes according to his or her own set of personal experiences and traditions; the repetition of scene types and redundancy of the ideological messages may have restricted individual readings. By drawing on older scene types (the royal hunt, battles, scenes of worship), the artists may have attempted to deploy visual codes accessible to the widest possible audience. The overall intention, however, was clear: to impart a sense of awe and admiration toward the Assyrian king.

Private contexts

In the private, restricted spaces of Neo-Assyrian palaces, a different set of images and readings occurred; this divergence should relate to differences in audience. In most cases, the decoration in the inner parts of the palaces focused more narrowly on religious and apotropaic scenes, as well as on more tranquil activities of the king, such as hunting and ritual. Assyrian temples also diverge from the militant, expansive emphasis of the palace decoration; Reade (1979a:339) has noted that the predominant decoration in first millennium temples depicts kings engaged in worship.

Finally, we can turn to the most restricted spaces of all, Mesopotamian houses. Unfortunately, domestic spaces have generally been underrepresented in excavation and publication in Mesopotamia, and much of their decoration may have been in perishable materials. Private houses have, however, yielded evidence for ritually protected space, overseen by apotropaic figurines and plaques (Stol 1995:498). Some Mesopotamians thus encountered visual imagery daily; they could have transferred knowledge and expected behaviors relating to representations from their residences into public spaces. In addition, a proportion of the population (which would have varied from period to period) also possessed seals and tablets with seal impressions. Seals and sealings were often present in residential areas; representational art thus extended into private contexts. The art from these areas, however, often differed in content and meaning from that available publicly, by supporting and affirming a personal link with the gods, here unmediated by royal intervention. Seal imagery available to private citizens was devoid of images of secular leaders during certain periods; seal inscriptions, however, may have made clear the relationship of the owner to the hierarchies and holders of power.

Composition

One of the principal compositional features of a work of art was scale. Size and scale appear to correlate cross-culturally with power; distinctions in size among individual figures, then, implied differences in authority. In different periods and contexts, Near Eastern artists deployed indications of status difference to a greater or lesser degree. On the Victory Stele of Naram-Sin (figure 16.1), the king is depicted as much taller and more muscular than his men (Winter 1996:21). Later, reliefs of Assurnasirpal II and Shalmaneser III (figure 16.2) depict these early Neo-Assyrian kings as just slightly larger than their soldiers and officials (Winter 1981b:12); here, the god Assur is the smallest figure, hovering above the field of action. In this example, additional details in the image convey the importance of the god, and of the king relative to his attendants. These differences may be due to changes in the ways of "reading" artistic representations between the periods.

Similarly, the placement or position of a figure in the two-dimensional pictorial field could indicate status; Mesopotamian artists used an array of available strategies for this, perhaps according to historically-contingent rules of representation and interpretation. Individuals of higher status might be placed in the center of a register, as on the "War Side" of the Standard of Ur (but not on the "Peace Side") (Hansen 1998:45–47). In other cases, however, this rule of centrality does not apply; in standard presentation scenes, the seated god (the individual with highest status) is located at the right edge. This may correlate with the preference for right over left, or convey motion toward the god (Winter 1996:12).

Much of the time, artists followed one important rule of vertical position: status accrued to the individual placed in the uppermost location. This hierarchization is employed on the Naram-Sin stele (figure 16.1), where the ruler stands above his soldiers and enemies; here the gods, though abstracted as astral symbols, take the uppermost position. Another example of the strategic use of vertical placement is the employment of registers to illustrate hierarchical distinctions; this is presumably at work on the Warka Vase, where the culminating and most important scene is at the top (Hansen 1998:46).

Figure 16.1 Victory Stele of Naram-Sin. Old Akkadian Period, Susa (Copyright Réunion des Musées Nationaux/Art Resource, NY; Photo: Herve Lewandowski; Louvre, Paris, France; reproduced by permission)

Horizontal registers could also be utilized to depict temporal developments, rather than hierarchy, in a narrative scene, as on the Vulture Stele of Eannatum (figure 16.3) and in Neo-Assyrian two-register reliefs, such as the throneroom decoration in Assurnasirpal II's palace. In both cases, the ruler appears in multiple registers, indicating the passage of time between scenes. The order of reading is inconsistent, however; Eannatum's victory progresses from bottom to top (Winter 1985:19), while in Assurnasirpal's reliefs, the upper scene takes place prior to the lower one (Winter 1983). This indeterminacy of order, or change in reading priority over time, suggests that Mesopotamian viewers could apply a number of potential readings to the horizontal and vertical dimensions of a work; differences in historical or spatial context may have affected the viewer's understanding of the images and could have led to misunderstandings of an early depiction when seen by a person in a later period.

Viewers were aided in their interpretation of an image by pose and gesture as well. The relationship of seated and standing figures in Mesopotamian art correlated with superior and inferior status, respectively. Additionally, a variety of hand

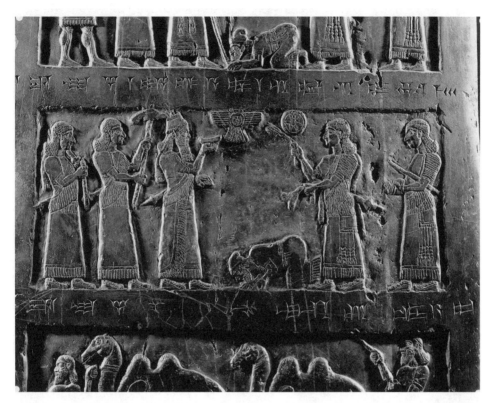

Figure 16.2 Black Obelisk of Shalmaneser III. Neo-Assyrian Period, Nimrud (Copyright Erich Lessing/Art Resource, NY; British Museum, London, Great Britain; reproduced by permission)

and arm gestures communicated details of relative status and circumstance. Thus, on the Law Code stele of Hammurabi, Hammurabi's pose, with his hand before his mouth, expressed his respect and reverence toward the sun god seated before him (Amiet 1980:No. 68). The intricacy of the gestural vocabulary in art is echoed by a similar complexity in Sumerian and Akkadian, in which a large number of verbal idioms (many not fully understood) denoted particular hand gestures and facial expressions.

Additionally, other features of the representations helped identify individuals by name, status, occupation, and other social parameters, and conveyed information about the situation portrayed. Dress, hair, and ornament were important signifiers in Mesopotamian art. Clothing could indicate status; Assyrian kings wore richly decorated robes in depictions of tribute delivery and in ritual (Oppenheim 1949:186). In battle scenes, however, their garments were not as ornate; dress therefore also depended on the particular circumstances underlying the scene. The artists who created Neo-Assyrian reliefs took particular care to distinguish the various ethnic and geographic groups that constituted the empire by dress, headgear, and hairstyle (Wäfler 1975). Intertwined with these pictorial distinctions were also

Figure 16.3 Vulture Stele of Eannatum. Early Dynastic Period, Girsu (Copyright Giraudon/Art Resource, NY; Louvre, Paris, France; reproduced by permission)

moral and conceptual ones: in this case, clothing communicated one's proximity to Assyrian values and authority. Mesopotamian artists also paid close attention to the proper representation of gods, distinguished from humans by stature and horned headgear, and from one another by attributes, usually the physical manifestations of their particular powers.

Finally, some individuals in Mesopotamian art lacked identifying features altogether. These could be enemies, naked or in simple clothing, shackled as prisoners, or lying dead on the battlefield. Mesopotamians of low social status were also depicted with few or no distinctive traits, particularly when they functioned as representatives of a social class or occupation. Thus, Eannatum's soldiers, backing up their ruler, hide behind shields or are rendered indistinguishable by their sheer numbers. Similarly, pig-tailed female laborers from Uruk period glyptic scenes are interchangeable except for their association with different objects (usually pots and textiles) (Pollock and Bernbeck 2000:159; figure 16.4). This lack of differentiation served as important an ideological purpose as the detailed depictions of king and god. It indicated to the maker and viewer that the undifferentiated masses, including women, played an economic or military role in the support of society, but were not to be singled out from their peers – thus reinforcing the symbolic and real hierarchies of power in society.

Another feature with the potential to add meaning, the use of an accompanying inscription, may have held significance for a smaller audience than the total number of viewers. In general, the principal readers of these inscriptions must have been Mesopotamian administrators and officials. An overlap in content between text and image would have reinforced the ideological statements expressed in the art, and upheld the superior position of the readers (Michalowski 1990:64–65). Elsewhere, discrepancies between image and text may indicate a different audience for each, or a complementarity of function. A mismatch of inscription and depiction may also be explained by inherent differences in the communicative capacities and techniques of language and art: the two modes of expression are not fully interchangeable. Together, however, text and image could have functioned to add redundancy to the message and meaning to the larger whole.

The selective adoption and adaptation of past styles and iconography was one final method by which artists affected viewer perceptions. Mesopotamian elites, especially rulers, were aware of past history, former kings, and "ancient" monuments. Old Babylonian period scribes recopied inscriptions from statues of Old Akkadian kings; Kassite rulers rebuilt and refurbished old and neglected temple buildings. The adoption of older iconographic elements, such as the "rod and the ring," signs of royal power, suggested continuity and legitimacy. But elements of past art were also consciously selected to communicate different ideologies and new meanings; this occurred, for instance, with Persian appropriation of Assyrian and Egyptian iconographic elements to convey a harmonious empire under their "benevolent" rule (Root 1990). The particular meanings read from borrowed iconography and style depended on the new historical and social context of artistic works. Perception relied on the audience's experience of imperial power, and on the precise details of style and iconography.

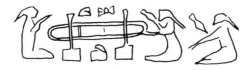

Figure 16.4 Late Uruk and Jemdet Nasr glyptic scenes (*source*: Pollock and Bernbeck 2000: Figure 13.2; reproduced by permission of the University of Pennsylvania Press)

Conclusions

The public art of the ancient Near East was produced under the direction of the ruling class, and with their interests and values embedded in its completed forms. Particular materials, genres, iconography, and styles were selected with intent and deliberation. The processes of artistic production, and the establishment of monuments in public settings, constituted material manifestations of elite ideology. These processes made possible public consumption of statements about societal order and proper governance. Ideological messages, however, were subject to renegotiation and renewal, challenge and change. Artistic changes therefore provide evidence and sometimes served as vehicles for the shifting sociopolitical and technological structures that stood behind them.

The methods of analysis outlined in this chapter are intended to help reveal the ideological messages and practices embedded within the visual codes of ancient Near Eastern art. The production of these codes was part of a socially and historically contingent process of meaning creation and interpretation. The components that constituted such meanings were multiple and overlapping. The art historian or archaeologist intent on drawing out ideological meaning and underlying social conditions must assess a variety of factors, including the locus of production: who was responsible for the design and creation of the images? An analysis of iconography produces an assessment of what is, and what is not, represented, and the ways in which depictions may have served to reinforce elite authority. Study of iconographic change over time may reveal shifts in the structures of power or in their representation.

The media of artistic representations also play a role in the selective dissemination of imagery through a population. We can ask what role material may have played in the expression of ideology. We must also consider how the circumstances of viewing, or the context of the representations, affected viewer perceptions of meaning, and even the identity of those viewers. Finally, compositional details such as (but not limited to) size, scale, position, pose, gesture, and inscription all had potential bearing on the reading of an image. These various components of artistic expression formed a compositional whole, but different makers and observers may have read from them distinct meanings. Both the artist/patron and the viewer held tools to generate and deduce meaning from representations; by applying the framework above, we may be better equipped to recognize the intended ideological content and its potential interpretation and reinterpretation in particular historical and sociopolitical circumstances.

Ideology is not monolithic: viewers, who brought their own perceptions to the interpretation of public art, had opportunities to develop alternative readings, or to resist the statements being communicated. At any time, multiple ideologies, sometimes "nesting" or complementary, sometimes conflicting, could be present in the appearance and interpretation of art. Subordinate individuals and groups may have had chances to interject their resistance and propose alternatives to the structures of power through art created and displayed in the private sphere, representations which have seldom been addressed archaeologically. Seals and sealings are forms of artistic expression that may have straddled the boundary between public and private spheres of activity by their use in public economic transaction with, often, consequences for private affairs; it is here, and in other forms of private art, that we may begin to look for alternative ideologies and strategies of expression.

NOTES

1   These terms, admittedly, derive from Western art historical discourse. In this chapter, I
     will consider their application within the representational and ideological practices of
     the ancient Near East.
2   Even such decorative scenes could have held particular meanings for their makers and
     viewers. See, for example, Benson's (1995) interpretation of ornamental friezes on
     Proto-Corinthian pottery as allusions to juxtaposed narrative scenes.
3   The use of the masculine pronoun here reflects the near-complete absence of female
     rulers from the artistic repertoire, and from most historical sources of the ancient Near
     East.
4   *Chicago Assyrian Dictionary (CAD)* Ṣ 78b–85b.
5   Cf. Cooper (1990) for an overview of these terms.
6   *CAD* N I 364b–367b.
7   *Akkadisches Handwörterbuch (AHw)* 3 1440.
8   *AHw* 3 1316–17.
9   See Van de Mieroop (1987:61) for evidence of an Isin-Larsa period workshop in which
     two teams of craftspeople alternated days of work.
10   Lambert (1987) presents a careful study of such attributions, based particularly on dif-
     ferent versions of the Gilgamesh myth.
11   Cf. Bloch (1986:167). For a more historicized interpretation of ritual, see Kelly (1988).
12   See Winter (2001:1–3) for a review of the principal trends, and remaining gaps, in glyptic
     research.
13   See Favro (1993) for an example of the use of structured movement to convey ideo-
     logical ideas in Rome. Research in this area owes much to the work of Thomas (1991).
14   Baines and Yoffee (1998) argue that this imagery, as one aspect of "high culture," was
     restricted to an elite audience. See also the responses to this thesis in Richards and Van
     Buren (2000).
15   In the Black Obelisk inscription, Shalmaneser III describes several of these practices
     (Grayson 1996:62–71).

References

Alden, John R., 1982 Trade and Politics in Proto-Elamite Iran. Current Anthropology
       23:613–640.
Algaze, Guillermo, 1993 The Uruk World System. Chicago: University of Chicago Press.
Amiet, Pierre, 1980 Art of the Ancient Near East. New York: Harry N. Abrams.
Azarpay, Guitty, 1990 The Canon of Proportions in the Art of the Ancient Near East. *In*
       Investigating Artistic Environments in the Ancient Near East. Ann G. Gunter, ed. pp.
       93–103. Washington, D.C.: Arthur M. Sackler Gallery.
Baines, John, and Norman Yoffee, 1998 Order, Legitimacy, and Wealth in Ancient Egypt and
       Mesopotamia. *In* Archaic States. Gary Feinman and Joyce Marcus, eds. pp. 199–260.
       Santa Fe: School of American Research.
Belfer-Cohen, Anna, 1991 Art Items from Layer B, Hayonim Cave: A Case Study of Art in
       a Natufian Context. *In* The Natufian Culture in the Levant. Ofer Bar-Yosef and François
       R. Valla, eds. pp. 569–588. Ann Arbor: International Monographs in Prehistory.

Benson, J. L., 1995 Human Figures, the Ajax Painter, and Narrative Scenes in Earlier Corinthian Vase Painting. *In* The Ages of Homer: A Tribute to Emily Townsend Vermeule. Jane B. Carter and Sarah P. Morris, eds. pp. 335–362. Austin: University of Texas Press.

Bernbeck, Reinhard, 1996 Siegel, Mythen, Riten: Etana und die Ideologie der Akkad-Zeit. Baghdader Mitteilungen 27:159–213.

Bloch, Maurice, 1986 From Blessing to Violence. Cambridge: Cambridge University Press.

Cauvin, Jacques, 1994 Naissance des divinités, naissance de l'agriculture: la révolution des symboles au Néolithique. Paris: CNRS Éditions.

Civil, Miguel, 1969 The Series lú=ša and Related Texts. Materials for the Sumerian Lexicon, 12. Rome: Pontificium Institutum Biblicum.

Collon, Dominique, 1981 The Aleppo Workshop: A Seal-cutters' Workshop in Syria in the Second Half of the 18th Century B.C. Ugarit Forschungen 13:33–40.

Collon, Dominique, 1985 A North Syrian Cylinder Seal Style: Evidence of North-South Links with 'Ajjul. *In* Palestine in the Bronze and Iron Ages. Jonathan N. Tubb, ed. pp. 57–68. London: Institute of Archaeology.

Collon, Dominique, 1987 First Impressions: Cylinder Seals in the Ancient Near East. Chicago: University of Chicago Press.

Cooper, Jerrold S., 1990 Mesopotamian Historical Consciousness and the Production of Monumental Art in the Third Millennium. *In* Investigating Artistic Environments in the Ancient Near East. Ann G. Gunter, ed. pp. 39–51. Washington, D.C.: Arthur M. Sackler Gallery.

Davis, Whitney, 1992 Masking the Blow: The Scene of Representation in Late Prehistoric Egyptian Art. Berkeley: University of California Press.

Davis, Whitney, 1993 Narrativity and the Narmer Palette. *In* Narrative and Event in Ancient Art. Peter J. Holliday, ed. pp. 14–54. Cambridge: Cambridge University Press.

De Marrais, Elizabeth, Luis J. Castillo, and Timothy Earle, 1996 Ideology, Materialization, and Power Strategies. Current Anthropology 37:15–31.

Edzard, Dietz O., 1997 Gudea and His Dynasty. Royal Inscriptions of Mesopotamia. Early Periods, 3/1. Toronto: University of Toronto Press.

Eisenstadt, S. N., 1979 Observations and Queries About Sociological Aspects of Imperialism in the Ancient World. *In* Power and Propaganda: A Symposium on Ancient Empires. Mogens T. Larsen, ed. pp. 21–33. Mesopotamia, 7. Copenhagen: Akademisk Forlag.

Favro, Diane, 1993 Reading the Augustan City. *In* Narrative and Event in Ancient Art. Peter J. Holliday, ed. pp. 230–257. Cambridge: Cambridge University Press.

Grayson, A. Kirk, 1996 Assyrian Rulers of the Early First Millennium B.C. II (858–745 B.C.). Royal Inscriptions of Mesopotamia. Assyrian Periods, 3. Toronto: University of Toronto Press.

Güterbock, Hans G., 1957 Narration in Anatolian, Syrian, and Assyrian Art. American Journal of Archaeology 61:62–71.

Hansen, Donald P., 1998 Art of the Royal Tombs of Ur: A Brief Introduction. *In* Treasures from the Royal Tombs of Ur. Richard L. Zettler and Lee Horne, eds. pp. 43–72. Philadelphia: University of Pennsylvania Museum.

Hauptmann, Harald, 1999 The Urfa Region. *In* Neolithic in Turkey: The Cradle of Civilization. New Discoveries. Mehmet Özdoğan and Nezih Başgelen, eds. pp. 65–86. Istanbul: Arkeoloji ve Sanat Yayınları.

Hodder, Ian, ed., 1996 On the Surface: Çatalhöyük 1993–95. BIAA Monograph, 22. Ankara: British Institute of Archaeology at Ankara.

Horsnell, Malcom, 1999 The Year-Names of the First Dynasty of Babylon. Hamilton: McMaster University Press.

Kantor, Helene J., 1957 Narration in Egyptian Art. American Journal of Archaeology 61:44–54.

Kelly, John D., 1988 From Holi to Diwali in Fiji: An Essay on Ritual and History. Man N.S. 23:40–55.

Kent, Roland G., 1950 Old Persian. Grammar, Texts, Lexicon. New Haven: American Oriental Society.

Kenyon, Kathleen, 1960 Archaeology in the Holy Land. London: Ernest Benn.

Lambert, Wilfred G., 1987 Gilgamesh in Literature and Art: The Second and First Millennia. In Monsters and Demons in the Ancient and Medieval Worlds. Ann E. Farkas, Prudence O. Harper, and Evelyn B. Harrison, eds. pp. 37–52. Mainz: Verlag Philipp von Zabern.

Liverani, Mario, 1979 The Ideology of the Assyrian Empire. In Power and Propaganda: A Symposium on Ancient Empires. Mogens T. Larsen, ed. pp. 297–317. Mesopotamia, 7. Copenhagen: Akademisk Forlag.

Mallowan, Max E. L., 1966 Nimrud and Its Remains, vol. II. London: Collins.

Mellaart, James, 1967 Çatal Hüyük: A Neolithic Town in Anatolia. New York: McGraw.

Michalowski, Piotr, 1990 Early Mesopotamian Communicative Systems: Art, Literature, and Writing. In Investigating Artistic Environments in the Ancient Near East. Ann G. Gunter, ed. pp. 53–69. Washington, D.C.: Arthur M. Sackler Gallery.

Mortensen, Preben, 1997 Art in the Social Order: The Making of the Modern Conception of Art. Albany: State University of New York Press.

Noy, Tamar, 1991 Art and Decoration of the Natufian at Nahal Oren. In The Natufian Culture in the Levant. Ofer Bar-Yosef and François R. Valla, eds. pp. 557–568. Ann Arbor: International Monographs in Prehistory.

Oppenheim, A. Leo, 1949 The Golden Garments of the Gods. Journal of Near Eastern Studies 8:172–193.

Parrot, André, 1974 Mari, capitale fabuleuse. Paris: Bibliothèque Historique.

Perkins, Ann, 1957 Narration in Babylonian Art. American Journal of Archaeology 61:54–62.

Pollock, Susan, 1999 Ancient Mesopotamia: The Eden That Never Was. Cambridge: Cambridge University Press.

Pollock, Susan, and Reinhard Bernbeck, 2000 And They Said, Let Us Make Gods in Our Image: Gendered Ideologies in Ancient Mesopotamia. In Reading the Body: Representations and Remains in the Archaeological Record. Alison E. Rautman, ed. pp. 150–164. Philadelphia: University of Pennsylvania Press.

Porada, Edith, 1980 Introduction. In Ancient Art in Seals. Edith Porada, ed. pp. 3–34. Princeton: Princeton University Press.

Reade, Julian E., 1979a Ideology and Propaganda in Assyrian Art. In Power and Propaganda: A Symposium on Ancient Empires. Mogens T. Larsen, ed. pp. 329–344. Mesopotamia, 7. Copenhagen: Akademisk Forlag.

Reade, Julian, 1979b Narrative Composition in Assyrian Sculpture. Baghdader Mitteilungen 10:52–110.

Reade, Julian, 1980 The Architectural Context of Assyrian Sculpture. Baghdader Mitteilungen 11:75–87.

Richards, Janet, and Mary Van Buren, eds., 2000 Order, Legitimacy and Wealth in Ancient States. Cambridge: Cambridge University Press.

Root, Margaret C., 1990 Circles of Artistic Programming: Strategies for Studying Creative Process at Persepolis. In Investigating Artistic Environments in the Ancient Near East. Ann G. Gunter, ed. pp. 115–139. Washington, D.C.: Arthur M. Sackler Gallery.

Ross, Jennifer C., 2001 Text and Subtext: Precious Metals and Politics in Old Akkadian

Mesopotamia. *In* Historiography in the Cuneiform World. Proceedings of the XLVe Rencontre Assyriologique Internationale, Part I. Tzvi Abusch et al., eds. pp. 417–428. Bethesda: CDL Press.

Russell, John M., 1993 Sennacherib's Lachish Narratives. *In* Narrative and Event in Ancient Art. Peter J. Holliday, ed. pp. 55–73. Cambridge: Cambridge University Press.

Sax, Margaret, Nigel Meeks, and Dominique Collon, 2001 Innovations in the Engraving of Near Eastern Cylinder Seals. Paper presented at the Annual Meeting of the American Schools of Oriental Research, Boulder, November 15.

Sigrist, Marcel, and Peter Damerow, 2001 Mesopotamian Year Names: Neo-Sumerian and Old Babylonian Date Formulae. http://cdli.ucla.edu/dl/yearnames/yn_index.htm.

Stansbury-O'Donnell, Mark D., 1999 Pictorial Narrative in Ancient Greek Art. Cambridge: Cambridge University Press.

Stol, Marten, 1995 Private Life in Ancient Mesopotamia. *In* Civilizations of the Ancient Near East. Jack N. Sasson, ed. pp. 485–501. New York: Scribners.

Thomas, Julian, 1991 Rethinking the Neolithic. Cambridge: Cambridge University Press.

Ungnad, A., 1938 Datenlisten. Reallexikon der Assyriologie 2:131–194.

Van de Mieroop, Marc, 1987 Crafts in the Early Isin Period. Orientalia Lovaniensia Analecta, 24. Leuven: Departement Orientalistiek.

Voigt, Mary M., 2000 Çatal Höyük in Context. Ritual at Early Neolithic Sites in Central and Eastern Turkey. *In* Life in Neolithic Farming Communities: Social Organization, Identity, and Differentiation. Ian Kuijt, ed. pp. 253–293. New York: Kluwer Academic/Plenum Publishers.

von Blanckenhagen, Peter H., 1957 Narration in Hellenistic and Roman Art. American Journal of Archaeology 61:78–83.

Wäfler, Markus, 1975 Nicht-Assyrer neuassyrischer Darstellungen. Alter Orient und Altes Testament, 26. Neukirchen-Vluyn: Neukirchener Verlag.

Weissert, Elnathan, 1997 Royal Hunt and Royal Triumph in a Prism Fragment of Ashurbanipal (82–5-22,2). *In* Assyria 1995. Simo Parpola and Robert M. Whiting, eds. pp. 339–358. Helsinki: The Neo-Assyrian Text Corpus Project.

Winter, Irene J., 1981a Is There a South Syrian Style of Ivory Carving in the Early First Millennium B.C.? Iraq 43:101–130.

Winter, Irene J., 1981b Royal Rhetoric and the Development of Historical Narrative in Neo-Assyrian Reliefs. Studies in Visual Communication 7(2):2–38.

Winter, Irene J., 1983 The Program of the Throneroom of Assurnasirpal II. *In* Essays on Near Eastern Art and Archaeology in Honor of Charles Kyrle Wilkinson. Prudence O. Harper and Holly Pittman, eds. pp. 15–32. New York: Metropolitan Museum of Art.

Winter, Irene J., 1985 After the Battle is Over: The Stele of the Vultures and the Beginning of Historical Narrative in the Art of the Ancient Near East. *In* Pictorial Narrative in Antiquity and the Middle Ages. Herbert L. Kessler and Marianna S. Simpson, eds. pp. 11–32. Studies in the History of Art, 16. Washington, D.C.: National Gallery.

Winter, Irene J., 1992 "Idols of the King": Royal Images as Recipients of Ritual Action in Ancient Mesopotamia. Journal of Ritual Studies 6:13–42.

Winter, Irene J., 1996 Sex, Rhetoric, and the Public Monument: The Alluring Body of Naram-Sîn of Agade. *In* Sexuality in Ancient Art: Near East, Egypt, Greece, and Italy. Natalie B. Kampen, ed. pp. 11–26. Cambridge: Cambridge University Press.

Winter, Irene J., 2001 Introduction: Glyptic, History, and Historiography. *In* Seals and Seal Impressions. Proceedings of the XLVe Rencontre Assyriologique Internationale, Part II. William W. Hallo and Irene J. Winter, eds. pp. 1–13. Bethesda: CDL Press.

Wolff, Janet, 1993 The Social Production of Art. 2nd edition. New York: New York University Press.

Yakar, Jak, 1991 Prehistoric Anatolia: The Neolithic Transformation and the Early Chalcolithic Period. Tel Aviv: Tel Aviv University.

Index